2-21-97

GARLAND STUDIES ON

THE ELDERLY IN AMERICA

edited by
STUART BRUCHEY
UNIVERSITY OF MAINE

A GARLAND SERIES

GROWING OLD IN THE EARLY REPUBLIC

Spiritual, Social, and Economic Issues, 1790–1830

PAULA A. SCOTT

GARLAND PUBLISHING, Inc.
New York & London / 1997

Copyright © 1997 Paula A. Scott
All rights reserved

Library of Congress Cataloging-in-Publication Data

Scott, Paula A., 1963–
 Growing old in the early republic : spiritual, social, and economic issues, 1790–1830 / Paula A. Scott.
   p.   cm. — (Garland studies on the elderly in America)
 Includes bibliographical references and index.
 ISBN 0-8153-2537-1 (alk. paper)
 1. Aged—United States—History. 2. Aging—Social aspects—United States—History. 3. Aging—Economic aspects—United States—History. 4. United States—Social conditions—To 1865. I. Title. II. Series.
HQ1064.U5S396 1997
305.26'09746—dc21
                                                              96-48389

Printed on acid-free, 250-year-life paper
Manufactured in the United States of America

To
Anita Walker Scott
and
Ernest L. Scott

Contents

List of Figures	ix
List of Tables	xi
Preface	xiii
List of Abbreviations	xxiii
1. Introduction	3
2. American Ideas on Aging and the Elderly to 1830	21
3. Making Sense of Old Age	57
4. Age and Economic Status	89
5. The Economic Challenges of Growing Old	121
6. Households of the Aged	171
7. Family Lives of the Elderly	201
8. Age, Wealth, and Community Leadership	231
9. Perspectives on the Elderly	271

Appendix A: Hartford Vital Records 279

Appendix B: Hartford Tax Records 283

Appendix C: Information on Hartford Leaders 291

Selected Bibliography of Primary Sources 295

Index 309

Figures

1.1	Age Structure of White Population, Hartford, 1830	14
1.2	Age Structure of Black Population, Hartford, 1830	15
4.1	Taxpayers by Age, North District Town Tax Lists	92
4.2	Taxpayers by Age, South District Town Tax Lists	93
4.3	Taxpayers by Age, Valuation Lists	94
4.4	Average List Size by Age, North District Town Tax Lists	98
4.5	Average List Size by Age, South District Town Tax Lists	99
4.6	Hartford Real Property Owned by Age Groups	105
4.7	Average Valuations by Age Group	106
6.1	Percentage of Households by Size, 1790–1830	174
6.2	Average Number of Household Residents by Age of Head	177
6.3	Household Sizes of Different Aged Men and Women, 1830	178
6.4	Percentage of Households Headed by Age Groups, 1790–1830	180
6.5	Proportion of Male Household Heads Compared to All Adult Males, 1830	182
6.6	Percentage of Age Groups Heading Households, 1830	183
8.1	Average Ages of Hartford Leaders, 1790–1830	234
8.2	Ages of Hartford Leaders by Decade, 1790–1830	236

8.3 Ages of Leaders Compared to Ages of All Adult Men	238
8.4 Average Ages of Leaders by Type of Organization, 1790–1830	240
8.5 Leadership by Age and Type of Organization Led, 1790–1830	242
8.6 Hartford Leaders' Tax Quartiles, 1790–1814	250
8.7 Leaders' Tax Quartiles by Type of Organization, 1790–1814	253

Tables

1.1	African-Americans and Foreigners as Percentage of Hartford Population	4
1.2	Age Structure of White Population, Hartford, 1830	16
1.3	Age Structure of Black Population, Hartford, 1830	17
4.1	Nominal and Real Average List Sizes by Age, North District, Hartford	102
4.2	Nominal and Real Average List Sizes by Age, South District, Hartford	102
4.3	Percentage Changes in List Size per Year by Age Group (Nominal)	112
4.4	Percentage Changes in List Size per Year by Age Group (Real)	113
6.1	Number of Households of Different Sizes, Hartford, 1790–1830	175
6.2	Household Size over Five Censuses, Hartford	175
6.3	Ages of Hartford Household Heads, 1790–1830	181
8.1	Mean and Median Ages of Officeholders by Type of Organization	241
8.2	Leaders' Ages in Government Offices, Hartford, 1790–1830	245

8.3 Leaders' Ages in Church Offices, Hartford, 1790–1830   246
8.4 Leaders' Ages in Voluntary Association Offices, Hartford, 1790–1830   247
8.5 Leaders' Ages in Institution Offices, Hartford, 1790–1830   247
8.6 Percentage of Leaders in Each Tax Quartile by Type of Organization   254
8.7 Percentage of Government Leaders in Each Tax Quartile by Office, 1790–1814   256
8.8 Percentage of Church Leaders in Each Tax Quartile by Office, 1790–1814   257
8.9 Percentage of Association Leaders in Each Tax Quartile by Office, 1790–1814   257
8.10 Percentage of Institution Leaders in Each Tax Quartile by Office, 1790–1814   258
8.11 Ages of White Males, Hartford, 1830   262
C-1 Average Age at Retirement and Interval to Death by Type of Organization   293

Preface

*The sun riseth upon us, and giveth us the
cheerful morning of youth; but how soon is it
that he setteth, and we are surrounded
with the shades of the evening of old age.*[1]

When these words were first articulated in 1829 everyone who heard them could bring to mind a picture of the aged in early national America. Men and women living in the years between 1790 and 1830 understood the special experiences and challenges that marked old age. Unfortunately, much of what Americans knew about old age in this period was lost as historians in the succeeding decades overlooked the aged's stories. Only recently have scholars begun working in earnest to reconstruct an understanding of old age in past times.

This book provides one building block for this new understanding. It looks at a specific time and place—Connecticut in the years between 1790 and 1830—to illuminate the spiritual and emotional aspects of being elderly, the economic consequences of growing old, and the ways social experience changed with advancing years. In doing so it demonstrates that life for the aged was risky and uncertain due to challenges on several fronts. Indeed, the research presented here reveals that early national Americans were quite accurate in referring to old age as the "declining years" and why old age was, as in the verse above, likened to somber shades of darkness. But challenges and risks were not the only important hallmarks of old age in this period. Indeed the way in which men and women approached old age is also significant. In the absence of institutional structures and pathways to guide the aging process, Americans in this "preindustrial" era negotiated old age on a highly individualized basis. Though we often think of the United States in this era as communally and family based, evidence on the elderly's lives shows that to a large extent constructing old age was an individual responsibility.

This book is not the first work on old age in America's past. In recent years scholars have focused more and more attention on the elderly and made many important findings. Interest in the aged has been spurred by the development of research methods that allow historians to better capture the experience of previously ignored groups. In addition, the proportion of old people in Western nations has increased to unprecedented levels and interest in the aged has burgeoned apace. As elderly people have become ever more visible in contemporary society, greater attention has been focused on the dynamics of growing old.

Scholarship on the aged has, in the last few decades, passed through several phases. Unlike long-established fields of inquiry which historians have mulled over for generations, the study of old age in the past was initially rooted in the concerns of non-historians. Social scientists, particularly those interested in modernization theory, were the first to seize on the topic. Modernization theory was originally developed in the social sciences to describe and predict how societies changed from "pre-modern" to "modern." Though advocates of the theory debated the precise nature of this transformation, most agreed it involved a shift from a precapitalist, artisinal, rural, and patriarchal social organization to one that was capitalist, industrial, urban, and democratic. Though there was considerable vagueness on the causes and linkages of these changes, advocates of modernization theory believed such a transition would, given time, occur in a predictable fashion in all societies.[2] Modernization theory thus provided a teleological view of historical change that could be applied globally.

A vision of the elderly in both pre-modern and modern societies formed part of this theory. Generally those embracing modernization theory argued that the history of the aged could be divided into two parts. The pre-modern period was one in which the old were few in number but uniformly respected. They held positions of power and authority which were accorded them by a society that valued old age and the wisdom that came with it. In addition, the elderly were well integrated into family and community life. They generally resided in extended families where they received whatever care they needed.

Preface xv

Thus there was no need for formal institutions to attend to the aged's welfare and old age was not a social "problem." This highly optimistic view of the aged in pre-modern society has sometimes been referred to as the "golden age" scenario.[3]

In contrast, the modern period tended to be considerably less ideal for the elderly. Though scholars argued that modernization generally resulted in more aged people, the position of these elderly was inevitably worse than in pre-modern times. In particular modern societies were marked by a decline in the leadership, power, and influence of the aged corresponding to generally lower status for elderly people as well as an increase "in the extent of disengagement of old people from community life."[4] These unpleasant changes were thought to stem from the many processes involved in modernization and, like modernization in general, to occur eventually in all societies regardless of cultural or other particulars.[5] Thus adherents of modernization theory unambiguously judged premodern societies better for the aged and modern societies worse.[6]

Despite early enthusiasm for this model of societal development and aging and a body of work demonstrating modernization's effects on the elderly, the theory was strongly criticized, particularly by historians. Indeed historians noted that "modernization theory, as it is generally formulated, actually may confound efforts to understand the aged in past times."[7] The theory's cultural biases, overbearing teleology, simplistic and erroneous periodization, and frequent failure to account for the experience of the aged all fostered doubt about its use as a tool for understanding the elderly.[8]

Not surprisingly, however, scholars who helped to tear down the modernization framework inadvertently perpetuated its influence. For example, the theory's ambitious claim to explain the situation of the aged in terms of vast sweeping change often required even those who rejected it to think in similar terms.[9] Also following modernization's lead, historians grew accustomed to thinking of the history of the aged in terms of "better" or "worse" periods, devoting much energy to analyzing exactly when and how a decline in the position of the aged occurred in American society.[10] In addition, though many scholars disputed the timing of change suggested by modernization theory, historians still assumed that the old were relatively homogeneous and that their fortunes rose or fell collectively. The tendency to describe the situation of the aged as a monolithic group stemmed partly from the evidence historians often relied on. In describing changes in the elderly's position, much more attention was given to ideas about old age and the aged than to the conditions in which the elderly lived daily life.[11] Finally, in charting changes in the history of old age, historians also carried over from modernization theory an emphasis on the aged's status, power, and authority in society.[12]

The continuing resonance of modernization theory in the work of its critics had some unfortunate effects. Local case studies were neglected as historians strove for grand vistas on par with those offered by modernization theory. In essence historians attempted to construct syntheses on the history of old age when the foundation for sweeping conclusions were only partially in place. In addition, concern over better and worse periods in old age history—as well as a focus on issues of status—meant that other interesting issues received short shrift. For example, topics such as the elderly's family life, social interactions, and daily activities were left almost untouched.

More recently, historians have been able to move beyond the boundaries imposed by modernization theory and its critics. Historians working on the late nineteenth and twentieth centuries have been particularly effective in addressing the shortcomings of modernization and modernization's critics. For example, much more is now known about the daily realities of the elderly's lives in these periods, allowing for a rejection of the notion of simple, unidirectional decline in the aged's circumstances and permitting an understanding of the diversity of the aged population.[13]

Unfortunately however, the period before 1850 has not benefited from these newer perspectives. As a result, the questions that modernization theorists initially posed and their vision of decline over time has continued to shape our understanding of old age before the mid-nineteenth century. This is because critics of modernization theory rejected its worst aspects but retained the notion that earlier periods of American history were better for the aged while recent times have been worse. Without question work by historians such as John Faragher, John Demos, Terri Premo, Thomas R. Cole, and others have taken strides toward broadening our understanding of America's earlier periods beyond the concerns of modernization.[14] Yet due to a continuing lack of concrete social history on the aged before 1850 the sweeping judgments of earlier scholars have been hard to refute. Thus

Preface xvii

the problems of overly simplistic periodization and a monolithic view of the old persist.

This book addresses these problems in several different ways. To begin with it offers solid information on the day-to-day experiences of America's elderly in a specific time and place, providing the kind of local study that has been sorely lacking. By bringing to bear a much wider array of evidence than most historians have used, this study reduces reliance on what people said or wrote about old age and increases knowledge of how old age was actually lived. Moreover, by asking a whole host of questions about how people experienced old age—from spiritual concerns, to economic circumstances, to domestic life and community involvement—it moves beyond the somewhat idiosyncratic concerns and facile generalizations inherited from modernization theorists to arrive at a fuller conception of what being old meant in the past. This book dispenses with the unidimensional portrait of old people that scholars have sometimes fallen back on and replaces it with a nuanced picture of great diversity among the elderly population. Meanwhile this book challenges the popular but simplistic periodizations of old age history presented in several surveys of American old age history. The evidence offered here calls into question the whole notion of a decline in the aged's lives over the last two centuries—a key component in these periodizations—and suggests that the turning points in the elderly's history are neither so sharp nor so well defined as once imagined.

Though this is a story of aged men and women in Connecticut in the forty years between 1790 and 1830, its findings reach beyond this relatively narrow scope. To begin with, it is probable that what I have found in Connecticut held true for other areas of the United States, particularly in the North, because this area was similar to much of the eastern seaboard where most of the United States' population was concentrated. In addition, for those concerned with the history of age relations this book provides a solid building block for more synthetic works which more accurately address the question of how the elderly's lives have changed over time.

This book also contributes to an understanding of American life more broadly. Much has been written about how societies treat one age group—children—because such treatment is considered a window onto the values and priorities of any given society. The way the aged are conceptualized and treated is no less revealing of the nature of social life. The elderly, for example, shed light on the debate over individualism versus communitarianism in early national America. In recent years historians have argued over whether America in this time was a patriarchal, family-oriented society which honored communal values above all or whether patriarchal structures had already disintegrated into an atomistic, individualistic society of faded communal commitments.[15] This study demonstrates that by the earliest years of the republic the family was already an unreliable institution as far as the aged were concerned and that an ethic of individual self-determination and self-support was already entrenched. The point is, of course, that the aged's circumstances merit interest not only from old age historians and gerontologists but from generalists as well. Indeed, studies of the past would be enhanced if historians took the category of age as seriously as they do race, class, and gender.

I hope that this book will also help to inform an understanding of the present. The elderly have become ever more numerous and visible in the late twentieth century. Correspondingly, the issues surrounding them have come to the forefront of public debate. The quality of old age, the degree to which the state should guarantee late life financial security, and how the elderly should be cared for are just some of issues modern Americans confront. In the swirl of discussion the aged's circumstances today are often compared to some earlier more secure time when society simply took care of its elders. This simpler time is usually thought to have been before industrialization, or urbanization, or any of the other upheavals that have so changed Americans lives in the last century and a half. This book demonstrates that the elderly did not enjoy such a simple or secure way of life even in much earlier periods of American history. It acknowledges that the old have always been a diverse population faced with great challenges. Indeed this book indicates that the elderly have been in an insecure position for a very long time—what has changed over time is only the kind of insecurity. In an age before large-scale institutions were developed to help manage the aging process and offer assistance, insecurity stemmed from the fact that responsibility for a good old age lay squarely on individual men and women while at the same time health, access to resources, family life, and social supports were maddeningly unpredictable. Recognizing these facts and drawing lessons from them will bring us closer to understanding and coping

Preface xix

with the complex situation of the aged in America today than will lamenting the loss of a past that never was.

The analysis that follows is organized thematically rather than chronologically. The first chapter defines the parameters of the study with an introduction to the geographical area being analyzed. Two subsequent chapters delve into the world of ideas and feelings to assess both the prevailing cultural norms regarding old age and how these notions actually played out in the lives of ordinary people. Chapter 2 focuses on the depiction of the aged in the printed literature of the period, while chapter 3 considers ideas about growing old from the perspective of ordinary Connecticut people. From there two chapters follow discussing the financial circumstances of the aged from different perspectives. Chapter 4 compares the aged as a group to other age groups in terms of economic standing. Chapter 5 details the ways in which the elderly of different classes coped with the financial challenges of old age. Household arrangements and the nature of family life are analyzed in the next two chapters. In chapter 6 census data show patterns of change in household arrangements over the life course and demonstrate the distinctiveness of the aged's domestic circumstances. Chapter 7 takes up the related subject of the aged's family relations. Chapter 8 then turns from the private, domestic realm to public life to show how old age reduced community involvement, particularly participation in leadership roles. The concluding chapter attempts to bring the evidence presented in earlier chapters into sharp focus to assess its overall significance.

In writing this book I have accumulated debts to scholars, institutions, friends, and family. To begin with I owe thanks to many people who have helped shape and improve this book. Joyce Appleby guided me from the start providing useful suggestions and encouragement. Ruth Bloch read drafts of the manuscript, offering suggestions that pushed me toward greater clarity and refinement. Kenneth Sokoloff challenged me to expand my project to include quantitative methods and spurred me on with practical advice and faith in the value of my project. I have also benefited from the comments and guidance of William Roy, Albion Urdank, Gary Nash, Clayne Pope, and Stanley Engerman. Members of the U.C.L.A. Early American Thesis Seminar helped me to clarify my project and critiqued early drafts of several chapters. The research for this project was made easier by several individuals and institutions in Hartford, Connecticut. I am grateful to the staff of the History and Genealogy Unit of the Connecticut State Library who patiently aided me over many months. Beverly Naylor and Kevin Johnson deserve special thanks for making me feel welcome in Hartford and helping me track down many obscure items tucked away in the library's mysterious vaults. The entire library staff of the Connecticut Historical Society was equally helpful. I am especially grateful to Alesandra Schmidt and Judith Johnson who tirelessly answered my questions and thought of new ways to find useful information, Ruth Blair who directed me to a particularly rich set of family papers, and Everett Wilkie, Jr. who freely granted access to needed documents. The Society also graciously allowed me permission to quote from its manuscript collections. Thanks also go to the Association for the Study of Connecticut History and the Organization of American Historians for offering a forum to present some of my findings. I am grateful too for the help of my editors at Garland who ably shepherded me through the publication process. Though my intellectual and practical debts are great, my greatest debts are personal. Jean-Laurent Rosenthal heard more about the aged in early America than he ever expected to, offered many helpful suggestions on research methods and writing, and buoyed me with optimism over the several years spent working on this project. My parents, Anita Walker Scott and Ernest L. Scott, also deserve sincere thanks. Their interest in my growth and education, love for their own work, and unqualified enthusiasm and encouragement have inspired me both as a scholar and a person. I dedicate this book to them.

NOTES

1. John Stanford, *Six Short Sermons Adapted to the Aged* (New York: T. and J. Swords, 1829), 42.

2. For a review of the origins and basic characteristics of modernization theory as well as the main criticisms leveled against it see Dean C. Tipps, "Modernization Theory and the Comparative Study of Societies: A Critical Perspective," *Comparative Studies in Society and History* 15 (March 1973): 199–226.

3. Donald Cowgill and Lowell D. Holmes, *Aging and Modernization* (New York: Appleton, Century, Crofts, 1972).

4. Donald O. Cowgill, "Aging and Modernization: A Revision of the Theory," in *Late Life: Communities and Environmental Policy*, ed. Jaber F. Gubrium (Springfield IL: Charles C. Thomas, 1974), 123. See also Cowgill, "The Aging of Populations and Societies," *Annals of the American Academy of Political and Social Science* 415 (September 1974): 1–18.

5. See Cowgill and Holmes, *Aging and Modernization* for schematic representations of how specific aspects of modernization adversely affect the aged.

6. It is ironic that adherents of modernization theory (who generally take a favorable view of the modern world) would be so pessimistic about the situation of the aged in modern times. Perhaps the desire to see the past as a "golden age" stems from a deeper source—a sentimentalized romanticism about earlier times—that not only predates modernization theory but will probably also outlive it.

7. W. Andrew Achenbaum and Peter Stearns, "Old Age and Modernization," *Gerontologist* 18 (1978): 307.

8. Historians of England and France have done much to discredit the claims of modernization theorists. For example, substantial energy has been expended in refuting the idea that extended families were once prevalent and the aged generally resided in them. See Peter Laslett, "Societal Development and Aging," in *Handbook of Aging and the Social Sciences*, 2d ed., ed. Robert H. Binstock and Ethel Shanas (New York: Van Nostrand Reinhold Co., 1985), 199–230; Jill Quadagno, *Aging in Early Industrial Society* (New York: Academic Press, 1982), 13–20; and David Troyansky, "Old Age in the Rural Family of Enlightened Provence," in *Old Age in Preindustrial Society*, ed. Peter Stearns (New York: Holmes and Meier, 1982), 209–231. In addition, scholars such as Keith Thomas have demonstrated that the position of the aged was far more ambiguous in "pre-modern" society than described in the golden-age view. ("Age and Authority in Early Modern England," *Proceedings of the British Academy* 62 [1976]: 205–248.) Georges Minois makes the same point very elegantly in *History of Old Age: From Antiquity to the Renaissance*, trans. Sarah Hanbury Tennison (Chicago: University of Chicago Press, 1989), see his introduction especially. Indeed, as the limitations of modernization theory became obvious it was generally abandoned not only by historians of aging but as a general theory as well.

9. Three ambitious surveys of old age in America appeared when the literature on old age was still quite undeveloped. These were: David Hackett Fischer, *Growing Old in America*, expanded ed. (New York: Oxford University Press, 1978); W. Andrew Achenbaum, *Old Age in the New Land: The American Experience Since 1790* (Baltimore: Johns Hopkins University Press, 1978); and Carole Haber, *Beyond Sixty-Five: The Dilemma of Old Age in America's Past* (New York: Cambridge University Press, 1983).

10. Several of the important surveys of American old age chart a decline of some sort in the elderly's fortunes over time, though each author rejects modernization's formulation of this decline. Fischer describes how Americans shifted from venerating the aged to despising them due to a "revolution" in age relations in the period from 1770 to 1820 (*Growing Old in America*, chapter 2). Achenbaum's *Old Age in the New Land* rejects

modernization's mechanistic linkage between ideas about the aged and social transformation as well as Fischer's analysis of change. Yet like Fischer, Achenbaum also sees a diminution in the value ascribed to old age over time as the idea that the aged were useful was undermined. Carole Haber, in *Beyond Sixty-Five*, likewise argues that old age was devalued through the course of American history, largely due to the development of a "scientific" notion of aging. Meanwhile, Thomas Cole's highly nuanced cultural history of aging in America describes how old age was stripped of meaning over time, depriving the aged of a satisfying existential experience. See *The Journey of Life: A Cultural History of Aging in America* (New York: Cambridge University Press, 1992).

11. Noting this trend Thomas Cole has gone so far as to remark that "we have not even allowed the actual experience of old people into our histories." (Thomas Cole, review of *Beyond Sixty-Five* by Carole Haber, *Journal of Social History* 18 (Spring 1985): 504.

12. Consideration of the aged's status is a central issue in Fischer's *Growing Old in America*. In addition, articles by Daniel Scott Smith ("Old Age and the Great Transformation: A New England Case Study," in *Aging and the Elderly: Humanistic Perspectives in Gerontology*, ed. Stuart Spicker, Kathleen Woodward, and David D. Van Tassel (Atlantic Highlands NJ: Humanities Press), 285–301) and John Demos ("Old Age in Early New England," in *Aging, Death, and the Completion of Being*, ed. David D. Van Tassel (Philadelphia: University of Pennsylvania Press, 1979), 115–164) also consider questions of the elderly's power.

13. For an excellent review of recent scholarship on the later nineteenth and twentieth centuries see Carole Haber and Brian Gratton, *Old Age and the Search for Security: An American Social History* (Bloomington: Indiana University Press, 1994), 10–19.

14. Several smaller studies avoid many of modernization's tendencies. See for example John Faragher, "Old Women and Old Men in Seventeenth-Century Wethersfield, Connecticut," *Women's Studies* 4 (1976): 11–31; Carole Haber, "The Old Folks at Home: The Development of Institutionalized Care for the Aged in Nineteenth-Century Philadelphia," *Pennsylvania Magazine of History and Biography* 101 (April 1977): 240–257; Barbara G. Rosenkrantz and Maris A. Vinovskis, "The Invisible Lunatics: Old Age and Insanity in Mid-Nineteenth-Century Massachusetts," in *Aging and the Elderly: Humanistic Perspectives in Gerontology*, ed. Stuart F. Spicker, Kathleen M. Woodward, and David D. Van Tassel (Atlantic Highlands NJ: Humanities Press, 1978), 95–125; John Demos, "Old Age in Early New England"; Michael Zimmerman, "Old-Age Poverty in Preindustrial New York City," in *Growing Old in America*, 2d ed., ed. Beth B. Hess (New Brunswick NJ: Transaction Books, 1980), 65–88. And two recent books also chart fresh directions in old age history. See Terri Premo, *Winter Friends: Women Growing Old in the New Republic* (Urbana: University of Illinois Press, 1990) and Thomas Cole, *The Journey of Life*.

15. The article that inspired much of this debate is James Henretta, "Families and Farms: *Mentalité* in Pre-Industrial America," *William and Mary Quarterly*, 3d series, 35 (January 1978): 3–32.

Abbreviations

CG   Hartford County, County Court Records, Conservators and Guardians 1739–1855, CSL.

CHS   Connecticut Historical Society, Hartford, Connecticut.

CSL   Connecticut State Library, Hartford, Connecticut.

HCC   Hartford County, County Court Records, 1798–1855, CSL.

HCiC   Hartford City Court Files, 1804–1902, CSL.

HTR   Hartford Town Records, Town Votes 3, 1796–1863, Town Clerk's Office, Hartford, Connecticut.

RPA   Hartford County, County Court Records, Revolutionary War Pension Applications, 1820–1832, CSL.

Growing Old in the
Early Republic

I

Introduction

The focus for this study is Connecticut and the city of Hartford particularly. In exploring different themes and experiences of the elderly I have necessarily adjusted my lens geographically, either broadening or narrowing the vista, according to the evidence available. Thus in examining some topics I draw evidence from all over Connecticut, and in other cases the county of Hartford forms the geographical limit. For the most part, however, the city of Hartford and the aged living there are the subject of this inquiry.

THE GEOGRAPHICAL CONTEXT

Hartford is an excellent locale for studying the aged for several reasons. Early national Hartford was large enough to encompass a diversity of activity—not everyone was a farmer, for example—and as a result, the elderly can be observed in a variety of circumstances. Yet the town was not so large that the details of its citizens' lives overwhelm the historian, making it difficult to trace individuals through time. It was feasible for this study to collect and analyze vital statistics, tax records, and census information for all of Hartford's inhabitants, while such a task would have been unreasonable or impossible for a larger place such as New York City or Philadelphia. In addition, Hartford boasts excellent records, including an indispensable set of birth and death notices that allow the historian to determine the ages of individuals whose names appear in the archival sources.[1] Hartford is also a suitable locale for study because it was a thriving place that participated in many of the trends affecting New England and the nation as a whole. Its population grew over time, its commercial and manufacturing activities expanded, religious diversity increased, and community life developed to support a wide variety of activities and institutions. Hartford was in these ways a typical small city of its time. The fact that it was typical in some ways, combined with its diverse character, manageable size and archival richness, make it a natural choice for studying the aged. Hartford is, however, a specific place and hence possesses a character all its own and peculiarities that must be understood. This chapter sets the stage for the analysis that follows by offering a portrait of the city as well as an introduction to its elderly population.

Hartford was first settled in 1635 and grew slowly at first, but by 1790 the town was home to some 4,072 inhabitants. Throughout the early national period, Hartford's population continued to grow. In 1800 the town held 5,347 souls. By 1810 it had reached 6,003 and in 1820, 6,500 people resided there. In 1830 Hartford's population had reached 9,789 and the town would continue to grow for many more decades. Thus from 1790 to 1830 Hartford's was a growing city with a population that more than doubled. This population consisted largely of native-born whites. As Table 1.1 illustrates, American-born whites far outnumbered both foreigners and African-Americans.

Table 1.1. African-Americans and Foreigners as Percentage of Hartford Population

Year	African-Americans	Foreigners
1790	2.1	—
1800	4.5	—
1810	4.7	—
1820	5.4	0.5
1830	5.0	1.1

Source: U.S. Censuses, Hartford, CT, 1790–1830.

Situated on the west bank of the Connecticut River, early national Hartford covered about thirty square miles, much of it land well suited to agricultural pursuits.[2] The town was bisected by another much smaller river—the Mill—into two divisions. The north side of town, as a gazetteer from 1819 explained, "comprises most of the public buildings, and a considerable proportion of the population, wealth & business of the city."[3] The south side of town, meanwhile, was considerably more rural. While its position on the river made Hartford

Introduction

accessible to both the hinterlands and the coast, it was also well-served by roads and stage routes. As early as 1800 daily stages to New Haven and Albany stopped in Hartford. And by 1819 many roads, mostly turnpikes, radiated from the city to New York, Boston, Providence, Hanover, New Hampshire and several other points. As one contemporary observer noted, "It is believed . . . that there is no town of its size in the United States, that unites so many facilities and conveniences for communication and intercourse abroad."[4]

Hartford's advantageous situation played a significant role in the pattern and rate of its economic growth. Agriculture and animal husbandry occupied some of the town's inhabitants—in 1817, for example, about three quarters of the town lands were employed as plowlands or pasture.[5] Farmers seem to have concentrated on growing hay, corn, rye, and potatoes as well as raising livestock while household gardens yielded a wide array of culinary vegetables and fruits. Though it is difficult to know exactly what percentage of Hartford's residents engaged in agriculture, farming remained an important activity throughout the early national period.[6]

Yet unlike many neighboring towns, Hartford was also a bustling commercial center where merchants gathered to trade the products of Connecticut's more interior areas—including grain, cider, spirits, butter, cheese, beef, lumber, and manufactured goods such as saddles and clocks—both in the coasting trade with other states and to destinations abroad.[7] Though the events surrounding the War of 1812 curtailed Hartford's mercantile business substantially, there were at least fourteen navigation concerns operating in 1819 and river traffic remained busy.[8] Indeed, "During the year 1816, two hundred and seventy eight ships, brigs and schooners, and more than two hundred smaller vessels ascended the Connecticut river to Hartford."[9]

Meanwhile, over the course of the early national period, manufacturing grew in importance. Hartford was the site of New England's first (though short-lived) woolen manufactory, built in 1788. Around the turn of the century residents made mirrors, paint, footwear, books, brass, furniture and cigars.[10] By the 1810s Hartford was home to numerous enterprises, large and small, producing items as diverse as hats, tinware, and paper. These existed alongside various artisanal shops that took care of everything from blacksmithing to baking. A list of the town's business establishments, taken from an

1819 gazetteer shows the variety of pursuits Hartford's citizens engaged in.

> 1 oil mill, 1 bell founder, 1 mill stone manufactory, 1 air furnace, 1 paper-hanging manufactory, 1 marble paper manufactory, 1 brush manufacturer, 1 button factory, 1 confectioner, 1 cotton factory, 1 pewter factory, 1 umbrella manufactory, 1 whip-lash factory, 1 machine card factory, 1 silk dyer, 1 sail maker, 2 gold leaf manufactories, 2 hat factories, 2 leather dressers, 2 looking-glass factories, 2 portrait painters, 2 tinware factories, 2 woolen factories, 2 carding machines, 2 wheelwrights, 3 auctioneers, 3 distilleries, 3 engravers, 3 exchange offices, 3 lottery offices, 4 carriage makers, 4 coppersmiths, 4 clothier's works, 4 shoe stores, 5 barber's shops, 5 merchant tailors, 5 wholesale dry goods stores, 5 grain mills, 5 potteries, 6 bakers, 6 book binderies, 6 master masons and brick layers, 6 sign, coach, and house painters, 6 tanneries, 6 tailor's shops, 7 bookstores, 7 druggist stores, 8 gold and silversmith's shops, 8 cabinet, furniture, and chair makers, 9 millinery and mantuamaker's shops, 9 printing offices, 10 coopers, 13 blacksmith shops, 14 houses concerned in navigation, 16 butcher's stalls, 16 shoe factories, 18 ale, porter, and small beer houses, 19 master house joiners and carpenters, 21 taverns or public inns, 26 dry goods retail stores, 61 grocery, crockery, and provision stores[11]

In addition to these activities, Hartford also had a complement of professional men including twenty-two practicing attorneys and twelve active physicians and surgeons.[12]

The early national period saw the beginnings of Hartford's insurance industry as well. After the first policy was written in 1794 by the Hartford Fire Insurance Company several other firms were founded including a marine insurance company in 1803 and Aetna in 1819. Meanwhile, banks opened to serve the needs both of businessmen and small savers. Hartford from 1790 to 1830 was a town of diverse economic activities with agriculture, commerce, manufacturing, and the professions each contributing to the mix.

Like other small cities during the period, Hartford had an active community life. As both the county seat and half-time state capital (an honor it shared with New Haven), Hartford was a locus of political activity when legislators and the courts held sessions. In addition Hartford had two local government bodies—town and city—adding structure to community life.[13] Politics in the city, as in Connecticut generally, tended to be staunchly Federalist, so it is not surprising that this locale was chosen for the Hartford Convention of 1814.

Religiously Hartford was also conservative. Congregationalism was the established denomination in Connecticut from the colonial period until 1818 and as a result the town in 1790 already had three Congregational churches with long histories. By 1790 a meeting of Baptists had also organized into a permanent church, as had an Episcopal group. Meanwhile, Methodist ministers preached sporadically in the town and a small band of Quakers met together for several years. Still, Hartford's Congregational tendencies waned only slowly as the effects of the Second Great Awakening began to be felt. Disestablishment weakened Congregational influence as well and by the 1820s Methodists, Universalists, and other rival denominations were attracting increasing numbers of followers.

Voluntary organizations also flourished in the early national period and Hartford, like many other towns, developed a whole host of associations that brought people together for many different purposes. In the 1790s a Masonic lodge was active, a Charitable Society was busy relieving poverty, and a social library had opened to circulate reading material. In each succeeding decade, new organizations were founded. Among them in the years between 1800 and 1830 were a Female Beneficent Society, a Cent Society, a Sunday School Society, a Mechanics Society, an Evangelical Tract Society, an Auxiliary Colonization Society, a Widows Society, a Linnean Botanic Society, and a Peace Society, which together created a dense web of voluntary activity in town.

Over the course of the early national period Hartford's institutions developed as well. In 1819 the town boasted a grammar school designed to prepare youths for college, three public schools, and fifteen private schools.[14] Among the latter was the American Asylum for the Deaf and Dumb, the first school of its kind in America, headed by Thomas Gallaudet. Washington College (later renamed Trinity College) was founded several years later in 1823. And by 1827 the town's citizens organized to establish the Hartford Female Seminary to educate "females in the liberal arts & sciences."[15] Interest in aiding the insane led to the founding of the Connecticut Retreat for the Insane, which pioneered more humane treatments of the mentally ill beginning in 1824.

Like so many other long-settled towns in the decades after the Revolution, Hartford was a place in which tradition was overlaid with change. Agricultural pursuits remained important alongside newer shops and manufactories. Federalism carried on in the face of a changing political climate. Congregationalism persisted as newer denominations earned adherents. And the older civic structures of the town were embellished by a flowering of associational activity. Yet while the developments of the early-nineteenth century did not pass Hartford by it was by no means a fully transformed "modern" city. For the most part Hartford's identity and activities were more firmly rooted in the past than in the future to come. This brief portrait of Hartford provides the geographical context for this study. Before beginning an analysis of the aged in early national Hartford it is equally important to understand the demographic setting.

WHAT WAS "OLD"?

The meaning of the word "old" for past times is not immediately obvious and therefore scholars have offered varying definitions. Carole Haber, for example, adopts our current chronological enumeration—sixty-five—as the definition of "old."[16] David Hackett Fischer employs contemporary measures such as the Biblical "threescore and ten years" for the colonial period.[17] Others, such as John Faragher, suggest that there may have been varying assessments of old age depending on when certain life-cycle criteria were met (such as marriage of a person's youngest child).[18] Some historians skirt the question altogether, implying that old age ensued around sixty but offering little explanation for this judgment.[19] Several of these definitions are asserted rather than demonstrated and they often fail to account for the possibility of changing notions of age over time and place. Yet we need not settle for these definitions of old age when printed works circulating in early national America and the personal papers of Connecticut citizens give insight into notions prevailing between 1790 and 1830 and effectively answer the question "what is old?"[20]

While Americans today tend to think of the life span as variable depending on genetic and environmental circumstances, many eighteenth and early-nineteenth century Americans believed God had set "the age of man" firmly at seventy years.[21] The seventy-year limit was a result of events described in the Bible, which many religious writers took literally. As Ebenezer Gay, an eighty-five year old minister, sermonized in 1781,

> The boundaries of human life have been different in the several ages of the world. There have been gradual abbreviations of it from the first man, Adam, who lived nine hundred and thirty years to Moses, who lived an hundred and twenty. But then, the term fixed by God was threescore years and ten. This hath ever been the gaol that stints our race—Some run beyond it, but the most do not reach it.[22]

A few decades later Caleb Tenney, also a minister, echoed this view and explained the reason for man's curtailed life span. In the past, he explained, men only "dimly saw death at the distance of many centuries" and hence indulged their sinful passions. Dissatisfied with man's ill use of time, God substituted a shorter span, providing a "check on human depravity" by keeping death close at hand.[23] These Biblical notions allowed Stanley Griswold, in a funeral sermon given in 1801, to conclude that "No living voice is to be heard on earth, of more than about threescore years and ten."[24] Joseph Lathrop, also a minister noted that "scarcely one in twelve" reach age eighty and that those who do were truly of a "great age."[25] The Reverend Joel Hawes of Hartford predicted in a more pessimistic sermon delivered in 1818 that "not more than one in a hundred lives to the age of seventy."[26] Though the Connecticut diarist, schoolteacher, and farmer Elisha Niles may not have heard the words of these ministers, his own clergyman may have made similar remarks. Thus on his seventieth birthday in 1834 he wrote, "This day I call my birthday . . . which makes me 70 years old . . . I may now call myself on Probation."[27] Seventy was considered the maximum life span for men and women in the early national period.

Clearly anyone who reached "the age of man" at seventy was "old." Those who persisted to eighty, ninety, or beyond could be called "far advanced in years" and were thought to have lived "beyond the ordinary limits of human life."[28] As Job Orton remarked in his *Discourses to the Aged*, "those who arrived to seventy years . . . know they must shortly put off the body; and they who, like Barzillai, are got ten years beyond it, are sure of a very speedy dismission."[29]

But when did old age begin? On this question there was less consensus. Unlike today's dictionaries which plainly state that old age is "generally considered to be the years after 65," early national dictionaries offered only vague definitions of the term.[30] For example, Samuel Johnson's *Dictionary of the English Language* defined old broadly as "Past the middle part of life; not young," reflecting the flexibility of the term.[31] Other dictionaries frequently defined the term "aged" simply as "old; stricken in years." Noah Webster's *American Spelling Book* noted that there were five states of human life—infancy, childhood, youth, manhood, and age—but declined to give general rules for when each stage began and ended.[32]

Evidence from other printed works and diaries of the period is somewhat more specific, often pointing to the fifties and sixties as likely starting points for old age. For example, *The New and Complete American Encyclopedia* (1805) divided life into four stages with old age occurring from age fifty until death.[33] With a similar definition in mind Rebecca Noyes, a diarist living in Stonington, Connecticut, concluded in 1809 at the age of fifty that "I should set myself about preparing for the approach of Winter (old age) which time rools on its swiftest wheels."[34] Her contemporary, the fifty-one year old merchant Peter Gallaudet of Hartford confided plaintively to his diary in 1807, "the days of my youth and middle age there is no recalling these stages of life, old age is advancing . . . I descend into the valley with a full view before me." A week later he confirmed, "I am now outbound & going down the stream of time."[35]

Others set the onset of old age slightly later in the fifties. John Hill's *The Old Man's Guide to Health* (1775) admitted that,

> It may be expected I should now say, at what period the state of it that we call aged begins, but nature has herself left this undeterminable. The weakness and infirmities of age come at different years, in different constitu-

tions . . . but to speak in general terms, [old age] begins about fifty-eight; tho greater infirmities of age do not advance till several years later.[36]

Similarly Isaiah Thomas included in his almanac for 1799 a nine-stage description of human life in which the period from fifty-six to sixty-three was identified as when "the infirmities of age come on."[37] The young schoolteacher William Pierson of Killingworth, Connecticut, seems to have agreed with these assessments since he referred to his fifty-nine-year-old father as "in his declining years."[38] The fifties thus appears to have been a rather loosely-defined boundary zone between middle and old age. Individuals in their fifties were judged old based on the presence of infirmities, while those who staved off debility may have avoided being labeled "aged" until a few years later.

Yet by sixty most thought old age began in earnest. Luigi Cornaro's oft-reprinted *The Probable Way of Attaining a Long and Healthful Life* promised those who followed his advice that they could avoid wrinkles and gray hair until age one hundred but he acknowledged that most people are infirm by about sixty.[39] Likewise Anthony Carlisle's *Essay on the Disorders of Old Age* (1819) noted that while old age has no precise boundaries, "The age of Sixty may, in general, be fixed upon as the commencement of senility—About that period it commonly happens, that some signs of bodily infirmity begin to appear."[40] One of the first American organizations founded to aid elderly women, the Association for the Relief of Respectable, Aged, Indigent Females in New York, adopted age sixty as the earliest age at which women could apply for relief "unless strongly recommended by necessitous circumstances."[41] This choice suggests that any individual over sixty could automatically meet the criterion of "aged." Other bits of scattered evidence support this idea. For example, Isaac Bickerstaffe's farcical play *He Would if He Could: Or an Old Fool Worse than Any* (1804) featured an "old fool" of sixty-six years. Likewise various Connecticut diarists not infrequently referred to individuals in their sixties as "old."

Though we are accustomed to considering the bureaucratically-mandated age of sixty-five as the boundary of old age, early national Americans gave the category more flexibility. These sources suggest that use of the term "old" was contingent both on individual circumstances and chronological age. In cases of ill health old age could begin as early as fifty. By sixty however, most seem to have been considered old for the simple reason that they had lived six decades, regardless of health or vivacity. By seventy, one was both old and at the limit of human life. After seventy one was living on borrowed time. The definition of aged in the early national period allowed for different kinds of old people—the "young old" below seventy, those at seventy who had reached "the age of man," and the "old old" over seventy.

HOW MANY OLD?

How many people lived long enough to meet the definition of "old" in past times? Were old people numerous or rare? Could men and women expect to grow old? A lack of reliable records for the United States before 1830 makes complete answers to these questions elusive. However, thanks to the work of demographers and historians, particularly on the colonial period, some basic facts are well understood.

For those living in colonial New England it is clear that life was relatively long. Studies by Philip Greven and John Demos, among others, point to the fact that reaching old age was not unusual.[42] For the generation that settled Andover, Massachusetts, for example, Greven demonstrates that "those who did survive to adulthood could anticipate long and healthy lives."[43] Indeed almost 80 percent of men who reached twenty survived on to age fifty, and half reached seventy. Women also "tended to reach advanced ages in appreciable numbers."[44] Demos has estimated that people aged sixty and over made up between 4 and 7 percent of the total population or from about 8 to 14 percent of the adult (aged twenty and over) population in established New England communities. As he points out, this means that old people were about half as numerous in colonial New England as in they were in the 1970s.[45] Taken together the evidence indicates that while there were certainly fewer aged people in colonial New England than there are today, to argue as some have that "there were not very many old people" overstates the situation.[46] The aged were not nearly as unusual as we might think.

Introduction

The early national period has received considerably less scholarly attention on these issues, but it appears that life expectancy, especially in New England, continued to be relatively high. Robert V. Wells has noted that, "In the absence of epidemic infections [nineteenth-century] Americans probably survived as long as any people in the world."[47] And Clayne Pope's study of mortality in America shows that both men and women could expect to live equally long in this period. However, in more settled eastern regions, including places like Hartford, "female life expectation tended to be higher than male life expectation."[48]

For the United States, Terri Premo indicates that those sixty or over made up at least 4 percent of the total population in 1830.[49] The percentage for New England alone was no doubt higher, due to the region's general healthfulness, and thus was probably comparable to Demos' estimates for New England in the colonial period.[50] Though more precise information on the age structure of the population is lacking, it is unlikely that major shifts in longevity or the proportion of aged people were underway from 1790 to 1830. Clayne Pope, for example, has recently demonstrated that life expectancy for people born at the end of the eighteenth century was remarkably similar to that of people born a full hundred years later.[51] Though the percentage of elderly people in the population increased very slowly over the course of the nineteenth century, it was not until the twentieth century that more major increases in the elderly population occurred.[52] Overall then, as Terri Premo has stated, "old persons" in early national America "were not rare and men and women could reasonably hope to live to old age."[53]

These trends were general. Because specific localities were likely to experience variations, evidence from Hartford itself improves our sense of how common the elderly were. Figures 1.1 and 1.2 display information from the 1830 census to show the proportions of various age groups in the white and black population in Hartford respectively. The general youthfulness of both the white and black populations is immediately striking. About 45 percent of all whites were under the age of twenty while a similar number of blacks were quite young. In addition, it is clear that the age distribution of both white and black men differed from that of women. Figure 1.1 also gives visual evidence that while the "young" old (those in their fifties and sixties) were not uncommon, people very advanced in years were scarcer.

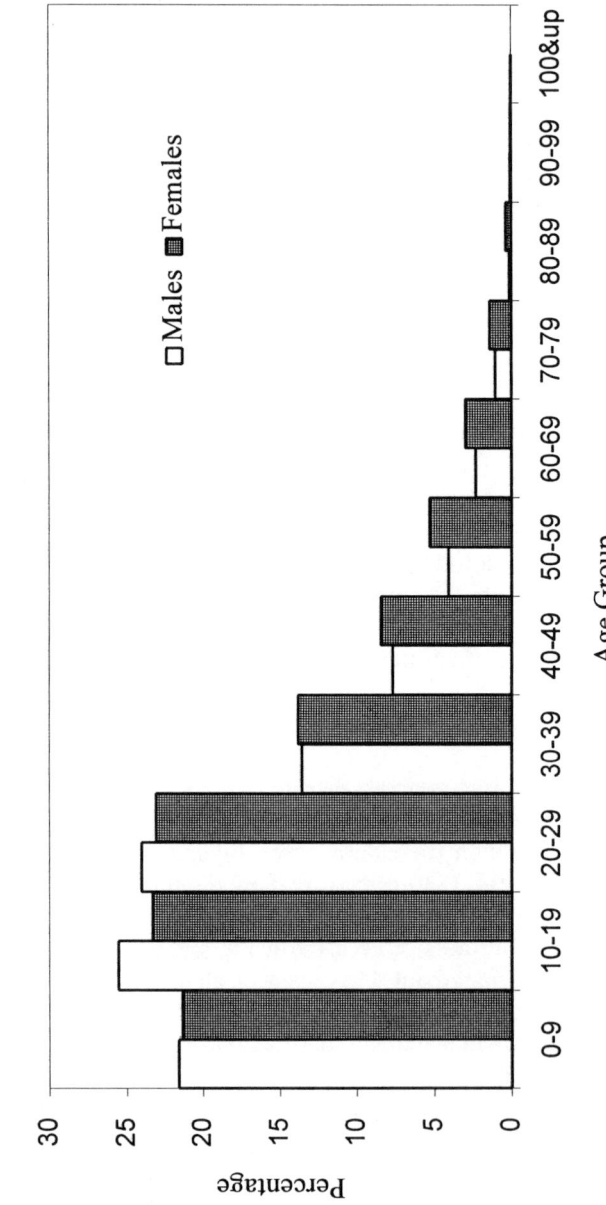

Figure 1.1. Age Structure of White Population, Hartford, 1830

Source: U.S. Census, Hartford, CT, 1830.

Figure 1.2. Age Structure of Black Population, Hartford, 1830

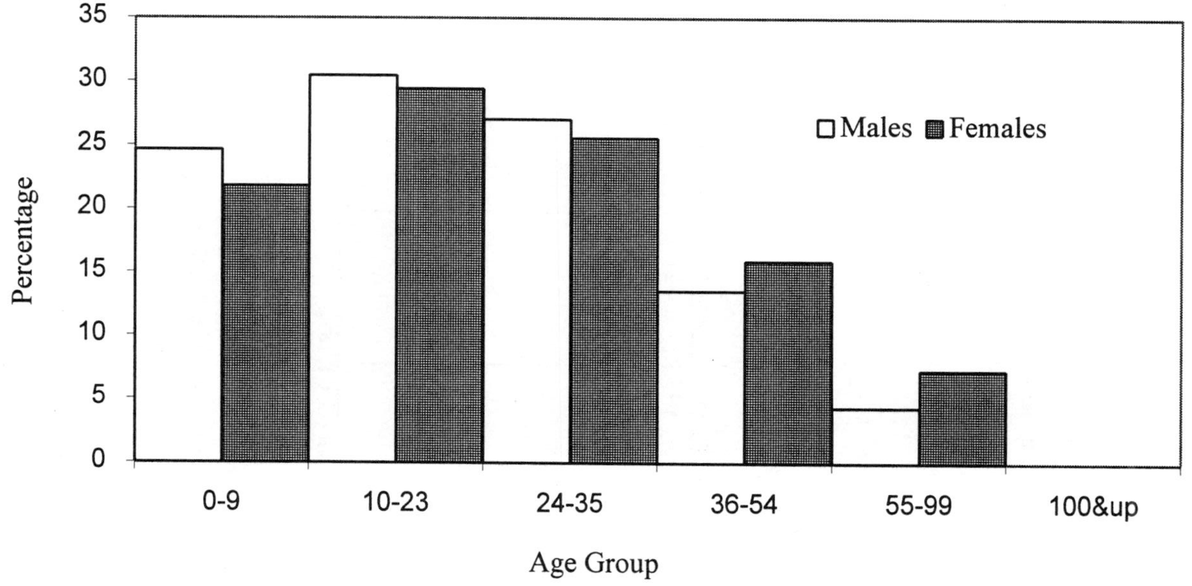

□ Males ■ Females

Source: U.S. Census, Hartford, CT, 1830.

Tables 1.2 and 1.3, showing the number and percentage of individuals in each age group allow a closer look at Hartford's demographics in 1830. Table 1.2 reveals that 7.4 percent of all white men and 9.7 percent of all white women were fifty or above. Meanwhile 3.4 percent of men were sixty or older compared to 4.5 percent of women. Because of the odd categories census enumerators employed, we know less about the structure of the small African-American population in Hartford. However as Table 1.3 indicates, 4.3 percent of black men and 7.2 percent of black women were aged fifty-five or more. Overall, the figures for both whites and blacks are comparable with Terri Premo's estimate that those over sixty comprised at least 4 percent of the population in early national America.

Table 1.2. Age Structure of White Population, Hartford, 1830

Age Group	Males		Females	
	Number	Percentage	Number	Percentage
0–9	999	21.60	997	21.30
10–19	1181	25.50	1087	23.30
20–29	1111	24.00	1077	23.00
30–39	626	13.50	643	13.70
40–49	354	7.60	393	8.40
50–59	188	4.00	246	5.20
60–69	106	2.20	138	2.90
70–79	48	1.00	65	1.30
80–89	6	0.12	16	0.34
90–99	3	0.06	2	0.04
100 & up	1	0.02	0	0

Source: U.S. Census, Hartford, CT, 1830.

In terms of sheer numbers these figures meant that in a city of about 9,800 people, 819 whites—or 352 men and 467 women—were aged fifty or over in 1830. The number of people over sixty amounted to 385 in total, or 164 men and 221 women. Because the black population was quite small there were naturally fewer elderly amongst them. Still, 30 African-Americans—including 9 men and 21 women—were fifty-five or older in 1830. Thus we can certainly say that encountering an aged person in Hartford must not have been an unusual occurrence. Elderly women would have been a particularly

Introduction

likely sight since among both blacks and whites a greater percentage of women were old than were men. Indeed women were present in greater numbers than men in most of the elderly age groups.[54] However, with both men and women a distinction between the "young" old and the "old" old should be made. Though good data on blacks are not available, Table 1.2 clearly shows that among whites the extremely aged were few in number. While there were twenty-two people in their eighties residing in Hartford, a mere five were in their nineties, and only one man claimed to be a centenarian.

Table 1.3. Age Structure of Black Population, Hartford, 1830

Age Group	Males		Females	
	Number	Percentage	Number	Percentage
0–9	51	24.6	63	21.7
10–23	63	30.4	85	29.4
24–35	56	27.0	74	25.6
36–54	28	13.5	46	15.9
55–99	9	4.3	21	7.2
100 & up	0	0	0	0

Source: U.S. Census, Hartford, CT, 1830.

Unfortunately, 1830 is the only year for which information on Hartford's age structure in the early national period is available. Hartford, as we have seen, was a changing city in this period and its mix of people of different ages may have varied over time. However, the information just presented, along with other findings for the period, show that while society was very youthful, the aged were nevertheless a significant fraction of the population. Not limited to only a few members, the elderly were an ordinary sight in the houses, fields, and streets of Hartford.

These concrete facts concerning the city of Hartford and its aged population begin to set the stage for understanding the elderly's experience. But understanding the ideological context for old age is equally important. The next chapter evaluates ideas about the elderly circulating in America's early national period to determine how old age was regarded and what expectations were associated with it. With this understood, we can then begin to peel back the multiple layers of experience in old age.

NOTES

1. I am referring to the Barbour Collection of genealogical records and the Hale Collection of headstone inscriptions housed at CSL. See appendix A.

2. Hartford was this size during the early national period, after East Hartford had broken off to form a separate town and before West Hartford incorporated as a separate town.

3. John C. Pease and John M. Niles, *A Gazetteer of the States of Connecticut and Rhode Island* (Hartford CT: William S. Marsh, 1819), 45.

4. Ibid., 41.

5. Ibid., 44, 38, reports that about 15,000 acres out of 19,200 fell into the category of taxable agricultural lands in the town's 1817 tax list.

6. The 1820 census counted the number of people engaged in agriculture, commerce, and manufacturing in Hartford. Of a total 1,522 individuals listed as engaging in one of these three pursuits 557 (or about 36 percent) were in agriculture, 235 (or about 15 percent) were in commerce, and 730 (or about 48 percent) were in manufacturing occupations. No doubt the balance of agriculture to other economic activities shifted substantially during the early national period. One would expect there to have been more farmers in 1790, for example, than in 1820. Thus these figures cannot be considered definitive for the entire period.

7. Pease and Niles, *A Gazetteer of the States of Connecticut and Rhode Island*, 13.

8. Ibid., 43.

9. Ibid., 50.

10. Viggo E. Bird, *Early Beginnings of Connecticut Industry* (Princeton NJ: Newcomen Society, 1937), 16–26.

11. Compiled from Pease and Niles, *A Gazetteer of the States of Connecticut and Rhode Island*, 43–44.

12. Ibid., 45.

13. Town government and city government existed alongside each other (fulfilling somewhat different functions and with different boundaries) from 1784 when Hartford incorporated as a city through the early national period.

14. Pease and Niles, *A Gazetteer of the States of Connecticut and Rhode Island*, 49.

15. Hartford Female Seminary, Records & Minutes of Meetings of Trustees, 1827–1890, CHS.

16. Carole Haber, *Beyond Sixty-Five: The Dilemma of Old Age in America's Past* (New York: Cambridge University Press, 1983).

17. David Hackett Fischer, *Growing Old in America*, expanded ed. (New York: Oxford University Press, 1978), chapter 1.

18. John Faragher, "Old Women and Old Men in Seventeenth-Century Wethersfield, Connecticut," *Women's Studies* 4 (Special Issue 1976): 16.

19. This is true for Daniel Scott Smith, "Old Age and the 'Great Transformation:' A New England Case Study," in *Aging and the Elderly: Humanistic Perspectives in Gerontology*, ed. Stuart Spicker, Kathleen Woodward, and David D. Van Tassel (Atlantic Highlands NJ: Humanities Press, 1978). John Demos offers somewhat more explanation in "Old Age in Early New England," in *Aging, Death and the Completion of Being*, ed. David D. Van Tassel (Philadelphia: University of Pennsylvania Press, 1979), 116–117.

20. In analyzing the definition of "old" I look at printed works published in the United States generally and the personal papers of Connecticut citizens.

21. It is important to note that none who attempted to define "old" in this period made gender distinctions. Those who adopted the Biblical measure of seventy years most likely believed it applied to both men and women. Sermons were directed to both sexes and most

people probably understood religious definitions of old age to include women. Yet it is difficult to know if other authors considered women as well as men. In the absence of a printed discourse on women's old age we must accept the definition of "old" described in this chapter only tentatively for women.

22. Ebenezer Gay, *The Old Man's Calendar*, 4th ed. (Dover NH: Eliphalet Ladd, 1793), 8.

23. Caleb Tenney, *Ministers Must Die. A Sermon Preached . . . After the Interment of the Rev. John Marsh* (Hartford CT: George Goodwin & Sons, 1821), 5. Ironically, though ministers saw the human life span as stunted, Americans and especially New Englanders in the late-eighteenth and early-nineteenth centuries probably enjoyed as long a life expectancy as any population in the world. See Robert V. Wells, *Revolutions in Americans' Lives: A Demographic Perspective on the History of Americans, Their Families, and Their Society* (Westport CT: Greenwood Press, 1982), 125–6.

24. Stanley Griswold, *The Good Man's Prospects in the Hour of Death* (Litchfield CT: T. Collier, 1801), 16.

25. Joseph Lathrop, *Old Age Improved: A Sermon* (Springfield MA: T. Dickman, 1811), 5, 3.

26. Oliver Boardman, Diary, 4 January 1818, CHS.

27. Elisha Niles, Diary, 28 February 1834, CHS.

28. Calvin Chapin, *A Sermon, Delivered at the Funeral of Rev. John Marsh* (Hartford CT: G. Goodwin & Sons, 1821), 20, 3.

29. Job Orton, *Discourses to the Aged* (Salem MA: J. Cushing for T.C. Cushing, 1801), 30.

30. *Random House Dictionary of the English Language* (New York: Random House, 1966). A sampling of the many other sources that employ sixty-five as the measure of old age are *Webster's Third International Dictionary* (Springfield MA: G. & C. Merriam Co., 1976); *Random House Dictionary of the English Language* 2d ed. (New York: Random House, 1987); *The World Book Encyclopedia*, vol. 14 (Chicago: World Book, Inc., 1989), 744; *Encyclopedia Americana*, vol. 20 (Danbury CT: Grolier Inc., 1991), 701.

31. Samuel Johnson, *Dictionary of the English Language* (Philadelphia: Jacob Johnson & Co., 1805).

32. Noah Webster, *American Spelling Book* (Boston: Printed for John West, 1805), 67.

33. *The New and Complete American Encyclopedia* (New York: John Low, 1805).

34. Rebecca Noyes, Diary, 18 April 1809, CHS.

35. Peter Gallaudet, Diary, 23 April, May 1, 1807, CHS. Terri Premo notes that some of the women she studied also considered themselves old in their early fifties. See *Winter Friends: Women Growing Old in the New Republic, 1785–1835* (Urbana: University of Illinois Press, 1990), 12 note 9.

36. John Hill, *The Old Man's Guide to Health* (Philadelphia: Dunlap, 1775), 4.

37. Isaiah Thomas, *Massachusetts, Connecticut, Rhode Island, New Hampshire, and Vermont Almanac* (Worcester MA: Isaiah Thomas, 1798), unpaginated.

38. William Pierson, Diary, 17 November 1808, CSL.

39. Luigi Cornaro, *The Probable Way of Attaining a Long and Healthful Life* (Portsmouth: George Jerry Osborne, 1788), 44.

40. Anthony Carlisle, *An Essay on the Disorders of Old Age* (Philadelphia: Edward Earle, 1819), title page, 13.

41. Association for the Relief of Respectable, Aged, Indigent Females, *The Constitution and First and Second Annual Reports* (New York: J. Seymour, 1815), 4.

42. Philip Greven, *Four Generations: Population, Land and Family in Colonial Andover, Massachusetts* (Ithaca: Cornell University Press, 1970), chapter 2; John Demos, "Notes on Life in Plymouth Colony," *William and Mary Quarterly* 22 (1965): 264–286.

43. Greven, *Four Generations*, 26.

44. Ibid., 27.

45. John Demos, "Old Age in Early New England," 122–123. David Hackett Fischer also ventures an estimate of the number of aged people in the population, though his figure is lower than Demos'. Fischer contends that in 1790 "less than 2 per cent" of Americans were aged sixty-five or older. He also argues that the proportion of old people in the population changed little from 1625 to 1810. (*Growing Old in America*, 3, 27.) Thus one can assume that Fischer's claim of "less than 2 per cent" applies not only to 1790 but to America's entire prior history. Part of the disparity in estimates between Fischer and Demos no doubt stems from the fact that Demos considers New England alone while Fischer seems to refer to America as a whole. As New England was generally healthier than other regions, an estimate for it alone would likely be higher than the figure Fischer offers. In addition, Fischer limits his estimate to those sixty-five and older while Demos includes everyone aged sixty and over. Thus, Fischer's estimate will necessarily be smaller.

46. David Hackett Fischer, *Albion's Seed: Four British Folkways in America* (New York: Oxford University Press, 1989), 104.

47. Robert V. Wells, *Revolutions in Americans' Lives*, 125.

48. Clayne Pope, "Adult Mortality in America before 1900: A View from Family Histories," in *Strategic Factors in Nineteenth Century Economic History*, ed. Claudia Goldin and Hugh Rockoff (Chicago: University of Chicago Press, 1992), 293.

49. Premo, *Winter Friends*, 11 note 2.

50. However it should be noted that Pope has recently shown that this New England advantage, while still perceptible in the early national period, decreased over the course of the nineteenth century. See "Adult Mortality in America before 1900," 284–287.

51. Ibid., 277. It should be noted however that Pope finds a decline in life expectancy in the decades surrounding the Civil War. Pope's overall findings are supported by other scholars. Robert V. Wells notes that life expectancy at birth for white Americans in 1850 was much the same as in the late eighteenth century. See *Revolutions in Americans' Lives*, 126. Looking at Massachusetts towns, Maris Vinovskis likewise finds stability in mortality rates in the first half of the nineteenth century. See "Mortality Rates and Trends in Massachusetts before 1860," *Journal of Economic History* 32 (March 1972): 184–213.

52. W. Andrew Achenbaum, *Old Age in the New Land: The American Experience Since 1790* (Baltimore: Johns Hopkins University Press, 1978), 60; Premo, *Winter Friends*, 11 note 2.

53. Premo, *Winter Friends*, 11 note 2.

54. Part of this is due to the fact that women were slightly more numerous than men in general in 1830 Hartford. However some of the differences may also be explained by higher life expectancies for women which could be expected in more settled eastern regions. On this last point see Pope, "Adult Mortality in America before 1900," 291.

II

American Ideas on Aging and the Elderly to 1830

All human societies infuse the aging process with norms and meaning, yet how old age is understood varies tremendously from one culture to the next. It has been argued that compared to earlier eras, current American culture lacks a shared meaning of old age, one that allows men and women to navigate the aging process with a sense of purpose and satisfaction.[1] Yet from an ideological perspective the early national period was no easier on the old. This chapter analyzes the particular set of ideas and expectations about senescence that circulated in America in the late eighteenth and early nineteenth centuries to show that ideas about growing old tended to be quite negative, stressing decline as the principle feature of old age. Cultural norms gave the aged little clear direction because contradictory ideas and prescriptions for behavior existed side by side. And even if one embraced the dominant set of notions about old age—that formulated by religious writers—ideals and expectations were demanding to the point of being unrealistic, while offering only harsh judgment to those unable to fulfill them. In short, the ideological environment of early national America was a difficult one for the aged. Bereft of a single guiding ideology men and women faced an array of ideas that were often at odds with one another, quite bleak, and difficult to put into practice.

The sources for this investigation are eighteenth and nineteenth-century books, sermons, poems, plays, almanacs, and newspapers, most of which were published in America. Diaries and letters of Connecticut people occasionally supplement these printed works. Though the elderly were less frequently the subject or intended audience for printed works than were children and youth, a significant body of material on aging and the elderly was published. Authors, who themselves ranged in age from seventeen to over eighty, offered a wide array of ideas about aging that resist simple explanation and differ substantially from our own.

In this overview of printed ideas circulating in America I have not focused on any one region. However, because most publishing activity in this period was concentrated in New England and the mid-Atlantic states, the sources from these areas tend to dominate. In the case of religious literature the voice of New England is especially strong. Thus if regions or religious groups seem neglected here it is because their ideas did not find their way into print rather than because they were purposely excluded.

OLD AGE AS DECLINE

Old age in the early national period was viewed as a distinct time of life. In defining the typical experiences of old age, early national Americans focused strongly on the negative. In countless sermons, books, and poems of the period, written by both lay and religious authors, little effort was made to discover positive aspects of growing old. Instead authors stressed the association between advanced years and physical and mental decline. They indicated that weakness, infirmities, and loss of mental powers were a given, to be expected by anyone who pushed beyond age sixty. Connecticut's diarists and letter-writers echoed these ideas. Some writers minimized the extent of decay in old age while others exaggerated it, but all agreed that deterioration and advancing years were two sides of the same coin.

Religious writers tended to describe the physical changes of old age most negatively, often referring to Solomon's Biblical assessment of old age as "the evil day" of human life in which pains and trials engulfed men.[2] Ebenezer Gay, for example, outlined the full bleakness of advanced years in 1793,

> the evil days ... are usually attended with such weaknesses, pains, diseases, disquiets, miseries of various kinds, as make folks (saith the Roman orator) complain of a load lying upon them heavier than mount Aetna.[3]

And in 1801 Stanley Griswold provided additional details on what his readers had to look forward to in old age:

> However alert, firm, active, or graceful our bodies may be in younger years . . . decays must come on, infirmities and pains must creep forward, the strong arm must become weak, the joints stiffen, the frame bow and totter, the graceful locks must whiten and fall, the face of beauty must be wrinkled.[4]

A tract entitled, "To the Aged" published in 1814 summed up the religious view of aging in a nutshell: "He that is old, should be, in his own estimation, a dying man."[5] Ministers urged their audiences to see old age in its worst light which they hoped would encourage redirection of hopes from the transitory physical world to the eternal realm. Emphasizing sickness and dependency highlighted the elderly's proximity to death and was meant to spur efforts to prepare for future judgment.[6] Yet whatever its intentions, the religious conception of old age in early national America provided a very pessimistic model of the nature of old age.

A second category of literature on old age—medical or health manuals—also focused on infirmity as the defining characteristic of old age. Yet though these works catalogued the physical ills associated with aging, they were somewhat more positive than religious literature in that they offered advice on how to ameliorate them. Many physicians drew on classical sources like Galen to understand old age. For example, Sir John Floyer's *Medicina Gerocomica* (1724) observed that "An old Man's body is like a plant dried by the sun; its Fibres are stiff, and Juices decayed, and less than in Youth."[7] John Hill's 1775 volume, *The Old Man's Guide to Health* similarly agreed that old people were "naturally too dry" resulting in problems ranging from "fullness of blood," to wasting, sharp humours, pains, inflammations, fluxes, gravel, asthma, and general weakness.[8] The existence of books devoted solely to improving health in old age indicates just how strongly the last phase of life was linked with debility. Indeed John Wesley's popular *Primitive Physic* included "old age" in its list of illnesses, suggesting that the idea of old age as a chronic disease state was by no means an invention of modern medicine.[9]

Other medical writers of the early national period also insisted on the physical withering brought on by old age, though they traced its cause less to dryness than to an overabundance of liquid in the body known as plethora. For example, John Scudder's *Inaugural Dissertation on the Diseases of Old Age* (1815) argued that plethora was especially prevalent in old age. In a rare mention of women in medical works on senescence, Scudder concluded that postmenopausal women were unusually prone to plethora, presumably because their bodies no longer discharged excess fluid monthly.[10] Benjamin Rush's *Medical Inquiries and Observations* similarly sought to understand the mechanisms of the aging body. He concluded that bone pain, weakness in the knees and ankles, difficulty breathing, costiveness, giddiness, deafness, imperfect vision, and inflammation of the eyes were among the problems plaguing the elderly.[11] Medical writers were somewhat more optimistic about physical health in old age than religious writers in that they felt decay could be ameliorated by therapeutics (unlike ministers who believed death was the only remedy). But medical and religious authors alike agreed with the basic assertion that old age was a time of fading corporal fortunes.

Limited evidence from almanacs and fictional sources such as poems suggests that infirmity as a defining characteristic of old age was not confined to religious and medical tracts. A humorous poem entitled, "The Old Bachelor" (1797) lamented "I'm not the same I us'd to be, My beard is long, my head is gray, My eyes are sore, my teeth decay."[12] Meanwhile, Andrew Beer's *The Farmer's Calendar* for 1805 described the life cycle of man. By sixty it explained, "disease and sullenness succeed... Thus he lives on till seventy, and may perhaps languish till eighty; but from thence forward all is pain and misery, not life but living death."[13] A poem entitled "Old Grandpapa" published in 1817 related the story of a boy who teaches his father to care for his elderly parent by telling him bluntly, "Papa, when I'm a man like you, Like you I'll then be smart and gay; Like Grand-Papa you'll then be gray, And feeble, helpless, weak, and bald."[14] Indeed it is quite difficult to find early national sources that do not include physical degeneration as an essential aspect of old age.

These views were not confined to published authors alone. Connecticut people seem to have shared the perception that old age was strongly linked to physical deterioration. Ordinary people took seriously the sermons delivered in their churches describing old age as "the evil day" of human life.[15] In addition, the words "declining years" appear in letters and diaries as synonymous with old age.[16] Physical decline was an expected part of this decay. Peter Gallaudet, a Hartford merchant, explained the aging process explicitly in 1813:

> If life is spared old age will bring its infirmities, the strength and activity will decline, the oil in the sockets of the joints will dry up & render them stiff and difficult to move. [T]he deep wrinkles in the face will tell its advanced age.[17]

Another man wrote his still-youthful sister of what she could expect as she aged:

> The revolution of times and seasons . . . remind us of our own decay . . . our bright morn of life will soon be succeeded by the meridian, and if still spared to live, the eve of age. You may already see those about you, who will soon be crowding you off the stage of action. Already you see those faultering, feeble tottering steps to which your own will soon compare.[18]

One who had already become old confirmed this negative prediction. Eliphalet Williams, a seventy-one year old Connecticut man, described himself to his brother like this: "My vitals with laborious Strife, Bear up the Crazy Load, and drag these poor remains of life, Along the Tiresome road."[19] Fifty-nine year old Daniel Wadsworth made clear that physical decay came as no surprise once the boundary into old age had been breached. Recovering from a fever he told a correspondent, "I find that my strength returns so slowly as hardly to be said to return at all.—This is to be expected as I am now so much more advanced in life."[20]

Yet debility in old age was not thought to be limited to the body alone. Many writers felt the aging process induced mental decay as well. Again, religious writers often took the most negative view. Discoursing at length on the troubles attending the aged, Stanley Griswold's 1801 book of sermons did not mince words:

> Many of those who sleep in the dust, once tasted with a high relish the pleasures of thought, of invention, or memory... but live to have their mental powers benumbed, memory fail, the force of mind abate, and second childhood return... Some were once luminaries... but became weak like other men, the light of their mind was put out, the strength of their genius decayed, and the last stage of life exhibited a mournful contrast of what they once had been.[21]

Joseph Lathrop's *The Infirmities and Comforts of Old Age* (published in 1805) was no more optimistic. Lathrop, a seventy-four year old himself, explained that memory failed first followed shortly by the other mental faculties. Ultimately, according to Lathrop, an old person must expect "the probable event of total decrepitude and confinement, and the entire loss of his feeble remains of sensibility and intellect."[22]

The only consolation (to Congregationalist writers at least) was that old age diminished the passions as well. Ebenezer Gay's *The Old Man's Calendar* noted that old age "abateth the violence of sensual inclinations; and it exempteth from many temptations to sin, in which youth betrayeth man."[23] This was the silver lining to the dark cloud ministers promised would envelop the aged and for some this promise came true. One seventy-one-year-old man from Connecticut was glad to tell his diary that "I have not so much pleasure in any thing as when I was young, but have the most Satisfaction in religious Exercises of any."[24]

As in their emphasis on bodily infirmity, clerics hoped their dire predictions of mental decline would spur religious reflection before it was too late. New England Protestantism required conscious, searching preparation for death that could not be performed under conditions of senility. Even if death seemed at a distance, the insidious effects of aging on the mind could curtail efforts to prepare and jeopardize salvation. Religious authors were interested in the long-term spiritual welfare of their readers, not in helping the aged to think positively about their circumstances.

Some secular writers shared an unfavorable view of the mental changes in the last stage of life. Andrew Beer's *The Farmer's Calendar* for 1805 included a description of the typical elderly man:

> He is tired by, and tiring every body, peevish and snarling, like an old cur, gnawing the present and licking over the past . . . destitute of sensibility, complaining at all hours and of all things.[25]

Though obviously a caricature of the worst tendencies of the aged, this passage echoed the ideas expressed by religious writers—that old age brought unpleasant changes to the minds and characters of ordinarily reasonable people.

While medical writers did not go to the same extremes as some religious writers in describing the mental consequences of aging, they often took for granted that some changes would occur. Benjamin Rush noted, as religious writers did, that

> The memory is the first faculty of the mind which fails in the decline of life. While recent events pass through the mind without leaving an impression upon it, it is remarkable that the long forgotten events of childhood and youth are recalled and distinctly remembered.[26]

Decay in "understanding" could also occur in old age, though Rush believed that constant stimulus of the mind could delay this. Thus, studious men rarely lost understanding in old age and "the same cause accounts for old people preserving their intellects longer in the cities than in country places."[27] Only in extreme old age, "In the absence of memory, and finally, in the extinction of every other faculty of the mind" would "second infancy" set it.[28]

Connecticut people of all ages, like published authors of various stripes, also linked age with declining mental acuity. For example, seventy-six year old Thomas Williams attributed a "blunder" he made to the "forgetfulness of age."[29] The forty-six year old Shubael Bartlett also seems to have expected less mental ability in the aged. Upon visiting an octogenarian neighbor Bartlett remarked in surprise that she was "remarkably intelligent for one of her age."[30] Similarly, an untitled poem copied into the memory book of Jennet Cowles of Farmington, Connecticut, called old age "The twilight of the mind."[31] Acceptance of a connection between old age and mental decay can also be detected in court records. In one of a number of similar cases, the Hartford County Court assigned a caretaker to Ebenezer Finch after it was shown that Finch "by age and infirmity has become deprived of his reason."[32]

People today often believe that old people in the past were valued for their wisdom. Yet such wisdom is difficult to reconcile with the mental and physical traits ascribed to the old in the early national period. In fact, wisdom was not often mentioned in association with the aged in the late-eighteenth and early-nineteenth centuries. Ministers, convinced of innate human depravity and of the urgency of preparation in the elderly probably avoided praising the wisdom of the old (if indeed they felt they possessed any) for fear of encouraging complacence. When wisdom was mentioned in connection with the elderly, it did not support the idea that the old were uniformly sage. For example, Job Orton noted that the aged "have most wisdom" but his book's condescending introduction also stated:

> What is abstruse, critical and difficult is here avoided, as it appeared improper and absurd to trouble persons who are in the decline of life with such things: and I have long observed that they are best pleased with what is plain, simple and affectionate.[33]

It is not clear what Orton thought the aged's wisdom could be applied to if complexities were beyond them. Lathrop also mentioned that the old have the authority and wisdom that comes with years, yet the context of this remark clearly confined these qualities to unstintingly pious Christians.[34] In fact, it is more accurate to say that people of this period felt the old should be wise but they were aware this was by no means the rule. Yet if ministers avoided the automatic connection between wisdom and age, they did occasionally allow that the elderly had more "experience" than their younger counterparts, which combined with the diminution of passion in old age could aid people in becoming more godly.

The writings of Connecticut people also tended to highlight the aged's experience rather than wisdom. Moreover contemporary diarists indicate that the experience that came from living a long life might be confined to the mundane. Indeed when diarists mentioned the elderly as repositories of information the weather tended to be the subject. For example, Mary Cowles told her diary on an exceptionally warm January day: "Probably the oldest man living cannot recollect such a winter as the present."[35] Similarly, Austin Williams noted on an especially cold May day: "it is a verry Cold day such as I have never seen or heard of by people quite advanced in life."[36] General wisdom in the aged was not often mentioned. Meanwhile, published fiction on the elderly rarely stressed wisdom in old age either.

Medical writers, for their part, were naturally more concerned with what was wrong with the old than what was right. As a result they were also unlikely to discuss good qualities such as wisdom in the elderly. Occasionally, however, they did point out the usefulness of prolonging life to old age. For example, John Hill justified his *Old Man's Guide to Health* by stating, "Healthful old age is the most valuable period of human life: Experience has rendered the ancient more able than those who have seen less, and felt less, to conduct themselves."[37]

John Hill's upbeat sentiment was unusual however. As we have seen, printed works circulating in early national America generally accentuated the negative. Over and over readers were informed that the years after fifty really were "evil years." A few might escape dramatic physical and mental decline but most did not. This in itself did not necessarily create difficulty for the aged. In the right context decay can be meaningful and indeed acceptable because it serves a larger purpose. Unfortunately writers who discussed the meanings and functions of old age did a poor job of providing a workable context in which men and women could effectively come to terms with growing old.

THE MEANINGS AND FUNCTIONS OF OLD AGE

Almost all authors could agree that old age was a time of serious decline, but the meanings and functions of old age were in dispute in early national America. Religious thinkers offered a full-blown system for understanding old age that fit the last stage of life into both the cosmic and worldly order and prescribed behavior and duties for the elderly. Secular writers on old age presented an array of less well-integrated ideas. However, a subgroup of these writers—health and medical authors—offered a way of thinking about aging that allowed for a systematic approach to old age. Meanwhile other secular publications, including fictional works, expressed a mix of ambivalent ideas about the aged and their place in society. These different strands of thought posed problems for people seeking guidance through the aging process. To begin with, the varying interpretations of old age often contradicted each other, resulting in no clear ideological path for individuals to follow. In addition, even if a person opted to embrace only one set of ideas (such as the religious) they discovered that such ideologies were both incredibly demanding and quite unforgiving. Meaning in old age came at a steep price for early national Americans.

The Religious Interpretation

"To everything there is a season, and a time to every purpose under the heaven."[38] This passage from Ecclesiastes provides an excellent starting point for understanding the religious conception of old age. Most religious authors who commented in print on old age were Congregational New England divines who brought their special brand of theology to bear on the question of old age. These men formulated an understanding of the purpose of old age, the duties of the elderly, and others' duties to them which changed little from the seventeenth to early-nineteenth century. As a result, this discussion of religious ideas draws on both colonial and early national publications. Congregational clerics found God's moving hand in every aspect of life on earth and old age was no exception. In preserving individuals to advanced age God had definite purposes which were elucidated and repeated regularly from the pulpit. Old age, according to these divines, was not a time of repose or relaxation but of serious and unrelenting soul-searching. For this crucial stage of life to be successful the aged were required to meet extremely high standards of behavior and were threatened with eternal damnation, the worst of all punishments, if they failed.

The first important purpose of old age was to provide the young with examples of both good and bad behavior. The pious elderly provided a salutary model for those in youth or middle age by "recommending" religion to others. As Joseph Lathrop put it,

> The aged man, taken off by his infirmities from the active business of life, can in no way do more service for

God and for mankind, than by exhibiting a visible example of contentment and humility, piety and spirituality, faith and hope ... He thus demonstrates the excellence and power of religion.[39]

Nathan Strong elaborated further on how the aged could be instructive to others. Answering the question "Why hath God spared a few of us to old age?" Strong suggested,

It might be to exhibit to the generations after us, the necessary decripitude of age ... When they look on us aged people, they find ocular evidence that [youth] cannot be; they see our palsied limbs, our failing memories, and our erring judgments; and from these ought to learn, that every man will soon come to his long home.[40]

Yet the old were not solely passive models of Christian principles, they played active roles as well. As Strong put it in another sermon,

What more venerable sight do we ever see, than an aged Christian, whose faith and good works have been an example and a blessing to others around him; who hath cautioned, warned, instructed and educated many to serve the Lord.[41]

This idea of the elderly as didactic examples for the rest of society promised an important function for old people and a way of influencing others after their involvement in more worldly cares had abated. At the same time it also laid a heavy responsibility on aged men and women.

Those who did not take this responsibility seriously provided a warning to youth. These "old transgressors, veterans in iniquity, who have grown grey in the practice of sin" were, according to ministers, frightful evidence of what could happen to those who allowed years to pass before concerning themselves with piety. Each year they became more hardened in sin and further from repentance.[42] Impious elderly men and women offered testimony to the perverse folly of misusing life on earth.

But serving as an example to others was far from the only purpose of old age. Old age was seen as an opportunity for an aged individual to improve in preparation for death. Indeed this was a duty the elderly were obliged to perform. Ebenezer Gay made clear the importance of the task, stating that old age "is the precious season of working out our salvation, and making our calling and election sure."[43] Advanced age is a blessing because "it gives the longest opportunity to prepare for entering on the rewards of another world," concluded Nathan Strong.[44] Preparation, a lifelong process of introspection combined with pious action, was essential in the Congregational view. As Charles Cohen has described, Congregationalists valued mature experience with religion, believing that "Time withers the body; grace improves with age."[45] Prolonged life allowed more time to reflect, to do good, and to spread the influence of God's word.

Preparation was conveniently aided by the very nature of old age. According to many divines, the debilitating effects of aging were God's method of weaning people from the world. By making earthly life very unpleasant God encouraged the aged to shift their attention to eternity and prepare accordingly. As William Bridge remarked, infirmities are "good warnings of our change approaching, and by them we dye daily, that at last we may dye graciously and comfortably."[46] These warnings could be welcomed as reminders of the promise of heavenly rest for the saved. Joseph Lathrop even suggested that an old person could "take pleasure in his infirmities, regarding them as kind intimations, that now is his salvation nearer, than when he believed!"[47] Indeed, sickness and pain had many good uses. Job Orton described how infirmity encouraged humility in the elderly while simultaneously offering the young a chance to express humanity and tenderness toward them. In this view, the pains and losses of growing old were far from purposeless, they were positive, functional aids on the path to sanctification.

Difficulties of any kind in old age—the death of a spouse, loss of hearing, or poor treatment by children—were seen as useful. God intended these trials to afflict and test the old, thereby pushing them toward spiritual betterment. Of course tragedy and loss could strike at any age and be useful tools for religious improvement. However because the aged were considered especially vulnerable to affliction, religious authors made a special effort to clarify the purpose of their suffering. Therefore, in reviewing the uses of old age, Nathan Strong remarked that the elderly were "preserved for [their] own trial." Good Christians, he felt, should respond to this test with redoubled obedience, humility, and "trembling."[48] Thus if religious writers played up the mental and physical suffering of old age they also imbued it with a purpose and meaning that potentially enabled believers to better bear their declining years.

God had definite purposes in mind when he spared people to old age, but for these to come to fruition man had many duties and obligations to perform. For old age to take on the weighty significance just described, old people were required to conform to specific and demanding behavioral instructions. These requirements contrast sharply with the twentieth-century American view of old age as a time for enjoyment of rest and leisure.

To begin with, the ideal old person behaved with sobriety. Cotton Mather insisted, "A trifling, & childish, & frolicksome sort of carriage, all Buffonery in an old man, is very disagreeable." He continued, "We cannot Reverence you, unless your grave looks, as well as your gray Hairs, demand it of us."[49] Joseph Lathrop, like many other clerics, agreed: "It becomes the aged to be grave and sober, for they stand on the brink of the eternal world. And who would not be sober there?"[50] Lathrop felt that the spectacle of old men (and presumably old women equally) engaging in "frothy discourse" or "guilty amusements" was shocking indeed and could only mean such a person was "totally alienated from God and religion, and completely stupefied by the habits of sin."[51]

Generally a higher standard of behavior was expected of elderly people, both because they were experienced and should know better, and because they were less tempted by passions. "Those that are ancient, have, or should have been frequent in holy duties, they therefore of all men are to live and walk most exactly," remarked William Bridge.[52] Part of this exactitude involved patience. Despite the fact that old age consisted of "evil days," the elderly were exhorted to resign themselves to any and all difficulties they encountered. Mather reminded his readers that "Old men are often froward, peevish, hard to please; you should lay aside that Morosity . . . Bear patiently the Infirmities of that Old Age."[53] In addition he and other divines recommended strongly against complaining, which smacked of ingratitude.

No matter how unpleasant old age became, a sense of submission and great thankfulness to God for continuing life was obligatory. This thankfulness would stem naturally from the recognition that "To God our escapes from death belong."[54] God was justified in cutting off life at any time. Therefore if he spared one to old age it was a munificent gift. Religious commentators felt that awareness of God's power and generosity, combined with reflection on his numerous past kindnesses, should be sufficient "cause to thank God . . . whatever inconveniences attend their old age" and to "prevent your murmuring under the burdens and infirmities of age."[55] Those who gave in to the temptation to murmur were chastised:

> It is too common a case for Christ's old disciples to grow sorrowful and dejected, and spend the conclusion of their days in fretfulness and complaining . . . But this is a very unreasonable and unbecoming disposition; very dishonourable to God.[56]

Humble submission, whatever old age might bring, was the proper attitude to take.

The virtues of sobriety, patience, submission, and gratitude were expected of both men and women. Both Mather and Orton specifically mention women's obligations to conform to these requirements. But the duties of aged Christians did not end there because a host of other tasks had to be performed. The most important of these was, of course, to take advantage of old age as an extended period to prepare for death. Though believers of all ages were enjoined to prepare, the aged were urged most forcefully because, as the popular expression stated, "Young men may die but old men must." "Remembering how old we are, and therefore have not long to live, we should review our actions, and repent of our sins," enjoined Ebenezer Gay.[57] In this way, "while our outward man is perishing, our inward man is renewed day by day."[58] Ministers assured aging people that religious study, attention at church meetings, introspection, and efforts at improvement would ease the transition to eternity. As Cotton Mather put it, "Old men have a Night coming upon them; and they above all, had need to get their Lamps lighted with such a knowledge, as may light them into the Chambers of Everlasting Glory."[59]

Worldly cares were thought to hinder preparation and distract the elderly from consideration of their future state. For this reason the old were told to wean themselves from the world. Joseph Lathrop called on the aged person to "dismiss his worldly affections and thoughts."[60] Many religious writers invoked the Biblical example of Barzillai who refused to go with King David to Jerusalem. Because he was old, he saw that sensual pleasures were useless to him, and he wanted to prepare for death.[61] Job Orton recommended that the aged "quit all worldly cares, as much as possible; and do not grasp the world, as too many do, with a dying hand."[62] However he conceded that this advice was difficult to implement and noted, "I do not say you should live like recluses, and shut yourselves up from all commerce with the world: but lessen your business and cares, as much as you prudently can."[63] In Orton's view the requirement to divorce from worldly cares conveniently matched the elderly's declining abilities. The aged, he argued,

> often manage their business aukwardly and unsuccessfully; are easily imposed upon; and their associates would conduct it better without them . . . indeed the aged ought, like Barzillai, to be the first to perceive themselves on the decline, and retire before the world is tired of them.[64]

Ebenezer Gay condemned those who failed to follow these suggestions:

> What is more absurd and shocking than to see men who are just going out of the world, loving it as fondly, and scraping for it as eagerly, as if they were never to leave it? . . . It is our shame and misery if our long experience hath not taught us the vanity of this world.[65]

Ideally the elderly disengaged from close personal relationships, business affairs, and other earthly cares and "retired" to a more spiritual realm. Religious authors thus recommended an almost monkish divorce from the world in favor of a life of spiritual contemplation. In the process the aged were expected to locate themselves in a liminal zone suspended halfway between the living and the dead.

Another duty of the elderly was to await death daily. While feeling constantly thankful for continued life the old were simultaneously expected to "converse much with death and eternity," to "hold themselves in readiness to depart," and ultimately to "reconcile their hearts to the approach of death."[66] Though Congregational theology often made one's eternal state uncertain during life and hence a source of significant anxiety for believers, the aged were enjoined not to fear death but to welcome it.[67] As William Bridge phrased it, "Let him long after Heaven, and not be afraid to dye."[68] The religious standard required the elderly, even those suffering from infirmity and loss, to transcend both their earthly environment and their apprehensions about the unknown world ahead.

However, these requirements did not release the aged from all duties on earth. Old age and its accompanying pains were no "excuse for sloth." Rather, the elderly were obliged to instruct others. Religious writers told readers that if "you are rich in Christian experience, communicate it freely for the benefit of others."[69] Nathan Strong recommended that the elderly give their families "the best advice, for we may very soon be taken from them."[70] William Bridge suggested "it is the work and duty" of the aged person to leave to posterity an account of his experiences with God including "some good exhortations and admonitions" for his relatives and friends.[71] Religious writers saw no contradiction between these weighty responsibilities and the injunction to withdraw from worldly involvements. Those who would live up to the expectations of the Congregational clergy had a very fine, perhaps even invisible, line to walk.

Ministers also urged another more practical duty on their aged audience—to set their houses in order. A pious old person, seeing his or her demise near at hand was obliged to make arrangements for the disposition of his worldly affairs—"make his Will, and leave his Legacies to his Children, Friends; and Posterity."[72] The ideal was to take care of all affairs and worries so that when death approached the aged had "nothing then to do but die."[73]

The final implicit duty of the aged was to accept and embrace reminders of their upcoming death, prodding questions about the state of their souls, and deprecating remarks on their physical and mental abilities. Caleb Tenney preached a funeral sermon in 1821 that displayed the candor typical of his time. Addressing his aged hearers he said,

> the time of your departure is at hand, Truly, your sun is disappearing; the graves are ready for you, and the night of death is brooding over you. Is your great work of preparation thoroughly made? . . . if you fail in preparation, the failure will be remediless and eternal.[74]

In a society such as ours in which even asking an older person's age is considered bad form, it is hard to imagine a world in which such bluntness was both accepted and encouraged. The aged of early national America, however, were asked to accept threats of eternal doom gratefully.

Congregational writers drove a hard bargain with the aged. They offered meaning and purpose in old age but only if elderly men and women conformed to very strict standards of behavior. Though the pains of age were great, complaints of any kind were unacceptable. Meanwhile the aged were expected to be pious exemplars for their families and communities while simultaneously withdrawing from the world to commune with God. And while earnestly preparing for an uncertain and unknowable afterlife (made vivid by ministers' fearful visions of damnation) they were supposed to remain perfectly calm.

Those who had difficulty imagining just how to implement these onerous prescriptions could turn to religious tracts for illustration of how all the qualities and behaviors described by ministers fit together in an ideal old person. For example, *Happy Poverty or the Story of Poor Blind Ellen* (1817) told of a destitute, lame, blind, aged woman who despite lack of food and infirmities worked all day, six days a week at spinning. Ellen also dutifully cared for a foul-tempered invalid for many years with little recompense. Through it all Ellen's mind was fixed firmly on God and his mercies for which she was exceedingly thankful. Ellen neither took support from her parish nor told others of her troubles or needs.[75] Another tract, *Account of Sir Matthew Hale* (1817) related the story of Hale, a prominent sixty-six year old man who became ill and immediately "determined to have nothing more to do with the affairs of this life." As his illness worsened Hale welcomed death. Despite his increasing pains he exercised remarkable patience and "forebore all complaints or groans, and with his hands and eyes lifted up was fixed in his devotion."[76] Other tracts idealized equally saintly behavior of aged people in difficult circumstances. This type of literature held up a model so demanding for the aged as to be unrealistic for most people.

Expectations of the elderly expressed by religious commentators were indeed high. In order to encourage efforts to live up to them, New England divines detailed the rewards due the faithful old and the punishments earned by aged sinners. The benefits to those who lived a good old age were numerous.[77] First, the pious elderly earned glory, honor, and respect. "The hoary head is a crown of glory, if it be found in the way of righteousness" was the frequently invoked Biblical proverb.[78] In addition ministers offered consolation to pious old people, reminding them that they would soon be in heaven, released from suffering, and at last united with God. John Dunlap told his readers that, "Your cup of suffering is nearly dry, your work is closing, your mansions of bliss are ready."[79] When the time did come to die, the faithful elderly could expect a good death. Reflecting the peace in their souls, they would expire without pain or violence. Finally, a godly aged person could expect to "leave a sweet perfume behind him, and many shall bless God for him when he is dead."[80]

Elderly believers also received assurances that others would treat them well. The Bible, according to many ministers, commanded respect and honor for the elderly, especially those who appeared to conform to religious principles. Though in theory everyone owed respect to all old people, most often writers emphasized the duties of family members in this regard. "The children and grand-children of aged, dying saints" were advised to "frequently visit them, reverence their instructions, hearken to their history of God's dealings with them, and desire and value their prayers."[81] Relatives, especially children, were also instructed to care for their elderly relatives if need be. Drawing on the Fifth Commandment to support his views, Martin Tullar, author of *A Concise System of Family Duty*, noted that if parents ever became the objects of charity "it becomes indispensably incumbent on children to minister to their support, and comfort."[82] Similarly *An Explanation of the Ten Commandments* (1794) instructed that "children should be ready to nourish and support their parents, if they are able, and there is occasion for it."[83] Job Orton castigated those who did otherwise:

> It is the duty of all to help and comfort the aged, especially of their own descendants ... Nothing can be meaner or viler than to use them ill; to impose upon their blindness, deafness, and decay of memory, or to despise them on account of their infirmities.[84]

Frequently injunctions to aid one's elderly parents were expressed in terms of reciprocity. Caring for aged parents provided an opportunity for "requiting the tender care they manifested to them in their helpless infancy."[85] By repaying parents, religious writers further suggested that children helped ensure their own future care. A tract entitled *Monitor to Parents* (1816) described the benefits that accrued to dutiful sons:

> And having richly paid back into the bosoms of his fond parents, with filial gratitude and attention, the returns due to their ardent love to him, he at length placidly fell asleep in the arms of his own children, who honored his memory with the same unfeigned affection he had done of his parents before him.[86]

Respecting and caring for aged parents both repaid the debt due from childhood and made a down payment on one's own future treatment. The care and respect of younger generations were an important advantage gained by the pious elderly.

Obviously, however, all these benefits did not accrue to those unable to meet the exacting requirements ministers set down. Elderly men and women who were unable to conform to religious standards received menacing warnings of the consequences of impiety. The unrepentant aged, if they believed these divines, had much to fear. First and foremost elderly sinners would feel God's stinging punishment. Nathan Strong told sinners advanced in age "that they are the most miserable of men; the years will not exculpate their transgressions; and that their long continued sin against the grace of God, will accumulate upon them a double weight of sorrow."[87] Besides the painful rebuke waiting after death, faithless old people could expect scorn to be heaped on them while on earth. Though ministers agreed that the elderly generally deserved respect and honor, they often argued that old sinners deserved far less. Cotton Mather concluded, "The Gray Hairs on the outside of your Heads, are not more Honourable, than the wrong thoughts in the inside of them are pernicious."[88] In fact being both old and wicked was especially detestable. "What more despicable character can there be, than that of a man who hath grown old in sin, and spent all his days in the service of the devil?" Job Orton demanded.[89] To make matters worse, some felt that the impious elderly would die painful deaths. Illustrating this point, a religious tract entitled *The Contrast* (1821) told of Voltaire's death at which even his physicians "called in to administer relief . . . [were] struck with horror, [and] retired [from his chamber], declaring the death of an impious man to be awful indeed." Even the field-marshal Richelieu "flew from the bed-side, declaring the sight was too terrible to be sustained."[90] Individuals who misused old age could expect contempt on earth, a horrible death, and eternal damnation.

Howard Chudacoff has recently argued that prior to the mid-nineteenth century prescriptive literature "almost never specified norms or demeanor appropriate to discrete ages or age groups."[91] Religious literature on the aged disproves this view. In fact, religious literature precisely specified the purposes of old age and how the aged were to behave. In doing so Congregational ministers provided a complete system for the elderly that fit aging into the cosmic order, outlined the obligations of others to them, answered timeless questions such as "Why do we suffer?," and gave hope for deliverance to a blissful afterlife. Religious authors thus gave great meaning and importance to the last stage of life. Unfortunately this system was problematic because its benefits were available only to those who could meet its stringent demands. As the following chapter will demonstrate, very few could actually do so. Thus religious thinking on old age may well have created more anxiety than satisfaction or comfort for men and women seeking guidance though the last stage of life.

The Medical Interpretation

Secular health and medical literature offered a very different view of old age than that offered by Congregational ministers. Health and medical advice books were generally unconcerned with cosmic meaning, eternity, or the spiritual nature of old age. Authors usually took for granted that long life was desirable and devoted themselves to addressing the practical questions of how to increase longevity and improve old age. As we have seen most medical writers conceded that physical and mental deterioration were likely consequences of aging. However, contradicting religious thinkers who counseled resignation, health and medical writers argued that infirmities could (and should) be mitigated by human efforts.

In this view health and long life were not solely the products of God's free grace but within the power of individuals to change through their own behavior. "By judicious management," Anthony Carlisle remarked, "the disorders of senility may often be relieved" and life extended.[92] These ideas had a long tradition in medical thought. *The Probable Way of Attaining Long and Healthful Life*, written by a sixteenth-century Venetian named Luigi Cornaro, enjoyed popularity through the early national period.[93] Similarly Sir John Floyer's *Medicina Gerocomica* (1724) and the anonymous *The Best and Easiest Method of Preserving Uninterrupted Health to Extreme Old Age* (1748) are two English examples of the type of books that were published in substantial numbers in Europe, England, and America. While there were variations in the methods prescribed by different authors most works published in the eighteenth and early-nineteenth centuries agreed on a few generic ideas.

Proper diet was perhaps the most important factor determining health and longevity in the writings of medical and health commentators. William Kitchener explained how, "without due attention to Diet, &c. the Third period of Life is little better than a Chronic Disease."[94] Alexander Thomson's *The Family Physician* (1802) articulated the basic principle to follow:

> Temperance in eating and drinking is doubtless advantageous to the prolongation of life: I do not mean a scrupulous exactness in point of quantity, but a general mediocrity in both, and an abstinence from habitual excess.[95]

Like many health manuals, Thomson's echoed Cornaro's contention that "when men were not addicted to voluptuousness, they had more strength and vivacity at four-score, than we have at present at forty."[96] Yet temperate habits were not valued for moral reasons but simply because they happened to suit the body best. Improper food brought sickness and shortened life, therefore authors prescribed dietary regimens for their readers. William Kitchener and Anthony Carlisle, for example, recommended heavy reliance on red meat. John Hill favored milk as the proper beverage of the aged while Benjamin Rush advocated wine. The virtues of these varying suggestions need not be explored here. The important point is that proper diet, however defined, was seen as a tool within human reach for improving the length and quality of life.

Likewise most aging manuals recommended moderate exercise. Sir John Floyer pointed out that "Hippocrates lived to 90 years, and his chief Art of preserving Health, was to eat moderately, and to use due Exercise."[97] Authors suggested horseback riding, bowling, walking, or if one was too infirm to leave the house, the use of the "flesh-brush" to stimulate the body. As with eating, moderation in exercise was the key to extending life healthfully.

One's environment also played a role in length of life and health. Many writers felt old age was better suited to warm and dry climates than cold and damp ones. John Hill, for example, was of the opinion that winter "hurts age, for age is cold and dry" while summer was conversely quite salutary. Others such as Alexander Thomson simply argued for constancy in climate:

> Uniformity in the state of the atmosphere, particularly in regard to heat, cold, gravity, and lightness, contributes in a very considerable degree to the duration of life. Countries, therefore, where sudden and great variations in the barometer and thermometer are usual cannot be favorable to longevity.[98]

The British author of *Hygeia; or Essays Moral and Medical* (1802), Thomas Beddoes, even looked forward to the day when "Edifices ... would rise under every inhospitable sky; and these CONSERVATORIES OF OLD AGE ... would afford compleat shelter against the inclemencies and the dangers of the seasons."[99] The quality of air was also considered by health writers who usually favored country air over stale interior air or putrid city air.

Maintaining a steady mental state was equally crucial to achieving a long, healthful life. After studying men and women over the age of eighty, Benjamin Rush concluded that "The violent and irregular actions of the passions tends to wear away the springs of life."[100] Luigi Cornaro explained how restraining his passions had helped him to live well past the age of ninety.[101] A chapter of *The Old Man's Guide to Health* (1775) by John Hill addressed the "Regulation of Temper, and of the Passions." Hill observed that anger, grief, terror, shame, and other "immoderate passions" were unhealthful. More agreeable feelings such as lust and joy were also to be avoided. "Of all passions," Hill explained, "let the old man avoid a foolish fondness for women . . . But if he will solicit that which he cannot enjoy, he will disturb his condition more than by any means whatsoever."[102] Hill would almost surely have also objected to older women indulging sexual passions. Joy was an equally destructive "violence of youth." Most authors did not inform their readers how they could banish strong feelings, apparently assuming that force of will was sufficient. Hill, however, recommended warm foods and cordials to those who were "melancholy and gloomy."[103]

Medical and health writers also expounded on lesser themes such as sleep, proper clothing, and intellectual exertion. In all these areas, as in those described above, there was general consensus—"moderation in every thing . . . is the means of greatest efficacy in prolonging life."[104] These were preventive measures, intended to ward off the symptoms of old age as long as possible. However, medical writers also offered help to those who were already stricken by illness and debility. In contrast with religious writers, who insisted on resignation or submission, medical men promoted an active approach to the problems of age.

The therapeutics described in medical manuals of the eighteenth and early-nineteenth century offered remedies based on the ancient humoral understanding of the body as well as more heroic measures. For example, Floyer's early-eighteenth century *Medicina Gerocomica* suggested treatments for the aged intended to balance their constitutions including bathing, sweating, purging, exercise, and oiling the skin. These measures aimed at correcting the "dryness" thought to be characteristic of the aged. Others mixed gentle non-invasive therapeutics with more aggressive practices. Benjamin Rush described how warming the aged body could be beneficial but he also advocated bleeding as effective in treating "the acute diseases of old people."[105] Likewise Anthony Carlisle felt that "the wholesome regulation of diet, clothing, exercise and air, are often more important than the administration of drugs, blisterings, or bleeding," yet these latter techniques were "most beneficial once disease has set in."[106] John Scudder, a young doctor in 1815 when he wrote *Inaugural Dissertation on the Diseases of Old Age*, embraced heroic measures wholeheartedly, reflecting the American trend toward greater use of dramatic therapeutics. Arguing that plethora (an overabundance of fluid in the body) was particularly likely to strike the aged and was related to many of the ailments of old age, Scudder concluded that the elderly needed more bleeding than other age groups. "Experience has proved that blood letting in old age is not only useful, but absolutely necessary."[107] Purges, beatings, pricking the skin, and mustard plasters were also beneficial. William Kitchener, for his part, was especially concerned with keeping the bowels in top form and urged the use of a variety of "peristaltic persuaders" on his readers. Over time, as medical practice in general shifted toward the dramatic intervention of heroic measures, treatment of the elderly followed suit.[108]

The medical approach to old age was clearly at odds with the religious. While religious writers gave God exclusive credit for preserving health and life, medical manuals suggested something quite different—that the adoption of a temperate lifestyle (the earlier in life the better) put individual men and women in control of their own health and longevity. Proper management of the body had a predictable result—long life and a comfortable old age. If infirmities had already commenced, medical writers offered a range of treatments that took for granted human power to alter the course of aging and illness. In this sense medical writings on the elderly conflicted with religious notions of aging that fostered a vision of human powerlessness in the face of divine omnipotence.

This contradiction between these two coherent strands of thinking on old age had the potential to cause problems for the elderly. Two clear choices existed and the stakes in selecting between them were high. Since religious and medical writers recommended conflicting prescriptions for behavior, the two systems could not work well together. Therefore, opting for physical well-being by following medical prescriptions might jeopardize salvation, while opting for spiritual well-being as counseled by ministers would deprive one of the chance to make old age physically more comfortable.

As an approach to old age, the medical view had flaws that went beyond the conflict with religious notions. The medical interpretation of aging was far less comprehensive than the religious view. Health writers were mute on the subject of the elderly's place in society and on the duties of others to the aged. Though they urged people to live temperate lives, this recommendation lacked a moral imperative and did not help the elderly to fit their experiences into a larger social or spiritual framework. Medical writers skirted the question of the value and meaning of senescence and made no original contribution to the question of the uses of old age. Their goals were to improve health and lengthen life—it was up to the individual to decide what to do with the extra years gained and to ascribe meaning to them. Therefore medical authors fell far short of offering the aged a satisfying way to think about growing old.

Furthermore, though the medical view gave individuals the power to influence the quality of old age through their own actions, it implicitly laid a heavy responsibility on the aged. If proper habits brought on a good old age then a sickly or unpleasant old age had to be the fault of the individual who persisted in bad habits. Therefore if an individual had health problems in old age he had only himself to blame. If the advice offered by medical authors had been truly effective against the infirmities of age, this would not pose a problem. Unfortunately the injunction to live moderately can not have been potent enough to combat the many problems the elderly faced. Therefore aged people who looked to medical authorities for direction in old age were given flawed advice but held accountable if it failed.

Other Interpretations in Secular Literature

Religious and medical literature provided the two coherent strains of thought on the elderly in the early national period and as we have seen each presented significant difficulties for the aged. Other published materials including poems, plays, almanacs, and newspapers commented on aging and old age but provided no systematic understanding of these issues. Instead these works added to the already contradictory array of ideas on senescence circulating in early national America. In them the aged might be praised but they were equally likely to be criticized. Old age might be described in positive terms but more likely it was not. Meanwhile readers searching for the meaning or purpose of the last stage of life would find little assistance.

In these types of publications explanations of the meaning of old age cropped up very rarely. Poems such as "Valedictory Address to a School by their Teacher" (published in 1797) suggested lack of meaning in old age rather than the period of spiritual renewal and usefulness envisioned by some. The poem's narrator addressed his pupils as he prepared to leave his teaching post:

> You'll see some grief and tears,
> Ere youth and childhood cease;
> But as you too advance in years,
> You'll find your griefs increase...
> Your Teacher walks away
> No more to come again;
> He'll spend, perhaps each summer's day,
> In sorrow, toil, and pain.
> He'll think on days that past
> When health and mirth did blend:
> Then grieve to think they slow'd so fast,
> And must so shortly end
> His youthful days, when fled,
> Shall see no glad return,
> Till he is numbered with the dead,
> And friends forget to mourn.[109]

This poem speaks of the decline and losses of old age yet offers no consolation. In it suffering brings no rewards, advanced years no legacy. Perhaps because religious literature so amply discussed the meaning of old age, poems like this that touch on the significance of advanced age were rare. However, fragments of evidence such as "Valedictory Address" indicate that doubt about the religious formulation of old age's purpose circulated in printed literature.

Non-medical secular literature was also relatively inarticulate on the duties of the aged, yet stories and anecdotes provide examples of the behavior of elderly characters. For example, an account published in 1803 of a very long-lived slave named Alice reported her zealous attention to religion. However, Alice seemed to have escaped the dire consequences of aging predicted by religious and medical writers, as "she has often been met on horseback, in a full gallop, at the age of ninety-five years."[110] Indeed she reached one hundred before her sight failed, though this did not prevent her continued activity. This story as well as the popular Old Mother Hubbard tales portrayed old women leading active lives engaged in worldly affairs.

Other stories showed the elderly in relationships with family members. Two companion poems published separately in 1817 were entitled *My Grandmother* and *My Grandfather*. Told from the point of view of grandchildren, these poems elucidated positive qualities in the old. Of the twelve stanzas of *My Grandmother* the first expressed appreciation of the aged woman's life-giving powers. Eight others extolled the grandmother's nurturing, affection, and generosity with gifts. For example, "Who came to see me far and near, With Cakes and Toys, throughout the year, And call'd me her sweet little dear? My grandmother."[111] Finally three other stanzas praised the elderly woman for her moral teachings, though these were not the heavy-handed preachings suggested by Congregational ministers. For example, "Who bade me duly keep in mind, 'To be to ev'ry Creature kind! And look with pity on the Blind?' My Grandmother."[112] Meanwhile the laudable qualities of *My Grandfather* were primarily his free gift-giving and playfulness. "Who when he saw me sad or cross, Would spin the top, or trap-ball toss; And let me make his cane my horse? My Grandfather."[113] These genial grandparents did not impart lessons to their descendants with stoic gravity, instead they loved and played with them, teaching the principles of common decency in the process. Such characterizations hint at the shift described by scholars such as Jay Fliegleman in this period from authoritative, hierarchical family relations to more affectionate, sentimentalized relations.[114] These portraits of old people suggest a contradictory vision of the elderly than that presented in religious or medical publications—one in which the aged were more like pleasant, ordinary people than disease-ridden, stern, and spiritually-distinctive exemplars of upright behavior.

But secular literature was far from uniformly positive in describing the elderly—indeed the elderly were sometimes singled out for criticism. We saw earlier how some writers associated old age with undesirable qualities such as peevishness or complaining. Besides these qualities only one other behavior in the aged inspired significant comment. If fictional publications are any measure, early national

Americans objected strongly to old men involving themselves romantically or sexually with younger women. It is likely that such objections were deeply rooted in the Western past. Historians such as Natalie Zemon Davis have detailed the ritualized punishments served on those who were involved in age-imbalanced love relationships in sixteenth-century France.[115] Indeed the foolish old man pursuing a young woman was a stock figure in early national literature. (Older women involved with younger men seem to have been much less frequent.) For example, the British author John Gardiner's *The Widowed Mourner*, reprinted in Boston in 1791, mocks an elderly man who "Absurdly falls in Love" with a youthful maid and "By false, mistaken Passion" ends up leaving his fortune to her rather than to his deserving children.[116] Similarly Isaac Bickerstaffe's *He Would if He Could: Or an Old Fool Worse than Any* tells the tale of an elderly man who falls for a youthful but duplicitous female servant. The "old fool" describes himself this way:

> Surely never mortal, at my age
> Was such a buzzard, such a calf:
> A man who years should render sage!
> I know not which to cry or laugh.
> In love at sixty-six!
> Ouns! infamy should fix
> A brand on the crime:
> Is threescore a time
> For beginning boyish tricks?[117]

Almanacs and newspapers not infrequently made aged lovers the butts of their jokes. Clearly threescore was not a time for love in the minds of fiction writers, especially with young women. These stories suggest that the grave demeanor and passionlessness recommended by both the clergy and medical writers had some broader cultural resonance. Secular literature tolerated a relatively wide range of activity for the aged but writers drew the line at May-December romances, perhaps because they confused age relations and jeopardized the smooth transfer of property from one generation to the next.

The duties of others to the aged received a fair amount of attention in non-medical secular literature. Most often the young were enjoined to respect the elderly. However, the way this moral was frequently

American Ideas on Aging and the Elderly to 1830

expressed indicates that respect may not have been the first impulse of youth. For example, *Father Abraham's Almanac* for 1805 counseled, "Laugh not at the grey headed declaimer, nor at thy aged grandsire. There often come forth from wrinkles of the skin words full of wisdom."[118] The story of *The Benevolent Old Man of the Rock* (1810) told of a poor, infirm, aged man "who hardly ever went to the neighboring village without being hooted, and even pelted at by the boys." As the story unfolds the old man rescues a small boy from death, becoming his "venerable protector and saviour."[119] The moral seems to be that the old man's humble exterior hides a diamond in the rough, deserving far better treatment than the village boys give him. Another children's book entitled *Old Age* (1810) gave more direct lessons on how to treat the aged. In one engraving an ancient man is supported by a staff on one side and a dutiful child on the other. The caption reads, "How much more beautiful is such a sight, than to see naughty children making a mock of the aged or infirm."[120] In these examples respect for the elderly is advised, yet each also indicates an undercurrent of hostility or ridicule directed at the old. Unalloyed expressions of goodwill toward the aged were rare in secular literature.[121] In these sources the young were supposed to treat the elderly with respect and kindness but they were frequently tempted to do otherwise.

A few fictional publications addressed the question of caring for the aged in their time of need though these expressed similar ambivalence toward the elderly. *Old Grand-papa*, for example, relates the story of an old man who turns his fortune over to his son. At first his son is grateful and treats his father respectfully, caring for him well as indicated by this passage:

> With down was puff'd his elbow chair
> And that was placed with punctual care,
> Snug, close beside the parlour fire,
> And when he speaks they all admire.[122]

But this happy situation does not last. As the son becomes more prominent he and his wife begin to find the aged father irksome, eventually relegating him to an outbuilding, both out of sight and out of mind.

> Behold! now in the coach-house loft
> Stretch'd on a bed nor warm nor soft,
> The venerable parent lies . . .
> Nor son nor daughter think of him.
> The servants have so much to do;
> The very dogs forget him too.[123]

Only when the old man's grandson threatens to treat his father the way he treats his father does the son repent and restore the old man to his proper place in the house. This story makes clear how children should care for their elderly parents but also illuminates the tension surrounding this requirement. Published fiction suggests that religious ideas of right treatment of the aged were taken seriously but that all too often fallible individuals had difficulty implementing them.

In our discussion of non-medical secular literature, one final work bears consideration—Cicero's *Cato Major; or a Discourse on Old Age*. This book, translated by Benjamin Franklin and reprinted several times in the late-eighteenth and early-nineteenth centuries, offers an vision of old age that stands in stark contrast with the views of either religious or medical authors. Unlike these writers, Cicero's goal was to divest "the prospect of old age . . . of every thing shocking or frightful."[124] To this end he systematically dispensed with the "four inconveniences charged to old age" (that it disables men from business, renders them infirm, deprives them of life's pleasures, and is "the next neighborhood to death.")[125] According to Cicero, rethinking old age in these ways could make "old age sit easy and light on me; and thus I not only disarm it of every uneasyness, but render it even sweet and delightful."[126] Cicero's work exposed readers to a far more positive view of senescence than found in other publications and thus added to the mix of opposing ideas on old age in early national America.

Poems, plays, newspaper articles, and almanacs cannot tell us exactly how early national Americans felt about aging and the elderly. Yet the shards of information they provide suggest that there was a significant difference between the characterization of old age articulated by religious and medical thinkers and more popular notions. In these secular works old people generally seem more "normal" and have a wider range of activity than in other publications. They appear in many forms—as pleasant grandmothers, lecherous old fools, golden-hearted saviors, and mistreated patriarchs. Scholars such as David Hackett Fischer have argued that a uniform view of the aged prevailed in this period—old people were respected and venerated.[127] The diverse portrayals of the elderly in non-medical secular literature and the ambivalence accompanying them suggest a far more complex conception of the aged than Fischer describes. Non-medical secular literature on old age never provided a systematic conception of aging and its purposes or a guide for behavior that the aged could follow. Instead it gave voice to a variety of notions—some positive and others negative—that did not mesh with the more coherent religious and medical formulations.

This chapter began by stating that early national ideas about old age created a difficult climate for the aged. It is now clear why this was true. The literature on old age was not reassuring. In general it insisted on the debility and disease of advanced years and rarely mentioned more positive qualities. Though authors of different stripes offered some solutions to the problem of decay, these came at a very high price. Religious meaning and purpose were only accessible to the small subset of the population who could meet the extremely high behavioral standards of Congregational clerics. For others, spiritual comfort in old age was denied. Relief from the physical strains of aging might come from following the advice of medical authors but only if the elderly adopted the recommended lifestyle and accepted full responsibility for their own health. Literature on old age made it clear that both spiritual and physical comfort required hard work from the aged. But not only were the paths to a good old age steep and difficult, there was no clear route to follow. An individual could not simultaneously satisfy the demands of both religious and medical writers, nor could he reconcile the many conflicting ideas that surfaced in non-medical secular literature. These problems were not mere abstractions. As the next chapter will demonstrate, the lack of a workable vision of old age played out in very real ways in the lives of men and women in early national America.

NOTES

1. Thomas Cole, *The Journey of Life: A Cultural History of Aging in America* (New York: Cambridge University Press, 1992).
2. The tradition of describing old age in this way was time-honored. For example, William Bridge's *A Word to the Aged* (Boston: 1679) expounded on this theme as did Cotton Mather's *Addresses to Old Men, Young Men, and Little Children* (Boston: R. Pierce, 1690).
3. Ebenezer Gay, *The Old Man's Calendar*, 4th ed. (Dover NH: Eliphalet Ladd, 1793), 22.
4. Stanley Griswold, *The Good Man's Prospects in the Hour of Death* (Litchfield CT: T. Collier, 1801), 15.
5. New England Tract Society, *Tracts Published by the New England Tract Society*, vol. II (Andover MA: Flagg and Gould, 1814), 277.
6. It should be noted that this was not a Congregational innovation. Indeed the emphasis on decay in old age as a spur to spiritual improvement was not a new feature of religious discourse even in the Middle Ages. See Georges Minois, *History of Old Age: From Antiquity to the Renaissance*, trans. Sarah Hanbury Tenison (Chicago: University of Chicago Press, 1989), 119–120.
7. John Floyer, *Medicina Gerocomica: Or the Galenic Art of Preserving Old Men's Health* (London: Printed for F. Isted, 1724), xvi.
8. John Hill, *The Old Man's Guide to Health* (Philadelphia: Dunlap, 1775), 11.
9. John Wesley, *Primitive Physic*, bound in Henry Wilkins, *The Family Advisor* 3d ed. (Philadelphia: Conrad for Cooper, 1801), 65.
10. John Scudder, *Inaugural Dissertation on the Diseases of Old Age* (New York: Van Winkle & Wiley, 1815), 15–17. It is worth noting however that menopause *per se* was not usually explicitly linked to old age. Most early national medical writers predicted the cessation of the menses would occur between ages forty and fifty. See for example William Buchan, *Domestic Medicine* (Leominster MA: Adams & Wilder for Thomas & Andrews & Whipple, 1804), 320–321; Richard Reece, *The Medical Guide for the Use of Families* (Philadelphia: B.B. Hopkins, 1808), 402; Joseph Brevitt, *The Female Medical Repository* (Baltimore: Robinson for Hunter & Robinson, 1810), 39; Thomas Ewell, *The Ladies Medical Companion* (Philadelphia: William Brown, 1818), 71; Samuel Bard, *A Compendium of the Theory and Practice of Midwifery*, 5th ed. (New York: Collins & Co., 1819), 78; William P. Dewees, *A Compendious System of Midwifery*, 6th ed. (Philadelphia: Carey, Lea & Blanchard, 1833), 58. None of these writers suggested that menopause marked the beginning of old age, though it did occur according to Ewell, "at the approach of old age," which would accord with the general view of old age described earlier as starting between fifty and sixty. Menopause was, without doubt, considered a significant time by medical writers of the period but it had not yet taken on the overweening importance ascribed to it later in the nineteenth century. For a full discussion of the later nineteenth-century literature see Carroll Smith-Rosenberg, "Puberty to Menopause: The Cycle of Femininity in Nineteenth-Century America," in *Clio's Consciousness Raised*, ed. Mary S. Hartman and Lois Banner (New York: Harper & Row, 1974), 23–37.
11. Benjamin Rush, *Medical Inquiries and Observations* (Philadelphia: Printed for Johnson & Warner, 1815), 245–247.
12. *The Old Bachelor's Masterpiece* (Fairhaven VT: J.P. Spooner, 1797), 33.
13. Andrew Beers, *The Farmer's Calendar; or New York and Vermont Almanack* (Troy NY: Wright & Wilbur, 1804), unpaginated.
14. *Old Grand-papa and Other Poems* (Philadelphia: Warner, 1817), 11.

15. Mary Treadwell Hooker reports on a sermon on this passage from Ecclesiastes 12.1. Record Book, 18 December 1808, CHS.

16. William Pierson, Diary, 17 November 1808, Connecticut State Library; Enoch and Julia-Ann Pond to John Maltby [Sr.], 22 May 1825, Julia-Ann Pond to John Maltby [Sr.], 14 February 1832, Maltby Family Papers, CHS.

17. Gallaudet, Diary, 1 September 1813, CHS.

18. Unknown to unknown, 6 July 1819, Maltby Family Papers, CHS.

19. Eliphalet Williams to William Williams, 15 January 1798, Williams Family Papers, CHS.

20. Daniel Wadsworth to Charles Chauncey, Esq., 1 May 1829, Daniel Wadsworth Papers, CHS.

21. Griswold, *The Good Man's Prospects*, 15.

22. Joseph Lathrop, *The Infirmities and Comforts of Old Age: A Sermon to Aged People* (Springfield MA: Henry Brewer, 1805), 7.

23. Gay, *Old Man's Calendar*, 26.

24. James Cogswell, Diary, 30 January 1790, CHS.

25. Beers, *The Farmer's Calendar*, unpaginated.

26. Rush, *Medical Inquiries and Observations*, 242.

27. Ibid., 243.

28. Ibid., 244.

29. Thomas Williams to John McClennan, Esq., 3 December 1811, Williams Family Papers, CHS.

30. Shubael Bartlett, Diary, 3 August 1825, CHS.

31. Jennet Cowles, Memory Book, undated, CHS.

32. Ebenezer Finch case, petition of May 1823, CG.

33. Job Orton, *Discourses to the Aged* (Salem MA: J. Cushing for T.C. Cushing, 1801), v.

34. Joseph Lathrop, *Old Age Improved: A Sermon* (Springfield MA: T. Dickman), 9.

35. Mary Ann Cowles, Diary, 11 January 1824, CHS.

36. Austin Williams, Diary, 14 May 1824, CHS.

37. Hill, *Old Man's Guide to Health*, 3.

38. Nathan Strong explicitly uses this passage in connection with a discourse on old age entitled *A Sermon on the Uses of Times; Addressed to Men in the Several Ages of Life* (Hartford CT: Peter B. Gleason & Co., 1813).

39. Lathrop, *Infirmities and Comforts of Old Age*, 10.

40. Strong, *Sermon on the Uses of Time*, 17.

41. Nathan Strong, *A Sermon, Delivered at Hartford . . . at the Funeral of the Rev. James Cogswell* (Hartford CT: Hudson & Goodwin, 1807), 5.

42. William Wells, *Eight Letters, from an Aged Minister* (Brattleborough VT: J.R. Caldwell, 1818), 20.

43. Gay, *Old Man's Calendar*, 13.

44. Strong, *A Sermon, Delivered at Hartford*, 6.

45. Charles Cohen, *God's Caress: The Psychology of Puritan Religious Experience* (New York: Oxford University Press, 1986), 103. Obviously the Puritan system Cohen describes for the seventeenth century is not identical to late-eighteenth and early-nineteenth century Congregationalism. However this particular feature seems to have persisted.

46. Bridge, *A Word to the Aged*, 6.

47. Lathrop, *Infirmities and Comforts of Old Age*, 12.

48. Strong, *Sermon on the Uses of Time*, 18.

49. Mather, *Addresses to Old Men*, 34–5.

50. Lathrop, *Infirmities and Comforts of Old Age*, 8–9.

51. Ibid., 9.
52. Bridge, *A Word to the Aged*, 12.
53. Mather, *Addresses to Old Men*, 37.
54. Gay, *Old Man's Calendar*, 10.
55. Ibid., 13; Orton, *Discourses to the Aged*, 203.
56. Orton, *Discourses to the Aged*, 139.
57. Gay, *Old Man's Calendar*, 16.
58. Ibid., 25.
59. Mather, *Addresses to Old Men*, 11.
60. Lathrop, *Infirmities and Comforts of Old Age*, 10.
61. For a detailed discussion of Biblical references to the aged see Minois, *History of Old Age*, chapter 2.
62. Orton, *Discourses to the Aged*, 23.
63. Ibid., 43.
64. Ibid., 40–41.
65. Gay, *Old Man's Calendar*, 20.
66. Lathrop, *Old Age Improved*, 7; Strong, *Sermon on the Uses of Time*, 19; Orton, *Discourses to the Aged*, 22.
67. There is a debate about just how uncertain a believer's status was. Cohen concludes that it was possible for Puritans to know they were saved while other disagree. See his discussion in *God's Caress*, 100–101 and note 103.
68. Bridge, *A Word to the Aged*, 13.
69. Orton, *Discourses to the Aged*, 19, 20.
70. Strong, *Sermon on the Uses of Time*, 18.
71. Bridge, *A Word to the Aged*, 15.
72. Ibid., 14.
73. Orton, *Discourses to the Aged*, 42.
74. Caleb Tenney, *Ministers Must Die. A Sermon Preached . . . After the Interment of the Rev. John Marsh* (Hartford CT: George Goodwin & Sons, 1821), 17.
75. Hartford Evangelical Tract Society, *Happy Poverty or the Story of Poor Blind Ellen* (Hartford CT: Hudson & Co., 1817).
76. Hartford Evangelical Tract Society, *Account of Sir Matthew Hale* (Hartford CT: 1817), 4.
77. Although a theological distinction existed between inward faith and outward works, prescriptive literature conflated the two. The assumption seems to have been that those who rigorously implemented religious prescriptions for behavior (performed works) were likely to be favored by God while those who ignored prescriptions were likely to be damned.
78. Proverbs xvi.31. quoted in Orton, *Discourses to the Aged*, 12.
79. John Dunlap, *Short Addresses to Children* (Cambridge NY: Tenney & Stock, 1804), 20.
80. Bridge, *A Word to the Aged*, 18.
81. Orton, *Discourses to the Aged*, 214.
82. Martin Tullar, *A Concise System of Family Duty* (Windsor VT: Nahum Mower, 1802), 104.
83. *An Explanation of the Ten Commandments* (Keene NH: Henry Blake & Co.), 31.
84. Orton, *Discourses to the Aged*, 13.
85. Ibid., 10.
86. Hartford Evangelical Tract Society, *Monitor to Parents* (Hartford CT: 1816), 8.
87. Strong, *A Sermon, Delivered at Hartford*, 5.
88. Mather, *Addresses to Old Men*, 21.

89. Orton, *Discourses to the Aged*, 252.
90. Hartford Evangelical Tract Society, *The Contrast* (Hartford CT: 1821), 3.
91. Howard P. Chudacoff, *How Old Are You? Age Consciousness in American Culture* (Princeton: Princeton University Press, 1989), 20.
92. Anthony Carlisle, *Essay on the Disorders of Old Age* (Philadelphia: Edward Earle, 1819), 6.
93. Luigi Cornaro, *The Probable Way of Attaining Long and Healthful Life* (Portsmouth: George Jerry Osbourne, 1788). Cornaro's work was reprinted at least thirteen times between 1788 and 1815.
94. William Kitchener, *The Art of Invigorating and Prolonging Life*, 2d ed. (London: Printed for Hurst, Robinson & Co., 1821), 48.
95. Alexander Thomson, *The Family Physician* (New York: James Oram, 1802), 80.
96. Cornaro, *The Probable Way*, 8.
97. Floyer, *Medicina Gerocomica*, 26.
98. Thomson, *The Family Physician*, 81.
99. Thomas Beddoes, *Hygeia; or Essays Moral and Medical* (London: Printed by J. Mills for R. Phillips, 1802–3), 94.
100. Rush, *Medical Inquiries and Observations*, 236.
101. Cornaro, *The Probable Way*, 12–13.
102. Hill, *Old Man's Guide to Health*, 26.
103. Ibid., 27.
104. Thomson, *The Family Physician*, 81.
105. Rush, *Medical Inquiries and Observations*, 249.
106. Carlisle, *Essay on the Disorders of Old Age*, 17.
107. Scudder, *Inaugural Dissertation*, 38.
108. I have offered a very simplified view of changing medical practices here. For a fuller picture see Richard H. Shryock, *Medicine and Society in America 1660–1860* (New York: New York University Press, 1960), chapter 2.
109. *Old Bachelor's Masterpiece*, 42.
110. *A Remarkable Instance of Longevity* (1803), 2–3.
111. *My Grandmother, A Poem* (Philadelphia: William Charles, 1817), 1.
112. Ibid., 2.
113. *My Grandfather; A Poem* (Philadelphia: William Charles, 1817), 2.
114. Jay Fliegleman, *Prodigals and Pilgrims: The American Revolution against Patriarchal Authority 1750–1800* (New York: Cambridge University Press, 1982).
115. Natalie Zemon Davis, "The Reasons of Misrule: Youth Groups and Charivaris in Sixteenth-Century France," *Past and Present* 50 (February 1971): 41–75.
116. John Gardiner, *The Widowed Mourner* (Boston: 1791), 3–4.
117. Isaac Bickerstaffe, *He Would if He Could: Or an Old Fool Worse than Any* (New York: David Longworth, 1808), 3.
118. *Father Abraham's Almanac for . . . 1805* (Philadelphia: Stewart for B., J., and R. Johnson, 1804), unpaginated. That the elderly were susceptible to mockery from younger people was remarked on earlier in America's past as well. Increase Mather, for one, warned against deriding the aged or making them laughingstocks. See John Demos, "Old Age in Early New England," 134–5.
119. *The Benevolent Old Man of the Rock: An Entertaining Story for Youth* (Boston: Thomas Wait & Co., 1810[?]), 7–8, 24.
120. *Old Age* (New York: Samuel Wood, 1810), 13.
121. One such example is the poem *My Grandmother*. Here the granddaughter vows that "O yes! and while I've breath will show The debt of gratitude I owe; Till heaven shall call thee from below. My grandmother." (*My Grandmother*, 6.)

122. *Old Grand-papa*, 5.
123. Ibid., 9.
124. Marcus Tullius Cicero, *Cato Major; or a Discourse on Old Age*, trans. Benjamin Franklin (Philadelphia: W. Duane, 1809), 251.
125. Ibid., 258.
126. Ibid., 294.
127. David Hackett Fischer, *Growing Old in America*, expanded ed. (New York: Oxford University Press, 1978), chapter 1.

III

Making Sense of Old Age

The published literature of the early national period presented two coherent systems of thinking about the aged—the religious and the medical—as well as a miscellaneous assortment of other ideas. The two major strands can be briefly summarized. Religious literature, composed mostly by Congregational ministers, provided an interlocking set of ideas and expectations for the aged. Religious publications told the aged to behave as grave, pious, and didactic examples to others, to use their old age in "preparation" for death, to accept pains and losses with submission, and to "wean" themselves from the world by severing earthly attachments and standing ready to die. Great rewards, including respect on earth and bliss after death, accrued to those who followed these prescriptions. Meanwhile great punishments—not the least of which was eternal damnation—piled onto those who disobeyed. Religious books and sermons also told the young to respect and care for their elders. In contrast, books by medically oriented authors provided a completely different—and incompatible—system for understanding and managing old age. Skirting spiritual concerns, medical authors stressed human control over the aging process. According to these writers, moderation in almost everything provided the key to a long and comfortable old age. Proper diet, exercise, and therapeutics were tools available to anyone wishing to take control of the aging process.

This chapter expands understanding of these ideas on aging and the elderly by analyzing just what men and women living in Connecticut made of these different formulations. What was, in fact, the connection between ideas expressed in print and the thought of ordinary people?[1] An answer to this question comes by comparing the thoughts and actions of Connecticut citizens—as revealed in diaries, letters, and other personal papers—with the ideas expressed on the published page. Early national New Englanders were prolific writers. Sifting through their reflections on daily life makes it possible to gauge how meaningful and accepted printed ideas were to ordinary people, and how successful men and women were at implementing them.

Inquiring into the connection between printed material and "real" life draws us into a number of intellectual thickets which must be cleared away before proceeding further. Most broadly it raises the epistemological debate over how humans come to have ideas in the first place. Do people merely absorb ideas like sponges, unwittingly mirroring their culture, or do they actively make choices among ideas to construct a meaningful ideology for themselves?[2]

For our purposes this large question can be reduced to a smaller, but no less difficult one: Does the reading of printed literature mean the absorption and adoption of it or simply that one has been exposed to an idea which can be freely embraced or rejected? In addition we must ask whether the very fact that a manuscript is published means it has greater authority as a cultural artifact than something that is never published. In other words, does an idea's existence in print signify its acceptance by the society that printed it? If so, what are the boundaries of this acceptance? These questions touch on our conception of the author as well. Are authors path breakers, holding ideological beacons that light the way for others to follow, or do authors serve simply to articulate inchoate ideas already circulating in society? And finally, on a very practical level, who reads printed literature and how? In other words, what sorts of people read the sermons, medical tracts, poems, and other works described in chapter 2 and in what contexts?[3]

My approach to these thorny issues is as follows. On the large question of how individuals come to have ideas there are two polar explanations. One states that individuals are the products of their culture—through the socialization process norms and values are impressed on the mind that cannot be unlearned. The opposing view sees individuals as rational actors. Free from the pressure of culture, individuals in this view select from a universe of ideas depending on what best suits their perceived needs. Shunning these extremes, I have opted for a middle approach. The evidence suggests that people do, either consciously or unconsciously, select from a universe of ideas. However, depending on the society, this universe may be quite narrow, thereby limiting possible choices. Thus, though a creative mind will occasionally devise new perspectives, most often people will construct their understanding of a given subject from the building blocks supplied by their culture.

Yet even a limited number of building blocks can create a number of different structures. Borrowing the language of transformational grammarians, we can call this process "rule-governed creativity," which as Nancy Streuver has pointed out, "suggests a model of culture as an abstract, rich, dynamic, and open-ended system."[4] What this means for us is that there will be variability in individual understanding even if there is general consensus on a subject such as old age.

However, where the ideas embraced by a society ordinarily originate—i.e. in the minds of ideological authors/leaders or in some sort of popular Zeitgeist—is unclear. A general answer to this question has eluded scholars and in the case of ideas about aging, there is little evidence on the subject.[5] As a result, I have not assumed that any of the Connecticut people I discuss read or were directly influenced by any of the published material discussed in chapter 2. Instead I search for overlap in the ideas expressed in print and by Connecticut people. The very fact that an idea was printed hints that it had some value to the society at large, if only because the decision to publish something is based on at least one person's judgment that it will be welcomed by the public. However, greater proof of the importance of an idea comes when ordinary people can be seen embracing it, or even better, trying to implement the idea in their own lives. My assumption has been that if an idea resonated both in print and in the thought or actions of an ordinary person, then the idea in question was probably more significant than an idea that did only one or neither. Thus I use personal papers to confirm the importance of ideas in print and vice versa. What matters here is understanding the resonance of ideas that did exist rather than seeking out their origins.

These issues at least partially resolved, we now turn to the evidence. The writings of Connecticut's women and men confirm what the previous chapter suggested: that the formalized conceptions of old age available in these years were faulty at best. Though the religious formulation of the aging process gained the most currency among ordinary people, those who sincerely tried to implement its prescriptions often had significant difficulty. Applied to daily life, religious ideology was often neither practical nor satisfying. As a result, many people modified religious ideas to better suit their circumstances. That religious notions required reworking by ordinary people to be made useful indicates the limitations of this approach to old age. Some did not even bother with this however. There were those for whom religious ideas gained no foothold at all, rendering formal notions irrelevant. Clearly early national society failed to offer its aging people a powerful and fully compelling way to come to terms with senescence.

IDEALS AND REALITY IN THE LIVES OF CONNECTICUT PEOPLE

Connecticut has long prided itself as "the land of steady habits" where tradition dies hard. True to this image, Connecticut remained religiously conservative through much of the early national period, only disestablishing Congregationalism in 1818. This tendency informed how its early national citizens thought about aging and the elderly.[6] Connecticut men and women who took the time to write down their ideas on old age often echoed themes expressed in religious literature, a genre dominated by Congregational clergymen. In some cases this is not terribly surprising since several diarists were themselves ministers. (Indeed pastors are better represented in the sources for this chapter than they were in Connecticut's general population.) However, because many of the non-ministers whose letters and journals survive also point to religious ideas as most significant and because no one articulated a competing system for understanding old age it seems clear that religion—to a lesser or greater extent dependi on the individual—was the primary lens through which people s... old age.

Religious ideas on aging undoubtedly were more widely disseminated and better understood than other ideas about old age because they existed not only in print, but were heard at church meetings and in private conversation as well. The following analysis illuminates how women and men strove to fit the inflexible ideas articulated by clerics into the contours of their daily lives.

Old Age is for Preparing to Die

In December of 1808 Mary Hooker, a Connecticut woman of fifty-three, expressed thanks in her diary that God had preserved her life, "Whilst many have fallen... [and] the shafts of death have been flying thick on every side." These reflections caused her to wonder "Whi am I spared another year?"[7] Hooker was not alone in seeking purpose as old age ensued. For many men and women purpose was found in the idea of preparation for eternity. Indeed, of all the ideas expressed in printed religious literature, the notion that old age was a time to make ready to meet God was the most powerful idea shaping perceptions and actions in the lives of Connecticut people.

Though the concept of preparation shaped the experience of old age, it was an idea that people of all ages were exposed to. Exhortation to prepare spiritually for the afterlife often began in childhood and continued throughout life. For example the Reverend James Cogswell recounted to his diary a conversation in which he "discoursed to ye Schoolmaster Jona. Devotion on the Importance of improving the Times of youth in preparation for old age & eternity."[8] However, Cogswell and other divines did not confine discussion of this issue to private conversation. People of all ages heard sermons on the topic. Twenty-four-year-old Oliver Boardman summarized an address he heard delivered in Hartford in 1817. The minister told his flock,

> Be ye also ready... it is of great importance to be prepared for death, those that are not prepared to die are not prepared to live, when any are going [on] a journey, they spend days and weeks in preparation, and is it not of far more importance to be prepared for eternity.[9]

Similarly a sermon by Hartford's Reverend Joel Hawes reminded this young man to "number" his days and "be sensible of their shortness one third of the people die under six years old and half die under twenty and not more than one in a hundred lives to the age of seventy."[10] Hawes' demographic figures were probably inaccurate but his point was clear—time passes swiftly and must be employed fruitfully. The fact that Connecticut men and women took note of sermons like these confirms that stress on preparation was not confined solely to books—it was part of everyday life for people of all ages.

There is significant evidence that religious injunctions were not simply heard but also taken to heart. Many diarists and letter-writers of various ages felt the need to prepare, usually stressing fleeting time as a strong motivator. Though only twenty-two, Eliza Staples was one who was alive to ministers' warnings. On the last day of 1826 she confided to her diary, "The year has gone, I am passing on toward eternity & O what improvement do I make of my time . . . and what preparation for another world." Then she resolved to live "more like a Christian."[11] Eliza Staples' concern over eternity was not uncommon, even in the young.

Yet increased age tended to add greater urgency to the need to prepare. The fifty-one-year-old merchant, Peter Gallaudet, let his impulse toward metaphor run free in order to express his impression that life was racing by ever faster:

> the year apparently lessens & come[s] round with more speed than formerly when I was ascending the hill of life . . . and as I descend the hill my speed apparently increases, like a descending stone its velocity is increased by the distance of space it passes through. O that I may be prepared for the closeing scene.[12]

For the very aged an even more heightened sense of urgency could prevail. At eighty-six, Eunice Stone knew that imminent death was no longer merely possible but quite probable. Stone described her situation in a letter: "life hangs on A slender thred—how soon or when this frail body drops I know not—Oh! may I but be prepar'd for the summons."[13] Connecticut people of all ages were enjoined to be prepared when their time came to die, but for the aged pressure to "work out" their salvation could be especially strong.

The end of a year, birthdays, or the death of loved ones were likely to spur reflection on one's spiritual state. For example, the aged spinster Rebecca Noyes remarked on the passing of her brother Peleg, "*He* departed this life I hope for a better world—Oh that I was prepared to follow him."[14] Birthdays were especially likely to provoke concern over adequate preparation. Noyes wrote with agitation on her birthday, "this day is my Anniversary Oh! that I cou'd realize *how short my time is.*"[15] Howard Chudacoff has argued that in America before 1850 "cultural values associated with age were imprecise" and Americans generally lacked "age consciousness." He reaches these conclusions based on the fact that age categories were not institutionally entrenched, that is, "age did not play an important role in the structure and organization of society." In Chudacoff's analysis, the celebration of birthdays is one indicator of the greater trend toward age consciousness he sees developing in the late-nineteenth and twentieth centuries. While Chudacoff is generally correct in seeing important changes in how age was conceived of and integrated into social and cultural life over time, evidence from early national personal writings suggest his conclusions are not altogether accurate. Individuals, at least in New England, could be intensely concerned (and anxious) about age and their advance through the stages of life. They were unlikely to mark birthdays with celebration but they often treated them, as in the case with Rebecca Noyes, as important warnings to make ready for death.[16]

Reminders to prepare came not only from the pulpit and from one's own conscience but from friends, neighbors, and family. Though today it would be considered impolite to ask an aged person if he were ready to die or to remind him of his impending demise, the elderly in early national Connecticut expected such questions and reminders. Indeed it was considered a service to the aged to warn them of their plight should they meet death unprepared. Sixty-year-old Abiel Baldwin warned his fifty-four-year-old relative John Maltby Sr. this way:

> My friend our time of working for god is short if we intend to do Any thing we must do it quickly or we shall soon be in Eternity I want to hear from all My friends in Northford whether they have repented of their sins or not if they have not do tell them from me they must repent or be wreched for Ever ... O my friend ... imbrace the Saviour if you do not do it immediately it may forever be to late.[17]

John Maltby Sr. also heard from his son on the same topic. John Jr. wrote, "I ... see you almost worn out—see you doubly burdened—& hear you sigh; yet, I trust [you are] not strangers to peace, not forsaken of God."[18] A year later John Jr. revisited the same theme, expressing hope that his parents were able "to contemplate [death] in relation to yourself, with composure . . . & the confidence of faith & hope."[19] The aged Rebecca Noyes received similar reminders. In 1826 Noyes recorded a visit with a friend who made clear that "He feels very much for us all to get that assurance of an happy eternity."[20] In 1828 another caller "was faithful in warning me to prepare for a better place."[21]

Thus even if Connecticut's readers never perused any of the printed material described in the previous chapter they were likely to be very familiar with one of its basic messages—old age was a time for preparing to meet God. Exposed to this theme in church meetings and in private conversations with friends and family, some aged people felt considerable pressure to perform this vital task well, knowing that eternal doom awaited if they failed. However, this vision of purpose in old age was not universally accepted. It must have had only limited appeal for those who expressed neither interest nor concern about meeting demands to prepare.

William Williams was one who took religious injunctions to prepare very seriously. Williams had once been a wealthy man, prominent in Connecticut politics, and had signed the Declaration of Independence. By the age of seventy-nine, however, he was much reduced in both health and finances. In an 1810 letter to his son he wrote, "my remaining days must be few & ought every minute be improved." To this end he explained, "I am seeking & striving to work out my Salvation with fear & trembling." Yet Williams did not feel sure of the results. He was unable to find "clear & satisfactory Evidence" of his salvation although the sermons he read offered a few "encouraging words." While he strove to have a "saving discovery of himself" he could not "say with confidence" that he had succeeded and as a result pledged to "seek for it with my soul, while I live." In the meantime Williams felt neither "ease nor freedom, nor shall [I] have any till I know that I am reconciled to God."[22] It is difficult to know exactly where Williams encountered spiritual difficulty. However his experience suggests that even for the religiously sincere, nagging infirmities, pressures to prepare, and the specter of looming death could make spiritual peace elusive.

Rebecca Noyes' life was entirely unlike William Williams', but she shared his anxiety about spiritual status. Yet while Williams' efforts to prepare gave him some encouragement, for Noyes the ideal of preparation in old age spawned nothing but frustration. Noyes' diary covered her quiet life in a household of siblings from age forty-two until her death at seventy-one. Her writings show both her awareness that old age should be a time of preparation and increased piety and the fact that she never mustered the energy to really devote herself to these tasks. A number of her comments on religious matters simultaneously recognize their importance and her own inadequacy. In 1813 she indicated she had discussed spiritual topics with a visitor and that "I wish I felt as zealous in the cause of religion as He does."[23] In 1816 Noyes marked the beginning of the new year, noting that "happy are those that are prepared for a better world."[24] That she did not consider herself among this "happy" group is evident. In 1827 she still felt insecure about her readiness to face eternity. The death of a brother reminded her that "how soon I shall follow him I know not Oh that I might be prepared for death."[25] And in the year of her own death she lamented, "what great reason of thankfulness to the giver of all things have I . . . that my life has been spared . . . and yet what an ungrateful wretch *I am*."[26] Unlike her sister Bridget who joined the Stonington church at the mature age of sixty-four, Rebecca failed in outward profession just as she did with inward preparation. Noyes knew what function old age was supposed to have but she also knew her own experiences did not measure up to the exacting religious standards of her time.

Mary Churchill, a Newington woman of fifty-four, had even more difficulty implementing religious prescriptions to prepare as old age advanced. She complained to a friend in 1812,

> At times I feel myselfe a grate sinner—for this year or two past, I have felt very careless and stupid . . . I don't know what will become of me, I have thought it a great wonder why I was spared to live here in this world so long as I have . . . I feel myself a poor lost sinner without divine mercy.

Part of the problem was that frail health kept her from attending church meetings and "a very careless memory" prevented her from remembering much even when she did go. Making matters worse, she confessed to being "indifferent" and "contented with my lot."[27] Like Rebecca Noyes, Mary knew full well how old age was supposed to be employed but somehow failed to effectively implement religious prescriptions. Instead of providing comfort and hope, religious demands made old age spiritually difficult for people like Mary Churchill.

Others avoided the whole issue of preparation. Though George Gillet, a surveyor from Hebron, faithfully kept a diary from the age of fifty-seven to eighty-one, religion seems not to have been important to him. Preparation is, of course, an internal process and a diary can never detail every aspect of life, yet such documents do provide a window onto the concerns of individuals. In Gillet's jottings work activities, social events, weather, and travel hold prominent places, while spiritual concerns are conspicuously scarce.[28] Gillet may well have been aware of religious injunctions to prepare for death but simply ignored them. But if he rejected the Congregational view of old age it is revealing that he proposed nothing in its place. Evidently Gillet found the formally stated purposes of old age offered by his culture irrelevant, electing to cope with aging on his own.

As these examples show, preparing for death and ensuring salvation in old age were easier said than done. Though the idea expressed in print of preparation as an essential task of old age resonated among Connecticut people, their responses to this concept were varied. Men like George Gillet seem to have avoided the challenge of preparation by ignoring unappealing religious prescriptions. Others who took religion to heart found that assurance could be elusive. Individuals invested energy in preparation but learned that these efforts did not always yield satisfying results. As a result, the spiritual rewards promised by religious writers were rarely reaped by ordinary people. Perhaps as the nineteenth century unfolded and the concept of universal salvation gained ground in Connecticut, believers were able to face death with a bit more confidence. For the early national period, however, ideas on old age created significant pressures on ordinary people, pressures that were hard to resolve but which threatened momentous consequences nonetheless.

Standards of Behavior for the Aged

Religious literature outlined not only the broad purposes of old age but also the particulars of proper behavior. These publications asked the aged to act with submission, gratitude, sobriety, and dignity, while offering spiritual instruction to others, weaning themselves from earthly attachments, and cheerfully awaiting death. According to authors of both religious and medical material, decreased passions in old age aided people in reaching this ideal behavior. The diaries and letters of Connecticut people help illuminate how seriously these demanding expectations were taken and with what consequences.

Old People Should Be Submissive

Ideally, according to religious writers, old men and women exhibited submission and its companion virtues, patience and gratitude. Though ministers felt a submissive attitude was desirable at any age, the elderly with their infirmities and trials were enjoined to be especially careful of questioning God's will or complaining. Indeed, authors emphasized the importance of resignation on the part of old people under the most trying and painful circumstances. No matter what ills or problems arose in old age, gratitude was the appropriate response. Not surprisingly, however, the reality of individual behavior often failed to measure up to these exacting expectations.

Diaries and letters of both men and women show that a submissive, uncomplaining posture was a valued attribute for the elderly. Religious people were especially motivated to face pains and trials with resignation, though even the most zealous found this a trying task. Yet though it was difficult, acceptance of God's will provided comfort by making sense of trials and misfortune. Eighty-four-year-old Eunice Stone, for example, was distressed that her relatives lived too far away to visit but found solace by reminding herself that "a wise & good ruler sits at [the] helm & directs every event in the best manner."[29] Such logic could also be applied to physical pain. Though Stone's infirmities made her "a prisoner of my chair" and her failing sight deprived her of the benefits of reading she recognized that "submission & patienc[e]" were the remedies to her problems.[30] This was also the response of seventy-five-year-old E. Dyer of Windham. He wrote, "I do not feel my health & strength as last year This time but hope to wait Patiently till my Change come."[31] After the Reverend Eliphalet Williams' wife died unexpectedly in 1800, the seventy-three-year-old widower similarly sought comfort in resignation. Though in losing his wife Williams felt "that off from my side my better half is torn, while the rest lies bleeding & to mourn," he wrote his brother that, "such is the will of the Lord, & I Desire to acquiesce in it as right and good."[32]

The idea that suffering was valuable in and of itself facilitated resignation. Not mere senseless exercises of power, God's afflictions acted to improve individuals. Faith in this purpose aided submission. John Maltby, for example, reminded his ailing father of the importance of suffering in 1831:

> I am pained to hear that you have been worse again . . . I hope that through the grace of God your afflictions, which for the present seem not to be joyous but grievous, will work out for you a far more exceeding & eternal weight of Glory.[33]

Sixty-year-old Abiel Baldwin employed similar logic to come to terms with his wife's bout of "tifus fever" which depleted her physically and rendered her "almost bereft of her mental faculties." He asked his nephew to pray for his family and hoped that,

> these Afflictions may be sanctified to us for our spiritual good & if your Aunt never has her Reason Restored to her Again we may kiss the Rod & Adore him that holds it noing it is god & believeing that he does Nothing but what is for the best.[34]

Resignation to trials in old age not only made sense of the experience but promised a reward of greater spiritual good to the submissive sufferer.

However, though resignation to God's will seems to have been a common goal in old age, not even the most sincere and pious people succeeded in complete submission. The efforts of Reverend James Cogswell probably represent the best fallible humans could do in implementing this difficult prescription. At seventy Cogswell set the standard for himself writing, "I desire to be wholly submissive to ye Providence of God in Life & at Death."[35] To this end, Cogswell ably turned what could have been complaints into opportunities for thankfulness. One December day he wrote, "cannot bear the Cold as I could once, but have Reason to be thankful that I can bear it so well."[36] Plagued by severe headaches throughout his older years as well as by "the infirmities of age," Cogswell nevertheless insisted, "I have no Reason to complain, but much to be thankful!"[37] However, Cogswell's resolve was tested often. When his beloved wife became feeble Cogswell admitted that though he desired to resign himself "to divine Disposal" he "look[ed] forward to the period of parting with her with Grief."[38] And later when Cogswell's son died in a musket accident, shock and pain overwhelmed his efforts at resignation. Indeed his wife had to refresh his sense of submission "by mentioning the Grounds for her Resignation & Comfort" when she had met with sorrows.[39] In moments like this, emotion could prove stronger than even the most ardent piety. In the case of his son's death Cogswell avoided "murmuring" against God but he had far more difficulty interpreting the event as positive in any way or feeling grateful for the loss. On other occasions Cogswell's efforts at submission broke down completely. In 1791 he reported, "have great reason for Thankfulness, but do not feel thankful as I ought. am sceptical, confused, headachy, inclined to fearfulness & Distrust—O God help me for Xts sake."[40] As Cogswell's case shows, submission was indeed valued but it posed a formidable challenge even for the most sincere and religiously dedicated individuals.

The infirmities and losses of old age could be vexing indeed and not everyone possessed the moral fortitude of a man like Cogswell. Seventy-seven-year-old John Bartlett found it impossible to bear up under the painful afflictions that accompanied his waning days. As a result he succumbed to complaining though such behavior was frowned upon as ungrateful. When Bartlett was suffering with a badly infected leg, his son described his situation: "father had a painful and wakeful night last night. Oh how many are the infirmities, and how childish are the complaints of old age!"[41] Even when physical pains were absent, old people could give in to negative thinking. Abigail Whitman described her grandmother's behavior: "she has been complaining about a week, she is not sick but appears verry gloomy and dejected."[42] Of course, Christianity is based on a premise of human fallibility so it is not surprising that ordinary people failed to be truly submissive even if they believed in the concept. Nonetheless, the existence of a demanding ideal juxtaposed with the reality of human inability to implement it undoubtedly created tension and anxiety.

Because total submission was so difficult to achieve, ordinary people lent the notion greater practicality by interpreting it loosely. Attitudes toward the use of medicine in old age provide a good example of this. If rigidly interpreted, the religious standard of resignation precluded human attempts, including medical intervention, to ameliorate suffering in old age. Yet Connecticut people used medicine and medical treatments freely, without concern that they interfered with submission. Reverend Cogswell, a man quite devoted to the concept of resignation, condoned the use of medicine to soothe the pains of growing old. When his wife was ill Cogswell wrote in his diary:

> Mrs. Cogswell was unwell in ye Night & could not sleep—I got up and gave her some Elixir, & it was very seasonable and comfortable. & she got asleep soon—what Reason have I of thankfulness for Remedies against Pain & Trouble in old age![43]

Evidently Cogswell felt that though God sent affliction he also provided medical means to relieve it.

A letter from sixty-nine-year-old Ezekiel William to his brother likewise indicates that the use of medicine was not considered by ordinary people to be at odds with an acceptance of God's will. Seeking help for back pain from faddish practitioners, Ezekiel went to Hartford,

> with a design to be Electerized by Mr. Strand who has an Instrument ... was very anxious about it as I had but little Faith in it or Expectations from it, as little as I had from the Metallick points which ... I have been scratched with almost to the Bone to as little purpose as to have been scratched with a pin. I have for some days past put myself under the care of Doct Stephens ... he did all he could, but to little purpose untill the Blister drawd which he put on to my wrist, which gave some temporary relief & yesterday gave me Physick ... could Eat something ... but as starvation is generally prescribed in such cases I am trying the

Experiences... Oh that God would give me patience and an Entire Submission to his holy will.[44]

Ezekiel's description of his manic search for pain relief and his yearning for "entire submission" appear inconsistent on the surface, yet simultaneous pursuit of these goals posed no problem in his mind. The widespread use of medical treatments to comfort the aged suggests that though religious ideas dominated the understanding of old age in Connecticut, the concept put forward by medical authors in printed literature that advanced age could be improved through therapeutics was accepted and grafted onto the religious system. In this way ordinary people adapted parts of the Congregational view to better fit their lives.

Others modified the notion of submission by preserving for themselves the right to question God's judgment. Rather than blindly accepting their lot, some wondered whether long life and its trials were always desirable gifts to be met with gratitude and acceptance. Indeed, though such doubts were incompatible with total resignation to divine will, Connecticut men and women sometimes harbored ambiguous feelings about the value of old age. William Williams—an infirm man of seventy-nine—told his son that it was "a wonder of Providence... that my blood yet flows in my veins & my pulse continues to beat" but he was unsure whether his continued life was "a Mercy or Judgment."[45] After a visit with an elderly neighbor, a much younger woman named Sophia Munroe recorded her similarly mixed feelings about the prospect of old age. Her aged neighbor was,

> truly melancholy in all the infirmities of decrepd old age—quite helpless and a sight that would sufficiently loosen the hold we have on life & our anxious wishes for its lengthened span.[46]

Likewise middle-aged James Robbins, upon describing the pathetic state of his elderly mother, opined that "old age, under the most favorable circumstances, seems scarcely to be desired."[47] A poem written by a Connecticut man named Robert Dinsmoor to an aged female friend also undermined the idea that old age was worthwhile. Dinsmoor's verses personify old age as a guide walking alongside an aging woman. In guiding the woman to death's door, old age prints wrinkles on his companion's face, shackles her feet, whitens her hair, and threatens her with deafness. Yet these actions give the old woman "no anxious care" because she knows she can "jilt" her guide when death comes, exchanging old age for "a better partner." In this poem old age has no inherent value and the trials of aging are devoid of spiritual meaning. Dinsmoor envisioned old age as an annoying phase to pass through on the way to a better situation. Religious authors insisted on gratitude for old age no matter what its price. Ordinary people may have subscribed generally to the ideal of submission to God's dictates, but they did not always refrain from weighing the costs of growing old and concluding that old age was not an unadulterated blessing.

The ideal of submission in old age was not confined to published materials alone. Pious men and women in Connecticut were likely to apply the concepts of patience, acceptance, and thankfulness to their own lives. However, because total resignation was almost impossible, even the most pious individuals failed to reach the high standard articulated in written works on old age. Encouraged by the idea that such behavior would be rewarded in the afterlife, some elderly people tried their best anyway, achieving only limited success. Others—though they may have hoped to be submissive—succumbed to complaining and dejection in old age, thereby failing to meet the challenge prescribed by religious writers. However, because true resignation was nearly impossible, it is not surprising that individuals did not always apply the notion as strictly as they might have. Suffering men and women reserved for themselves the comfort of medical treatment and the right to question whether an old age wracked by disability and pain was really worthwhile. Men and women therefore salvaged the rigid and difficult ideas offered by religious authorities by bending them into more practical shapes.

The Elderly Should Live Between Life and Death

Religious writers saw the task of weaning oneself from the world as another important goal of old age. Feeling that the proper focus of the elderly should be the afterlife, clerical authors suggested that men and women untangle themselves from earthly attachments of all kinds. Severing ties to sensual enjoyments was especially important. Pains and trials could aid the aged in weaning by lessening their desire to continue on in the world. Once detachment was accomplished the elderly could place themselves in a state of suspension—neither clinging to life nor fearing death—as they waited for their "change" to come. Religious literature praised those who matched these expectations, while condemning as depraved those who failed to wean their affections from life's vain pleasures and ambitions. To test the resonance of these ideas in the lives of ordinary men and women we can again look to diaries and letters. They show, as we have seen with other religious prescriptions for behavior, that aspects of the religious formulation of old age were both unrealistic and unattractive to Connecticut people. Though some may have felt that weaning was desirable in theory, personal papers suggest it was rarely attempted and never successfully practiced.

Lack of familiarity with the idea was probably not the reason the aged failed to detach themselves from the world. Just as in printed material, at least one Connecticut minister drew on the Biblical tale of Barzillai to illustrate and recommend the concept. Zeloda Barrett, a young diarist from New Hartford, reported hearing such a sermon in 1820. The minister described how Barzillai, "a very aged man even four score years old," was invited by the king to go with him to Jerusalem and enjoy the comforts of life at the royal court. Barzillai refused because of his age and the conviction that his short time was best spent contemplating religion rather than immersed in the world, however great its charms.[48] A sermon presented in Hartford in 1817 explored a corollary to these notions, arguing that if one successfully detached from the world death would hold no terror but would, in fact, be welcomed. On this occasion the minister explained that "it is no mark of the Christian to live in fear of death." Therefore rather than existing in a state of "continual alarm," the reverend recommended that every Christian possess a "desire to depart" from the world.[49]

Yet even the most spiritually-minded Connecticut citizens only embraced these prescriptions partially. The Reverend James Cogswell, whose exceptional piety and sincerity has already been described, provides a good example. Cogswell prayed that "I may live for Eternity, & be willing—yea ardently desirous to leave the world whenever God shall call me hence."[50] He also attempted to shift his focus from earthly attachments to God more exclusively. For example, after a trip away from home in 1791 Cogswell wrote, "it is very pleasant being among friends abroad, but they take up too much of my attention . . . and leave the less for God."[51] Yet as an active minister Cogswell could not really distance himself from work responsibilities, interactions with parishioners, or community doings. Nor was Cogswell able to detach from his role as a husband and father. In old age Cogswell kept busy comforting others, catechizing children, reading, studying, conversing with his wife, and performing more mundane tasks like getting his horse shod. In addition, the world's temptations continued to beckon Cogswell in old age. At seventy he wrote, "have reason to be greatly humbled that I am stil in old Age no more Spiritually minded—but have an inordinate Attachment to animal Enjoyments & pleasures. I pray God forgive me."[52] A few months later he confided again, "find too much attachment to animal Enjoyments, tho I endeavour to live above the world."[53] Most likely these enjoyments were relatively innocent, as when he remarked, "fear I eat too much apple & milk—must be more temperate in my old age."[54] Yet innocent or not, Cogswell was well aware that sensual pleasures were incompatible with living "above" the world yet he found resisting them quite difficult. Indeed the example of James Cogswell suggests the impossibility of simultaneously living in the world with all its cares and pleasures and maintaining a detached posture in suspense waiting for death. Rather than helping people like Cogswell improve their remaining time on earth, the ideal of weaning raised an unrealizable standard that led only to feelings of failure when it was not met.

Cogswell's effort to meet religious standards of behavior in old age was exceptional. Most elderly people never even attempted to wean themselves from the world, even if they believed in the idea in principle. Elisha Niles, for example, gave only lip service to the concept. On his seventy-third birthday Niles expressed the hope that "I may live the few Days I have remaining In a Constant Readiness to Leave the World."[55] Though on some level Niles may have been ready to cast off his earthly form, most of his attention seems to have gone to the practical aspects of living. Niles remained actively working at planting, gardening, and other tasks until his death at eighty-one. Religious writers suggested limiting worldly activity in old age. For most aged people engaged in making a living, family affairs, and other pressing concerns, this ideal simply could not be integrated into daily life.[56]

The tension between life and the injunction to transfer one's focus to the eternal realm is suggested in a letter from Enoch Pond to John Maltby on the occasion of the death of Maltby's wife. In an effort to console his correspondent, Pond urged Maltby to "raise your thoughts & affections much toward that world, where, you may now truly say your *best friends*, your *kindred dwell*." An instant later however, Pond suggested that "It may help to divert your mind to visit your children."[57] Weaning one's affection from the world struck Pond as a good suggestion but so did seeking comfort from relatives who were still alive.

Given these problems most aged people seem not to have even tried to detach themselves from the world. Rebecca Noyes kept a diary from the age of forty-two until her death at seventy. Though she knew she must be spiritually prepared for death, Noyes never mentioned any plans to curtail her affectionate family life and transfer her focus to the afterlife.[58] Terri Premo's study of aged women in early national America suggests that withdrawal from the world may have been especially difficult for women because their lives were defined by relations with others. As Premo puts it,

> Supported and strengthened throughout their lives by a morality of connection and interdependence, women in old age were expected to 'improve' on this earlier model by withdrawing from earthly connections . . . to sever those ties which nourished them throughout life.

Yet Premo notes that this "was a task requiring more than some women will willing or able to undertake."[59]

Men could be equally unwilling to withdraw from the world. At eighty Humphrey Pratt showed little concern with any religious objectives at all. Instead, right up until his death the entries in Pratt's diary remained firmly rooted in the here and now. His reflections two weeks before his demise are typical: "quite unwell but have been out to day very bad cold in my head my head akes some and ear akes & nose runs very much but I hope I feel some better looks like rain."[60] Finally, there were those who not only failed to wean from the world but actively plunged into it in a way authors of religious literature would have found most unseemly. The husband of Martha Lewis was one. The aged Mr. Lewis created scandal in Middletown by carrying on an adulterous dalliance with a young widow.[61] The Reverend Thomas Robbins, to give another example, surely knew well the Congregational counsel to withdraw from the world as age advanced yet at fifty he continued to find earthly temptations irresistible. So much so that in 1827 a group of his parishioners complained that he had kissed and fondled several female members of his flock against their wishes, resulting in discharge from his post.[62] Sensual temptations—whether in the form of apples and milk or women—as well as the facts of daily living made detachment from the world an unreachable challenge for aged people.

The prescription to withdraw from work, emotional attachments, and sensual enjoyments in old age did not serve the old well because it made little practical sense. As diaries and letters suggest (and later chapters will confirm), the aged were frequently as absorbed with family life, economic concerns and other preoccupations as younger people. Perhaps if the modern nursing home, with its segregated elderly population, detachment from work and family, and atmosphere of decay had existed in the early national period, the aged would have found institutional support for efforts to wean from the world. However this institution had yet to be invented, leaving the elderly too enmeshed in life with all its cares and joys to detach effectively from earthly existence.

The Aged Should Be Grave, Sober, and Dignified

In addition to the behavioral prescriptions already discussed, the aged also received instruction from religious writers to behave with gravity, sobriety, and dignity. As one author phrased it, "trifling, & childish, & frolicksome" carriage were inappropriate.[63] Yet though religious tracts informed readers that these qualities were expected in the aged, such general expectations are rarely found in the personal papers of Connecticut people. One discovers instead only occasional hints that a different standard of propriety for the elderly existed. In addition, it is not at all clear that these notions of propriety were religiously based. Connecticut sources therefore suggest that while ordinary people accepted certain components of the religious formulation of old age—such as submission for example—others components were simply irrelevant.

A few shards of evidence suggest that propriety for the aged was defined differently than for other groups. At the age of forty-nine Mary Hooker explained in her diary that she had joined the choir and indicated that "it is a privilige, of which I can not bare to be denied, so long as I am able, and it shall be thought decent and proper on account of my Age."[64] A poem written in the inside cover of Rebecca Noyes diary likewise hinted that age played a role in determining appropriate behavior. It read:

> The wild Fox-glove and Wallflower hung
> In fantastic wreaths, intermingling with the
> mantling Fog, and, like ill-suited
> ornaments upon age, rendered but more
> conspicuous its decay.[65]

Though the poetic value of the stanza is dubious, the message that the aged should avoid ornamenting themselves is clear. Both these examples suggest that, for the aged, correct conduct was defined differently than for younger people, though the age at which the standard changed is left unstated.

Another case concerns a letter from an adult son to his widowed father on the subject of his father's wish to remarry. The son agreed that remarriage was "proper" but expressed concern about one candidate on account of her youth. The son explained,

> I should rather see you connected with a person, about [my deceased] mother's age. I think there is a propriety in it. The person in question is nearer our ages than your's. True there are cases of marriage where the difference of age is much greater, but I should be very sorry to have my father thought of & talked of as such individuals are.[66]

Chapter 2 showed that age-imbalanced romances inspired disgust and ridicule not only in religious writings but in medical and fictional works as well. Clearly the son quoted above was sensitive to this notion of propriety and felt the community shared his views.

Yet despite these limited examples, so little was written by Connecticut people about the ideal of sobriety and dignity in old age that it is difficult to argue that it was an important concept for ordinary people. A look at the behavior of some of Connecticut's elderly suggests that if even the ideal did exist in the minds of ordinary people, in reality old people ranged from quite proper to downright undignified. Peter Gallaudet, a Hartford merchant, qualifies as a dignified old man. Gallaudet cultivated propriety and expected others to appreciate him for his upright behavior. A diary entry from 1813 highlights these aspects of his character. In it he relates the story of an unpleasant stage ride during which he shared space with some young men and a couple of women:

> [During] the forenoon the younger part said but little. [I]n the afternoon one of them took the lead & others soon followed in the most trifeling conversation bordering on rudeness ... when those in more advanced life give up the lead in conversation in mixed companies, to the young ... they too frequently take advantage.[67]

As an older person Gallaudet felt responsible for guiding the conversation of his fellow travelers, despite the fact that they were strangers to him. Accordingly he expected the group to look to him for proper behavior in the complicated situation of mixed company travel.

But elderly people were not always so anxious to set an example of gravity. One diary recorded the conduct of an itinerant aged man in Simsbury:

> A traveler calling himself 'Doct. Elijah Remington 74 years old' called & staid two or three hours & entertained me with several *Indien stories*. At night saw the Doct. again at Wm Adam's where he lied abominably.[68]

Unlike Gallaudet, the man described showed no preoccupation with maintaining reserved dignity or raising the moral tone of his listeners. Nor does the diarist who preserved this event indicate that the old man's behavior was objectionable because he was old. Likewise the adolescent William Pierson, son of a respectable Killingsworth man, noted a number of occasions in his diary when "Old Moses Blackley" entertained the town's youth with fiddling. On these evenings "a great number of young people" would gather to dance or have a "spinning frolick" while Moses lightened the mood with music.[69] Though far from religious prescriptions of proper behavior for the aged, Pierson relished these performances rather than disapproving of them. Connecticut people seem to have had little use for the limited range of behavior recommended for the elderly by religious publications.

Even when an aged person acted contrary to prevailing morals, disapproval did not necessarily stem from the person's age *per se*. Martha Lewis was in late middle age when she penned the story of her tumultuous marriage to a sheriff in Middletown. Mr. Lewis was a deceitful man whose indiscretions included carrying on an affair with a young widow in town. Though his wife, and indeed the whole town, was aware of his egregious behavior—a party of townsmen having witnessed the adulterers in *flagrante delicto*—Lewis lied about it and threatened to deprive his wife of financial support if she acted against him. But while Martha Lewis described her husband as "The Wily Old Gentleman on whose head many years ago the Almond-tree had blossomed," his age was not the crux of the problem.[70] It was his conduct as a husband, not as an aged man that most concerned those involved.

If the ideal of propriety advocated by clerics was not widely subscribed to in Connecticut, what took its place? Diaries and letters suggest that the elderly were valued more for what they brought to personal relationships than for abstract characteristics such as dignity. For example Frances Ann Brace, a woman from Hartford, wrote to her grandparents after marrying and moving away,

> I want to tell you too, how frequently I have been reminded during my stay here of the pleasant hours in the society of you both that have passed in former days, and the recollection of which inspires grateful feelings for your unremitted kindness, and attention to my wants.[71]

Frances' appreciation for these aged people was sentimental, based on affectionate interaction over the years, rather than grounded in high moral principles. When appreciation of an aged person was not based on sentiment, it often involved practical attributes that would have been appealing in a person of any age. To the twenty-four-year-old Sophia Munroe good qualities in an old person were summed up in her acquaintance, Mrs. Thursten. Munroe wrote: "This day Mrs. Thursten—an old lady more than 90 years of age, is here upon a visit—& 'tis delightful to see old age so social—so free from infirmities & so very useful as she seems."[72] William Pierson similarly enjoyed the company of an "old gentleman" one evening because he was "very sensible."[73] In extolling the sentimental and practical characteristics of the aged over more high-flown moral attributes, Connecticut people echoed fictional works about the aged such as the poems *My Grandmother* and *My Grandfather* discussed in chapter 2. In these fictional works the elderly behaved like normal people, just older ones, rather than as the stern figures envisioned by religious writers.

Religious literature stressed that the aged should display a sober demeanor. However, Connecticut sources do not strongly indicate that this was an important concern for ordinary people. There are hints that propriety for the aged may have been defined differently than for other age groups but there is also evidence that a relatively wide range of behavior was acceptable in the old. Moreover, it appears that what made elderly people attractive to their contemporaries were not the special characteristics extolled by clerics but instead the virtues that were pleasing at any age Meanwhile, the passionlessness that supposedly marked the aged went entirely unmentioned in diaries and letters. That Congregational notions of propriety resonated neither in the thought nor action of ordinary people suggests a failure on the part of religious authorities to offer appealing and useful approaches to behavior in old age.

The Old Should Instruct Others Spiritually

In religious material published on old age, the aged were assigned another important duty—that of instructing others in spiritual matters and sharing their experience with God. Ideally such activity made the aged useful while simultaneously improving younger people. Again however, Connecticut people apparently did not find this a serviceable suggestion and as a consequence fell short of published expectations. Few aged men or women expressed interest in fulfilling this duty or recorded any efforts at instruction. In fact, only two instances of attention to this duty have been uncovered, and in both cases the old men doing the instructing were ministers, making it difficult to distinguish between their teaching motivated by professional obligations and teaching stemming from advanced age.

The first case concerns the Reverend James Cogswell, whose earnest piety has already been remarked upon. At seventy, Cogswell described his efforts to instruct others in his diary. In March of 1790 he explained,

> have been to catechise the Children at Brunswick[?] School House this afternoon... pray God to bless my weak but sincere Endeavours to instruct the rising Generation & form theirs to Religion.[74]

Yet this would have been his duty whether he was old or not. Cogswell also made an effort to spur his son Mason to greater piety. For example, he "discoursed largely with Mason this Morning on the Importance of being devoted to God & publicly assuming the Xtian character without Delay."[75] Again, however, the question of motivation is problematic—was Cogswell acting as a minister, a father, or an old man? Given his devotion to his calling and his fond love for Mason, the first two roles would have provided ample reason for instructing his son. Because the Reverend Cogswell does not mention his age as a factor spurring him to teach others, there is little positive evidence to suggest such an idea was influential.

The second case provides even less evidence that ordinary people took the ideal of instruction seriously. In this instance, William Pierson, a young Connecticut man reported in his diary on a sermon delivered by Dr. Lathrop of Springfield, Massachusetts. Lathrop expounded on Philemon, verses 8 and 9, telling his audience that he hoped they would "especially regard" his message "on account of his age, being an one as *Paul* the aged."[76] Yet that Lathrop echoed the idea expressed in printed literature that the aged should be especially effective religious instructors comes as no surprise—Lathrop himself was the very author of a tract discussed in the previous chapter that counseled the aged to act as teachers.[77] This case, therefore, provides no support that the idea of the elderly as sage instructors had wide resonance beyond the printed page.

The almost total absence of remark in personal papers on the aged's obligations or activities as religious instructors does not prove the idea was meaningless to ordinary people. However it does suggest strongly that ordinary men and women were not preoccupied with this prescription, and may have chosen to ignore it as an ineffectual component of religious thinking on old age.

Duties of Others to the Elderly

The previous chapter described how printed literature not only outlined the roles of the aged but also the duties of others toward the elderly. When prescriptions were made they tended to stress that the elderly deserved respect and that younger people were responsible for needy older relatives. Children especially were told to provide support and care for their aged parents. Religious authors described a sort of moral economy in which children repaid the debt they owed their parents by caring for them, thereby helping to insure their own future care. How important were these principles to ordinary people, and how well implemented? A full answer to this question must await later chapters which explore family relations in greater depth. However, the evidence here indicates that religious formulations of the aged's place in society were not compelling enough to be embraced fully by ordinary people.

Though there is limited evidence that older people felt respect was due them from all young people, most Connecticut people who commented on duties to the aged focused on what was expected from immediate family.[78] Most often, the fact of parenthood, rather than old age, was what bound the young in obligation to their elders. In other words a relational hierarchy, rather than an age hierarchy, dictated proper behavior. For example, the fifty-three-year-old merchant Peter Gallaudet told his diary with dismay of a man who refused to pay a debt of his father's, forcing the older man to languish in debtor's prison. Gallaudet branded the son's behavior "unnatural" since "Children are bound by gratitude to releive their Parents, could they but realize how much their Parents have done for them they could not but aid them."[79] A number of other men and women echoed Gallaudet's formulation of a child's duty to his parents. The diary of Austin Williams reveals his expectations of help from children as he aged. Though these expectations were thwarted by his son's untimely death, Williams had hoped that his son "might grow up & become useful; a comfort to his parents in their declining days, support for them on the bed of languishing, & smooth their dying pillows."[80] Similarly, the widow Anna Goodwin told her seventeen-year-old son that she looked "forward with Pleasure thinking that I shall have a Prop on whom I can lean" in later life.[81]

For the elderly Jonathan Brace, hopes for care and attention in old age were extended to grandchildren as well, perhaps because he played a large role in their upbringing. Brace counseled his granddaughter to learn domestic skills from her grandmother so that,

> when she is old and unable to manage herself, you can take the charge and care of managing the affairs of the family in her place. In this way you will be able to recompense her for all her care and trouble in bringing you up.[82]

At seventy-seven Bunce reminded his granddaughter and grandson-in-law that "I avail myself on this occasion, to say to you both, that on you especially . . . I rely, for comfort and support in old age." In Brace's case, the fact that he had helped raise his granddaughter, had financed her schooling, and had maintained a close and affectionate relationship with her meant he could expect a lot in return.

Respect and support from all young people was probably not expected by the aged, but parents and grandparents evidently felt such attention was due from offspring. Young people tended to agree that filial duty should be honored. For example, Julia Ann Pond, a woman of thirty-five, acknowledged that if she were living closer to her parents, "I should know better how to pay the debt which all children owe their parents."[83] Her brother John also expressed awareness of his obligation to his parents. After receiving a gift of money from them John wrote: "I feel one more cord drawn with the many which already bind me to my parents & my duty."[84] A few months later he elaborated on his vision of duty, telling his parents, "if the will of the Lord were so I should be glad to return & be their companion & their staff as the withering influence of age comes over them."[85] Likewise, when Solomon Williams' brother-in-law Lemuel went to visit his aged father, Solomon noted approvingly,

> I am very glad ... Lem[u]el has gone to Woodstock to give a little satisfaction to his Father—it is a duty which he owes to the grey hairs of an aged Parent—whose years have been uncommonly spent in *laborious anxiety* for his Children.[86]

Solomon also adopted a filial attitude toward his own parents, based on the gratitude he felt towards them for their care and nurturing of him.[87]

Clearly the idea that the young—especially children—should comfort and assist their relations had importance not only in religious publications but in the lives of both young and old.[88] However the reasoning behind this idea varied from that offered in printed works. Rather than constructing this duty in terms of age relations, as religious authors sometimes did, ordinary people more likely viewed in it terms of family relations—that between a parent and a child. Connecticut citizens generally avoided explicitly religious rationales for a child's duty to his parents, relying instead on a straightforward sense of fairness to justify filial responsibility—parents take care of children when they are young and helpless, therefore children should care for parents when they are old and need help. Thus ordinary people accepted that old parents could expect help and comfort from children, but they broke from religious writers on a number of points. None of the religious notions discussed so far made the transition from the printed page to daily life without alteration. Published notions of behavior toward the aged provide no exception.

Of the different ideas about old age circulating in America's early national period, the array presented by religious authors resonated most in the lives of Connecticut's men and women. Yet as the writings of ordinary people have shown, the formally stated religious conception of old age was too limited and unyielding to be of great service to the elderly. There is no question that these ideas were promising—they offered the possibility of making sense of old age, lending purpose to pain and suffering, and fitting the last stage of life into the cosmic order. Unfortunately, few were able to reap these rewards for several reasons. Those who took religious prescriptions seriously often found that they were difficult, if not impossible, to live up to. As a result a sense of guilt and failure were more likely consequences than spiritual comfort for aged people striving to implement religious ideas. When prescriptions were not extremely demanding they were impractical instead, as with the advice to wean from earthly attachments. Ordinary people were aware of religious expectations but they simply could not make some aspects of the religious program work. Moreover, some aspects of the religious formulation simply failed to capture the interest of ordinary people. In this sense, religious notions were simply irrelevant and consequently of little use to the aged. Given these limitations, individuals were forced to modify religious thinking to make it serviceable. But in doing so, they risked losing the benefits promised by clerics and experienced the stress of trying to navigate between a real world and an ideal world that were fundamentally incongruous.

The examination of printed works in chapter 2 demonstrated that early national America offered several ways of coming to terms with old age. These conflicted with one another and therefore provided the elderly no sure path to a good and meaningful old age. Ordinary people seem to have solved this problem by cutting through the thicket of conflicting notions about old age and opting primarily for the religious conception. However this choice did not end the ideological problems the elderly faced. Though the religious view may have been the best of the lot, the elderly were nevertheless working with a difficult system. Having made their choice, men and women were required to do the best they could with the stiff materials available. On them fell the responsibility of refracting these rigid ideas through the prism of individual experience and fitting them into a complicated and imperfect world.

NOTES

1. By "ordinary" I mean the vast majority of men and women who were not authors of printed material on aging.

2. The underlying question here is even broader, namely how do we understand the "black box" that mediates experience and meaning/structure both on the individual level and the larger social level. Nancy Streuver raises this issue when she writes of the gap in understanding of how "input and output, between external 'causes' or stimuli and the complex social mechanisms invented to cope with experience" relate to one another. See "The Study of Language and the Study of History," *Journal of Interdisciplinary History* 4 (Winter 1974): 410.

3. The complexities of interaction between reader and text are explored at length in Roger Chartier, "Texts, Printing, Readings," in *The New Cultural History*, ed. Lynn Hunt (Berkeley: University of California Press, 1989), 154–175.

4. Streuver, "The Study of Language," 415.

5. Clifford Geertz's seminal article, "Ideology as a Cultural System" articulates some of the difficulties encountered by social scientists attempting to describe the origins and functions of ideas. In *Ideology and Discontent*, ed. David Apter (London: The Free Press of Glencoe, 1964), 47–76.

6. The early national period was, of course, a time of religious flux. The Second Great Awakening and the rising influence and appeal of evangelical ideas were important characteristics of the period. Yet there is little evidence in Connecticut personal papers to 1830 that evangelical ideas had much effect on ideas about aging and the elderly.

7. Mary Treadwell Hooker, Record Book, 31 December 1808, CSL.

8. James Cogswell, Diary, 23 January 1790, CHS.

9. Oliver Boardman, Diary, 23 February 1817, CHS.

10. Ibid., 4 January 1818.

11. Eliza Ann Staples, Diary, 31 December 1826, CSL.

12. Peter Wallace Gallaudet, Diary, 23 April 1807, CHS.

13. Eunice Stone to John Williams, Esq., 1831, Williams Family Papers, CHS.

14. Rebecca Noyes, Diary, 2 March 1825, CHS.

15. Ibid., 23 February 1813.

16. Howard P. Chudacoff, *How Old Age You? Age Consciousness in American Culture* (Princeton: Princeton University Press, 1989), 9–10. For his discussion of birthdays see chapter 6. Looking closely at the evidence, one might even argue that pre-1850 Americans were more conscious of age than people are today. For example in the colonial period, New Englanders often put more age information on tombstones than we do today. They included not only years lived, but months and days as well. This could be construed as signifying greater age consciousness than possessed by modern Americans.

17. Abiel Baldwin to John Maltby, Sr., 19 May 1822, Maltby Family Papers, CHS.

18. John Maltby Jr. to John Sr. and Elizabeth Maltby, 11 November 1829, Maltby Family Papers, CHS.

19. Ibid., 27 December 1830.

20. Noyes, Diary, 19 May 1826.

21. Ibid., 8 June 1828.

22. William Williams to Solomon Williams, 16 July 1810, Williams Family Papers, CHS.

23. Noyes, Diary, 18 February 1813.

24. Ibid., 1 January 1816.

25. Ibid., 17 September 1827.

26. Ibid., 1 January 1830.

Making Sense of Old Age

27. Mary A. Churchill to Martha Deming, 16 April 1812, Norman Brigham Correspondence, CHS.
28. George Gillet, Diary, CSL.
29. Eunice Stone to Abigail Williams, 3 December 1829, Abigail Williams Correspondence, CHS.
30. Eunice Stone to John Williams, Esq., 1831, Williams Family Papers, CHS
31. E. Dyer to Amelia Wyllys, 21 April 1796, Wyllys Papers, CHS.
32. Eliphalet Williams to William Williams, 27 January 1800, Williams Family Papers, CHS.
33. John Maltby Jr. to John Maltby Sr., 22 April 1831, Maltby Family Papers, CHS.
34. Abiel Baldwin to John Maltby Sr., 14 February 1822, Maltby Family Papers, CHS.
35. Cogswell, Diary, 14 February 1790.
36. Ibid., 23 December 1790.
37. Ibid., 25 November 1790.
38. Ibid., 21 June 1790.
39. Ibid., 2 September 1790.
40. Ibid., 29 January 1791.
41. Shubael Bartlett, Diary, 24 July 1831, CHS.
42. Abigail Whitman to Eliza Whitman, 10 February 1811, Whitman Family Correspondence, CHS.
43. Cogswell, Diary, 12 February 1791.
44. Ezekiel Williams to William Williams, 15 January 1798, Williams Family Papers, CHS.
45. William Williams to Solomon Williams, 16 July 1810, Williams Family Papers, CHS.
46. Sophia Munroe, Diary, 7 March[?] 1812, CHS.
47. James Robbins to Thomas Robbins, 13 August 1828, Thomas Robbins Papers, CHS.
48. Zeloda Barrett, Diary, 19 November 1820, CHS.
49. Boardman, Diary, 23 February 1817.
50. Cogswell, Diary, 8 May 1790.
51. Ibid., 21 September 1791.
52. Ibid., 31 January 1790.
53. Ibid., 2 March 1790.
54. Ibid., 26 September 1790.
55. Elisha Niles, Diary, 28 February 1837, CHS.
56. For many, reduced work was an impossibility for financial reasons. See chapter 5, especially the sections on the destitute and middling aged.
57. Enoch Pond to John Maltby Sr., 4 January 1831, Maltby Family Papers, CHS.
58. Noyes, Diary.
59. Terri Premo, *Winter Friends: Women Growing Old in the New Republic, 1785–1835* (Urbana: University of Illinois Press, 1990), 157–158 and chapter 6 in general.
60. Humphrey Pratt, Diary, 27 March 1828, CHS.
61. Martha Mortimer Starr Lewis, Record Book, CHS.
62. Complaint by Elihu Wolcott, 3 May 1827, Thomas Robbins Papers, CHS.
63. Cotton Mather, *Addresses to Old Men, and Young Men, and Little Children* (Boston: R. Pierce, 1690), 34–35.
64. Hooker, Record Book, 19 February 1804, CSL.
65. Noyes, Diary, inside cover.
66. John Maltby Jr. to John Maltby Sr., 23 August 1831, Maltby Family Papers, CHS.
67. Gallaudet, Diary, 22 September 1813.

68. Ransom Warner, Diary, 2 June 1829, CHS.
69. William Seward Pierson, Diary, 15 January, 18 February, 28 February, 13 March, 25 April 1805, 25 November 1808, CSL.
70. Lewis, Record Book, 23.
71. Frances Ann Brace to Jonathan Brace, 24 June 1831, Bunce-Brace Correspondence, CHS.
72. Munroe, Diary, 26 March 1812.
73. Pierson, Diary, 25 September 1810.
74. Cogswell, Diary, 16 March 1790.
75. Ibid., 8 September 1790.
76. Pierson, Diary, 8 January 1809.
77. Joseph Lathrop, *The Infirmities and Comforts of Old Age: A Sermon to Aged People* (Springfield: Henry Brewer, 1805).
78. Peter Gallaudet for example felt that youth owed "respect for the aged which they should ever pay." (Gallaudet, Diary, 22 September 1813.)
79. Ibid., 22 May 1809.
80. Austin Williams, Diary, January[?] 1835, CHS.
81. Anna Goodwin to Daniel Goodwin, 4 May 1794, Goodwin Papers, CHS.
82. Jonathan Brace to Frances Ann Brace, 21 October 1818, Bunce-Brace Correspondence, CHS.
83. Julia Ann Pond to John and Elizabeth Maltby, 26 February 1826, Maltby Family Papers, CHS.
84. John Maltby Jr. to John Sr. and Elizabeth Maltby, 2 April 1825, Maltby Family Papers, CHS.
85. Ibid., 27 August 1825.
86. Solomon Williams to John McClellan, 19 October 1801, Williams Family Papers, CHS.
87. Harriet and Solomon Williams to Mary and William Williams, 1 January 1807, Williams Family Papers, CHS.
88. Due to its complexity, the question of how successfully these ideas were actually implemented must be put aside for the moment. A great many factors influenced behavior including economic circumstances, personality, family size and structure, and place of residence. Chapter 7—devoted entirely to the family relations of the aged—takes up these issues in detail.

IV

Age and Economic Status

While it is valuable to understand the ideas and attitudes held about the elderly in America's early national period and how the aged coped with these, ideas cannot stand alone. Equally important is an analysis of the material conditions that formed the concrete outlines of old people's lives. Access to money and property has always been an important determinant of quality of life, social standing, and power. Therefore it is essential to chart the fortunes of the elderly if we hope to grasp their place in society. This chapter investigates the economic circumstances of Hartford's elderly by using tax records to address two major questions. First, what position did the elderly hold economically in relation to other age groups? Second, how did age affect a person's material circumstances? Though in all stages of life a wide variety of economic experiences were possible, the evidence presented here indicates that youth generally meant low but rising fortunes, while middle and early old age brought peak economic health. In contrast greater age signaled a decline in material resources. Indeed, growing old tended to have an adverse effect on material well-being and stability. This chapter—based as it is on quantitative sources—describes the typical or average experience of different age groups in Hartford. The subsequent chapter, chapter 5, builds on this view by exploring in detail the sources of financial difficulty in old age and ways individuals coped with the many economic hurdles that came their way.

Tax records from the city of Hartford are the basis for this analysis, providing an excellent window onto the fortunes of different age groups. A number of tax record books survive from Hartford's early national period. These records are of two main types—town lists and valuation lists.[1] Town lists were made annually for the purpose of calculating individuals' obligations to their parishes, towns, and other government bodies. Quite of few of these lists—though not all—are available for the early national period. Made separately for the North and South districts of Hartford, they are analyzed here according to this division since the character of these areas was rather different.[2] In making town lists, tax assessors attempted to distribute the tax burden evenly among community members. Because Connecticut's taxation system was based on the premise that a person's income was the best indicator of his ability to pay taxes, assessors estimated the yearly revenue value of various kinds of property as well as income from the practice of trades. In addition they assessed a flat poll tax. Combined, these elements made up what was called a "list" for each individual, from which his taxes were calculated. Once poll assessments—which as flat taxes bore no relation to income or wealth—are subtracted from individuals' lists, these figures are quite useful for estimating the relative economic standing of individuals or groups.[3] Indeed they capture a sense both of individuals' income (which tax assessors explicitly set out to measure) and their wealth (which tax assessors inadvertently measured by basing income estimates mostly on property holdings).

Valuation lists, the second type of tax document used here, are also useful sources for understanding economic patterns among Hartford citizens. Valuation lists exist for three years in our period—1813, 1815, and 1816—and include both North and South districts together. Simpler than town lists, valuation lists recorded the names of all owners of real property in Hartford and the market value of that property. Thus they permit a fairly complete picture of the distribution of real estate among various age groups. In addition—because valuation lists counted the market value of each taxpayer's real property rather than its income value—these lists provide additional insight into the wealth of Hartford's residents.

Though both these types of tax records are quite helpful in analyzing the economic fortunes of Hartford people, they do have several biases which must be borne in mind. Town lists did not include everyone in Hartford. For a variety of reasons poorer people were less likely to appear on tax lists than more middling or wealthy individuals. As a result taxpayers as a group were unlikely to be a cross-section of Hartford's population as a whole, but rather the middle and upper strata. In addition, men over seventy were less likely than others to be included in tax lists because they automatically received exemption from the poll tax. Those who persisted on the rolls after seventy tended to be wealthier than those who were excluded.[4] Consequently, the situation of those seventy and over probably appears more favorably in the data that follow than it actually was. Women, of course, are also less common on tax lists than men since they were never assessed poll taxes and infrequently held taxable property. Hence tax lists tell us little directly about women's fortunes. Valuation lists are somewhat less problematic since they simply recorded the holdings of all real estate owners.[5]

However, because neither town lists nor valuation lists included any age information, names from both had to be matched to birth and death information gleaned from elsewhere to make them useful.[6] The analysis that follows is based on the roughly one half of all names on valuation lists and town lists that were successfully matched to age data. Because the available birth and death data are themselves biased—towards somewhat wealthier and better established Hartfordians—these biases have been transferred to the tax data used here. Tax records are an invaluable source revealing quite a lot about the financial life-cycle of Hartford people, but they are best understood when these minor problems are kept in mind.[7]

A PROFILE OF HARTFORD TAXPAYERS

A look at the age composition of Hartford's taxpaying population will help illuminate the pool being analyzed and aid in understanding the data presented a bit later. Figures 4.1, 4.2 and 4.3—for the North District, South District and Valuation years respectively—reveal the age composition of the taxpaying pool and give a rough portrait of the age breakdown of Hartford's adult population.

Though the North and South districts vary in some respects and there are differences in the data by decade, general observations can be made. Very young people—under twenty—are rare for the obvious reasons that they rarely owned property independent of their parents. Those in their twenties are far more numerous due in large part to the fact that at age twenty-one men became eligible for the poll tax.

Thirty-year-olds in general were more numerous still.[8] In the North, twenty to thirty-nine-year olds made up almost 50 percent of

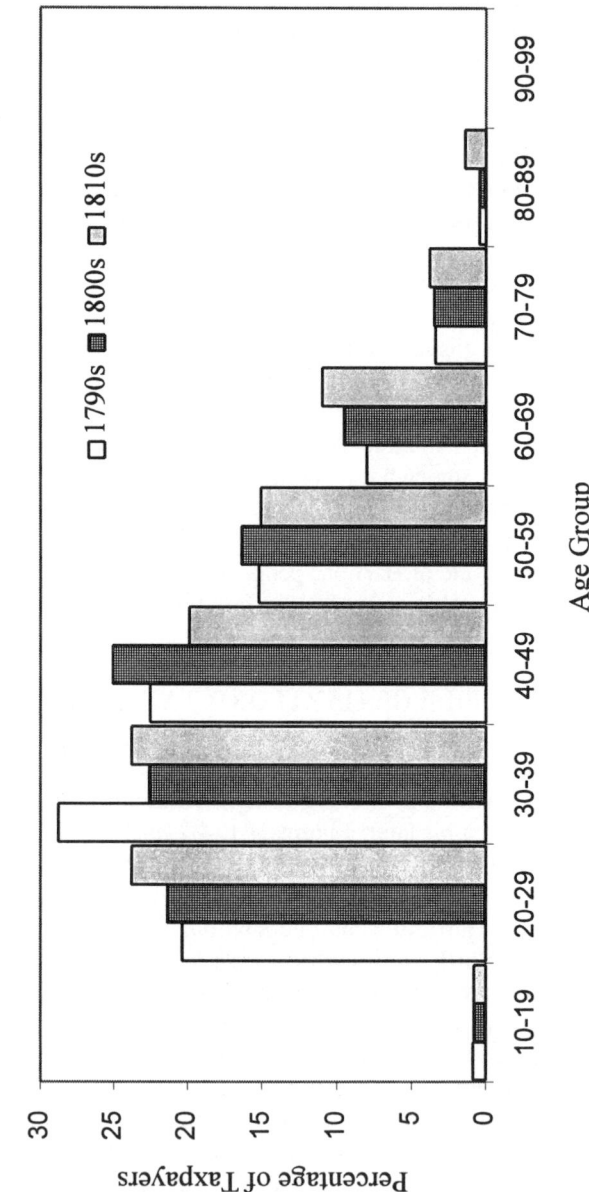

Figure 4.1. Taxpayers by Age, North District Town Tax Lists

Source: Hartford, CT Town Tax Lists, North District, CHS. See appendix B.

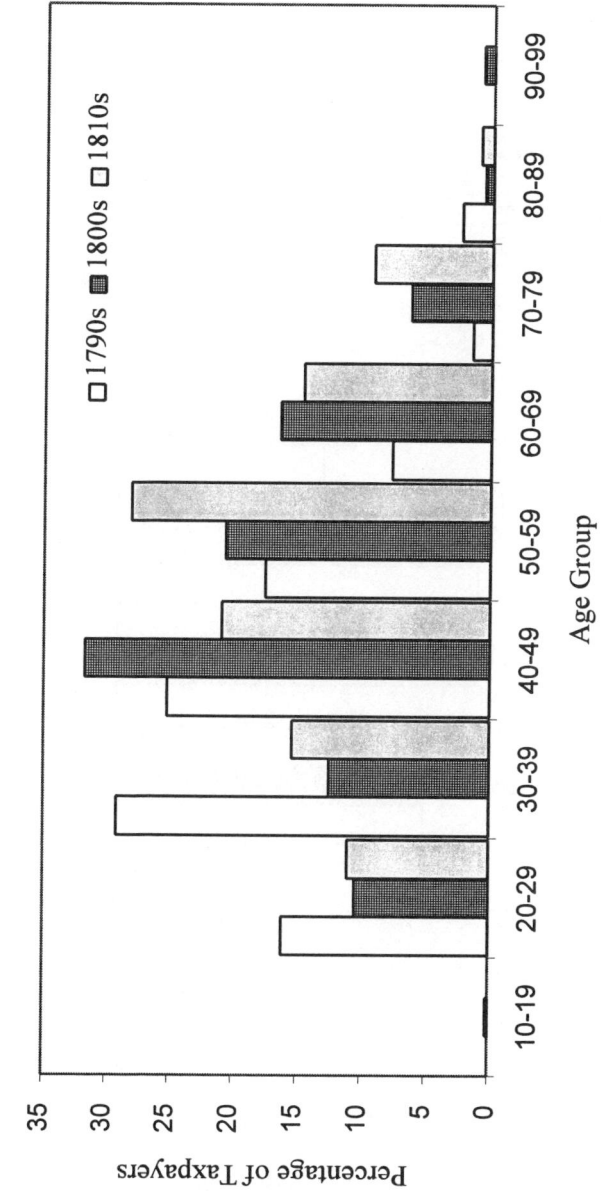

Figure 4.2. Taxpayers by Age, South District Town Tax Lists

Source: Hartford, CT Town Tax Lists, South District, CHS. See appendix B.

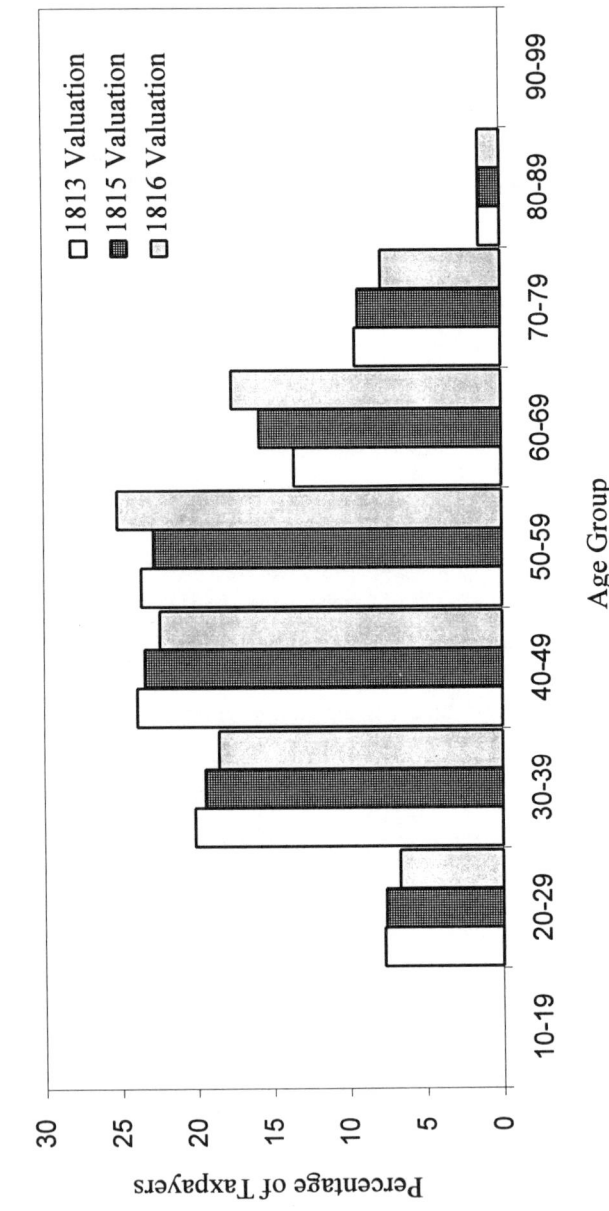

Figure 4.3. Taxpayers by Age, Valuation Lists

Source: Hartford, CT Valuation Lists, CHS and CSL. See appendix B.

the adult population and the thirties group is the largest of all age groups. In the South, with its older population, the forties group makes up the largest segment of taxpayers. A similar curve is observed in both cases as, after these peaks, the numbers of taxpayers steadily declines with increasing age. In both districts there is a significant drop from the fifties to the sixties. In the North and South as well, the number of seventy-year-olds is less than half that of sixty-year-olds. Taxpaying octogenarians are even scarcer, always accounting for less than 2.5 percent of all taxpayers, and ninety-year-olds are rare indeed.

There are two important reasons why the numbers of people on the tax rolls declined so clearly with age. Death, of course, was an important factor in eliminating taxpayers as they aged. We can estimate that from age fifty to sixty about 30 percent of all taxpayers died, accounting for most of the decline in taxpayers seen in these years. From sixty to seventy approximately another 31 percent of taxpayers passed away.[9] A second factor reducing the number of aged taxpayers was the fact that after age seventy men were automatically exempted from poll taxes. Another 5.2 percent of men dropped off the tax lists because of this relief—having no other property that would have required continued taxation.[10] So together death and poll relief account for about 36 percent of the decline in taxpayers between sixty and seventy years of age. Yet the drop in taxpayers seen in figures 4.1 and 4.2 collectively is slightly more that 59 percent—leaving about 23 percent of the decline unexplained. Some of this might be due to men moving out of Hartford. A more likely solution for most of these aging men, however, is diminishing resources. It is quite possible that in this 23 percent were men who had had taxable property (i.e. they paid taxes other than the poll) in their sixties, but that by their seventies had it no longer. Thus for older men we can add a third factor to our list of reasons why men disappeared from town lists—decaying fortunes—a hypothesis for which additional support is provided later.

Figure 4.3, showing the percentage of taxpayers by age on the valuation lists of the 1810s, offers further information. Unlike figures 4.1 and 4.2, this graph displays the age breakdown of taxpayers who owned real estate. (The one criteria for inclusion on a valuation list was ownership of land, lots, or dwelling houses in Hartford.) While figures 4.1 and 4.2 show a bell shape that is pushed toward the left, indicating heavier concentrations of younger people, this graph is better centered. This fact indicates that older people tended to own more real estate than their proportions of the taxpaying population would suggest. For example, the proportion of taxpayers in their twenties is relatively small on the valuation lists—about 7 percent—indicating that young men might be present on the town lists in large numbers but they tended to own less real estate than their sheer numbers would lead one to conclude. Even though the age composition on the valuation lists is older, we still observe a relatively rapid fall-off in taxpayers after age fifty-nine, as we saw in figures 4.1 and 4.2.

We can conclude from these three figures that, in general, men from twenty to forty were numerically dominant among taxpayers in any given year. Those in their fifties continued to persist in significant numbers (especially on valuation lists) but men in their sixties or older became increasingly rare on tax lists. Death played a role in this decline. However, for those who survived to seventy, worsening financial circumstances, reflected in the lack of any taxable assets, meant fewer old men persisted on the tax lists.

ECONOMIC STANDING OF DIFFERENT AGE GROUPS

This discussion becomes more meaningful when figures 4.4 and 4.5 are introduced. Based on the town lists for the North and South districts respectively, these show the average amount of taxpayers' "lists" broken down by age groups. If we accept a person's list amount (minus his poll tax if any) as a proxy for his or her general economic standing in the community, some important trends are readily apparent.

It is clear that people in their twenties had the lowest average list amount in every single year in both the North and South districts. For both the North and South sides of Hartford the average list size of thirty-year-olds begins about $40 higher than for twenty-year-olds'. Over time thirty-year-olds' fortunes dip and rise but remain pretty close to the twenty to twenty-nine group, though occasionally intersecting with older age groups. In both the North and South districts the average list size for the forty-year-old cohort is almost always higher that the list size of people in their thirties.

The figures for people in their fifties are more ambiguous. While it is obvious that fifty-year-olds were better off in general than those in their twenties and thirties, they were not always wealthier than men in their forties. Figures from the North district show that in two years forty and fifty-year-olds had very similar average list sizes (1792 and 1802), and in one year (1814) the forties cohort surged about $40 higher than people a decade older. In the South district average list sizes for forty and fifty-year-olds were close in 1794, 1808, and 1811. However, in other years the fifties group either fell well below the forties group (1809) or moved above it (1816). Thus, by age fifty the pattern linking increased age with increased list size was broken. Those in their fifties were clearly better off than those in their twenties and thirties but they could not always expect to surpass the forty-year-olds.

The findings on those sixty and over are harder to interpret. Knowing as we do that some men began dropping off the tax lists by this age, it becomes more difficult to argue that those who remained were typical of taxpayers in general. We can see however that those who did persist on the tax rolls in the North district resembled the forties cohort most closely through the 1790s. However, by 1802 the sixties group's fortunes were on the upswing and they had the highest average list size in 1802 and 1805. Were it not for one remarkably wealthy woman in the 1806 group of seventy-year-olds, the sixties group would also be dominant here. This woman, Mehitable Wadsworth, was the widow of the most prominent man in Hartford. If we remove her and recalculate the average, it falls well below the sixty-year-olds to around $80 for 1806. The results in the South district are similarly ambiguous. Here those in their sixties approach or even exceed those in their seventies in the first four years, but then decline to the level of the thirty-year-olds by 1811. Given the relatively small number of people on the Southside lists it would be a mistake to over-interpret these fluctuations. However, it is clear that increasing age did not necessarily bring improved fortunes. Those in their sixties were likely to be better off than those in their twenties or thirties, but they were vulnerable to greater volatility than the solidly middle-aged.

People still on the tax rolls in their seventies were more economically secure than Hartford's septuagenarians in general, since poorer men would have dropped off the list by this age, having been freed from the poll tax obligation. Therefore the results we see in figures 4.4 and 4.5 represent the more affluent of the aged and

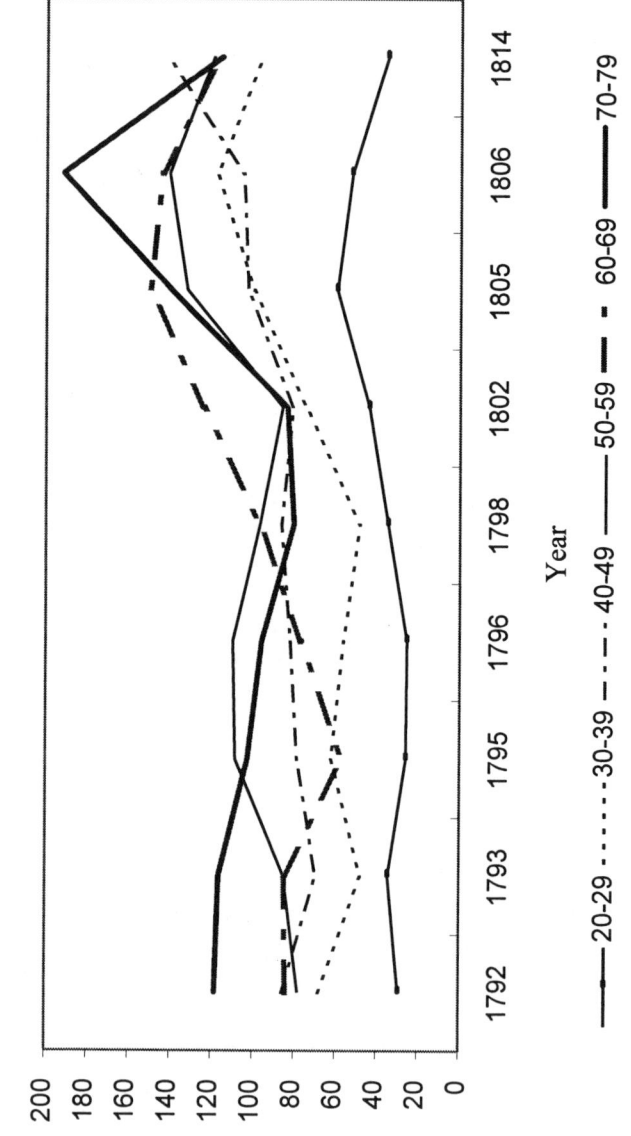

Figure 4.4. Average List Size by Age, North District Town Tax Lists

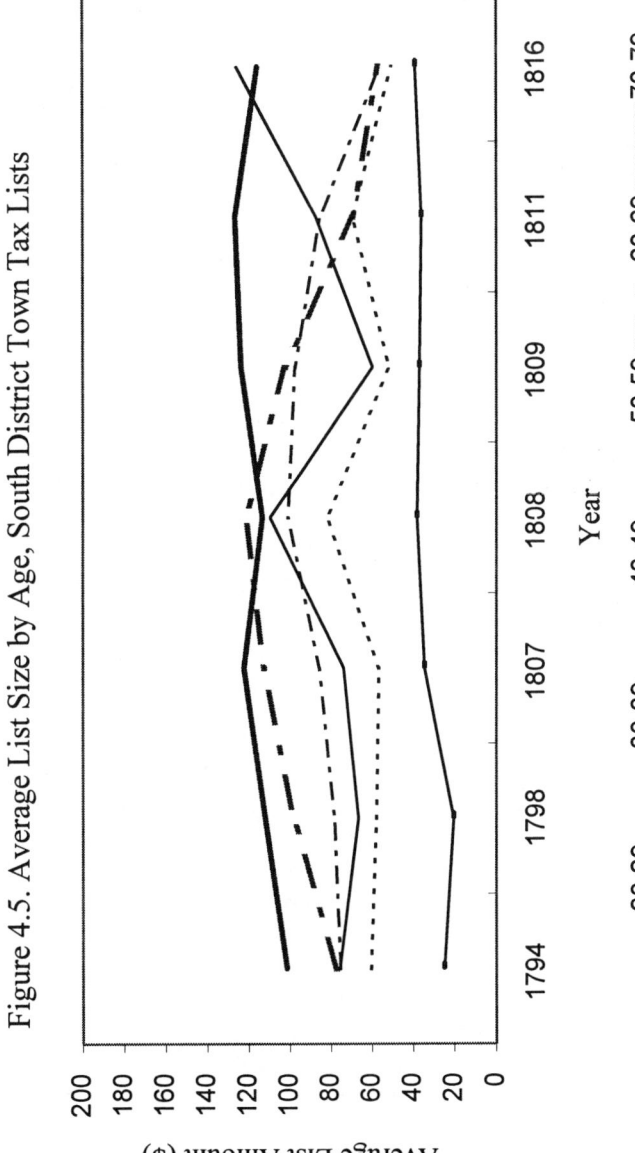

Figure 4.5. Average List Size by Age, South District Town Tax Lists

Source: Hartford, CT Town Tax Lists, South District, CHS. See appendix B.

exaggerate the economic success of this group. As the North district picture shows, their fortunes fluctuated—though this fluctuation is in part due to their small numbers, and as we see in 1806, the ease with which one exceptional person (again Mehitable Wadsworth) could alter the curve dramatically. The seventy-year-olds begin in 1792 with the highest list size, but from about 1795 onward their list size converges with that of more middle-aged taxpayers, and falls significantly below the curve for the sixty-year-olds (again, if we ignore Mehitable Wadsworth and put the figure for 1806 around $80). Thus, like sixty-year-olds, North district septuagenarians' financial fortunes could vary widely. For the South district the fortunes of the seventy-year-olds who continued on the tax lists seem more stable. Here the seventies cohort enjoys the highest list of any age group for five out of seven years. Only those in their fifties and sixties ever exceed the list size of the seventy-year-olds. Firm conclusions on the seventy-year-old group are difficult to formulate. The North district data illustrate how widely their circumstances could vary even when poorer people are not included in the analysis, while the South district data make clear that those who remained on the tax lists—presumably the cream of all seventy-year-olds—could remain in control of formidable assets and outdo their younger neighbors.

A few eighty-year olds occasionally continued to appear on the tax rolls in some years. They are not included in the graphs because their small numbers make an average figure rather misleading in a number of years. For example, in the Northside list for 1806 identifiable eighty-year-olds had an average list size of $67. The next Northside list however has five identifiable eighty-year-olds with an average list size of over $287. This does not reflect any gain in status for this age group—rather, Mehitable Wadsworth has now entered the cohort and her wealth skews the average accordingly. Suffice it to say that the fortunes of taxpayers in this age group were very unpredictable and probably represent, even more than the sixty and seventy-year-olds, only a small and atypical segment of all eighty-year-olds in Hartford.

This group is even narrower by age ninety. We can identify only one ninety-year-old in the tax records. The widow Anna Boardman lived in the South district and appears in 1807 with a list of $32. This list declines in 1808 to $17 and remains at this level for the final year of her life, 1809. In her case death was clearly the cause for her exit from the tax rolls.

Age and Economic Status

The data presented in figures 4.4 and 4.5 are nominal—that is they have not been adjusted for changes in the value of the dollar over the period. Yet even when the figures are recalculated to account for price fluctuations we see similar results. Tables 4.1 and 4.2 provide both the nominal and real average list sizes for the North and South districts of Hartford. As the tables makes plain, adjusting for changes in the dollar's value over time has the effect of compressing the list sizes of different age groups into a somewhat tighter band than seen with the nominal figures. However, because we are concerned with the relative position of different age groups rather than in estimating wealth or income, these differences between nominal and real average list sizes do not alter the trends already discussed.

The data presented above allow for some general conclusions about average list sizes, and consequently, the financial circumstances of different age groups. Overall, youth (the twenties) was a time of relatively low financial fortunes. This makes sense since young men had not yet had the time to accumulate much property through work or inheritance or to establish a trade or business. The thirties seems to have brought significant improvement in material circumstances, a trend that persisted through the forties as well, as people continued to rise economically. The graphs show the fifties, sixties, and seventies as the peak of financial health. Presumably by early old age a man had capitalized on whatever abilities he had and accumulated what he could before physical decline set in or he had begun to distribute property to his offspring. However, with the seventies group we must be cautious. While those who remained on the tax lists seem to have kept pace with more middle-aged men or even bettered them, we know that a significant fraction of all seventy-year-olds had probably dropped off the tax lists by this age due to worsening financial circumstances. Thus the findings on septuagenarians are ambiguous. By eighty, however, though a few exceptional cases muddy the findings somewhat, even those who remained on the tax lists had lower average lists than those from fifty to seventy-nine years of age, suggesting that these people were either drawing down their assets by consuming them in old age, by giving property to their descendants, or both.[11] In addition, these aged people may have slowed their work pace or quit productive labor altogether, thereby reducing income. If eighty-year-olds on the lists—representing the most financially

Table 4.1. Nominal and Real Average List Sizes by Age, North District, Hartford

Age	1792 Nom	1792 Real	1793 Nom	1793 Real	1795 Nom	1795 Real	1796 Nom	1796 Real	1798 Nom	1798 Real	1802 Nom	1802 Real	1805 Nom	1805 Real	1806 Nom	1806 Real	1814 Nom	1814 Real
20–29	29	29	35	32	26	18	25	16	35	27	44	35	60	40	53	37	35	18
30–39	68	68	48	44	62	44	56	36	48	37	74	59	100	66	118	82	96	49
40–49	86	86	70	64	79	56	82	53	87	66	81	65	103	68	105	73	142	73
50–59	78	78	85	78	109	78	110	70	97	74	86	69	132	88	141	98	120	61
60–69	84	84	85	78	57	41	77	49	97	74	124	99	150	99	144	101	116	60
70–79	118	118	116	106	103	73	96	62	81	62	84	67	140	93	192	134	115	59

Source: Hartford Town Tax Lists, North District, CHS. Note: Figures are rounded to nearest dollar.

Table 4.2. Nominal and Real Average List Sizes by Age, South District, Hartford

Age	1794 Nom	1794 Real	1798 Nom	1798 Real	1807 Nom	1807 Real	1808 Nom	1808 Real	1809 Nom	1809 Real	1811 Nom	1811 Real	1816 Nom	1816 Real
20–29	25	21	20	16	35	25	38	31	37	27	36	27	39	24
30–39	61	52	58	44	57	41	82	67	52	37	70	52	51	31
40–49	75	65	78	60	86	62	101	82	98	70	85	63	56	35
50–59	76	66	67	51	74	53	110	89	60	43	87	65	126	78
60–69	77	67	98	75	113	81	121	97	103	74	70	52	57	35
70–79	102	88	112	86	122	88	113	92	124	89	127	94	115	72

Source: Hartford Town Tax Lists, South District, CHS. Note: Figures are rounded to nearest dollar.

successful of this age group—had fewer resources than before, we can assume that eighty-year-olds off the lists experienced similar declines. By ninety almost no one remained both alive and with taxable property. Indeed only one ninety-year-old taxpayer appears in the dataset, testifying to both the rarity of such extreme old age and the unliklihood that truly superannuated people would continue to hold property.

The findings here seem to accord well with a general description of the life cycle formulated by Alice Hanson Jones, in which

> a young man . . . leaves his parents' household to make his own start and gradually acquires more possessions through work and savings. He may acquire land as his family expands and his experience grows, and perhaps he receives an inheritance upon the death of his father. His wealth reaches a maximum somewhere in late middle age or old age. Thereafter, as his energy declines and his children leave home, he may engage less actively in farming or other productive activities and may dispose of some of his assets to meet his current needs, or may transfer some of them, as land to sons, to help them get a start.[12]

Such a process, while not the experience of everyone, was typical for Hartford men.

But how would such a cycle apply to women? Though derived from looking at the overwhelmingly male population presented in tax lists, the trends presented above can to some extent describe the fortunes of married women as well. We can assume that married women shared in the rising and falling fortunes of their husbands, though because they were likely to be somewhat younger than their husbands, the age at which changes occurred was slightly younger.[13] As with men of lower material circumstances, the figures probably do not capture the situation of poorer women very well. For women, financial status was also complicated by widowhood, which became more and more likely the older a woman became. We know that some widows like Mehitable Wadsworth were extraordinarily wealthy and enjoyed great material ease throughout old age. However, many widows, even of relatively well-to-do men, experienced a decline in resources when the family property was divided among heirs. Relying on scholarship on widows and spinsters in other places, we can assume that such women in Hartford were at a disadvantage. Tax lists are unfortunately rather uninformative in this respect. Qualitative evidence from other sources explored in chapter 5 will provide more insight on these women.

Figures 4.6 and 4.7 help to put the information on average list sizes in perspective. While figures 4.4 and 4.5 looked at the average list size of taxpayers by age group, figure 4.6 shows the percentage of real property owned by each group—that is how much of the total value of Hartford real estate each group owned. The information provided in figure 4.7 supplements figure 4.6 and helps clarify trends. Because these graphs are based on the valuation lists rather than town lists, we need not be concerned about the older age groups being less complete. Figures 4.6 and 4.7 present pictures of all landowners for whom we have age information. Because real estate ownership was a strong sign of economic success in early national New England, by comparing age groups we can get a sense of relative standing.

From figure 4.6 it is clear that people in their twenties—though they constituted from about 13 to 22 percent of taxpayers on the town lists (figures 4.1 and 4.2)—owned less than 5 percent of Hartford's real property. If we compare the percentage of twenty-year-olds on the valuation lists (figure 4.3) with their percentage of real estate holdings, it becomes clear that on average this group owned less per person than other age groups. Only 5 percent of Hartford's property was distributed among about 7 percent of taxpayers. Therefore, those who did own real estate in this group owned less proportionately than those in other age cohorts. This is borne out by figure 4.7 showing that indeed those in their twenties tended to have smaller holdings than any other group.

These trends continue with the thirties group. Thirty-year-olds appeared less often on valuation lists than on town lists, meaning they tended to own real estate less often than their elders. When they did own real property, on average their holdings were smaller than their numbers would suggest. Thus, though people in their thirties make up around 19 percent of all people included in valuation lists, they owned slightly less than 15 percent of Hartford's real estate. A look at their average property valuation confirms that, like those in their twenties, people in their thirties generally had holdings worth less than their elders.

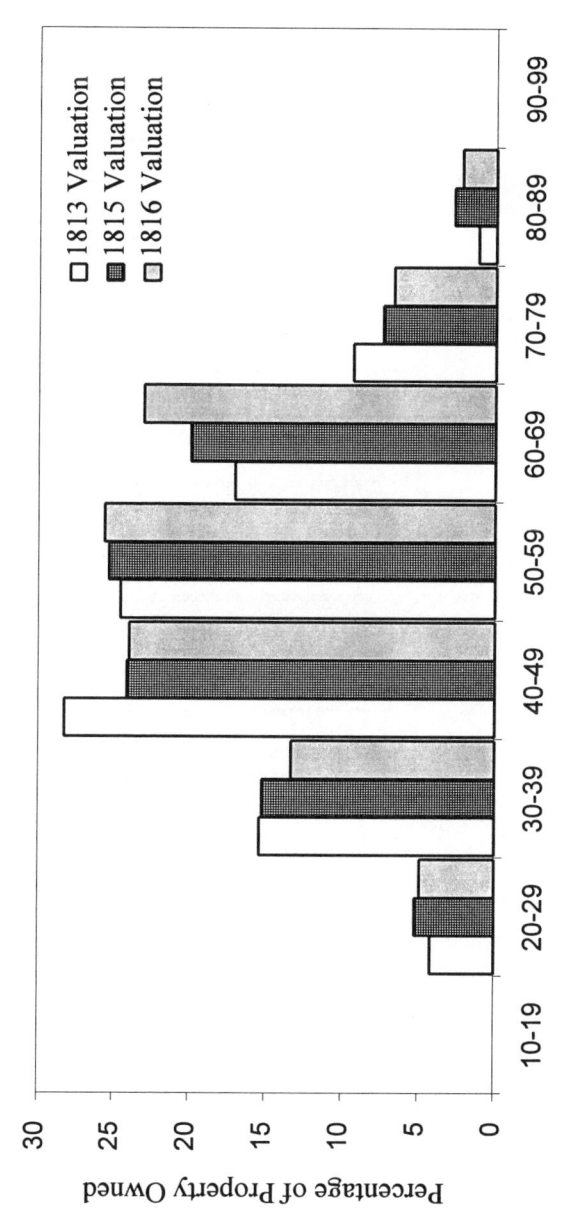

Figure 4.6. Hartford Real Property Owned by Age Groups

Source: Hartford, CT Valuation Lists, CHS and CSL. See appendix B.

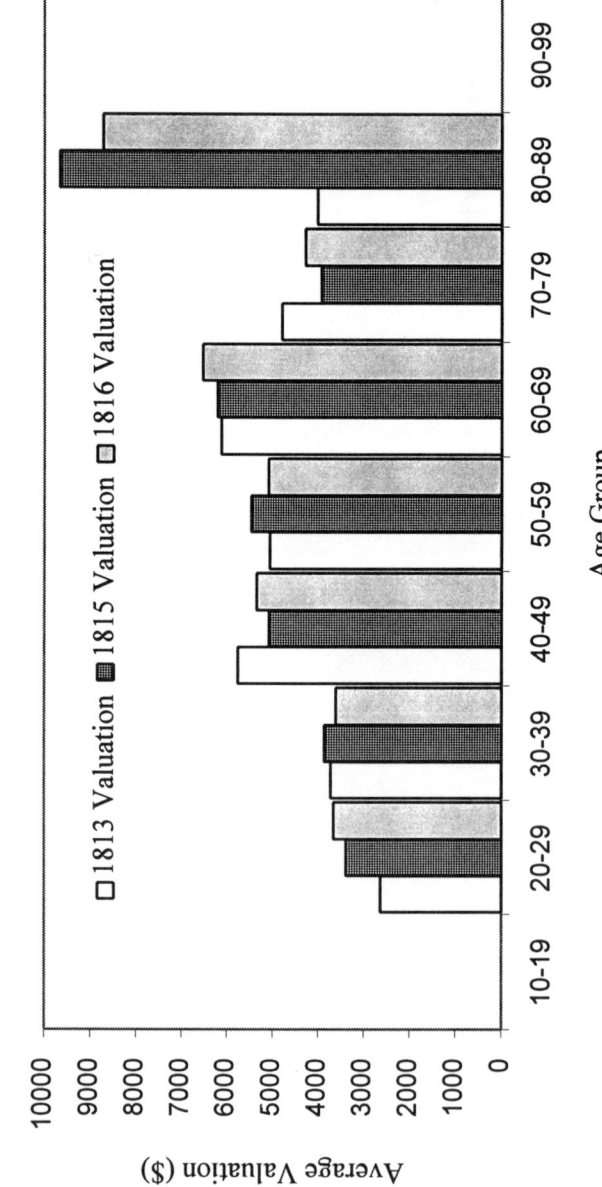

Figure 4.7. Average Valuations by Age Group

Source: Hartford, CT Valuation Lists, CHS and CSL. See appendix B.

With the forties group, we begin to see closer correspondence between the percentage of the taxpaying population the group comprises and the proportion of property owned. In fact this group owned slightly more property than we would guess from their percentage of the population. People in their forties constituted slightly more than 23 percent of those on the valuation lists and owned a little more than 25 percent of Hartford's real estate. Not surprisingly the average valuation of this group is more than $1,000 larger than for those a decade younger.

This tendency to control slightly more than a proportional share of real estate continues with the fifties group. This group made up from about 16 to 23 percent of the taxpayers on the town lists but closer to 24 percent of those on the valuation lists—in other words, fifty-year-olds tended to own real estate significantly more than their youngers. In addition, like those in their forties, the value of their holdings was greater on average than that of "the rising generation." This is clear from the fact that their share of Hartford's real property was about 25 percent, reflected in average valuations similar to the forties cohort. Thus those in their forties and fifties owned the largest shares of real estate—accounting for about 50 percent of the total.

This figure is even more dramatic when compared with their share of the total population. Though the federal censuses in this period are only broken down into rather large age groups, they still add some insight. In the federal censuses of 1800, 1810, and 1820, the group of people aged forty-five to sixty-four made up about 30 percent of Connecticut's adult population.[14] Though this group is not identical to our forty to fifty-nine-year-old group it is close enough to suggest that roughly 30 percent of the adult population owned 50 percent of Hartford's real property.

With the sixty-year-old group, however, we see an even greater difference in the percentage of the taxpaying pool they make up and the percentage of property owned. While those in their sixties account for from 10 to 13 percent of the town lists, they account for approximately 16 percent of people on the valuation lists. Thus, a disproportional number of sixty-year-olds owned real property. In addition, their holdings were on average even larger than those of the fifties group—amounting to about 20 percent of all of Hartford's real property. Indeed if we dispose of Mehitable Wadsworth (whose presence among the eighties cohort pushes their average valuation to astronomical heights in 1815 and 1816), it becomes clear that people in their sixties owned property worth more per capita than any other group.

With the seventies cohort, however, we again see a narrowing between the proportion of people who owned real estate and the fraction of property they owned. Seventy-year-olds appear more frequently on valuation lists than on town lists, hinting that they were still more likely to own real property than much younger taxpayers. But they composed approximately 9 percent of taxpayers on the valuation lists and owned about 8 percent of property, suggesting that per person their real estate amounted to less than men in their forties, fifties, or sixties. Indeed the average valuation for this group was from about $1,200 to $2,000 lower than for fifty-year-olds. From these figures we can hypothesize that by around seventy, those who still held assets had begun to divest themselves of at least a portion of their real property, most likely handing it on to children, which may in turn help account for some of the rise in holdings among twenty and thirty-year-olds. It is possible that in transferring assets to children or others that elderly people received annuities in exchange, allowing for their maintenance through old age.[15] Or septuagenarians may have simply sold off portions of their property for their own support as increasing age diminished the ability to work.

A few eighty-year-olds did continue to manage real estate holdings. Though octogenarians made up only about 1 to 1.5 percent of those included in town lists, they accounted for slightly more on valuation lists. Overall their holdings accounted for 2 percent of Hartford's real estate. Yet if we remove Mehitable Wadsworth from the equation their share was much tinier—0.6 percent in 1815 and 0.3 percent in 1816. In addition, though it appears from figure 4.7 that people had huge prosperity to look forward to in old age, this was not in fact the case. Again, once Mehitable Wadsworth and her real estate worth $37,310 is subtracted from the average we see that eighty-year-olds on average held property worth $2,745 and $1,572 respectively in 1815 and 1816. These figures make them more similar to people in their twenties and thirties than to any other age groups. The falling average valuations for octogenarians suggests even more strongly that the older one became, the more likely he or she was to either consume or to give away resources that had been accumulated over a lifetime.

Age and Economic Status 109

A number of conclusions can be drawn from this data. People in middle and early old age dominated Hartford in terms of real estate ownership, collectively controlling about 70 percent of all holdings. Of this dominant group, the sixty-year-olds seem to have had the largest holdings per capita, exerting greater control over resources than their numbers would suggest. The seventies cohort was significantly smaller in numbers and per capita holdings declined from the peak just described. Those eighty-year-olds who persisted on the valuation lists generally had significantly smaller holdings per capita than even the seventy-year-old group, and in terms of sheer numbers were much scarcer than people just ten years younger. In general then, the data describe a curve with the sixties cohort at the top and all other groups falling off to the sides. These trends are compatible both with the findings from our earlier analyses and with the generalized life cycle described above.

Of course Hartford was populated by many more people than owned real property. Indeed the people represented in figures 4.6 and 4.7 probably represent the upper strata of Hartford society. Yet the overall trends found in valuation lists are similar to those found in the town lists, which tended to more inclusive.

Though the fortunes of poorer people are not well illuminated by tax data, their economic lives likely followed a similar pattern. Poorer men and their families, relying on their own talents and physical strength rather than on inherited property, struggled in their twenties and thirties for a livelihood. Like their social betters, if they were to enjoy comforts it would have been in middle age and perhaps early old age, when they had had a chance to accumulate some meager resources or establish themselves in farming or a trade. However, old age—with the ill health it so often brought—probably hindered the ability to work, throwing a person's fortunes into jeopardy. Evidence in chapter 5 indicates that this scenario played out frequently among poor men.

In terms of age and material resources, Hartford was far from egalitarian. Tax records—both town lists and valuation lists—show that youth was a time of modest holdings but significant upward mobility. Meanwhile people in middle and early old age were fewer in number but nevertheless dominated Hartford economically—holding a disproportionate share of taxable property and real estate. People over sixty, though often better off than other groups, were vulnerable to declining resources, a trend that seems to have accelerated with advancing age.

HOW INDIVIDUALS FARED OVER TIME

So far we have looked at tax records in cross-section, essentially treating each year's records as if they were for different populations. Yet many people appeared year in and year out on Hartford's tax lists. By looking at the rising or falling fortunes of the same individuals over time, we gain another perspective on the circumstances of people at different ages. Using the tax records of people for whom I had birth and death data, I was able to discover how aging affected the size of individuals' lists. The results of this analysis are summarized in tables 4.3 and 4.4. Though both tables present information on the same set of individuals, the figures in table 4.3 are nominal (they have not been adjusted for fluctuations in the value of money over the period) while the figures in table 4.4 are real, having been adjusted for inflation and deflation.

Both table 4.3 and table 4.4 show the average (mean) percentage change in individual's lists per year by age groups. The percentage change in average—another means of assessing the data—is also shown.[16] In addition, the median change in list size per year, as well as the standard deviation from the mean, are presented to allow for an accurate assessment of the numbers. The most striking finding from the data in both tables is the tendency for people's lists to grow in youth, stagnate in middle age, and decline in old age. Also highly significant are the large differences for most age cohorts between the mean and the median, and the correspondingly high standard deviations for many groups. These provide strong hints that Hartford was not only economically diverse by age but also within age groups.

Youth appears on tables 4.3 and 4.4 as a particularly dramatic time of life for taxpayers, especially if we focus on the mean list change. We see in table 4.3 that in the years from twenty to twenty-four, individual's list sizes shot up by an average of slightly more than 60 percent per year. The next five years are even more amazing. From ages twenty-five to twenty-nine, individuals experienced a yearly average increase of over 209 percent. And the years from thirty to thirty-four, while apparently a time of less explosive upward mobility, still show a dramatic increase. However, the standard deviations for these same years are very large, alerting us that the mean does not describe the data very well since the data points are spread widely apart rather than clustered around the average. Such deviations suggest that only a small fraction of the population experienced the huge increases in list size that the mean figures show.[17] When we look at the median percentage increase in list size per year, this point becomes even more clear. The median for twenty to twenty-four-year-olds reveals that while list sizes certainly grew, this growth was nowhere near as astronomical as the average would lead us to believe—indeed half of the twenty to twenty-four-year-old group had list increases of less than 2.8 percent per year. Likewise the median growth rate of lists in the years between twenty-five and twenty-nine was 4.6 percent, a striking contrast with the mean of over 209 percent per year. The same can be said for the thirty to thirty-four-year-old results. These trends in the nominal data are also observed in the figures adjusted for fluctuations in the value of money over the period shown in table 4.4.

The important finding—illustrated by both the nominal and real figures—is that youth was a time when people's material resources, reflected in the size of their tax lists, grew. However, given the large discrepancies between the means and medians as well as the large standard deviations, we can posit that for most people such growth was relatively modest, though a small number of people came to control extraordinary resources in their young years—most likely through inheritance. This bifurcation of the taxpaying population in youth suggests that while age played a role in Hartford's economic stratification, other factors made it possible for a few young men to catapult to the top of Hartford's economic heap.

The years from thirty-five to forty-five also appear from the figures in tables 4.3 and 4.4 as a time of growth in list size, mirroring improving financial footing. However we can see from the mean list changes, as well as the change in average figures, that this growth had slowed compared to the twenties and early thirties. Meanwhile the medians in both tables indicate that only a relatively small portion of taxpayers in these ages continued to move rapidly ahead of their neighbors in terms of economic resources. The unadjusted information for the thirty-five to thirty-nine-year-old category shows a median gain of a bit more than 2 percent per year, declining to 0.98 percent in the forty to forty-four-year-old group and to 0 percent by the late forties. The figures adjusted for price changes likewise suggest that slow growth or even no growth characterized the financial experience of many in these age groups. Standard deviations, though still quite large, are smaller than before, suggesting somewhat less heterogeneous experiences in the population. In general, then, it appears that while early middle age tended to be a time of upward movement financially, for most people this movement was rather slow.

Table 4.3. Percentage Changes in List Size per Year by Age Group (Nominal)

Age Group	Mean List Change	Change in Average	Median List Change	Standard Dev.	Obs.
14–19	10.15	1.47	0	35.06	8
20–24	60.42	16.18	2.82	194.48	113
25–29	209.57	12.66	4.68	1190.18	250
30–34	53.84	7.64	1.87	320.46	239
35–39	17.09	5.44	2.01	74.11	251
40–44	22.84	3.86	0.98	100.36	296
45–49	17.52	4.87	0	89.98	226
50–54	14.65	-0.35	0	95.11	214
55–59	11.95	-0.80	0	98.65	144
60–64	2.01	0.58	0	31.22	103
65–69	-1.35	-0.75	-0.90	136.15	82
70–74	-2.30	0.66	-3.54	17.81	47
75–79	-3.03	-3.21	-0.71	10.21	22
80–84	-4.47	-5.67	0	7.92	66
85–89	—	—	—	—	0
90–94	-23.43	-30.61	-23.43	23.43	2
95-99	—	—	—	—	0

Source: Calculated from all extant Hartford town tax lists from 1792–1816, Hartford Town Tax Lists, CHS.

The years from fifty to sixty-four appear in the tables as another distinctive period for individual's financial fortunes. Though both the nominal and real means for this age group indicate some still experienced growth in list size, there is more evidence that most people in early old age faced economic stagnation or even decline. For example, the medians in table 4.3 all stand at zero—indicating that half of all taxpayers either saw no change in their list size or experienced a loss. Meanwhile the change in average figures in table 4.3 are negative for the first time for most of those between age fifty and sixty-four. The equivalent figures presented in table 4.4 are even more strongly negative, as are the medians. Clearly, as both tables indicate, early old age was not the time to make one's fortune. Indeed for most people, a more realistic goal would have been to merely shepherd accumulated resources in preparation for the years after sixty-five. However, many failed to do even this. As such, early old age marked a turning point in the financial life cycle of Hartford people when declining fortunes became more likely than not.

Table 4.4. Percentage Changes in List Size per Year by Age Group (Real)

Age Group	Mean List Change	Change in Average	Median List Change	Standard. Dev.	Obs.
14–19	4.43	-0.22	0	38.41	8
20–24	60.12	13.89	4.89	186.07	113
25–29	183.35	7.54	4.09	1150.10	250
30–34	49.32	5.73	1.77	302.09	239
35–39	12.86	1.69	0	70.13	251
40–44	17.73	1.87	0	84.96	296
45–49	14.69	2.46	0.85	81.82	226
50–54	16.42	-2.64	-1.79	111.44	214
55–59	3.00	-2.90	-1.97	59.92	144
60–64	2.16	-1.17	-1.44	34.31	103
65–69	197.33	-2.71	-5.93	1829.70	82
70–74	-3.88	-0.59	-5.35	19.01	47
75–79	-7.11	-9.22	-5.18	12.30	22
80–84	-9.37	-13.73	0	13.42	66
85–89	—	—	—	—	0
90–94	-25.85	-29.20	-25.85	13.62	2
95–99	—	—	—	—	0

Source: Calculated from all extant Hartford town tax lists from 1792–1816, Hartford Town Tax Lists, CHS. Note: Adjustments have been made to 1792 dollars based on the Warren and Pearson, "Wholesale Price Indexes by Major Product Groups: 1749–1890" in U.S. Department of Commerce, Bureau of the Census, *Historical Statistics of the United States, Colonial Times to 1970*, Bicentennial ed., part 1 (Washington D.C.: 1975), 201–202.

After sixty-five one was even less likely to reap new material harvests. The unadjusted figures in table 4.3 show that almost across the board individual's list sizes were likely to get smaller with every year. For example, those aged sixty-five to sixty-nine lost an average (mean) of 1.35 percent of their list size each year. From age seventy to seventy-four, losses were even greater at 2.3 percent per year. And lists declined even more dramatically after seventy-five; in these years the medians are also negative. Similar results are seen in table 4.4, showing figures adjusted for fluctuations in prices over the period. (The exception is the mean for the sixty-five to seventy age group. This figure is exceptionally large and positive due to one individual. When he is removed, the figure drops to -3.47, well in line with all the other results.)

It is interesting to note also that in both table 4.3 and 4.4, the means and medians are generally much closer after age sixty-five than before and the standard deviations shrink. Reaching seventy meant exemption from the poll tax and as a result eliminated many poorer men from tax lists who were liable for no other taxes. Those who remained on the tax rolls after seventy were thus generally wealthier than men of that age generally. The similar means and medians and smaller deviations in the tables reflect the fact that the taxpaying population was indeed more homogeneous after seventy then before. However, because those who remained on the tax lists after seventy were better-off than those who did not, their declining list sizes are doubly interesting. The data confirm that even the best off of the elderly were subject, either by design or circumstances, to diminishing material circumstances. Those not on the lists were, at least in the eyes of tax assessors, too poor to pay taxes on their property. These people must have experienced the pinch of declining resources all the more strongly since they had less property to begin with than those who still made an appearance on the tax lists.

A number of scholars have noted the tendency for New England men to hold on to property late in life rather than pass it on to sons who were probably eager to get settled in life. Philip Greven, Daniel Scott Smith, and others have explored the extent to which fathers used control over property as leverage to control their sons' behavior.[18] Yet the Hartford data suggest that those aging men who had property may have had very good reasons to maintain control of what they could as they faced declining economic prospects and uncertainty about how long old age would last. While some men probably took advantage of control over property to influence their children's lives, their basic

Age and Economic Status

motives may have been simpler—the desire to influence the course of their own lives.

Of course, it would be useful to know much more about the economic experiences of Hartford people over the life cycle. Ideally one would investigate the upward or downward mobility of individuals from youth through old age to find out whether aging fundamentally reshuffled social standing. The data presented here show that on average resources declined in old age, but undoubtedly there was significant variation among individuals based on factors such as occupation, family circumstances, and health. Unfortunately, Hartford tax records cover too short a period to make such investigation possible and systematic occupational data are missing as well.[19] However, the subsequent chapter presents a wealth of qualitative evidence touching on these issues that illustrate some of the determinants of economic experience for the aged.

Because the work habits of the aged and their patterns of retirement have interested scholars, it would also be ideal to apply Hartford tax data to these questions.[20] For example, as a proxy for retirement one would like to determine the exact age at which individual men's resources began a steady decline, suggesting a decrease or cessation of work activity. Again however, the lack of long-term records (as well as gaps in the records that do exist) make pinpointing the time when specific individual's resources began a steady decline impossible.[21] Fortunately, qualitative evidence discussed in chapter 5 sheds some light on the character and frequency of retirement from work.

While the longitudinal data presented above cannot tell us all we wish to know, they nevertheless compliment the cross-sectional analysis by providing a different perspective. Cross-section data showed how age groups generally fared relative to each other. Our notable findings were that youth was a time of rather low material circumstances; middle age and early old age were times for consolidating resources and often appear as the peak years for economic attainment; and old age—though the data are muddied by a number of factors—seems to have had the potential for continued financial health but could also be characterized by dispersal of assets and unpredictable fortunes. The data just presented enhance this picture by showing that by early old age, though many people were at the height of their material well-being, growth was stagnant or perhaps even beginning to decline. Though economic standing could be good in old age, each passing year was likely to decrease assets, either because people elected to distribute property to their heirs or because they had to draw on resources to support themselves. These different perspectives on tax data describe a world in which the elderly, materially at least, were likely to be at a disadvantage.

For some, the dispersal of assets accompanying old age was manageable and perhaps even desirable, as in the case of a father electing to pass on his property to his children. Yet for others, perhaps with smaller holdings to draw on, poverty (at least as measured by tax assessors) was the result. For such people, declining fortunes undoubtedly had less to do with choice and more to do with necessity, as the debility or illness that often came with old age stymied productive activity. Whatever the cause, the last stage of life usually meant descent from the economic dominance of middle and early old age, with the result that old men in Hartford began to resemble younger men once again.

What are the larger implications of these findings? First, they provide a case study that confirms and extends the work of other scholars. For example, the data presented here agree strikingly with the findings of Alice Hanson Jones on the colonial period. In *Wealth of a Nation to Be*, Jones describes three factors as having a major influence on wealth: personal freedom or lack thereof, sex, and age. In terms of the latter, her data drawn from a sample of 1774 probates

> show a pattern of rising wealth, starting from a low point under age 25, up to a peak around age 60, or a plateau from about age 60 to 65 or even older. Thereafter, there is some dropping off in average wealth in later years to successively lower levels.[22]

This description is almost identical to the life cycle of wealth in Hartford and suggests two things. First, in terms of the connection between age and wealth, the early national period did not differ greatly from the colonial period described by Jones. Second, it is clear that Hartford was not atypical in terms of its citizens' economic experiences. In fact, Hartford's trends of wealth and age resemble those found in a number of other studies. As Jones explains, similar patterns have been documented for colonial Guilford, Connecticut, colonial Maryland, Wisconsin in the mid-nineteenth century, Texas in 1860, Oklahoma in 1960, and for the United States in general at different times.[23]

The findings for Hartford also accord with Daniel Scott Smith's work on seventeenth-century Hingham, Massachusetts. Smith finds that "Hingham in the late seventeenth century was not a society of the young ... Before the age of forty, few men ... held substantial amounts of property." Though middle age brought increased property-ownership, he notes that

> these indicators of status do not keep rising with age ... after the fifties mean wealth dropped ... Old age was honored and respected but it did not command continued wealth or leadership position.[24]

Smith sees the decline of the aged's fortunes in Hingham as a necessary cost of maintaining a valued family system. He argues that Hingham's "commitment to generational succession and the autonomy of family heads meant that the old could not have the same status and authority as the middle aged."[25] Resources were limited and in this "Christian, communal, patriarchal, English, pre-industrial society," the elderly had to step aside for the younger generation.[26]

Smith's conclusions raise an important question: Do similar trends in age and wealth in different societies mean that the societies themselves were similar? Can we conclude, for example, that nineteenth-century Hartford was like seventeenth-century Hingham? Do certain age and wealth patterns clearly indicate communal values, family systems, or individual motives? While the evidence from Hartford could be used to support the idea of a communally-oriented, "patriarchal," family-based society, the data could also be interpreted as showing the "individualistic" tendencies of Hartfordians, who allowed the elderly to slip into decline once their useful days were over.[27] The truth is that from this data alone we cannot chose between such alternatives. However, when the quantitative proof of material decline presented here is combined with qualitative sources in chapter 5, some interesting conclusions emerge.

NOTES

1. A third type of tax records—assessments—exist for many Connecticut towns for the years 1795 to 1798. However, they are not useful for this project. These records list names of individuals by their town of residence and include an assessment (presumably made by taking a percentage of the town list). Unfortunately these records are poorly documented, though the assessment may well have been for a state tax. These documents are held by CHS under the title "Conn. Assessors 1797-1798."

2. See chapter 1 for a description of the two districts.

3. Poll rates were the same for everyone and hence do not reflect differences in wealth. Therefore they were subtracted from taxpayers' lists prior to analysis. For more information on this see appendix B.

4. For additional information on poll tax exemption after age seventy and its effects see appendix B.

5. For a survey of Connecticut's system of taxation see Diana Ross McCain, "As True as Taxes: An Historian's Guide to Direct Taxation and Tax Records in Connecticut 1637-1820," (Master's thesis: Wesleyan University, 1981).

6. See appendix A for a full account of the sources and methods used in compiling vital statistics for this project.

7. For a complete description of Hartford tax records from the early national period and the methodological problems associated with them refer to appendix B.

8. For reasons that are difficult to fully explain the South district's taxpayers were not as youthful as those of the North district. Possibly Hartford's South side, being primarily agricultural, had already begun to be hit by outmigration of younger people in search of land, while the North side with its craftsmen, traders and small factories attracted younger people in this same period.

9. These estimates of mortality were calculated by counting the number of people in each age group on each town tax list who died in the year immediately following the year the list was made. (For example, I counted all the people in each age group on the 1806 town list who died in 1807). Results from the different tax lists were then averaged to produce an estimate of mortality for each age group. For the group of men in their sixties, about 3.8 percent died per year. Over ten years this produces an estimated death rate of 31.25 percent (i.e. 3.8 to the tenth).

10. It is possible to estimate the number of men who disappeared from tax lists in this way by noting that the percentage of men in their sixties who had lists equal to zero (that is, they had no tax obligations save the poll) was on average 7.5 percent of identifiable sixty-year-olds on the town tax lists. If we assert that approximately 70 percent of these men survived to age seventy (given a mortality rate over ten years of about 30 percent) we can imagine that about 5.2 percent were left to drop off the tax list due to poll relief.

11. Some colonial period research indicates that sixty-six to sixty-seven was the average age at which farmers "retired" from work by turning over land to sons. Such a pattern fits this data well. See David Hackett Fischer, *Growing Old in America*, expanded ed. (New York: Oxford University Press, 1978), 54-55.

12. Alice Hanson Jones, *Wealth of a Nation to Be* (New York: Columbia University Press, 1980), 214.

13. A number of scholars have shown that women's age at first marriage tended to be younger than men's. See David Hackett Fischer's compilation work on this subject in *Growing Old in America*, 279.

14. Adult is defined here as fifteen and over. The figures from the Connecticut censuses are gleaned from *Historical Statistics of the United States, Colonial Times to 1970*, part 1 (White Plains NY: Kraus International Publications, 1989), 25.

Age and Economic Status

15. Unfortunately information on annuity arrangements in early national Connecticut is scarce. What little qualitative evidence I have uncovered is presented in chapter 5.

16. Both the mean and the change in average figures are averages but they are arrived at differently. The change in average is found by adding up all the changes in individual's lists over a given interval, adding up the total sizes of the lists in the starting year of the interval, and then finding the ratio of these figures. As the figures in the tables show, this method of assessing the data is less sensitive to extreme values than that used to find the mean.

17. The tendency toward greater extremes of wealth in youth than in other periods of life has been confirmed by Lee Soltow for the United States in general somewhat later in the nineteenth century. See Jones, *Wealth of a Nation to Be*, 383.

18. Philip Greven, *Four Generations: Population, Land, and Family in Colonial Andover, Massachusetts* (Ithaca: Cornell University Press, 1970); Daniel Scott Smith, "Parental Power and Marriage Patterns: An Analysis of Historical Trends in Hingham, Massachusetts," *Journal of Marriage and the Family* 35 (August 1973): 419–428.

19. Hartford tax records cover 1792 to 1816 so the maximum numbers of years observed is twenty-four. Most people have far fewer years of records than this because they died or left Hartford during the period or they entered the records after 1792. As a result, it is impossible to track more than a fraction of any one person's financial career.

20. See for instance Roger L. Ransom and Richard Sutch, "The Labor of Older Americans: Retirement of Men On and Off the Job, 1870–1937," *Journal of Economic History* 46 (March 1986): 1–30.

21. Because records for many individuals cover only a relatively short span of their lives, it is not possible to say when a steady decline in holdings may have begun (or ended). In addition, tax records do not exist for every person for each year between 1792 and 1816, compounding the difficulty to charting individual fortunes. See appendix B for more on the quality of extant tax records.

22. Jones, *Wealth of a Nation to Be*, 214.

23. Jones summarizes these results in *Wealth of a Nation to Be*, 382–3.

24. Daniel Scott Smith, "Old Age and the Great Transformation: A New England Case Study," in *Aging and the Elderly: Humanistic Perspectives in Gerontology*, ed. Stuart Spicker, Kathleen Woodward, and David D. Van Tassel (Atlantic Highlands NJ: Humanities Press, 1978), 290.

25. Ibid., 292.

26. Ibid., 296.

27. Though this dichotomy between communal and individual was established quite some time ago by modernization theorists, these issues came to the fore afresh in a well-known article by James Henretta and response by James Lemon. See Henretta "Families and Farms: *Mentalité* in Pre-Industrial America," *William and Mary Quarterly*, 3d series, 35 (January 1978): 3–32 and Lemon, "Comment on James A. Henretta's 'Families and Farms: *Mentalité* in Pre-Industrial America'," *William and Mary Quarterly*, 3d series, 37 (October 1980): 688–700. The polemics of this debate have obscured the fact that human motives are often complex and that concern for family is not incompatible with economic striving.

V

The Economic Challenges of Growing Old

Since old age tended to bring declining fortunes, as shown in the previous chapter, how materially secure were the elderly? This chapter demonstrates that they were not very secure at all. By looking at the circumstances of poor, middling, and wealthy old people in Connecticut several salient facts become clear. From a material standpoint, growing old was risky, as evidenced by a significant number of aged people suffering in destitution. The only way to definitively ensure a comfortable old age and avoid the threat of penury was through individual effort. If a person's savings were insufficient or he was unable to labor for his own support there were no guarantees of safe passage over the many pitfalls threatening the aged. Family did sometimes assist older members economically but many times they did not. Meanwhile community support for elderly people in need was neither reliable enough nor generous enough to sustain an easy old age. In early national America dependence on others was best avoided because dependence was only a few steps removed from indigence.

These points are illuminated first by looking at the destitute aged for evidence of what they owned and how their holdings, or lack thereof, affected the quality of life. Scrutiny of the very poor reveals the manifold economic quagmires that could entrap elderly men and women, as well as the system of social supports that offered only limited help. The next section considers those whom I will call "middling"—the large majority of elderly who were neither very poor nor rich. These men and women were getting by but often faced many of the same challenges that afflicted the poor. By relying on their own resources, or because they were lucky enough to enjoy help from others, they managed to maintain a measure of independence and comfort in old age. Finally I consider the wealthy aged who, by maintaining economic independence, succeeded in sheltering themselves from the trials less fortunate people faced. In the case of each group we can observe how the strength or weakness of four crucial pillars of security—wealth, the ability to labor, health, and family—interplayed to determine people's fortunes in old age.

THE POOR ELDERLY

Despite the claims of some historians, poverty among the elderly was a significant problem in early national Connecticut.[1] Many of the women and men who were destitute in old age had been relatively poor all their lives, but poverty could also strike the well-educated, the once-prominent, and the formerly prosperous. Though the details of individual lives differed, all too often the causes of indigence can be traced to the failure of three, if not four, of the important financial supports of old age. Lack of savings, coupled with health problems, the inability to work, and a family that either could not lend a hand, or worse, added to the aged's burdens, almost always resulted in penury. Revolutionary War pension applications from Hartford County—our main source here—provide an intimate look at the lives of elderly men and women who, heavily burdened with misfortune, succumbed to destitution.

In 1818, Congress acted to provide pensions to men who had served for at least nine months in the Continental services during the Revolutionary War and were materially needy.[2] While earlier pension acts had restricted payments only to those disabled in the war, this act was the nation's first to extend benefits to those who had merely served but suffered no injuries.[3] Its aim was to relieve men who had sacrificed for their country of the indignity of indigence. In 1820, Congress passed a second act requiring that veterans submit detailed proof of their need.[4] Together these actions produced thousands of pages of documentation. For our purposes, a set of 244 pension application files, dating from 1820 to 1832, in the records of the Hartford County Court are most significant.[5] Because by the 1820s Revolutionary veterans were getting on in years (in Hartford their ages ranged from the fifties to the eighties), these documents describe aged people almost exclusively. And because veterans had to prove they were destitute in order to receive a pension, the information these applications provide concerns some of society's poorest members.

Pension applications are wonderfully rich documents. Each application included a veteran's age, occupation, place of residence, a description of his military service, an inventory of real and personal property, an explanation of how any property had been disposed of recently, his family circumstances, and an account of why he could no longer support himself. Veterans, who frequently composed and penned the applications themselves, often added many extra descriptions of their daily lives as well.[6] In addition, pension applications are also quite reliable. Though there may have been some applicants who exaggerated their circumstances in an effort to receive an undeserved pension, the fact that county courts checked applications and the United States War Department rechecked them carefully before final approval reduced the likelihood of fraud.[7] In any case, only applications that were accepted under the strict 1820 act requiring detailed proof of indigence are used here.[8]

Pension documents indicate that destitution in old age was more common in early national Connecticut than some have been tempted to believe. In all, 239 men in Hartford County were granted pensions under the 1818 act of Congress because they were needy. Of these, 198 remained on the rolls after the stricter 1820 rules requiring greater proof of poverty went into effect.[9] This figure corresponds to about 0.8 percent of Hartford County's total adult population. However, when we look only at the population of males aged forty-five and over, the percentage of pensioners rises to 5 percent.[10] If we had the figures to narrow the population down further—to those men fifty and over—the percentage would rise again. It is plain then that at the very least 5 percent of older men in Hartford County were destitute. Because many pension applicants had wives who were also indigent, it is safe to assume that at least 5 percent of older women were also poverty-stricken. In short, a minimum of one in twenty older men and women were without the means to pay for their basic needs. Considering that poor widows, non-veterans, and veterans who served less than nine months or had served in a militia rather than in the Continental forces were ineligible to apply for pensions, a conservative estimate of the actual percentage of indigent elderly would be higher—perhaps around 10 percent. If approximately 10 percent of Hartford's aged population suffered in abject poverty, surely many more were only barely eking out a living.[11] Clearly, though those men who filed for pensions were among Hartford County's most abject citizens, they were not unusual in their misfortune.[12]

Still, the number of pension requests from indigent veterans that flooded into Washington after 1818 surprised even contemporary observers. For example, Calvin Goddard, a lawyer and Connecticut legislator wrote in 1818, "I have on hand a great number [of applicants]—all of them miserably poor—I have made their [application] papers because when I began I supposed there not be more than ten or a dozen in my jurisdiction."[13] Congress likewise was somewhat shocked to find so many veterans in need of assistance.[14] Perhaps this was because it was widely believed that "in America there are few without families, and the ease of procuring subsistence removed all apprehensions of suffering in old age."[15] However, though contemporary observers seem to have thought that old age poverty was rare and historians have sometimes taken them at their word, this view was clearly incorrect.

Material Life of the Destitute Aged

As we will see later, wealthy old people often had estates valued in the thousands of dollars. Men who applied for pensions had property that was better measured in the tens of dollars. Over one third of all applicants owned nothing but the clothes on their back and perhaps some bedding. Of those who possessed nothing, many were substantially in debt. For all pension applicants, the median value of both real and personal property (not including clothing and bedding) was only $13. The mean, though higher, was still only about $34. Pension applicants did not own much as a few examples make clear.

Sharp Camp, a seventy-five-year-old black man from Granby, could count up his property easily—he had a walking cane, a "testament" and a hoe valued together at 96 cents.[16] Ira Clarke, aged sixty-four, was a little better off—with a half acre of land, two small hogs, two tables, and some kitchenware he was worth about $54.[17] Even those with larger holdings had precious little. James Francis' entire estate came to just over $93 and included a motley collection of items among which were:

1 small cart, 1 cow, 8 poor old Windsor chairs, 1 poor stand, 4 old tables, 1 looking glass, 10 old pictures, 1 doz. common earthen plates, 2 cyder barrels being old, 1 barrel half filled with pork, 2 old axes, 2 iron candle sticks, 1 old iron pot.[18]

Men with resources as meager and dilapidated as these did not live comfortably. As the language used by the petitioners suggests, possessions tended to be old and worn. Though one veteran listed his sole item of property as a "silver French watch," few had such luxuries.[19]

Housing, for those who owned any, tended to be correspondingly shabby. Many owned no real property at all, but the descriptions of houses among those who did suggests how unfortunate these pension applicants and their families were. Sixty-four-year-old James Anderson described his residence as a "small dwelling house" that "barely affords a shelter for the family."[20] Another man's "old house standing on the public highway" in Granby was ramshackle enough to be appraised at only $10.[21] Pension applicants described their dwellings as a "small hut," a house "old and poor," an "old hut without chimney," "an old one story dwelling House ... out of repair," or "one poor board hut on another man's ground."[22] And some who had these wretched dwellings were on the verge of losing even them. William Smith's application explained that, "His house ... is almost decayed and will not much longer be tenantable." Nevertheless he lived in this one-room dwelling with his wife and two children.[23]

Many pension applicants owned no real estate. Of these men, some lived in the homes of grown children. Others rented whatever they could afford, though for many even this expense was too great. As a result, finding shelter could be a matter of catch as catch can. Relief provided by public or private charity allowed some to pay for boarding in the homes of neighbors or strangers. Some found temporary shelter among friends or former employers. Amos Curtis, a man with no belongings save his clothes, wrote, "I have no family and have for several years past subsisted by the charity of friends residing in different families."[24] The seventy-year-old debtor Timothy Stephens reported, "I have ... no place of residence but with those who employ me at work," and, as he explained, his ability to labor was declining.[25] For men who requested pensions life was far from comfortable.

The Failure of Wealth, Labor, Health, and Family

Why were these men utterly unable to support themselves? For most the answer had four parts—wealth, work, health, and family. The four were often closely intertwined.

Savings, the first pillar of material stability elderly people relied on, was obviously lacking for all those who became indigent. Why did a portion of the aged population fail to put away resources for old age? One important answer is that they had never had much money even in their younger years. Information on occupations provided by pension applicants suggests that many had brushed with straightened circumstances even before old age. Indeed, 31 percent of indigent Revolutionary pensioners described themselves simply as "laborers" possessing no occupational skills whatsoever. As hired hands, such men performed agricultural chores and other tasks on a relatively temporary basis. Another 29 percent were or had been craftsmen. Of these, one third were shoemakers—an occupation that had fallen onto hard times as the shoemaking industry was more formally routinized in the early nineteenth century.[26] If we add the laborers and shoemakers together, men from these very humble walks of life account for about 40 percent of all Hartford County pensioners. Meanwhile 36 percent of pensioners were or had been farmers who may once have been successful but no longer were by the time old age set in. Less than 2 percent were professionals and only one merchant was obliged to request a pension. Those employed in these more lucrative occupations rarely needed pensions. Thus the occupations of these poor veterans indicate that many had never risen very high economically or had much chance to save for the challenges that old age could bring.

Still, with no savings to speak of or property to sell if hard times worsened, wages gained from even relatively unremunerative occupations offered at least slim protection from indigence. Unfortunately, as Revolutionary War pension applications show, the ability to labor in old age was frequently compromised. In almost every case, by the time their petitions for aid were made veterans' ability to work was a thing of the past. Almost to a man, pension applicants had lived beyond their capacity to gain a livelihood because of deteriorating health.

Diverse physical ailments plagued the destitute elderly. Sometimes long life had simply taken its toll. For example, seventy-eight-year-old Abel Alling, wrote that he was "old & worn out." As such he suffered from partial deafness and blindness and a "Rheumatic complaint."[27] Though Alling had been a farmer, not surprisingly he swore that "my ability to pursue said occupation is very small & daily failing ... I am unable to earn my living by manual labor."[28] For other men a combination of illness and accident eliminated their productive abilities. Timothy Olmsted had once been a farmer and a music instructor but by the age of sixty generally poor health, as well as the fact that "one of his legs has been broken & renders him a cripple for life," made obtaining a livelihood all but impossible.[29] Not surprisingly, a decline in health often sufficed to push men who had just been scraping by into destitution. Jonathan Pasco, a seventy-year-old farmer, had once "laboured hard" on sixty acres of land he owned. But when his health failed the property was mortgaged to pay some of his debts and finally he landed in debtors prison. By the time he made out his pension application he owned less than $40 worth of property.[30] Mental infirmities could be equally devastating. For the eighty-two-year-old physician Asa Hillyer who "by reason of age and a Succession of Fits has lost his mind and memory," continued practice of his profession was clearly not an option.[31]

When health problems hit, a number of men made valiant efforts to prolong their earning abilities. Aware that only continued labor separated them from penury, some men changed occupations when their original callings became impossible. Amasa Green, for example, took an occupational step down in old age to accommodate worsening health. A shoemaker until age fifty-four, Green took to peddling "through the various states of the Union" once age and infirmities reduced his ability to follow his trade. However, after seven more years even this proved too difficult and he became "wholly dependent on public charity."[32] Elijah Deming also took to peddling, though he worked only locally "for my neighbors." Formerly an agricultural day laborer, Deming probably chose peddling because it was less physically demanding. Unfortunately it was also less rewarding and despite his efforts, Deming was poverty stricken by the age of sixty-one.[33] Perhaps the most pathetic example of this effort to earn a living even after one's body had ceased to cooperate was the farmer Peter Magira. At seventy-four he could no longer support himself or his wife due to "losing the use of both of my hands" and other debilities. Six dependent children, all looking to him for succor, intensified his problems further. Begging was the only means he could devise to bring in sustenance but even with this effort he and his family "suffered greatly."[34] In each of these cases, men whose health was faltering adopted new and often less remunerative employment that could be performed despite infirmities. Yet such adaptation usually only postponed rather than prevented the onset of poverty.

Many pension applicants had depended not only on their own labor for sustenance but on that of their wives as well. But the health of veterans' wives was frequently just as precarious as that of their husbands. Applicants often reported that their wives were weak, infirm, or feeble. For some aging women, the basic running of a household could prove too much of a burden. Elkanah Smith reported that his fifty-nine-year-old wife Mary was "very infirm by age and dropsical complaints so that she is unable to do the ordinary work of my small family & much of the time unable to take care of herself."[35] Elijah Deming was more fortunate. His wife, a weaver, managed to "laber about half of her time."[36] Still, her limited earnings could not save the family from penury. Even those wives who could work failed to earn enough to support themselves, their husbands, and perhaps other dependent family members.

Poor health, therefore, was a principle cause of poverty because it interfered with work. But infirmity also contributed to indigence in other ways. Just as the elderly today must contend with hefty medical expenses, the aged of the early national period could be similarly burdened. "I am a very poor man," John Collar wrote on his pension application. Collar was also crippled because he had "lost part of one of my feet." This condition along with his wife's "weakly" state served to indebt him to "Doctor Neasly" for almost $100—a sum greater than twice his total estate of $38.[37] Likewise a sixty-four-year-old mariner named Joseph Clark suffered from two "ruptures" and a lame hand, racking up $18 in physician's bills. For Clark, with an estate worth only $27, such expenses were simply unmanageable.[38] Health crises and the costs they incurred overwhelmed men already teetering on the brink of financial ruin.

If health problems were short term, some men might have been able to spring back from them to resume their usual productive activities. Unfortunately, in many cases disability lingered for years.

At seventy-two, one former unskilled worker wrote that "for the last twenty years I have not been able to do any labor whatever in consequence of having a very offensive, distressing, painful & troublesome fever sore upon my right leg & ancle."[39] Few people, and especially those already on the margin of poverty, could scrape together enough to support themselves through such protracted debility.

In the absence of any institutionalized system to provide for elderly citizens, work in old age—on the part of both men and women—was important for maintaining financial stability. For those already close to poverty, labor was absolutely essential if total financial collapse was to be avoided. Not unique to early national Connecticut, such a state of affairs had long prevailed in the western world.[40] Yet for many, it was only a matter of time before age and accidents reduced or cut off entirely the ability to work. Some would try to cope with diminishing strength and prolong their productive years by changing occupations. Yet this strategy could fail, exposing the individual afresh to indigence. Thus, for men like those who applied for pensions, "retirement" from work only occurred when forced on them. Retirement was not a choice but an imperative required once the mind and body were literally incapable of laboring another day. This sort of retirement, anticipated with dread by elderly people struggling to get by, played a large role in reducing poorer elderly to destitution.

Once a person's own efforts to maintain security failed, family became the one remaining buttress preventing economic catastrophe. As seen in chapters 2 and 3, family members, especially children, were often expected to assist their aged kin. These expectations were codified into Connecticut laws requiring family relations who were able to provide support for needy parents and grandparents.[41] Nevertheless, for a significant fraction of the aged adequate aid from kin never materialized. Indeed, rather than assisting the elderly, family often worsened their economic circumstances. Those who were reduced to destitution in old age learned the hard way just how unreliable family could be.

Hartford County pension applicants lived in diverse family circumstances.[42] The largest proportion—about 38 percent—lived with both a wife and children. Another 30 percent lived with their wives only. About 20 percent lived on their own and another 5 percent lived with children only.[43] The remaining applicants lived with other relatives or non-kin. Clearly, poverty could strike the aged in all kinds of households.[44] Yet though household arrangements varied, the destitute aged shared one of three common family problems: 1) their kin's assistance was too meager to help much, 2) their kin offered no help at all, or 3) their kin actively drained away their resources. A host of factors including the ages, gender, and health of family members played important roles in creating these outcomes.

Connecticut law required close relatives of indigent people to assist them financially if they were able.[45] A few elderly poor did receive some support from relatives. In the cases of several pension applicants, adult sons lent a helping hand in times of crisis. For Elijah Smith, aged sixty-four and quite infirm, financial dependence on two sons "who each of them have families" was a necessity.[46] Likewise Elijah Monroe—a fifty-nine-year-old with less than $17 worth of property and several large debts—found himself "so far reduced . . . that I have been dependent on the charity of my son for a house in which to live, & and on his charity for the last two years for my support in part."[47] Some applicants had sons who had moved far away, as was the case with Timothy Hatch, whose son Frederick sent monetary aid from Virginia.[48] Yet in each of these cases the sons' resources seem limited. Young men in their twenties and thirties were likely to be struggling themselves as they began careers and started families. And the children of pension applicants probably struggled more than most men their age since their fathers had little property to give them to ease their start in life. Thus, though the law asked children and other kin to provide when aged relatives required, if the children themselves were poor such aid was likely to be limited.

Daughters and younger children of either sex were probably even less able than adult sons to provide adequate support for aged parents. The family of sixty-one-year-old William Steel provides the most extreme example of such a situation. Steel's household consisted of himself, his wife, his ninety-four-year-old father, and his ninety-one-year-old mother. The only person in the household with any earnings at all—on whom the entire family relied—was Steel's son Henry, aged fourteen.[49] When four elderly people past the ability to work and without savings looked to one boy for support, poverty was the only possible outcome. Conversely, dependence on children who were too old to labor could be a problem too. Nathaniel Humphrey, a pauper in his ninth decade of life looked to his fifty-six-year-old daughter Lucy for assistance. However Lucy was "unable to do but little labour except taking care of me," Nathaniel wrote.[50]

The limited aid elderly pension applicants got from their relations failed to protect them from indigence, much less offer much material comfort. Pension applications suggest that the lack of a reasonably successful mature son or well-off daughter to fall back on in old age meant reliance on less capable bread-winners—namely young or unhealthy women or boys—and ultimately penury. Thus the elderly described above were aided by their families, but despite their kin's efforts this help was insufficient.

Pension applicants who received even small assistance from kin were relatively rare. Applicants with families wholly unable to aid them appear more frequently. First there were applicants who had no family at all. As Philo Treat, aged sixty-four, stated his case, "I have no family having never been married, & no friend, or relative who are obliged by law to contribute to my support."[51] Equally trying was the case of Daniel Brewer. If the Revolution had never occurred Brewer might have avoided indigence in old age. As it was, the war brought the deaths of all three of his sons—effectively and permanently destroying his chance for help from children in old age. It is no wonder Brewer felt that, "the liberty of my Country was a severe purchase to me."[52] With his wife also dead, Daniel Brewer, like Philo Treat, lacked even the most rudimentary safety net if misfortune hit.

For many other elderly poor the problem was not lack of relations *per se* but lack of relations, especially children, with anything to spare. For example, John Warren explained, "I have one child only, & she is a married woman with a family, & her husband is poor."[53] And even when Abraham Wright's possessions dwindled to a single item—a cask full of currant wine—his grown daughters could not assist him as they were "barely capable of maintaining themselves."[54] Nor could the aged farmer Thomas Stedman look to his thirty-one-year-old son for aid because his son possessed only "small mental capacity and affords no support or assistance to the family."[55] Sometimes children, who may once have been able to aid their needy parents, fell victim to misfortune themselves, reducing their ability to help. Eighty-three year old Benjamin Reed had once been able to count on his son for support. Unfortunately he noted, "My son on whom I leaned has entirely lost his sight and has become poor."[56] Not surprisingly, his son's troubles brought an end to any aid.

In the cases described above the kin of poor aged people acted to aid them, albeit in a limited way, or gave nothing. Yet the most common scenario was one in which family members actively drained resources from the elderly poor's small holdings. This occurred when family members—most often children and sick relations—depended on the aged person for support. About 41 percent of pension applicants lived with both their wives and some children. Without reading the descriptions of family provided by the applicants, one is tempted to think that these elderly veterans and their wives had moved in with adult children who were caring for and supporting them. This was not the case. Of the seventy households in which parents and children lived together, only eight fit this description. The other sixty-two households consisted of elderly parents and dependent children—both minor and adult—and sometimes grandchildren. Interestingly, these households contained significantly more dependent daughters than sons.[57] Whether the presence of dependent children caused poverty among pension applicants or simply exacerbated it is impossible to tell from the sources. Clearly, however, an association existed between dependent children in the household in old age and indigence.

Couples in early national New England generally did not practice fertility control. As a result women often bore children over the entire span of their reproductive years. With the end of fertility occurring in the late thirties or early forties, and old age commencing as early as fifty, old people with young children were not anomalous. Because men tended to marry women younger than themselves, old men were especially likely to have young children. Pension applications offer numerous examples of this phenomena. Peter Magira's case is not unusual. At the age of seventy-one this infirm farmer was the father of children aged fourteen, twelve, nine, and six. In addition, his forty-year-old wife had recently presented him with twins. Though old age had already encroached on his bread-winning abilities, Magira contended with a large brood of dependents.[58] Lack of control over fertility posed formidable problems for aging couples. Rather than being cared for by adult children, many pension applicants struggled to raise young children in extremely straightened circumstances.

Older children and other dependent relatives could also drain away the small holdings of the aged poor. When sickness reduced the prospects for independence of young adults, they turned to aged parents for support. Yet for the already poor elderly, such a burden

The Economic Challenges of Growing Old 133

was too much to bear. At age fifty-nine Richard Belden had six children ranging in age from eight to thirty-three depending on him. Of these he explained,

> My daughter Lina [is] aged 33 years born blind and unable to do anything. Ralph my son [is] aged 18 years born blind & is an unfortunate being unable to labor. My son Richard [is] aged 16 years deformed & blind & unable to do anything.

It is no surprise that he was "unable from my own situation & the unfortunate state of my family to subsist without charity."[59] Grown daughters seem to have been a special liability, since in times of trouble they appear to have fallen back on parents more often than their brothers.[60] For example, an unskilled laborer of sixty-two named Josiah Steel found himself responsible for "a daughter Cynthia with two children" who, like the rest of the family, were not "able to do anything towards their support." Only semi-productive himself and with a crippled wife and an estate worth less than $5, the burden of three generations weighing on him far outstripped his abilities.[61]

Grandchildren, sometimes accompanied by their parents and sometimes not, could also put pressure on the resources of their aged grandparents. Thomas Palmer, a failing day laborer troubled by constant rheumatism, found himself responsible not only for his own upkeep and that of a disabled wife but also for that of two orphaned grandchildren aged eight and ten.[62] The household of Elijah Noble contained three generations of people, most of whom were ailing. Elijah himself was infirm. His son Harry was "in the last stages of a consumption" and his three daughters were "feeble, of delicate constitutions." Two grandchildren aged eight and eleven were well, but helped to stretch the family's small resources thin. Though he owned twenty-three acres of land, these were "sandy and unproductive" and mortgaged besides.[63] With very little to his name, this sickly patriarch was in no position to support his children or grandchildren.

Finally, some pension applicants had their own very aged parents to support. The Sash family of Hartford consisted of Moses, a pension applicant of sixty-four, his wife aged fifty-six, and his mother-in-law aged ninety-seven. Moses Sash's application revealed he had no property whatsoever nor the health with which to gain any. Even more pathetic was Lemuel Fox on whom ten others relied namely,

> Prudence aged 37 Nichumah aged 35—Parmelia aged 33 a *cripple*—Silas aged 30 Lemuel 27 years old lost an eye Manson aged 24, Betsey aged 21 Jane aged 16 Sarah Brooks my wifes mother aged 85 who is helpless.

His own health was bad "by having a cart load of wood run over me."[64]

When individual efforts to remain economically afloat faltered in old age, family played a potentially key role in rescuing the aged. Yet this assistance was far from guaranteed. Indeed, a significant fraction of old people forced to fall back on their families found support lacking and descended deeply into indigence as a result. Though we will see in our discussion of middling people that family was sometimes the saving grace that protected them from poverty, ironically family could also act—as it did in many pension applicant's cases—to drive aged people into poverty or worsen their already difficult economic circumstances. Dependence therefore was risky yet impossible to avoid once efforts at self-sufficiency floundered.

Sources of Support for the Aged Poor

When savings, the ability to labor, good health, and family broke down and failed to provide sustenance the lives of aged people became unpleasant indeed. Yet such failure was not uncommon in early national Hartford County. As shown earlier, roughly 10 percent of people over forty-five were completely unable to support themselves. In addition to the truly destitute, many more aged people must have been in narrow circumstances, requiring occasional aid to make ends meet. But once the normal supports caved in, where did such aid come from?

Early national America had its share of social problems, yet it was not a world that employed elaborate social policy or large-scale institutions to manage these. David Rothman has shown that an interest in formalized institutional solutions to ills such as poverty and crime was on the rise at this time.[65] However, such structures were only in an embryonic phase before 1830 and none existed to serve the aged, because the aged as a special group with unique problems was not yet recognized. While creative thinkers such as Benjamin Franklin and Thomas Paine occasionally proposed measures to assist the destitute elderly, their ideas went largely unheeded.[66] Perhaps the republican idealism of the new nation was ill suited to consideration of dependence, old age or otherwise. Or perhaps the youthfulness of the American population made old age poverty seem remote, and solutions to it far from urgent. Whatever the reason, several more decades would pass before Americans turned serious attention to devising formal measures for managing the problems associated with growing old.[67] It is not surprising therefore that few efforts were made between 1790 and 1830 to assist the aged poor in particular. (Even Revolutionary pensions, which did much to aid needy old people, were intended as a service to veterans, not the elderly more broadly.) Instead, the indigent aged were largely undistinguished from the ranks of the poor. What help they received when destitution struck came from the hodgepodge of efforts—both public and private—to relieve paupers. Such assistance did not address the unique problems of the needy elderly, much less offer them comfort and security in their final years.

Public efforts to aid the poor were almost all locally based. Of the New England states, Connecticut had an especially strong tradition of town responsibility for paupers. Colonial statutes ordered each town to "maintain their own poor" and designated town selectmen as the agents of this policy. To raise funds for the provision of "Victuals, Cloathing, Fire-Wood, and any other thing necessary" for the relief of paupers, towns like Hartford levied a yearly tax on their citizens.[68] Hartford's colonial records indicate that the selectmen were helping needy residents as early as 1658.[69] At least until 1714 town assistance took numerous forms. Some people were given cash to purchase needed goods while in other cases the town offered clothes, house repair, board and care, food, or help with medical expenses.[70]

Unfortunately, for the period from 1716 through the early national period, Hartford's town records concerning the poor are lost.[71] The sparse evidence that remains indicates that the town continued to tax its citizens for support of the poor throughout the late-eighteenth and early-nineteenth century.[72] Outdoor relief as practiced during the colonial period seems to have continued as the principal aid to the needy until at least 1782, when the town fathers built a poorhouse.[73]

Once the poorhouse was in place, the selectmen continued to provide some outdoor aid as an alternative to the almshouse "in some special & extraordinary cases."[74] Then by 1797, for reasons that are obscure, the selectmen sold the poorhouse and may have eliminated the institution altogether. By 1810, however, according to federal census takers, some paupers were again residents of a "Poor House."[75] This may have been an arrangement by which Hartford contracted with a private individual to care for the town poor. Soon after in 1811, perhaps responding to greater economic hardship provoked by the trade restrictions leading up to the War of 1812, the selectmen again concluded that an official institution was needed. They established a temporary almshouse "to have all the town poor supported at that place," with the exception of a few cases at the discretion of the selectmen.[76] This system seems to have persisted until 1822 when a new combination workhouse/almshouse was erected and began operations.[77] The rules for this institution were set down in twenty points dictating hours of work, meals, rest, and worship, as well as guidelines for inmates' conduct. The rules specified that "All the Poor whom this Town is liable to support shall be placed in the Almshouse." However, as they had earlier, the selectmen reserved the right to give other kinds of aid "in cases where œconomy, humanity, or necessity require it."[78] Unfortunately, neither lists of outdoor relief recipients nor of poorhouse inmates survive.

Hartford's poor records are scant, but Revolutionary pension applications indicate that support from towns was a significant source of assistance, though clearly only as a last resort, for the elderly poor. At least twenty-four pension applicants from all over Hartford County (or about 14 percent of all applicants) explicitly stated that they were receiving partial or complete support from their towns. More probably benefited from town aid but failed to mention it in their applications. Of the fifteen veterans resident in the city of Hartford itself who successfully applied for pensions, five (or 33 percent) acknowledged some support from the town.

It is difficult to know exactly what sort of aid these men and their families received. None of the applicants from any Hartford County towns stated they had ever resided in a poorhouse, though one applicant expressed fear that if he did not receive a federal pension, "I must be carried to the poor house of the town of Hartford."[79] Indeed, when 1810 census takers counted the residents in Hartford's

The Economic Challenges of Growing Old

poorhouse they found that at least 55 percent were aged forty-five or older. Some of these men and women were surely elderly.[80] The fact that the *Hartford Times* recorded the death of more than one elderly pauper while resident at Hartford's almshouse also suggests that the aged were considered suitable candidates for institutionalization. In addition, once the permanent almshouse was built in 1822, we know that the selectmen took steps to limit the amount of aid given in outdoor relief, preferring to spend funds on supporting the needy in the poorhouse and thereby ensuring that needy old people would be incarcerated.[81]

Though evidence on local public relief for the aged is spotty, a few conclusions are possible. Throughout Hartford County, town aid was an important component in the support of the elderly indigent. How much help was provided as outdoor relief, compared to relief in an almshouse or in the residence of a contractor for poor relief, is unknown. In many smaller towns without poorhouses, outdoor assistance in the form of cash, food, firewood, or medicine was probably the norm through much of the early national period. In larger towns like Hartford, once a central almshouse was established, the aged poor became likely residents. Indeed, as the nineteenth century progressed and imposing almshouses began to dot the New England landscape, there was a trend towards greater institutionalization of all poor, and the aged probably participated in this trend as much as other age groups.[82] Old age *per se* did not seem to be a sufficient reason to excuse a person from the poorhouse on the grounds of "humanity." Probably Hartford's selectmen decided the fate of the penurious aged on a case by case basis, just as they did for paupers of any other age. Economic decline was associated with old age but towns made no effort to distinguish elderly paupers from the poor of other ages or to address their special needs.

The state of Connecticut was another less frequent source of aid for destitute people. Though poor relief efforts were almost exclusively a town concern in Connecticut, the state took responsibility in cases when a pauper was both ill and had no official town of residence.[83] Only three successful pension applicants in Hartford County mentioned receiving such assistance. Never very extensive, state aid became even rarer after 1820 when the state took measures to reduce the expense of state-supported poor.[84]

Though the federal government provided no poor relief specifically for the aged, the pensions offered to Revolutionary veterans (beginning in 1818) ultimately helped support hundreds of elderly people in Connecticut alone.[85] As described earlier, an application sworn to and certified in court was the first step to receiving a pension. If proof of poverty—which came to be defined as having neither a yearly income of more than $96 nor an estate worth over $960—and military service were acceptable to the War Department in Washington D.C., applicants were added to the rolls. Pensions were intended "to provide for the absolute wants of the poor but meritorious soldier of the revolution & the highest rate of pension is supposed to be the smallest sum that will afford a comfortable support to an individual."[86] In practice this meant that veterans received $96 a year in semiannual installments, except for a few former officers who got a liberal $240 yearly.[87]

Ninety-six dollars was not a large sum, especially for men with many dependents, medical expenses, or debts. Even some of the lowest paid workers—agricultural laborers—could expect to earn about $124 a year, while many artisans brought in closer to $416 a year and some Hartford ministers took home from $900 to $1,000 annually.[88] Compared to these yearly incomes, $96 dollars offered only the barest maintenance. Yet without this money most pensioners would have been forced to rely on local charity (either public or private) to survive. Indeed, it is important to note that pensions did not really provide for a group that had previously been unprovided for, they merely shifted responsibility from towns to the federal government. Still, for elderly paupers a federal pension must have been an attractive alternative to town relief. First, being a revolutionary pensioner—recognized by the federal government for services in the war—may have been a slightly more dignified status than "town pauper."[89] Second, pensions provided a predictable income and allowed individuals to manage their own affairs. This condition was preferable to town outrelief which dispensed small sums or goods as needed to paupers, or to life in the poorhouse which squelched all independence.

Private efforts to aid the poor also contributed to the support of the indigent elderly. Charity by individuals to needy acquaintances or friends seems to have been a fairly common form of private assistance. Quite a few pension applicants stated the importance of this sort of aid in helping them get by. For example, Jehiel Latimer, aged sixty-eight, revealed that "much private aid and charity from my neighbors and friends" combined with "some public aid" had preserved him.[90] The septuagenarian David Jerome also had his "friends and relations" to thank for supporting him over more than twenty years.[91] For others, such as Isaac Cluff, intermittent private aid helped him over times when other sources of assistance were lacking. Cluff wrote, "I was supported by the charity of individuals at times and at other times by the state of Connecticut."[92] While some benefactors seem to have offered assistance freely, other indigent men had to plead for help. Richard Case, a seventy-eight-year-old East Hartford man explained that he "subsisted partly on charity begged from my neighbors."[93] Charity could also come from social superiors. Local lore tells of Daniel Wadsworth, Hartford's wealthiest man after the death of his father in 1804, setting out occasionally with a "big gunboat sleigh . . . laden with food for the poor and delicacies for the sick."[94]

Friends may have been motivated by affection for the needy person, who perhaps they had known in better days. For neighbors and men like Wadsworth the impetus may have been a communal sense of responsibility for the poor in their midst. Mary Cowles, a young woman in Farmington, expressed such feelings in a diary entry from 1823:

> The number of individuals, who depend entirely on others for support is immense. To these it is our duty to show pity, & relieve them of their misfortune: we have more than is needful for our necessity or convenience, & the surplus we should reserve for those who really need our charity.[95]

A sense of religious duty played a role for others. Shubael Bartlett, a minister living in East Windsor, told his diary of aid he offered to an aged widow. He justified his assistance by citing the injunction, "Thou shalt open thy hand to thy poor neighbor."[96] However, because records of individual charity rarely survive, we know very little about the motivations of the givers, the effect on the recipients, or the scope of assistance.

Like most New England communities in early national New England, Hartford was home to numerous voluntary associations, another source of private charity for the aged. Founded in 1792, the

Charitable Society had perhaps the greatest impact on the lives of the aged poor. The Society recognized the inadequacy of public support in some cases and set about providing assistance to "sober and industrious" people,

> for whom the poor Laws of the State do not provide the relief suitable to their condition and circumstances, or adequate to their necessities: among whom the Widow, the Orphan, the Aged, labouring people depressed by sickness or inevitable misfortune, persons or Families of decayed fortune, will be distinguished as objects of the Society's care and munificence.[97]

To accomplish these worthy goals the Society raised funds from membership dues, donations from the congregations of various Hartford churches, gifts from individuals, and interest on loans as well as bank and stock holdings.[98]

The Society's records indicate that from 1790 to 1830 outlays were made on 1,807 occasions to hundreds of individuals—the majority of them women. Indeed almost 73 percent of all payments were made to women of whom at least 16 percent were widows.[99] Women, and aged women particularly, were especially vulnerable to poverty in part because early national law deprived them of control over property. Women also had fewer opportunities to earn wages and received smaller remuneration for their efforts than did men. The fact that women could not apply for pensions placed them at a disadvantage as well. In a society organized around the male as principle economic actor, it is not surprising that women were forced to rely more heavily than men on private charity.

Though occasionally the records indicate "Old Mrs. Burham" received some cash or some "very old people" were aided, exactly how many recipients of either sex were old is unclear.[100] However we can be sure that many widows receiving assistance were aged and that the elderly were frequently objects of the Society's charity. A few cases illustrate the experience an aged person might have with the Society. "Widow Hender" first came to the Society's attention at the age of thirty-seven in 1794, when she seems to have lived with her elderly mother. She continued to receive aid as she herself became old, that is at least until she was seventy-three in 1830. Though the duration of

The Economic Challenges of Growing Old 141

aid to Widow Hender was unusual, the type of assistance she received was not. Almost every year Widow Hender was provided with cash, "sundries," or a load of wood. Never worth more than $10 each, such infusions cannot have supported her by themselves. The Charitable Society's aid only supplemented whatever slim resources Widow Hender had of her own or other charity she received. Similarly Daniel Hinsdale was fifty-six when he received his first aid (a load of wood) from the Society in 1800. Perhaps a temporary illness precipitated this assistance because he seems to have received nothing more until 1814 at age seventy. After this age, however, cash help came almost every year varying in size from $3 to over $20.[101] It appears that as he aged, and perhaps poor health set in, Hinsdale came increasingly to rely on the aid of the Society. Like Widow Hender however, Hinsdale's principal source of support came from elsewhere. While the indigent elderly could look to the Charitable Society to ease them over economic rough spots, such help did not replace public support.

The Widows' Society, founded in 1825, had similar goals but aided only women. Perhaps feeling the precariousness of their own economic circumstances, the female founders of the Society hoped to assist women "who had seen better days and lived in easy circumstances" but were now destitute. In their first year the Society succeeded in aiding twenty-six widows who were in many instances "aged, sick, lame, deaf, or blind." Few records survive, but a historian of the society noted that aid given widows was "small."[102] Probably, like the larger Charitable Society, the Widows' Society offered assistance to supplement other charity.

Churches also aided the needy. Though many church archives lack information on poor relief efforts—either because the information is lost or because no such efforts were ever undertaken—records from two churches survive. We know therefore that the small Society of Friends in West Hartford collected money from members for "the use of the poor."[103] Whether these poor were other Quakers or simply needy people is not known. Whether aged people received assistance is also a mystery. Of the Quakers the most we can say is that they may have aided some aged people in their attention to assisting the poor in general. More is known of the activities of Hartford's oldest church—the First Church of Christ (Congregational). No mention is made in the records of attempts to assist the poor prior to 1817. In this year, however, church leaders voted to begin allocating funds "for relief of Poor members." After this decision the church earmarked money for the needy regularly. By 1824 approximately twenty people were receiving aid in varying amounts. As with voluntary associations, women (including widows) seem to have been the principal beneficiaries of the church's charity. Outlays to the fifty-one-year-old widow Lydia Prudden illustrate the type of assistance the church gave. On four occasions in 1830 Prudden received $3 payments, and once she was given $4. Gifts of between $1 and $4 were the norm.[104] The ages of most recipients are impossible to recover, but the elderly must have benefited in some measure from church aid. However, like the Charitable Society and Widows Society, the church did not attempt to fully support its needy members. Rather, cash gifts were probably intended to supplement other resources—an hypothesis that is at least partially confirmed by the fact that some recipients of the First Church's charity also benefited from Charitable Society assistance.

Once individual efforts to make a living faltered and support from family failed, communities offered no seamless safety net for the elderly to fall back on. In terms of public aid, a federal pension (for those who qualified) provided the best alternative. Pensions offered only the barest subsistence, but recipients maintained their independence. Less lucky were those aged poor who were compelled to depend on their towns for relief. Instead of a bi-yearly pension allowance, such individuals probably received very small cash payments or goods to cover immediate needs. As a result, their economic futures were more uncertain and more worrisome than that of pensioners. In addition, in cities like Hartford, the elderly could find themselves incarcerated in the poorhouse with their freedom severely restricted. Yet for those ineligible for pensions, town aid at least offered enough assistance to get by. Private charity was more variable. While some paupers struggled along by depending on friends and neighbors, for many private aid could only supplement help from other sources. Voluntary associations and churches seem to have made the lives of the indigent aged—especially more vulnerable women—easier, but their aid was insufficient to depend on fully. Indeed the wretched living conditions many pension applicants describe suggest that even when help from all available sources was pieced together, hardship and privation (though not starvation) were the result. Communities did not let the needy elderly perish but neither did they provide comfort and security to their aged neighbors.

Revolutionary pension applications reveal destitution in old age as a multi-step process. The first step to penury came when individuals arrived in old age without substantial savings. The second step came when health failed and labor consequently became impossible. The third step occurred when family failed to intervene with sufficient aid, or worse exacerbated the financial difficulties of the old person. Anyone, no matter how prosperous he had once been, who experienced these steps became indigent. Unfortunately, once this process was completed, early national society had no well-established method of rescuing aged people. At best the needy elderly found themselves dependent on a poorly-organized patchwork of public and private charity ill suited to their compound problems.

THE MIDDLING ELDERLY

The stories of the destitute aged point to the many pitfalls facing aging men and women. Yet though most old people were threatened by economic difficulties, not everyone succumbed to financial crisis in old age. The middling elderly—men and women who were neither poverty-stricken nor wealthy—managed to weather the financial trials of old age fairly successfully. Such success was possible because at least one of the major supports for economic well-being—wealth, health, the ability to work, or family—remained intact.

Though middling old people made up the largest segment of the aged population, comparatively little is known about them. The very poor constituted a social problem and therefore generated records useful to historians. Wealthy people tended to be eulogized by contemporaries and genealogists alike, creating a body of information in the process. Those in between often failed to catch the attention of their contemporaries either as objects of envy or of charity. Thus, though it may seem inelegant to lump all those falling between the two economic extremes together, the qualitative records do not allow much finer distinctions. Nevertheless a careful reading of the evidence allows for a discussion of the economic challenges facing middling people and the methods they employed to avoid serious economic trouble.

Material Life of the Middling Aged

Though not lavish, the material life of the middling aged stood above that of the very poor. A few examples, taken from the ranks of ordinary Hartford taxpayers, suggest that middling people enjoyed at least some comfort and economic security in old age.[105] Yet within the category of middling, material circumstances varied. Unfortunately, occupational and other information that might allow finer gradations of understanding of the middling aged is scarce. The sketches below serve to indicate the range of possessions held by those who were neither wealthy nor very poor.

Among the better-off middling were men like Daniel Seymour. With a tax list of almost $137 in 1808, the seventy-nine-year-old Seymour was quite comfortable, though not rich.[106] Like other men with tax lists his size, his holdings included land (fifty-nine acres in all) as well as livestock including six cows, four steers, and a horse. Most likely he also owned a dwelling house. Unlike wealthier men, however, Seymour owned little in the way of luxury goods. Instead of a silver or gold watch, Seymour possessed a wooden clock.[107] Less well-off among the middling was fifty-three-year-old Consider Burt, with a list worth $47. Burt owned no land at all and although he owned livestock like Seymour, his barn held only one horse and one cow. Burt's tax list suggests that he had a house of his own. He also counted among his possessions a carriage, though it was a significantly cheaper model than those used by wealthier Hartfordians.[108] Lower down on the economic scale but still not very poor were people like William Whitman, a fifty-six-year-old trader with a list of about $15 in 1816. He held a small parcel of land (four acres for mowing), a relatively inexpensive silver watch, and must have rented a dwelling since he did not own one.[109] Compared with the destitute aged, whose belongings often amounted to little more than clothes and a few personal items, men like Seymour, Burt, and even Whitman enjoyed financial success in old age.

Financial Responsibilities of the Middling Elderly

Though middling people had some resources, they (like their poorer neighbors) also had a host of financial responsibilities, not the least of which was their own upkeep. For some this meant maintaining a home and paying for or producing provisions. Others paid for boarding. For example the elderly sisters Rebecca and Bridget Noyes both paid their brother annually "for boarding with him the year past."[110] Elisha Niles, a farmer and teacher in his fifties, "hired" a house and paid the rent by laboring for his landlord.[111] Added to these basic costs of living, unexpected expenses due to an illness or accident could impinge on the middling elderly's holdings.

Expenses related to children could also claim a share of the aged's resources. Just as with poor elderly people, some middling parents had minor children to support. For others such as the aged Morris Maltby, an ill daughter increased his expenses. He wrote of her in a letter to his brother:

> Fidelia our youngest, 16 last May, has never enjoyed a Comfortable health never did but part days work in a day in her life . . . I think she would be able to help her aged mother through the trials and hard labour she has had to endure but [she] never has been able.[112]

Rather than contributing as a productive member of the household, Fidelia was an extra burden on her aging parents.

The cost of setting children up in the world could also weigh on older parents. William Pierson, a young man fresh from Yale reflected on his father's prospects at the age of fifty-six. Though Pierson needed financial help from his father he realized that

> I with my health and education can better gain myself a livelihood than he in his declining years upon a rough farm that affords no income beyond a competence, can support his family, & pay debts incurred by my education & Lydia's [his sister's] furniture.[113]

Though children could sometimes offer financial assistance in old age as we will see shortly, they could also put demands on their aged parents resources.

The machinations of unscrupulous people also occasionally had an unwholesome effect on the aged's economic well-being. People with diminished mental acuity seem to have been the most likely victims.

Hezekiah Griswold, a Windsor man who "through age and great bodily Infirmities" was "unfit and unable to transact any Business," was one who fell prey to designing people. The selectmen of his town testified in court that Hezekiah "is frequently induced by Artful Men, to make improvident and foolish Bargains, whereby he hath been deprived of part of his Property."[114] Hezekiah was not the only elderly person taken advantage of, indicating that scams to bilk the elderly out of their holdings are not a recent invention.

Qualitative information on the financial responsibilities of the aged is sketchy. A detailed breakdown of the relative costs of food, medical care, care of dependents, and other expenditures is impossible. However, it is evident that those who remained middling in old age faced many of the same financial hurdles that tripped up the indigent aged. The question is, what allowed some people to retain middling status in old age while others succumbed to penury?

Sources of Support for Middling Old People

While all sources of support fell through for those who became destitute, middling people hung on to financial stability because they entered old age with some modest resources, decent health allowed them to continue laboring, they maintained a frugal lifestyle, or their families, instead of dragging them into penury, actively helped them.

Middling people held more resources than the poor, but their savings alone were frequently too small to carry them through old age comfortably. Therefore, like the poor, middling men and women often depended either partially or entirely on income from work for their maintenance.[115] Often aged people continued to do the same kind of work they had done in younger days, though sometimes at a slower pace. Rebecca Noyes continued to sew for others through much of her old age, but in her final years reduced the number of projects she took on.[116] Elisha Hinman, a seaman from Southbury, also slowed down as age advanced. At seventy-three he wrote a friend of his activities: "I have done going to sea but am doing a little in that way—I have a Brig now in Jamaica Commanded by Ebenezer Hotchkiss by acc[oun]t is like to make me a good voyage."[117] Hinman thus remained involved in his lifelong occupation but in a less active capacity, ensuring at least some income as old age advanced.

For others continued work was more of a challenge. The Reverend James Cogswell began his labors as a minister in 1744 as a youth of twenty-four and continued until the ripe age of eighty-four.[118] As he aged, his ability to work was compromised by frequent severe headaches and what he called "luminous appearances" accompanied by mental confusion. At the age of seventy he already felt hard pressed to work as he once had, telling his diary, "laboured some, partly for Health and partly for Necessity. felt Tired, a little work Tires me [I] find by Experience that I grow old."[119] The Sabbath became especially fatiguing so when neighboring ministers relieved him occasionally Cogswell appreciated the "Respit from public labours."[120] Yet despite his trials Cogswell did not rest until only three years before his death. Describing himself as having "lived comfortably tho always poor," the necessity to earn a living probably played an important role in his long exertion. Indeed the circumstances of another minister, the seventy-six-year-old Eliphalet Williams, suggest what Cogswell may have feared. Williams continued as a minister until his death but serious health problems threatened his performance. He wrote his brother in 1804 complaining that "I take a pen to write a Line, but with a trembling hand. Such is my debility that I can scarcely make a mark." Probably as a result of his diminished abilities to perform his office, Williams was "greatly stritened for *Cash*, in consequence of the diminution of Sallary &c."[121] Already pressed economically Williams could not risk quitting his labor altogether. Despite physical problems Williams, like Cogswell, pressed on at least in part because the money earned was essential to his maintenance.

The case of the farmer Timothy Maltby further illustrates the need for continued productive labor by aged middling people. At fifty-eight, Maltby described himself as suffering from "Rheumatism and palpitation of the heart." In consequence he explained, "I have not so much as been able to drive a team one day this spring having but one boy to work my farm it is hard meeting my debts."[122] Despite his sickness, he evidently managed to get by at farming for a few more years. By the age of sixty-five, however, he wrote, "I have discontinued the labour of my farm with my own hands and as a substitute for a pastime &c I have taken up weaving carpets."[123] This work probably brought in some small income that helped him through his declining years.

Work was an important component of economic stability. As we have seen the poor were halted in their productive efforts by bad health. Those who maintained middling status did so in part because their health allowed labor to continue. Thus for many middling people retirement, as an abrupt and complete termination of work, was neither a hoped for ideal nor a viable reality. In old age there was no abrupt ceasing of labor to make way for rest or relaxation. Commentators on modern old age have criticized the system of mandatory retirement which pushes elderly people out of productive activity and into forced leisure. Yet the early national system, which demanded continued work from people whose abilities were failing, cannot be seen as superior. Elderly people in early national American knew that their economic security rested on their own efforts and thus bore the heavy responsibility of remaining productive into old age.[124]

A parsimonious lifestyle was another active measure the aged employed to protect themselves economically. Mary Vinton, a widow in her fifties, knew the importance of frugality as she managed the small estate left for her use by her husband. She told her son that, "Having food & raiment, & shelter by night & day ... y[ou]r *real* wants are supplied, & the rest are *imaginary*, & may be resisted & contrould."[125] Vinton practiced what she preached with the justification that "*self-denial* is the ordeal wh[ich] God has appointed to purify the character."[126] For many women, widowhood was a financially precarious time yet Vinton's careful planning and management of limited resources preserved her from severe problems. Benjamin Gilman, an aged man with grown children living at a distance, likewise had only small means. He wrote his son-in-law that in terms of money, "I expect to always continue in want of it myself."[127] Though very eager to see his children and grandchildren, Gilman economized by not traveling to see them. "I cannot afford the expence of Travelling" he told his children, "therefore I must count the weeks that were spent with you, and if possible try to derive that satisfaction that would arise from frequent short visits."[128] Such penny-pinching was a necessity for elderly people with limited resources.

Though the best way to ensure economic stability in old age was through one's own efforts, dependence on others—especially children—was sometimes unavoidable. In earlier chapters we saw that early national Americans often expected children and other relatives to assist their aged kin. We have also seen that dependence on kin was risky because if help failed to materialize, destitution followed. Those who hung on to middling status in old age faced this risk but were lucky enough to have children or other relatives who were both willing and able to lend a helping hand once the ability to cope economically had waned.

Children offered a variety of material assistance to parents in need, ranging from occasional practical gifts to complete support. For example, the minister Shubael Bartlett of East Windsor provided his septuagenarian father-in-law Mr. Leffingwell with frequent food gifts. Bartlett's diary entries in July of 1825 reveal he gathered currants and "made it into jelly & shrub for ourselves and for Father Leffingwell" and that he "Carried a quarter of veal, which was butchered in the morn[in]g to Father Leffingwell's."[129] Later Bartlett sent his son to Leffingwell's with "24 bushels of winter-apples which we give him as a token of our gratitude for his many and great gifts to us."[130] Practical items such as provisions were likely welcome gifts from children allowing an aged person to live more comfortably.

For others, children's assistance took the form of labor on behalf of the aged person. William Williams was once a prosperous man and signer of the Declaration of Independence. Yet at seventy-nine he was much reduced both in health and fortune. Williams' son, living nearby, helped by working on his father's farm, even when his own farm needed attention.[131] Likewise, when old age rendered Robert Cogswell incapable of "performing much business," his daughter stepped in to manage his property and affairs.[132]

In other cases—when aged parents were needier—children offered complete support. Elizabeth Robbins was fortunate enough to have sons who relieved her of all material worries. Widowed in 1813, Robbins lived on her own resources until 1825 when her son noted that "her means of support are nearly expended . . . She has nothing to depend on." Yet perhaps because she "was never a great economist," she knew nothing of her own financial problems and her three sons did nothing to disturb her complacence. Instead they agreed amongst themselves to each "pay as much as 20 dollars a year, or five dollars quarterly" for her support. Their exertions allowed Widow Robbins to "get along comfortably" as well as "feel a kind of independence—& . . . have the enjoyment which results to a parent from receiving expressions of kindness & affection from children."[133]

Until her death at eighty-three, Widow Robbins remained free from the "fears, which often haunt old people, of being a burden to her children, or of becoming poor." Indeed the benefits of such aid were great—without it Widow Robbins would have joined the ranks of the indigent, depending entirely on charity for her upkeep.[134]

Material assistance from friends and neighbors also helped the aged maintain their middling status. Neighborly reciprocity came in handy in old age as James Cogswell's diary reflects. In 1790 when Cogswell's aged wife fell ill, female neighbors "sent butter &c." Their help—which both provided the family with food and replaced Mrs. Cogswell's labor—was extensive enough to make Cogswell worry that they "will lay themselves out too much."[135] But when Cogswell had the opportunity to aid other aged neighbors he did not hesitate to lay himself out. He recorded, for example, how in the winter of 1790 he "carried . . . some apples" to a local ninety-one-year-old woman.[136]

Neighbors' help could be extremely generous at times. In 1780 at around eighty years of age John Thomas was childless, having never married. Indeed he had no family whatsoever since he had emigrated alone from Great Britain years before. Though he owned some land, his other possessions were few and his health interfered with his ability to provide for himself, especially in winter. Yet Thomas' last years were comfortable because a neighboring farmer named Wetmore took the unusual step of welcoming Thomas into his household. Thomas wrote:

> I know not but that I would have suffered had it not been for the kindness shewn me by said Wetmore who . . . invited me to come and live with him and board at his House and Table which invitations I have accepted.

Wetmore also managed Thomas' land which the old man could no longer make use of himself. Ultimately Thomas willed his land to his benefactor. Altruism may have been Wetmore's motive in caring for the old man (indeed his townsmen vouched for his "honest" behavior) but if Thomas had not possessed adjoining land and been heirless his neighbor's generosity may not have extended as far as it did.[137] Whatever the impulse, however, Thomas benefited from his neighbor's willingness to sustain him comfortably until his death.

Personal arrangements with kin and friends were important economic supports for the middling aged in Connecticut's early national period. However, a few more formal possibilities existed as well. Corporate insurance for old age—in the form of annuities or reversionary payments—were in their infancy from 1790 to 1830. The first commercial venture specializing in life insurance, the Pennsylvania Company for Insurance on Lives and Granting Annuities, was chartered in 1812. Most of the policies this company wrote were for annuities in which an individual paid a sum to the company in return for smaller annual payments while he lived. However, the industry remained quite small through most of the period. Indeed in 1828 one observer noted that life insurance was only then "slowly but gradually attracting the public attention and confidence in our principle cities." Not surprisingly then, no evidence has surfaced to suggest that such schemes were much used in Connecticut.[138]

However, annuities agreed upon between individuals may have been more common. As one historian of insurance has remarked,

> Arrangements . . . whereby persons of advancing years made over their property to the eldest son, less frequently to several of their children or to others, in return for maintenance during the remainder of life, are met with from early times, and have perhaps existed in all societies.[139]

Unfortunately, only hints of such arrangements survive from our period. In one colonial court case, for example, a "covenant" made between an elderly man named Elizur Stockwell and another individual named Stratton obliged the latter to pay for the support of Stockwell and his wife.[140] The exact terms of this agreement are lost. Documents relating to the Widow Anna Rudd also indicate that she had a bond agreement with her son requiring him to pay a yearly sum for her support.[141] A Hartford man named Pantry Jones also arranged an annuity for his aged wife before his death.[142] Finally, a letter penned by the wealthy Daniel Wadsworth to a friend in Hartford tells of an arrangement to provide an aged woman with an annuity so that "the good Lady will have no occasion to fear the very great evil of poverty, in her old age."[143] These fragments suggest that private annuities did exist, but exactly how and why they were arranged and how effectively they operated is uncertain.

Voluntary associations may also have offered annuities that benefited the elderly, though again evidence is sketchy. A Ministers Annuity Society, composed of pastors, met in Hartford in the 1820s and was devoted to mutual aid. The group footed bills for burial expenses, but whether the society provided support to its aged members before death is unknown.[144] Similarly, a Mechanics Society formed in Hartford in 1816 for mutual aid and other purposes. The Society consisted of respectable "master mechanics or manufacturers" and sought to protect and aid "such of its members as by sickness or accident, may stand in need of assistance."[145] Such assistance may have been extended to members as they aged. In any case only a small fraction of the elderly population would have qualified for help from either the Ministers or the Mechanics societies. In general, the paucity of records on formal provisions for financial security in old age indicate their embryonic stage in the early national period.

Indeed, the only well-documented source of formal economic assistance to the middling elderly came from the law. In particular, Connecticut law allowed local courts to appoint a conservator to any individual who through incompetence, idleness, or infirmity was unable to manage her or his own property.[146] Thus the law provided aid in the form of managerial help rather than cash or provisions. Court-appointed conservators were an important mechanism by which incapable aged people could protect their property and maintain middling status. In practice mentally and physically impaired old people accounted for about one quarter of all conservator cases in Hartford between 1739 and 1855. Dorothy Eno was one aged person who benefited from court intervention. Eno owned about $3,250 worth of property, but

> for want of discreccion in the management of s[ai]d Estate ... Dorothy is like to be reduced to penury and want and to suffer for want of the conveniencies & necessaries of life unless some suitable person is appointed to take care of the person and estate.[147]

Eno, like scores of other ill elderly, was saved from economic distress by the formal provision of a caretaker who maintained her property when she herself could not.[148] But like the assistance voluntary societies may have offered, this formal assistance was limited to a narrow segment of the aged population.

Holding on to middling status in old age was a matter of patching together solutions. The most important of these—continued work and frugality—required the active planning and participation of the aged themselves. Other solutions such as family and neighborly aid were also important, though the elderly had less control over them. Those who retained financial stability in old age faced many of the same risks and challenges that proved the undoing of those who became destitute. However, because health held out and allowed for continued labor, or because family, friends, or neighbors came through with adequate aid, some men and women avoided sliding into penury.

THE WEALTHY AGED

So far we have considered the circumstances that entrapped some elderly in poverty and how, using a variety of methods, the middling aged managed to avoid these pitfalls. There are still those who enjoyed great prosperity in old age to consider. Though rare, a few individuals effectively insulated themselves from the risks of declining productive activity and dependence on others. What allowed a handful of women and men the luxury of solid economic security in old age? The answer, as before, revolves around wealth, health, work, and family. However, where health, work, and family were more significant to middling and poor people, savings not surprisingly played a larger role among the rich. Yet even for the wealthy, it was a rare individual who possessed enough resources to rely on this pillar of financial stability alone. The four vignettes that follow illustrate how wealthy individuals, through rather different means, maintained their economic status in old age.

We begin with Mehitable Wadsworth—not only Hartford's wealthiest old woman, but by leaps and bounds Hartford's wealthiest woman of any age. (Financially Mehitable outdid most Hartford men as well—only her own son Daniel held more assets than she did at the time of her death at age eighty-two in 1817.) Mehitable's tax list amounted to $1,295 in 1806 when the average was around $80. Such a list reflected holdings that included livestock, two coaches, one chaise,

324 ounces of silver plate, $18,800 in bank stock, and extensive real estate holdings including a store.[149]

How did an elderly woman come to own so much property? Put simply, she was the widow of Jeremiah Wadsworth, the scion of a distinguished family and a successful businessman in his own right. Jeremiah's ancestor William Wadsworth was an original proprietor of Hartford who by 1675 had already amassed a sizable estate worth £1,677.[150] From these beginnings the Wadsworths played an active part in Hartford's civic affairs through the nineteenth century. Jeremiah increased the family wealth through trade with the West Indies and local entrepreneurship. In addition, Jeremiah combined his business acumen with patriotism and held important posts during the Revolutionary War. In short, Jeremiah Wadsworth was "the foremost citizen of Hartford during the Revolutionary period and the years following."[151]

Jeremiah Wadsworth's assets were so large that when he died in 1804 at the age of sixty he was able to leave both his wife Mehitable and his son Daniel huge legacies—setting up his son did not require him to deprive his widow of any comforts. Unlike most widows who received only use rights to property, Mehitable was given her inheritance outright. During her marriage, Mehitable had been accustomed to genteel living. Control of enormous wealth assured that even if her physical and mental strength failed and family members deserted her, her thirteen-year widowhood would remain materially easy.[152] If Jeremiah had elected to give Mehitable only use rights to property as was customary, she would still have been comfortable, but perhaps far less so than she was. Sheer material abundance and the independence it afforded was one way to vanquish financial worries in old age.

Because almost no one had assets like the Wadsworths, most who remained well-off in old age had to rely on different methods. Mason Fitch Cogswell was a Yale-educated physician and surgeon who came to Hartford in 1789 to set up a practice. Mason's family was respectable (his father was a minister) but far from wealthy. When he came to Hartford as a young man Mason had neither independent wealth nor status as a member of an established family. His tax list for 1793 reveals he owned neither land, real estate, animals, nor taxable luxury goods.[153] Nevertheless, the newcomer built financial success upon a combination of raw ability—he was once described as "the youngest scholar, but the most distinguished, of his class" at Yale—and unceasing toil. As one observer put it, "he was a rare example of the amount of fatigue which can be undergone, and of the arduous labor which can be performed by one who is willing to spend and be spent in the discharge of his duty."[154] Mason made thousands of professional calls every year (including many to the Wadsworth's home) and helped organize the American Asylum for the Deaf at Hartford and the Connecticut Medical Society.[155]

Over time these exertions paid off. By 1814 his tax list had quintupled in size from 1793. Now aged fifty-three, Mason owned a horse, forty-one acres of land, a chaise, a gold watch, and $200 in bank stock and could be counted among Hartford's prosperous.[156] Yet the onset of old age did not slow Dr. Cogswell's pace. Perhaps the desire to settle his five children propelled him to continue his frantic work schedule. Though "in his latter days he would sometimes complain that his friends had deserted him . . . and wondered that they did not continue to employ him as before," he maintained enough clients to keep him "active and assiduous in the performance of his professional engagements" until the very week of his death in 1830 at age sixty-nine.[157] Mason Cogswell's formula for continued financial health in old age was the same self-reliant strategy that had earned him prominence in the first place—intense work. Because his health remained good until the last few days of his life he was able to maintain in old age the hard won assets he had accumulated over his active career. If his health had failed, forcing him to slow his pace, Cogswell may well have been less financially secure.

Pantry Jones, a Hartford farmer, was also fairly well-to-do in old age. Though Pantry was related to one of Hartford's founding families, there is no evidence that he inherited any sizable estate. We know little about his early life except that he married Jerusha Cadwell in 1741 and that the marriage produced no children. Perhaps because he had no immediate heirs, Pantry seems to have held on to most of his property as he aged. In 1795—one year before his death at age eighty-one—he owned two oxen, four cows, two horses, 102 acres of land, a chaise, a brick house and some other buildings.[158] The men sent by the Probate Court to inventory his estate after his death listed among his belongings such niceties as a set of china cups and saucers, silver buttons, a silver tankard, and silver shoe buckles and valued his total worth at about £4,227 (about $14,100).[159] All told his estate brought him an income of around $3,000 annually.[160]

Without children to work his land, Pantry may have hired laborers or leased out his property when he himself became to old to work it properly. Whatever his system, he extracted more than enough income from his estate to avoid selling off property.[161] Ironically, not having children probably allowed Pantry to remain financially comfortable until his death—if he had had offspring, he might have parceled out his holdings earlier. For poorer people, the lack of children to provide support in old age could mean the difference between comfort and destitution. Pantry Jones offers an interesting contrast to this scenario, showing that for those with sufficient resources the absence of children's financial support had no negative consequences.

Yet the Jones story is only half told if we stop at Pantry's death. Though Pantry sailed through old age unencumbered by and independent of family relations, his widow Jerusha could not. Her experience, stemming from inheritance practices that made most women temporary users of property rather than owners, shows how easily even a well-to-do woman could fall into financial difficulties once a spouse died.[162] Jerusha was younger than Pantry but still an old woman of seventy-three when her husband died. Most likely, the productive abilities she possessed in her younger years were largely dissipated by this age. Thus in her old age she depended entirely on the provisions Pantry made for her in his will. No doubt Pantry himself was aware of this and hence set out a generous plan for her support. He willed Jerusha the use of their conjugal house, garden, and outbuildings as well as the use of two cows, a horse, "my riding chair," and all his household furniture and implements. He also decreed that she would receive an annuity of $150 paid by two nephews who, in exchange, received large gifts of real estate that more than offset the annuity. These nephews, John and Nathaniel Jones, were also supposed to provide Jerusha with pasture and hay for her animals and firewood for herself.[163]

This arrangement effectively eliminated the independence from kin that the Joneses had enjoyed when Pantry was alive and placed Jerusha at the mercy of her nephews-in-law. Pantry's provisions for his widow were generous but did not take into account the unscrupulousness his heirs were capable of. The rest of Jerusha's life was spent embroiled in one lawsuit after another as she attempted to collect the money and goods due her. The records of the Hartford City Court include at least ten lawsuits from 1804 to 1809, all revolving around the fact that neither John nor Nathaniel Jones ever paid Jerusha's annuity or provided her with firewood or animal fodder. In almost every case the court decided in Jerusha's favor but somehow the nephews still never paid.[164] It is likely that Jerusha died without ever seeing a cent of her promised annuity.

Pantry Jones remarked in his will that his wife Jerusha had "been industrious and Assisting in procuring our Estate."[165] Despite Pantry's wish to recompense Jerusha's contribution, Jerusha had to fight for her due portion and even then got nothing. Had she been given full possession of her husband's estate, and hence independence from kin, such problems would have been avoided. Unfortunately, no matter how financially secure a married woman was, inheritance practices that denied women outright ownership of resources in widowhood could dramatically reduce financial security and leave women vulnerable to difficulties. In old age Jerusha Jones experienced both wealth and want, independence and dependence, illustrating just how porous economic boundaries could be for the elderly.

Luther Savage, a farmer and merchant, provides our final example of a wealthy old person. Whether he was born in Hartford we do not know, but by 1792 he appeared on Hartford's tax rolls with modest holdings. Like Mason Cogswell, Luther Savage seems to have built his estate from the ground up. At the age of thirty-four he held no land in Hartford though he had a horse and perhaps a dwelling house. About ten years later his property had grown substantially, now he held livestock, fifty-six acres of land, a chaise, two silver watches, a three-story store and other buildings.[166] By the time of his death in 1835 at age seventy-six, he had accumulated over $20,000 of real and personal property that included bank stock and shares in Hartford's budding Aetna Fire Insurance company.[167] Luther Savage, like the other wealthy people seen so far, seems to have elected to hold on to his property rather than disperse large portions of it to relatives before his death.

Unfortunately, late in life Luther's health failed so dramatically that he became "incapable of managing his affairs and of taking care of himself."[168] As a result his brother Timothy Savage instigated legal proceedings to have a conservator appointed to Luther who would have the power to manage his financial affairs and the responsibility of seeing that Luther was provided for. Typically the rationale in such cases was that the old person left to his own devices might be taken advantage of, or might dispose of property unwisely. The court agreed that Luther Savage was in such danger and Timothy himself along with his son and another relative seem to have been appointed caretakers of Luther's estate. Luther Savage's case is interesting because it illustrates one of the few institutionalized means an old person had to safeguard property.[169] Overtaken by sickness, a fate he shared with many poorer elderly, Luther remained safe from financial distress because the court stepped in to aid him. When he died soon after, his property was intact.

These four cases illustrate the differing strategies people devised to maintain a privileged economic position in old age. For Mehitable Wadsworth the strategy was simple—control of great wealth swept away financial worries and made work or help from others irrelevant. Yet this method depended more on her husband's planning than any preparation she herself could make. The fact that her husband had made her the outright owner of her property (rather than just the user of it while she lived, as most widows were), allowed her a degree of economic security very few women knew. Men like Mason Cogswell adopted a more active approach. Having toiled hard for material success all his life, Cogswell remained at labor in old age to ensure continued financial well-being. Of course, such a strategy required good health. Had Mason become feeble and been forced to curtail his medical practice, his finances would surely have suffered. Pantry Jones probably employed a variation of the work strategy just described—he made his land work for him once he could no longer work himself. Still, the formula that worked for him was impossible for his widow. Jerusha Jones, unlike Mehitable Wadsworth, saw her fortunes fade once her husband died and control over conjugal property passed out of her reach. Finally, Luther Savage (though unwittingly, of course) used court intervention to safeguard his resources in old age.

Significant wealth in old age, however it was maintained, made for a rare independence which protected a lucky few from the economic effects of health crises, the inability to labor, or the failure of family to provide support. Unlike their poorer neighbors, the rich elderly had a wide margin of security to fall back on if these calamities occurred. However, as the examples offered above make clear, remaining wealthy in old age was partly a matter of planning, but good fortune also played an important role.

Having looked more closely at the economic experiences of elderly men and women we can now return to the question posed at the end of chapter 4. Just what kind of a society was early national America and what place did the aged have in it? The answer is that it was a society that stressed self-reliance and independence over familial or communal responsibility. For the aged this meant that the best way to ensure a comfortable old age was to provide it for oneself. Individual efforts at maintenance were therefore the most important economic supports in old age. For some, these supports remained strong and reliable throughout old age resulting in a materially easy experience. But despite the importance of retaining independence in old age, threats to autonomy were serious. Poor health was a principle menace, one which elderly people could neither predict or control (despite the claims of medical writers), yet which routinely threw aged people into economic crisis. For some the chance of economic stability in old age was threatened further by the fact of being female or of having always been poor. Less prosperous men and women of all kinds were especially likely to encounter economic trouble as they aged since their labor generally brought less remuneration and their access to property was often blocked. Therefore self-reliance was the best economic strategy in old age but it was not universally available.

The fact that it was impossible for a substantial number of elderly people to maintain themselves does not, in itself, prove that the aged were especially vulnerable to hardship in early national America. That proof comes when we acknowledge that once individual efforts failed, other supports were unreliable. Both family and community have been much vaunted as cushions for aged people in need. The truth is that family *might* work to protect aged people economically, but family failed often enough to make poverty a real fear for those entering their "declining years." When family assistance fell short the consequences were grave, because the larger community had no coherent or well-developed system to ensure economic stability for the aged. Old people's needs were addressed through a poor relief system that extended only the barest subsistence and never acknowledged that the challenges facing indigent aged people were different from the poor of other ages. Though Americans would slowly come to confront the economic problems of growing old and devise formal, institutionalized solutions to them, these efforts lay in the future.[170]

Chapter 4 demonstrated that economic fortunes tended to decline in old age. We are now in a better position to understand why. Early national society was not ruthless to its aged citizens, it simply expected them to make their own way much of the time. Unfortunately, because old age and decline went hand in hand the aged were at particular risk of economic uncertainty and hardship due, in many cases, to factors beyond their control. Under such circumstances many middling and wealthy people did manage to handle their economic affairs on an almost exclusively private, individualized basis, successfully avoiding the worst pitfalls in their path. Yet the elderly poor were numerous enough to serve as a warning, both to contemporaries and historians alike, that the economic hazards of growing old were formidable indeed.

NOTES

1. Those who see earlier eras of American history as more favorable for the elderly, such as David Hackett Fischer, suggest that most people enjoyed at least modest comfort in old age. As for the poor elderly, "There were not many of them." See David Hackett Fischer, *Growing Old in America*, expanded ed. (New York: Oxford University Press, 1978), 61.

2. Eventually needy came to be defined as having neither an annual income of more than $96 nor an estate worth $960. Department of War, Revolutionary Pensions, 26 December 1828, manuscript in Hartford County Court Records, Revolutionary War Pension Applications, CSL.

3. Theda Skocpol shows how Civil War pensions eventually evolved into America's "first large-scale nationally funded old age and disability system." (*Protecting Mothers and Soldiers: The Political Origins of Social Policy in the United States* [Cambridge: Harvard University Press, 1992], 1.) The 1818 pension act for Revolutionary veterans set the stage for this development by pioneering the concept that service (as opposed to disability or death) justified state-supported pensions. Though the 1818 act restricted service pensions to indigent veterans only, the concept was broadened in 1832 when another act extended federal pensions to all who had served whether needy or not. For the text of these various pension acts see W.T.R. Saffell, *Records of the Revolutionary War* (Philadelphia: G.G. Evans, 1860), 511–525.

4. Specifically each applicant was asked for an inventory of his estate and an explanation of how any property had been disposed of since 1818.

5. RPA.

6. Pension applications are a significant but underutilized source for the Revolutionary and early national period. John C. Dann's *The Revolution Remembered: Eyewitness Accounts of the War for Independence* (Chicago: University of Chicago Press, 1980) is one of the few books that has taken advantage of some of the unique information they provide.

7. Of the Hartford County applications still extant some were indeed rejected by the War Department, but the reason was as often insufficient military service as being too well-off to qualify. In the majority of cases, however, both the Hartford County Court and the United States War Department were satisfied with the accuracy of applicants' testimony. We know this by comparing names of applicants with the names listed in *Report from the Secretary of War... in Relation to the Pension Establishment of the United States* (Washington: Duff Green, 1835), 37–45.

8. Of the 244 applicants represented in the Hartford County Court records, 171 were granted pensions under the 1818 act and also met the stricter 1820 requirements for proof of indigence—either remaining on the pension rolls continuously, or if removed, subsequently reinstated after having successfully reproven their indigence. This chapter uses only data from this group of 171 as there can be little doubt that the information provided in their applications was accurate and reliable. To establish the outcome of applications, names were checked against *Report from the Secretary of War*, 37–45, showing the status of Hartford County pensioners.

9. These figures are derived from the list of names presented in *Report from the Secretary of War*, 37–44. The 198 figure includes some that were initially dropped after 1820 but were eventually reinstated. Though there were 198 successful pensioners in Hartford County, the applications of only 171 of these men are preserved among the Hartford County Court records. This chapter is based on this latter group.

10. These figures come from calculating the age breakdown of Connecticut's population in 1820 from census data and applying the same percentages to Hartford County's population. Connecticut census data is from *Historical Statistics of the United States Colonial Times to 1970*, part 1 (White Plains NY: Kraus International Publications,

1989), 25. Hartford County population data is from Charles Hopkins Clark, "The Growth of the County," in *Memorial History of Hartford County*, vol. 1, ed. J. Hammond Trumbull (Boston: Edward L. Osgood, 1886), 208.

11. Though these figures might reflect a sudden upsurge in elderly paupers after 1818, this is unlikely. While the precise percentage of aged poor probably varied somewhat with larger economic fluctuations, evidence from pension applications—in which veterans testified of indigence lasting years or even decades—suggests the chronic nature of such poverty.

12. Michael Zimmerman reaches a similar conclusion for New York City in the first half of the nineteenth-century stating that, "the aged ... were a significant segment of the poor and dependent population of the city." ("Old Age Poverty in Preindustrial New York City," in *Growing Old in America* 2d ed., ed. Beth B. Hess [New Brunswick, NJ: Transaction Books, 1980], 70.) How the number of elderly poor in early national America compares to today is a difficult question. A report from the Government Accounting Office estimates that in the 1980s roughly 14 percent of those sixty-five or older fell below the poverty line, with women, minorities, and the "old" old particularly at risk. Unfortunately an accurate comparison of this finding with those from 1790 to 1830 (adjusting for differences in age categories, social services provided, etc.) would require far more extensive study than is possible here. See Government Accounting Office testimony in U.S. House of Representatives, Select Committee on Aging, *Old, Poor, and Forgotten: Elderly Americans Living in Poverty* (Washington D.C.: Government Printing Office, 1992), 66–93.

13. Letter from Calvin Goddard to Ebenezer Huntington, 8 April 1818, A–H Miscellaneous Letters, CHS.

14. At the time of the 1818 act, no one in Congress had much sense of how many destitute veterans existed and would apply for pensions. However, the number that were granted pensions under the 1818 act exceeded most expectations and led many to conclude that some applications were fraudulent. This conclusion resulted in the 1820 act requiring more detailed proof of destitution. As a result of these new requirements (and probably a less sympathetic attitude toward applicants) about 35 percent of those initially granted pensions were removed from the rolls. Of about 18,880 original pensioners, about 12,331 remained in 1822. However by 1823 many who had been so removed had succeeded in proving their destitution and were again granted pensions. Thus the level of fraud in applications from 1818 was probably far lower than suspected at the time. For the history of pension legislation see, William Henry Glasson, *History of Military Pension Legislation in the United States*, Studies in History, Economics and Public Law, vol. 12, no. 3 (New York: Columbia University Press, 1900); and *Index of Revolutionary War Pension Applications in the National Archives*, rev. ed. (Washington D.C.: National Genealogical Society, 1976), x.

15. Fischer, *Growing Old in America*, 61.

16. Sharp Camp, 2 August 1820, RPA. Camp is one of a few Hartford County African American veterans whose pension records survive. Unfortunately, such records are insufficient to analyze the role of race in old age poverty.

17. Ira Clarke, 1 August 1820, RPA.

18. James Francis, 2 April 1822, RPA.

19. Josiah Bicknell, 1 August 1820, RPA.

20. James Anderson, 10 August 1830, RPA.

21. Cato Black, 2 August 1820, RPA.

22. Mark Filley, 21 August 1820; William Francis, 1 August 1820; Peter Freeman, 2 August 1820; Daniel Wright, 3 April 1829; Thomas Palmer, 1 August 1824, RPA.

23. William Smith, 22 November 1821, RPA.

24. Amos Curtis, 9 August 1820, RPA.

25. Timothy Stephens, 1 August 1820, RPA.

26. Paul Faler describes the difficulties shoemakers faced in this period. Beginning with the War of 1812 there was "a sharp decline in [shoemaking] business activity . . . and almost complete stagnation in the depression that followed the war." Indeed in the 1820s business was still only "slowly and haltingly" recovering. ("Workingmen, Mechanics and Social Change: Lynn, Massachusetts, 1800–1860," [Ph.D. diss., University of Wisconsin, 1971], 162.) As a result practitioners of this trade may have been especially likely to experience destitution.

27. Abel Alling, 3 May 1828, RPA.
28. Ibid., 1 August 1820.
29. Timothy Olmsted, 2 August 1820, RPA.
30. Jonathan Pasco, 18 February 1831, RPA.
31. Asa Hillyer, 2 August 1820, RPA.
32. Amasa Green, 18 August 1825, RPA.
33. Elijah Deming, 2 August 1820, RPA.
34. Peter Magira, 1 August 1820, RPA.
35. Elkanah Smith, 17 August 1820, RPA.
36. Elijah Deming, 2 August 1820, RPA.
37. John Collar, 1 August 1820, RPA.
38. Joseph Clark, 1 August 1820, RPA.
39. David Jerome, 1 August 1820, RPA.

40. Georges Minois describes how in early-medieval Europe "the poor man had to go on working for as long as his strength permitted." If he could not and he had no family "he was immediately relegated to the ranks of the beggars." (*History of Old Age: From Antiquity to the Renaissance*, trans. Sarah Hanbury Tenison [Chicago: University of Chicago Press, 1989], 138.) Likewise Keith Thomas relates how "for most manual workers old age meant, first, a move to lighter (and lower-paid) work, then a decline to abject dependence." ("Age and Authority in Early Modern England," *Proceedings of the British Academy* 62 [1976]: 240.) This finding holds true for New York City in the early-nineteenth century as well. See Zimmerman, "Old Age Poverty in Preindustrial New York City," 68. Jill Quadagno also identifies labor as a necessity for many elderly people in *Aging in Early Industrial Society: Work, Family, and Social Policy in Nineteenth-Century England* (New York: Academic Press, 1982), 22. The pattern of continued work for the aged, though often in lower paid, less demanding occupations, appears to have extended into the twentieth century as well. See Roger L. Ransom and Richard Sutch, "The Labor of Older Americans: Retirement of Men On and Off the Job, 1870–1937," *Journal of Economic History* 46 (March 1986), 1–30.

41. For a detailed discussion of Connecticut's statutes on family responsibility see Edward Capen, *The Historical Development of the Poor Law of Connecticut*, Studies in History, Economics and Public Law, vol. 22 (New York: Columbia University Press, 1905), 75–76, 116.

42. Almost 95 percent of the 171 veterans who successfully applied for pensions in Hartford County described their household's composition, from which the household-type percentages are derived.

43. It should be noted that the 20 percent who reported living alone did not necessarily head households. Though some did, others were solitary transients or poorhouse residents. See chapter 6 for more on households of the aged.

44. However, the fact that 20 percent of applicants lived alone strongly hints that family supports for many were weak, thereby increasing the chance of destitution.

45. Connecticut statutes made clear that close relatives—that is fathers, mothers, grandparents, children, and grandchildren—were legally obliged, if able, to "relieve" any poor family they might have and set a penalty for those who failed to do so. Law of May

1715 in J. Hammond Trumbull, ed., *The Public Records of the Colony of Connecticut*, vol. 1 (Hartford CT: Brown & Parsons, 1850), 503. How strongly enforced this law was is unclear. However at least one case of grandchildren being sued for failure to support their indigent grandmother was seen in Hartford County Court in the early national period. The suit was brought against the grandchildren by town officials who had been saddled with the aged woman's expenses. Olive Montague case, March and August 1820 sessions, HCC. In any event, the state could only require those who had assets to support needy kin. Since the relations of pension applicants were often poor themselves, they could not have been prosecuted for failure to help.

46. Elijah Smith, 2 August 1820, RPA.
47. Elijah Monrose, 2 August 1820, RPA.
48. Timothy Hatch, 2 August 1820, RPA.
49. William Steel, 1 August 1820, RPA.
50. Nathaniel Humphrey, 1 August 1820, RPA.
51. Philo Treat, 1 August 1820, RPA.
52. Daniel Brewer, 1 August 1820, RPA.
53. John Warren, 1 August 1820, RPA. Indeed, the anecdotal evidence presented in pension applications suggests that elderly people with daughters and no sons had a thinner margin of economic safety than those with sons. This would not be surprising for two reasons. First, women did not control property as men did and some husbands may have been more reluctant or tardy in contributing to the support of their parents-in-law than their own parents. Secondly, when women did have income or property it was likely to be substantially smaller than that of male counterparts. This observation comes from the greater frequency with which daughters unable to provide support are mentioned by applicants than sons unable to provide support. Further study drawing on other sources would have to be done to confirm this finding.

54. Abraham Wright, 9 August 1820, RPA.
55. Thomas Stedman, 1 August 1820, RPA.
56. Benjamin Reed, 19 August 1824, RPA.
57. Among this group there were a total of fifty-seven dependent sons compared to seventy-five dependent daughters.
58. Peter Magira, 1 August 1820, RPA.
59. Richard Belden, 1 August 1820, RPA.
60. This speculation comes from a reading of pension applications only. Further research is needed to show it definitively.
61. Josiah Steel, 10 August 1820, RPA.
62. Thomas Palmer, 1 August 1824, RPA.
63. Elijah Noble, 1 August 1820, 13 August 1823, RPA.
64. Lemuel Fox, 1 August 1820, RPA.
65. David Rothman, *The Discovery of the Asylum: Social Order and Disorder in the New Republic* (Boston: Little, Brown & Co., 1971).
66. James H. Cassedy notes Benjamin Franklin's interest in a plan for housing the aged poor in *Demography in Early America: Beginnings of the Statistical Mind, 1600–1800* (Cambridge MA: Harvard University Press, 1969), 245. Thomas Paine's proposal for a nationally-funded pension system for the elderly is briefly discussed in W. Andrew Achenbaum, *Old Age in the New Land: The American Experience Since 1790* (Baltimore: Johns Hopkins University Press, 1978), 83.
67. Very small-scale institutions to aid the poor elderly existed in Europe as early as the fifteenth century. See Minois, *History of Old Age*, 245–6. However a conception of the aged as a special group of needy was slow in emerging and elderly women initially drew more attention than aged men. The first American organization to aid elderly women specifically was founded in New York City around 1815. By 1817 Quakers in Philadelphia

had organized a society to house elderly poor women. See Carole Haber, "The Old Folks at Home: The Development of Institutionalized Care for the Aged in Nineteenth-Century Philadelphia," *Pennsylvania Magazine of History and Biography* 101 (April 1977): 240–257. In France, likewise, the first half of the century saw the beginning of the Little Sisters of the Poor, a religious order focusing on care of the elderly poor. For more on the latter see, Paul Milcent, *Jeanne Jugan: Humble, So As to Love More* (London: Darton, Longman and Todd, 1980).

68. *Acts and Laws of his Majesties Colony of Connecticut in New England* (1702; reprint, Hartford CT: The Acorn Club, 1901), 94–95.

69. "Hartford Town Votes Volume I 1635–1716," *Collections of the Connecticut Historical Society* 6 (1897): 121.

70. Ibid., 123, 224, 233, 248, 253.

71. The system of keeping town records in the home of the town clerk, rather than in a central and permanent repository, undoubtedly contributed to the loss of many records.

72. HTR.

73. Mary K. Talcott, "The Town Since 1784" in *Memorial History of Hartford County*, vol. 1, ed. Trumbull, 361.

74. Resolution of the 3d Monday, January 1812, HTR.

75. U.S. Census (manuscript), Hartford CT, 1810.

76. Talcott, "The Town Since 1784," 361–2.

77. Connecticut law differentiated between "beggars" and other unsavory people who were generally sent to workhouses and paupers (poor but not criminal) who were candidates for almshouses. Edward Capen traces the development of this distinction in *The Historical Development of the Poor Law of Connecticut*.

78. At an Adjourned Meeting of the Inhabitants of the Town of Hartford, held on the 30th Day of December, 1822... (N.p., n.d.). This broadside is in the collections of CHS.

79. Prince Hull, 2 August 1820, RPA.

80. U.S. Census (manuscript), Hartford CT, 1810.

81. Vote of 30 December 1822, HTR.

82. Rothman, *The Discovery of the Asylum*, documents this trend toward institutionalization well.

83. The rules for establishing "settlement" in Connecticut towns changed over time and were the source of confusion due to their complexity and ambiguity on some issues. The best review of these rules is in Capen, *The Historical Development of the Poor Law of Connecticut*.

84. Ibid., 139–141.

85. Pensions had been given before 1818 to veterans who had been disabled in the war and to officers who had remained in service until the war's end. Widows of Revolutionary casualties had also been provided with pensions from 1780 on. The 1818 legislation, however, greatly broadened the numbers receiving federal money.

86. Department of War, "Revolutionary Pensions."

87. *Report from the Secretary of War.*

88. The wage rate for agricultural laborers comes from Donald R. Adams, Jr., "Wage Rates in the Early National Period: Philadelphia, 1785–1830," *Journal of Economic History* 28 (September 1968), 420. Adams provides daily wages which I converted to yearly wages on the basis of a 310-day work year. Artisans wages from the Northeast come from Robert A. Margo and Georgia C. Villaflor, "The Growth of Wages in Antebellum America: New Evidence," *Journal of Economic History* 47 (December 1987), 893. Because of fluctuations in the 1820s I averaged wage rates for the decade to arrive at $1.34/day or $416/year (for 310 days). See also Kenneth L. Sokoloff and Georgia C. Villaflor, "The Market for Manufacturing Workers during Early Industrialization: The American Northeast,

1820 to 1860," in *Strategic Factors in Nineteenth Century American Economic History*, ed. Claudia Goldin and Hugh Rockoff (Chicago: University of Chicago Press, 1992), 29–65. Information on ministers' salaries comes from *History of the Parish of Christ Church Hartford* (Hartford CT: Belknap & Warfield, 1895), 70–71.

    89. However only slightly. Given the apparently widespread concern about fraudulent claims arising from the large number of applicants after 1818, one senses that Revolutionary pensioners were looked on by some as the early national equivalent of today's vilified "welfare mothers." Evidently public indignation over possible fraud was especially strong in Connecticut. See Glasson, *History of Military Pension Legislation in the United States*, 37–39.

    90. Jehiel Latimer, 2 August 1820, RPA.

    91. David Jerome, 1 August 1820, RPA. For a fascinating account of the life of another poor Revolutionary veteran who subsisted in part by the charity of friends see Alfred F. Young, "George Robert Twelves Hewes (1742–1840): A Boston Shoemaker and the Memory of the American Revolution," *William and Mary Quarterly*, 3d series, 38 (October 1981): 561–623.

    92. Isaac Cluff, 1 August 1820, RPA.

    93. Richard Case, 1 August 1820, RPA.

    94. Henry Baldwin, "Social Life After the Revolution," *Memorial History of Hartford County*, vol. 1, ed. Trumbull, 602.

    95. Mary Ann Cowles, Diary, 14 January 1824, CHS.

    96. Shubael Bartlett, Diary, 9 June 1829, CHS.

    97. *Constitution of the Charitable Society* (Hartford CT: 1793[?]).

    98. Charitable Society Papers, 1792–1871, CHS.

    99. In the 1790s outlays to men and women were about equal. However, with each passing decade the Society made increasingly more outlays to women than men so that by the 1820s there were at least 521 payments made to women and only about 117 made to men. For more on the special circumstances of poor widows and relief given them see Lisa Wilson, *Life After Death: Widows in Pennsylvania 1750–1850* (Philadelphia: Temple University Press, 1992), chapter 3.

    100. Charitable Society Papers.

    101. Ibid.

    102. *A Review of the Records of the Widows' Society of Hartford 1825–1892* (Hartford CT: Case, Lockwood & Brainard Co., 1892), 6.

    103. West Hartford Society of Friends, Quaker Records 1800–1823, reel 404, CSL.

    104. Hartford First Church of Christ, Records 1684–1930, vol. 15, reel 503, CSL.

    105. As seen in chapter 4, average list sizes for taxpayers in their fifties, sixties, and seventies were between $60 and $150 in any given year. Since taxpayers as a group tended to be better off than the overall population, I use as examples here people with lists sizes below $150. This figure does not include any poll taxes that may have been assessed as flat taxes polls bore no relation to wealth.

    106. An individual's "list" was not the total value of his estate but a fraction, based on complicated assessment rules. The list amount was used much as today's adjusted gross income is employed—as a base from which to calculate taxes due. See appendix B for further information.

    107. Hartford Town Tax List, South District, 1808, CHS.

    108. Hartford Town Tax List, South District, 1808, CHS.

    109. Hartford Town Tax List, South District, 1816, CHS.

    110. Rebecca Noyes, Diary, 1801–1831, CHS.

    111. Elisha Niles, Diary, 13 April 1816, CHS.

    112. Morris Maltby to John Maltby [Sr.], 23 July 1834, Maltby Family Papers, CHS.

    113. William Seward Pierson, Diary, 17 November 1808, CSL.

114. Hezekiah Griswold case, petition of 5 April 1793, CG.

115. It would be nice to be able to discuss the occupational differences between the poor and the middling people. Unfortunately such information is lacking. One suspects that middling people were able to accumulate more resources during life than the poor in part because they pursued more remunerative occupations than those who became destitute in old age.

116. Rebecca Noyes, Diary, 1801–1831, CHS.

117. Elisha Hinman to Shadrach Osborn, 12 March 1795, Shadrach Osborn Papers, CHS.

118. Franklin Bowditch Dexter, *Biographical Sketches of the Graduates of Yale College*, vol. 1 (New York: Henry Holt & Co., 1885), 701–2.

119. James Cogswell, Diary, 1 May 1790, CHS.

120. Ibid., 11 July 1790.

121. Eliphalet Williams to William Williams, 9 February 1803, Williams Family Papers, CHS. Lifetime pastorates were quite normal in Congregational churches of the time. However, when age and infirmity diminished a pastor's abilities arrangements were sometimes made to hire a co-pastor. In such cases the senior minister might accept a lower salary. Williams may have been in such a situation. For more on the long tenures of clergymen see Donald Scott, *From Office to Profession: The New England Ministry, 1750–1850* (Philadelphia: University of Pennsylvania Press, 1978), 3–6.

122. Timothy Maltby to John Maltby, 12 May 1828, Maltby Family Papers, CHS.

123. Ibid., 30 April 1835.

124. In the few exceptional cases when retirement did occur in the abrupt modern sense, public offices were involved. For example the seventy-four-year-old Joseph Cooke decided after forty years of public service to "retire" from his post as a Connecticut Assembly member citing "the burthen which the personal responsibilities attached to every man who hath been in Council must have experienced." Such a post with its fixed duties was more than Cooke wanted to manage in old age. Yet even Cooke practiced the tapering off of labor described above—though he quit the Assembly, he retained his post as judge in his county's probate and county courts. Joseph P. Cooke to William Williams, 27 May 1803, Williams Family Papers, CHS.

125. Mary Vinton to Francis Vinton, 11 January 1825, Francis Vinton Correspondence, CHS.

126. Ibid., 22 July 1827.

127. Benjamin Gilman to Samuel Odiorne, 11 May 1819, Benjamin Clark Gilman Correspondence, CHS.

128. Ibid., 17 April 1821.

129. Bartlett, Diary, 14, 26 July 1825, CHS.

130. Ibid., 28 September 1830.

131. William Williams to Solomon Williams, 16 July 1810, Williams Family Papers, CHS.

132. Cogswell, Diary, 18 February 1791.

133. James W. Robbins to Thomas Robbins, 31 March 1825 and 5 February 1827, Thomas Robbins Papers, CHS.

134. It should be noted that technically, relatives (parents, children, grandparents, and grandchildren) of needy people were legally obliged to aid in their support. Thus is could be argued that the Robbins sons were merely fulfilling their legal obligation. However the fact that they did so voluntarily suggests that their interests went far beyond simply fulfilling the legal minimum.

135. Cogswell, Diary, 17 May 1790.

136. Ibid., 9 December 1790.

137. John Thomas case, petition of 28 March 1780, CG.

138. Chancellor Kent of New York quoted in R. Carlyle Buley, *The American Life Convention 1906–1952: A Study in the History of Life Insurance*, vol. 1 (New York: Appleton-Century-Crofts, Inc., 1953), 33. The public was probably exposed to the concept of corporate annuities through advertisements in almanacs and other publications. For example, the 1816 diary of Samuel Talcott was penned on old almanacs, one of which announced the incorporation of the Pennsylvania Company and explained its basic policies. (Samuel Talcott, Diary, 1816, CHS.)

139. A. Fingland Jack, *An Introduction to the History of Life Assurance* (New York: E.P. Dutton & Co., 1912), 177.

140. Elizur Stockwell case, petition of 2 February 1768, CG.

141. Untitled page dated 19 January 1819, Coventry, Norman Brigham Correspondence, CHS.

142. Pantry Jones, probate packet, will of 28 February 1794, Hartford County Probate Packets 1641–1880, CSL.

143. Daniel Wadsworth to Charles Chauncey Esq., 4 October 1824, Daniel Wadsworth Papers, CHS.

144. A letter from J.A. Flint to Thomas Robbins indicates the Society paid a "dividend" for headstone expenses. (28 July 1825, Thomas Robbins Papers, CHS.) Societies to aid the families of unfortunate clergy had existed in America for some time. For example, the Society for the Relief of the Widows and Orphans of the Clergy of the Protestant Episcopal Church was established in 1762. Records of a state branch of this society in 1818 indicate it collected dues from members and paid out benefits to clergy suffering under "age, sickness, or misfortune." See *Rules of the Society... in the State of South Carolina; Adopted the 21st day of October, 1818* (Charleston: A.E. Miller, 1819). It is possible that Hartford's Ministers Annuity Society operated similarly.

145. Mechanics Society of Hartford, *Act of Incorporation and By-Laws of the Mechanics Society of Hartford* (Hartford CT: P.B. Gleason & Co., 1829), 11, 3.

146. Between 1821 and 1824 the law limited conservators to "idiots" and the insane only. In all other years between 1750 and 1830 conservators could be appointed to anyone unable to manage their own affairs for any reason. The only permanent alterations to the statutes concerning conservators were those that afforded greater protection to the ward by codifying the conservator's responsibilities more explicitly. See Capen, *The Historical Development of the Poor Law of Connecticut*, 76, 118.

147. Dorothy Eno case, petition of 29 March 1819, CG.

148. Whenever conservators were appointed to old people with property, their heirs stood to gain as much from the arrangement as the elderly person himself. Indeed, it should be noted that some attempts were made to use the conservator system against old people to deprive them of full control over property.

149. Hartford Town Tax List, North District, 1806, CHS.

150. Mary K. Talcott "The Original Proprietors," in *Memorial History of Hartford County*, ed. Trumbull, vol. 1, 264–5.

151. Mary K. Talcott, "Prominent Business Men" in *Memorial History of Hartford County*, ed. Trumbull, vol. 1, 656.

152. Its worth noting that Mehitable's family did not desert her. Her son Daniel was quite dutiful and affectionate and she seems to have been surrounded by family in Hartford. (Wadsworth Family Papers, 1756–1866, CHS.)

153. Hartford Town Tax List, North District, 1793, CHS.

154. George Sumner and Gurdon W. Russell, *Sketches of Physicians in Hartford* (Hartford CT: Case, Lockwood & Brainard Co., 1890), 12–13.

155. Records of Mason Fitch Cogswell's practice are preserved in his daybooks held by CHS.

156. Hartford Town Tax List, North District, 1814, CHS.
157. Sumner and Russell, *Sketches of Physicians in Hartford*, 31, 14.
158. Hartford Town Tax List, North District, 1795, CHS.
159. Pantry Jones, probate packet, Hartford County Probate Packets 1641–1880, CSL.
160. John Stanton and wife v. John and Nathaniel Jones, May term 1805, HCiC.
161. The tax records show Pantry Jones with less land in 1796 than in 1795. However the 1796 list may have been made after death so I do not consider it evidence that he divested himself of property while living.
162. For an explanation of women's legal rights to property at this time see Marylynn Salmon, *Women and the Law of Property in Early America* (Chapel Hill: University of North Carolina Press, 1986).
163. Pantry Jones, probate packet, will of 28 February 1794 and codicil of 9 April 1796, Hartford County Probate Packets 1641–1880, CSL.
164. John Stanton v. John Jones, October term 1804; John Stanton and wife v. John and Nathaniel Jones, November term 1804; John Stanton v. Nathaniel Jones, October term 1805; John Stanton and wife v. Nathaniel Jones, October term 1805; John Stanton and wife v. John and Nathaniel Jones, May term 1805; John Stanton and wife v. John Jones, May term 1805; John Stanton v. Nathaniel Jones, August term 1805; John Stanton v. Nathaniel Jones in mutilated 1806 packet; John Stanton and wife v. Nathaniel Jones, October term 1806; John Stanton and wife v. John Jones, May term 1809, HCiC.
165. Pantry Jones, probate packet, will of 28 February 1794, Hartford County Probate Packets 1641–1880, CSL.
166. Hartford Town Tax Lists, North District, 1792, 1814, CHS.
167. Luther Savage case, 1835, CG.
168. Ibid.
169. Conservatorships were a relatively recent development in Connecticut law. Established in 1750 as a device to manage incompetent people with resources, they remained in force throughout Connecticut's early national period with minor changes. For a discussion of these developments see Capen, *The Historical Development of the Poor Law in Connecticut*, chapters 2 and 3.
170. Of course there is some argument over how well modern American methods of managing the elderly's financial problems have succeeded. There is evidence that even today a significant fraction of the old population is poor, in part because many fail to take advantage of government programs to assist them. For more on this see, U.S. House of Representatives, Select Committee on Aging, *Old, Poor, and Forgotten*, 66–93.

VI

Households of the Aged

In describing the spiritual and economic experiences of the aged we have gone a long ways towards capturing the nature of old age in early national America. However several facets of social experience—among them household arrangements and family life—must also be addressed. No institutions were more significant in the lives of the aged than the household and the family. This chapter begins an analysis of the elderly's domestic environment by focusing exclusively on the household; that is, the people who resided in the same dwelling with the aged. An old person's household largely determined the quality of an elderly person's daily life because it provided his or her most frequent social contacts as well as the setting for the basic tasks of living. The subsequent chapter complements and expands our understanding of the aged's daily experience by focusing on the nature and quality of their family lives. Composed of relations by blood or marriage, family members were often also household members. However, whether family members lived with their aged kin or not, their lives were interwoven with those of the elderly on many different levels.

What sorts of households did the aged live in and what led them to these arrangements? How did the households of old people differ from those of younger men and women? What changes in living arrangements could aging people expect to encounter? This chapter approaches these questions on the aged's domestic environment in two ways. We begin with an analysis of the United States census for Hartford to discover general trends in household composition in old age. Connecticut diaries, letters, and court records then help to put a human face on these findings, illustrating the variety of household arrangements employed by elderly people.

The evidence indicates that as people progressed through old age they had to accept more marginal and dependent roles within the household than they had in their younger years. First, old men and women lived among fewer people than middle aged people. The aged's households were thus reduced from the bustling social centers they had once been. Second, many old people surrendered their roles as heads of household and became subordinate members of other households. Autonomy was valued and aged individuals adopted various strategies in order to prolong control of independent households. Unfortunately, the same causes that often made the elderly economically dependent—poor health and a lack of resources—could cut off the chance to retain one's own household as well. Once a subordinate role in someone else's household became inevitable, there were several possibilities. Some were pleasant enough, some were harder to bear, and others were quite bad indeed. But whatever situation an aged person found himself in he had to be prepared for change. Due to vicissitudes in health and resources old age was a time of flux. One individual might experience several different household arrangements in old age as life was modified to meet changing needs. Overall, this was a process in which solutions to where and how the elderly lived were arrived at on an individualized basis, demanding significant flexibility from the aged at a time when resilience was likely to be low. Therefore, just as the aged were confronted with spiritual challenges and economic decline, they faced difficult adjustments at home as well.

GENERAL TRENDS IN HOUSEHOLD ARRANGEMENT

Before discussing household life for the elderly, we must first understand households generally in Hartford's early national period. The United States censuses from 1790 to 1830 are helpful in this respect, but a word about their peculiarities is in order. Unlike modern censuses with their carefully delineated categories, the first censuses enumerated the population rather idiosyncratically. Though all people in each household were counted, census takers only recorded the names of household heads. The relationships of other household members to the head were not indicated. And while census takers noted the ages of residents according to crude categories, it is

Households of the Aged 173

impossible to link age information from the census with names directly.[1] As a result, household heads' names on the censuses had to be matched with birth and death records from elsewhere.[2] About half the names on each Hartford census from 1790 to 1830 were so matched and much of the analysis that follows is based on this group.[3]

Household Size and Its Determinants

Despite these limitations, early national censuses provide important information on households in Hartford. To begin with, the censuses from 1790 to 1830 show the prevalence of different sized households. Figure 6.1 summarizes the percentage of households having different numbers of residents for all five census years. (Table 6.1 provides the exact numbers.) There are two notable features to figure 6.1. First, it is immediately obvious that most households in Hartford were large by today's standards. Residences with between four and six members account for about 33 to 42 percent of all households. Dwellings with between seven and thirteen residents comprised an equally sizable chunk of Hartford households—about 35 to 46 percent. In addition, the city had a sprinkling of even bigger households. The great majority of Hartford's people lived in relatively large households, with half the households in every census year containing six or more members.

The second notable feature of figure 6.1 is the close correspondence in the curves for all five censuses, suggesting little change in the sizes of Hartford households over the forty years between 1790 and 1830. When calculations of mean and median household size are made for the same period we find similar stability. As table 6.2 indicates, the mean was between six and seven for all years with no clear upward or downward trend. The median stayed steady at six throughout the entire period except for 1820. A number of scholars have argued that the early national period was part of a transition to a new sort of family life in America characterized by fertility control and hence smaller households.[4] We might expect such changes to have some impact on the elderly. Yet Hartford census data do not show such a change and it is therefore safe to conclude that demographic changes were not yet reshaping the experiences of the old or young in any dramatic fashion.[5]

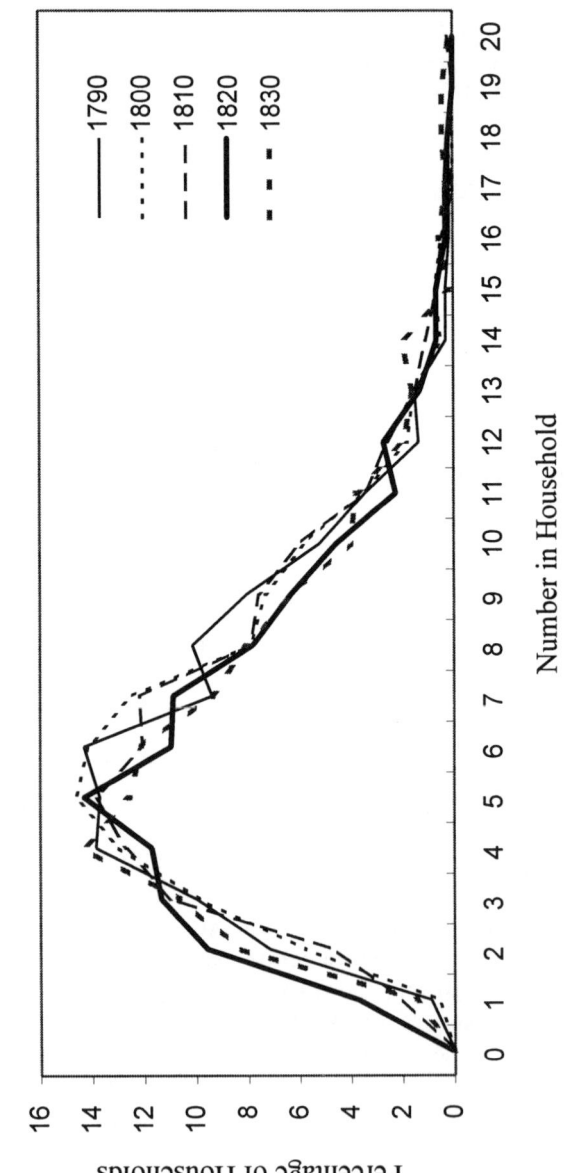

Figure 6.1. Percentage of Households by Size, 1790-1830

Source: U.S. Censuses, Hartford, CT, 1790-1830. Includes all households listed in 1790 to 1830 censuses except those few with more than twenty members.

Households of the Aged

Table 6.1. Number of Households of Different Sizes, Hartford, 1790–1830

Number in Household	1790	1800	1810	1820	1830
1	6	5	19	40	21
2	48	49	44	103	121
3	67	84	103	122	155
4	93	110	119	126	209
5	92	124	130	154	183
6	96	120	113	118	176
7	63	106	114	117	137
8	68	67	74	84	117
9	54	62	71	68	91
10	35	49	56	49	58
11	23	30	32	24	55
12	9	15	24	29	28
13	10	13	14	14	23
14	2	4	10	7	29
15	2	6	6	7	2
16	0	4	4	3	8
17	0	0	0	3	4
18	0	0	2	2	6
19	0	0	0	0	6
20	0	0	2	0	2
Total Households[a]	668	848	937	1070	1431

Source: U.S. Censuses, Hartford, CT, 1790–1830.
[a] These figures are slightly lower than the total number of households actually listed in each census because they do not include the few very large households with over twenty members.

Table 6.2. Household Size over Five Censuses, Hartford

Census	Mean	Median
1790	6.10	6
1800	6.30	6
1810	6.40	6
1820	6.00	5
1830	6.63	6

Source: U.S. Censuses, Hartford, CT, 1790–1830.
Note: Figures include all households listed in each census.

Hartford households were generally large by today's standards. However, several factors influenced just how large a specific household would be. The age of the household head was one such factor. Figure 6.2 illustrates the effect of age alone on household size using all households for which age data were available for all five censuses. As before, we see similarity in the curves for the different census years suggesting limited change over time in the organization of households. These curves describe a situation in which youthful household heads had compact households. Yet heads in their forties presided over much larger households containing an average of eight residents each. By this age the full, or nearly full, complement of children would have arrived and heads would often have accumulated the resources to employ hands or servants. After the forties, the head's increasing age is correlated with shrinking household size. The decline from the forties to fifties is gentle, but by the sixties, most heads had households smaller than their thirty-year-old neighbors. This decline continues into the seventies where heads presided over even smaller numbers than men and women in their twenties. (The pattern in extreme old age is mixed—the product of very few observations due to the rarity of very old household heads.) The data indicate that age was related to household size and elderly household heads were likely to live in smaller assemblages than middle-aged heads, or even very junior heads.

The 1830 census, the only one offering a breakdown of population by ten year groups, helps to extend the findings above on household heads to the entire census population. Figure 6.3 shows the average number of residents in a household when one resident is of a certain age.[6] Figure 6.3 presents a similar curve as in figure 6.2—the main difference in shape is due to the inclusion of minors here when there were none among the household heads. This figure shows that it was not only the age of the household head, but of any member, that helped determine household size. Once both men and women passed their forties they were likely to live with fewer and fewer people progressively until late old age. Indeed men and women in their sixties and seventies lived, on average, in significantly smaller households than any of their younger counterparts. The tendency of older people to live in smaller households is highlighted when single-person households in the 1830 census are analyzed. Living alone was rare—only twenty-one cases existed in Hartford when the census

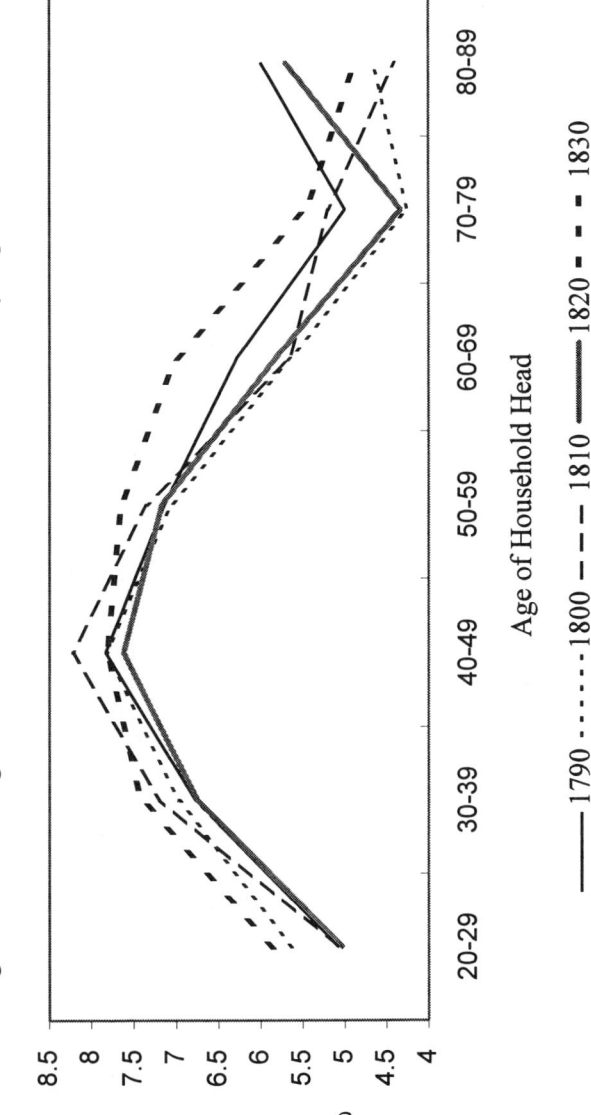

Figure 6.2. Average Number of Household Residents by Age of Head

Source: U.S. Censuses, Hartford, CT, 1790-1830. Includes all households for which age data (for household head) are available.

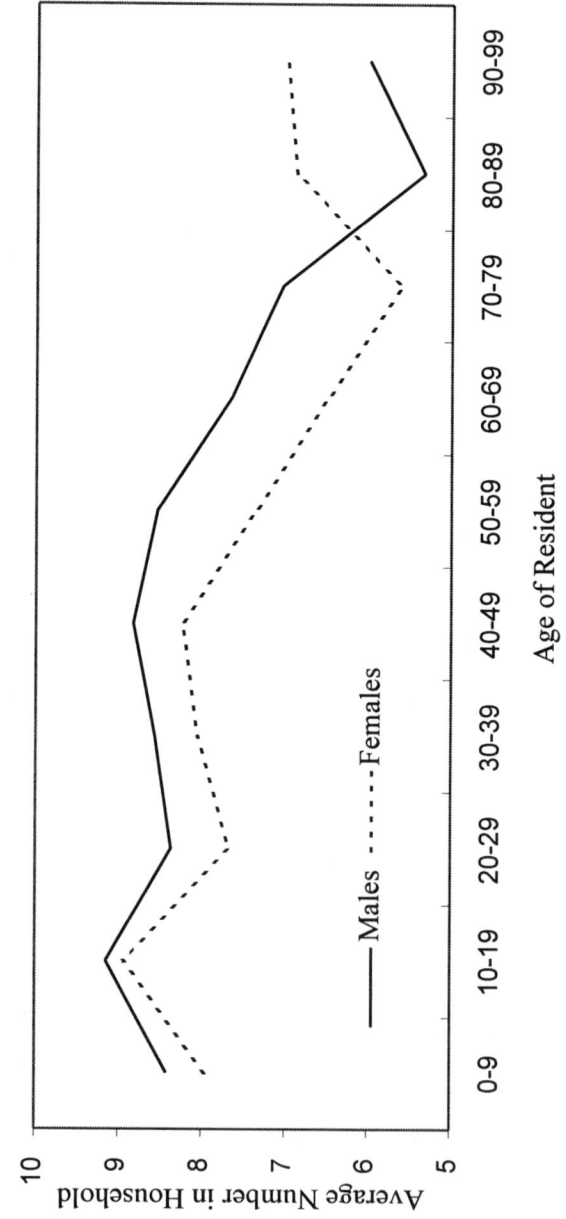

Figure 6.3. Household Sizes of Different Aged Men and Women, 1830

Source: U.S. Census, Hartford, CT, 1830. Includes all households listed in the census. Note: Because many households have more than one member, each household may be figured into the average for several different age groups.

enumerators made up the Fifth Census—but it was largely the province of older people. Indeed over 80 percent of all single households sheltered someone aged fifty or over. In most of these cases (about 76 percent) that someone was a solitary woman.[7]

However living in a truncated household seems to have given way in later old age to another pattern. As figure 6.3 indicates, after age seventy for women and age eighty for men, people once again lived in larger households. Perhaps responding to a sense of isolation or the need for help from others, it appears that very old people traded their own hollowed out households for subordinate positions in larger and more youthful residences. Overall then, though age was not the sole determinant of household characteristics (wealth for example played a role as well), it was an important one.[8] Census data indicate that old people could expect their households to dwindle dramatically as they aged, eventually giving way entirely when the elderly accepted dependence in households not their own.

Who Headed Households?

So far we have been concerned primarily with household size and its determinants. Yet census enumerations allow for more detailed analysis of the household heads themselves to reveal what age groups were likely to have the responsibility of heading a home.[9] Figure 6.4 shows the percentages of households headed by different age groups in the five censuses from 1790 to 1830. One is struck initially by the similarity of curves for the different census years over the forty year period. Indeed when mean and median ages of household heads are calculated for each census, as in table 6.3, no definitive pattern of change over time in household headship emerges. These facts again suggest that if change over time in family structure was occurring in early national Hartford, it must have been quite gradual.

Figure 6.4 also yields insight into who was likely to preside over households. Individuals in their thirties and forties dominated household leadership in every census year. Less common, but still important as a group, were those in their fifties. Yet not surprisingly, there were fewer and fewer household heads as age increased. These findings are best evaluated with reference to the larger population. Using the 1830 census—the only one for which adequate age data are

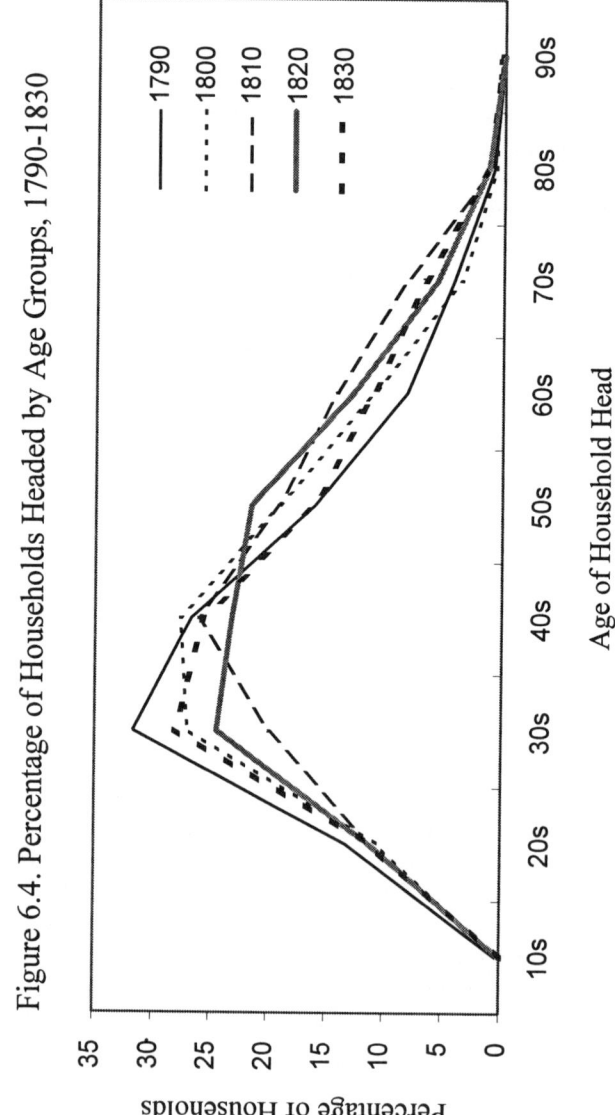

Figure 6.4. Percentage of Households Headed by Age Groups, 1790-1830

Source: U.S. Censuses, Hartford, CT, 1790-1830. Includes all male-headed households for which age data are available.

available—we can compare the proportion of household heads of different ages to their proportion in the population at large.

Table 6.3. Ages of Hartford Household Heads, 1790–1830

Census	Males		Females	
	Mean Age	Median Age	Mean Age	Median Age
1790	43.4	40	46.7	46.0
1800	44.6	43	56.2	52.5
1810	46.9	46	59.5	61.5
1820	45.6	44	56.0	55.5
1830	44.6	42	53.3	52.0

Source: U.S. Censuses, Hartford, CT, 1790–1830.
Note: Figures include all households for which age information on heads was available.

Figure 6.5 represents the male household head population compared to the total male population in 1830.[10] Male household heads and adult males are broken down by age so we can readily compare the prominence of each age group in each population. In youth, many fewer men headed households than we would expect from their numbers in the total population. However by the forties this pattern is reversed. Men in their forties comprised 25 percent of all household heads, despite the fact that they accounted for only about 15 percent of adult males. Indeed men in their forties were the most heavily represented as heads of any group of adult men. After the forties men continued to head households more than expected, but with increasing age there was a steady reduction in the extent to which they did so. Middle-aged and older men clearly held a disproportionate share of household leadership at the expense of younger men. Nevertheless, increasing age did loosen this dominance so that by very late in life household headship became increasingly less likely.

Figure 6.6 provides another perspective on household heads. While the previous graph showed the prevalence of different aged heads (household heads of a certain age divided by all heads) and compared this to the general population, this graph shows what proportion different aged heads made up of all men or women of that age. Looking first at the males, we see a similar trend as described in the previous graph. In the twenties, a relatively small percentage of all men in their twenties headed households—only about 24 percent. This rises rather dramatically among the next age group in which about 70

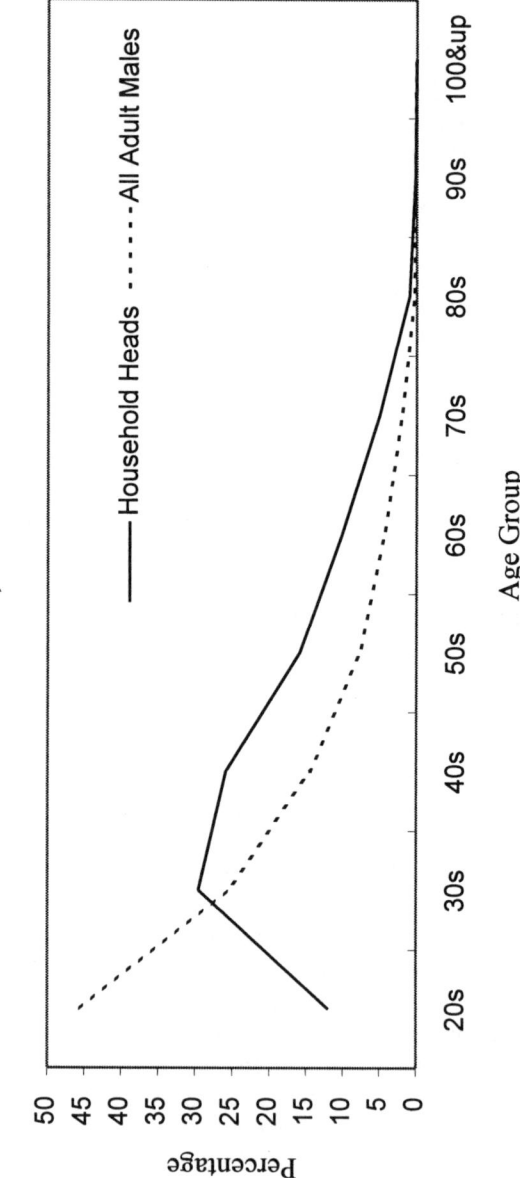

Figure 6.5. Proportion of Male Household Heads Compared to All Adult Males, 1830

Source: U.S. Census, Hartford, CT, 1830. Includes all male household heads for whom age data are available, compared to all adult males (over twenty) in all households.

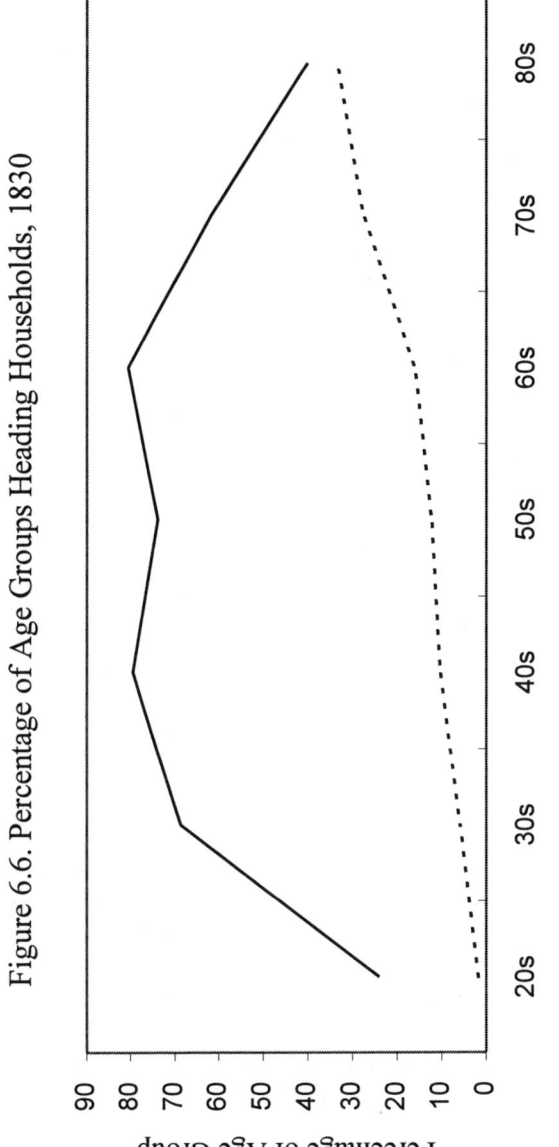

Figure 6.6. Percentage of Age Groups Heading Households, 1830

Source: U.S. Census, Hartford, CT, 1830. Includes all white households for which age data are available.

percent of all men in their thirties headed households. By the middle of life—in a man's forties, fifties, and sixties—household headship was clearly the norm, with 75 to 80 percent of men in these groups heading households. However as age advanced even further, fewer men remained in charge of homes. Of all septuagenarians, about 60 percent headed households. Therefore 40 percent of men in their seventies resided in the homes of other men or women—a sizable fraction. By the eighties, the majority of men lived as secondary members of other households while only about 40 percent presided over their own households. These figures offer additional proof that as men advanced into old age they were increasingly likely to surrender household headship and take up residence in the fold of another household head.

The life course of men in this period provides an explanation of these patterns. For men in early national Hartford, household headship was a predictable consequence of maturity. The authority to head a household rested in part on the head's (and his wife's) ability to support and maintain a family. As we know from chapter 4, men in middle age through their sixties were best equipped financially to do this as they held more resources than other age groups. Thus it is not surprising that men of these ages should so frequently have stood as leaders of households. However in later old age—the seventies and eighties—a man's ability to labor, support a household, and take responsibility for others could easily be compromised by illness or debility. Under such circumstances, men left their own shrunken homes and moved in with others still possessing these abilities—perhaps children or other relatives. Such a scenario seems to explain how, by age eighty, only 40 percent of men remained in charge of households.

Figure 6.6 also sheds light on female household heads. Due to social and legal norms that subordinated women, the female experience of household headship was quite different from that of males. Female heads were invariably rarer than male—in 1830 women headed only about 14 percent of all Hartford households. There was no stage of life in which the majority of women headed households. And, as table 6.3 makes plain, female household heads were generally older than their male counterparts. While headship among men reached a plateau in the forties, fifties, and sixties and then declined, this was not the case for women. Headship among females rose slowly but steadily throughout middle age and into old age. In contrast to males, women therefore reached their peak of household headship in extreme old age when about 33 percent of all octogenarian women presided over their own homes. Women's patterns of household headship, like men's, can be explained by considering the typical life course. Young female household heads were rare because social and legal norms generally disqualified youthful women from domestic leadership roles. As women aged, however, the likelihood of widowhood increased and as a result so did the proportion of women heading households. Indeed the elimination of the male household head (the husband) through death probably accounts for most of the increase in female headship seen in figure 6.6. Female household headship, unlike male, increased with age. This different pattern should not, however, obscure the fact that even in very old age most women resided in households headed by someone else.

Census Overview

Growing old generally brought significant changes to households and therefore to the day to day lives of the elderly. Both household composition and leadership were transformed as individuals moved from middle to old age. First, the elderly's households were smaller than that of their younger neighbors, with the result that many aged lived their daily lives in a more isolated context than younger people. At the same time the old were prone to losing control of their own households. With increasing age men frequently surrendered their leadership roles and the authority that went with them. Both men and women, especially in very old age, could expect to become dependents in someone else's household.

These facts suggest connections to previous findings. We have already seen that economic security generally declined with old age. This chapter indicates that men were increasingly likely to lose their status as household heads during the same period. These two phenomena were almost surely linked—loss of resources likely played an important role in men's loss of control over their own homes, an hypothesis for which we will see qualitative support shortly. The finding that men were less and less likely to maintain household leadership also harkens back to chapter 2. In that chapter we saw that prescriptive authors sometimes counseled withdrawal from the world and a shedding of earthly responsibilities. Though chapter 3 indicated that such withdrawal was not generally sought after by Connecticut people, this prescription may have provided a comforting rationalization for those who found themselves in old age lacking the influence, responsibility, and sense of centrality they had once experienced as household heads.

These household transitions seem simple enough in the aggregate. But behind these general trends were men and women seeking to work out appropriate living arrangements while juggling the many challenges of old age. The choices and constraints aging people confronted are best revealed by turning to personal papers and court records.

LIVING ARRANGEMENTS OF THE AGED

What were the specific living arrangements of the elderly and how were they arrived at? Census data have already shown that change was a fundamental characteristic of the domestic experience of the old. Qualitative sources confirm this fact—showing that the same person might experience a series of different living arrangements as he progressed through old age. Though it has often been assumed that these arrangements were restricted to retention of their own homes or residence in the homes of their children, a host of other possibilities also existed. Indeed, great variety marked the living situations of aged people. Independence, however, was generally preferred by the aged and therefore strategies that allowed individuals to maintain control over the domestic setting were eagerly employed. Unfortunately, illness, the loss of a spouse or other family member, a change in economic status, or other more idiosyncratic forces often upset established arrangements and worked to push aged men and women into dependence. For some this dependence was secure and comfortable but for others it brought only disruptions and uncertainty, adding extra afflictions to the ordeal of growing old.

Maintaining Independence in Old Age

Census data indicate that some people continued to maintain independent residences in old age. Remaining in charge of a household was probably attractive for several reasons. First, it permitted individuals to pass their aged years in familiar surroundings, among belongings accumulated over a lifetime, and perhaps near friends and acquaintances. Second, it allowed people the freedom to organize daily living according to their own preferences. And third, it extended the long-accustomed authority of household headship into old age, creating reassuring continuity between middle and old age and postponing the day when concessions to decline would have to be made. To reap these benefits elderly people used different strategies: some were self-reliant, others received help from family, and others purchased hired labor to help them manage their own households.

Some married couples continued to maintain homes they had raised families in even after children had departed. William Williams (a Harvard graduate and prominent figure in public affairs) and his wife maintained their own household in Lebanon until his death at age eighty after their children had all moved away.[11] Likewise John and Elizabeth Maltby occupied the family home in Northford throughout old age, receiving periodic visits from their children and grandchildren who resided elsewhere.[12] Though neither couple was wealthy, each could afford to maintain an independent home in old age.

Couples like these were not the only ones who continued to keep independent households in old age. Aged people without spouses sometimes persisted in maintaining their own independent residences. This was the case with Mary Vinton—a widow in her fifties in the 1820s. With four children—all of whom seem to have lived away from her town of Pomfret—Mary Vinton had the use and care of her deceased husband's estate. This included a dwelling that she made efforts to improve for her children's eventual benefit. Envisioning "the *home* I occupy" as "the *only* possession of the family & a retreat in cases of misfortune and sickness," Vinton took her role as household head seriously.[13] As her own health was good, it made perfect sense for Vinton to remain in charge of the family home.

In some cases help from family was what allowed aged men and women to keep house in old age. For example, Jonathan Brace—a prominent man and a mayor of Hartford—and his wife raised a granddaughter in their home who probably assisted Mrs. Brace in her housework.[14] Similarly, the septuagenarian Reverend James Cogswell and his wife shared their dwelling with a granddaughter named Polly as well as a boy named John. Such dependents could provide important services for the elderly. The Cogswells' granddaughter Polly performed many chores around the house and was invaluable at times when Mrs. Cogswell was infirm. Likewise John's labor eased their workload further, a fact made clear in a diary entry from 1790. When John was away temporarily, James Cogswell found that he "met with some difficulty having so much to Do myself" and that Mrs. Cogswell had "more to do than she ought."[15] Help from younger relations and other dependents thus aided some elderly in maintaining their own homes.

Relatives were not the only solution in situations where additional care was needed. Indeed some old people shared their homes not with relatives, but with hired help. This appears to have been most likely in cases of illness when an individual or family could no longer manage without extra assistance. Sixty-year old Abiel Baldwin of Durham faced such a situation when a "distressing sickness" overtook his wife Ann resulting in her "declining both in Body & mind" to the point where she "is now in such a state as to be Almost bereft of her mental faculties and we fear she will never regain them." Ann obviously could no longer perform her usual domestic duties, so Abiel concluded that "the situation of our family is sutch that we must have a housekeeper & we think it would be best to git one for A year." Therefore he set about looking for someone "to take the charge of our business that could spin & weave & do all kinds of house work."[16] We do not know if the Baldwins lacked female relatives who could step in to help or if they preferred to hire a stranger but for them hiring a housekeeper was a practical way to maintain their home in the face of a serious health crisis.

Elizabeth Robbins, a frail woman in her late seventies and early eighties also found hired help useful in retaining her independence. Robbins was a widow subject to "frequent poor turns" and was "quite feeble, and her memory appears doubtful."[17] Alone she could not have managed the basic tasks of household management. Though Robbins' home was only a few steps from that of her daughter and son-in-law in rural Norfolk, Robbins elected to head her own household until her death at eighty-three. This was possible because she employed the services of a woman named Sally Lawrence. Close family members were near at hand and could have cared for Widow Robbins in their dwelling, but the old woman and her family agreed that she was better off in her own house with a servant. As her son phrased it, "She will live at the old place & with Sally Lawrence more comfortably than she would anywhere else."[18] Widow Robbins enjoyed good relations with her nearby family, receiving visits from kin almost every day in old age. She might have lived with them had she chosen to. Instead, Robbins and her family found it both convenient and attractive to keep independent households. Not all aged people could afford to hire a helper, but for those with sufficient resources such help could enhance old age by permitting continued residence in a familiar home.[19]

James Henretta has argued that in pre-industrial America, families were largely self-sufficient entities that served a wide array of social functions for their members. Henretta writes, "the lineal family remained predominant in large part because there were few other institutions in early-nineteenth century America that could assume its social and economic functions," including providing "comfort and security for the old." In Henretta's view, this arrangement was not only necessary (because social and economic functions had to be performed) but also preferred by individuals who viewed the world "through the prism of family values."[20] Yet the cases of Abiel and Ann Baldwin and of Widow Robbins—residents of small, largely farming communities—suggest that Henretta's view may not be fully justified. Even in rural areas hiring helpers from outside the family in old age was evidently not unusual and families were capable of adopting the practice even when family labor was available. Thus though there was no formal institutional alternatives to family care of the aged, non-institutional options arranged to fit individual circumstances were available. Hiring servants provided an extrafamilial solution for some aged people wishing to maintain the independence of their own residence.

Accepting Dependence in Old Age

Independence was valued in old age, but at some point many elderly surrendered their own places of residence to live in households managed by others. Why did they make this sometimes difficult transition? Often dependence was imposed on people for reasons out of their control. Various factors—among them declining health and shaky economic status—made residence in another's household a necessity rather than a choice.

Physical or mental debility was an important reason elderly people gave up their own homes to seek residence among others. The case of John Bartlett illustrates this process. Bartlett was seventy-five years old and had been a widower for nine years when he decided to abandon the home he had lived in for forty years in Lebanon to take up residence in the home of his son Shubael, a minister in East Windsor. Yet though he informed his son, "that he had made his plan to spend the remainder of his life at our house," the elder Bartlett was none to happy about the move and on leaving his old home he complained "very forcibly and justly" to his son Shubael that "we cannot know to the full extent how he feels in his old, widowed state, leaving his home and going to a new place of abode!"[21] What compelled John Bartlett to undergo this unwanted transition was probably an infected leg that rendered him lame. Indeed by the time John Bartlett joined his son's family he really needed the nursing services Shubael and his wife could provide. His leg had gotten worse and Shubael reported that, "We are grieved and distressed to find that the sore on our hon[ore]d father Bartlett's leg has the same kind of worms in it that prey upon dead flesh."[22] Despite the aid of a physician, Shubael soon found himself "called upon every day . . . to spend as much as an hour and a half and sometimes 2 hours attending on my Hon[ore]d & Dear lame sore father."[23] By the time John Bartlett died after two months residence in his son's home, his need for care and attention had become constant. For John Bartlett living alone, especially as a widower without the nursing a wife could provide, was untenable due to declining health.

While infirmity compelled some to live with children, living with non-relatives was another possibility for decrepit men and women. John Thomas found himself at the age of seventy-five with "no relations or kindered in this part of the world." Though he had lived alone in his own house for a number of years, as age advanced Thomas found this "not convenient or comfortable especially in the very cold winter." Given these difficulties, Thomas was relieved when a neighbor named Wetmore invited him "to come and live with him and

Households of the Aged

board at his House and Table." Thomas accepted the offer and "Rejoyced that my life has been so much more Comfortable & convenant since I have lived with s[ai]d Wetmore than before." Evidently Wetmore's offer was initially made without expectation of payment, as Thomas had few liquid assets. However, after living with Wetmore for about a month, Thomas decided to recompense his neighbor for his kindness by willing him the eighty acres he owned.[24] For a lone man like Thomas, maintaining a separate home in old age was too burdensome to manage.

Boarding with non-relatives was for those suffering from poor health who lacked family willing or able to provide care. While Thomas did not explicitly pay for his room and board, more commonly old men and women disbursed agreed upon sums for their upkeep. In this sense, though not formally institutionalized, boarding served a function similar to today's nursing homes. Joanna Teel of Farmington provides a good example of how dependence in the households of non-kin operated. In 1797 the selectmen of Farmington described Teel as someone who "for a long time has been by reason of age, & infirmities, non compos mentis, & infirm, & utterly incapable of taking care of herself or her property." As a result of these disabilities, Teel was appointed a conservator to look after her and manage her property. This conservator arranged for Teel to board at the home of another man named Benjamin Butcher. Teel remained with Butcher for over six years, paying $1 per week for his "boarding & taking care of her."[25] Perhaps Butcher felt warmly toward his charge but humanitarian motives were not the basis of his long-term care. Butcher opened his household to Teel to provide a service that she, in her decrepit old age, needed and could pay for. Utterly unable to maintain a residence of her own, Teel had no choice but to accept this kind of dependence.

With self-sufficiency completely out of the question, very infirm elderly had little control over their own living arrangements and could only hope that some kind of stable situation could be worked out. Unfortunately this was not always the case. Dorothy Eno of Simsbury was, like Joanna Teel, too physically infirm to care for herself. Like Teel, Eno was also assigned a conservator who arranged for her board and care. However Eno's living arrangements were much more unstable as she moved frequently from household to household. Over a ten year period Eno bounced back and forth among at least six different households. Never settled anywhere for very long, Eno's living arrangements were constantly in flux. In 1814, for example, Eno began the year boarding in one location. Then in April she came to live with her conservator, Daniel Willcox, for eighteen weeks. For some reason she then left Willcox, presumably to board elsewhere until October, when she rejoined the Willcox' household for only four and a half weeks. After that she boarded elsewhere for the rest of the year. This itineracy characterized all her years as a paid boarder. Some of her keepers were non-relatives while others may have been relations but apparently no one wanted to keep her for very long.[26]

Paid boarding offered a solution to the question of how to house and care for the most infirm, helpless, or poor of the aged population when family was unwilling or unable to do so. Like earlier examples of people who paid servants to live with them, this evidence of paid boarding shows that family was not the only provider of care for the needy elderly. Historians looking for formal institutions to aid the aged in the past have rightly found that few existed. Yet this does not mean that family was the only source of such assistance. Early national Americans had recourse to a number of less formalized options external to the family when care in old age was needed. However, while these options ensured that elderly people were not completely abandoned, they did not guarantee a comfortable old age. As we have just seen, Dorothy Eno paid for her upkeep but she was in no position to ensure an easy or settled existence for herself.

For some elderly people health problems played the major role in reducing autonomy and requiring dependent living arrangements in the households of others. For others economic trouble was the deciding factor that closed off options. This was the case of the parents of one Mr. Brown of Hartford and his wife Phebe. According to Phebe her aged in-laws had "moved back from the state of New York in a state of deplorable penury and cast themselves upon our protection." Evidently, the younger Browns first attempted to set the aged couple up on their own, procuring "houseroom, fuel, and Medicine for them ... to make them comfortable in some measure."[27] However, when Mr. Brown's father died, his infirm widow moved in with the Browns, presumably to depend on them for the rest of her life. For an aged woman without property, she had few options other than living with her son and daughter-in-law.

Among Revolutionary War pension applicants there are other examples of aged parents moved by financial necessity to take up residence with children. Unable to support himself, the poor and infirm sixty-three-year-old Ebenezer Darrow found himself "dependent almost entirely on his Son for support, eats at his Sons table and in his Son's house."[28] Likewise Charles Miller, seventy-nine-years-old and very poor, reported that he resided "with and am dependent on a daughter for my support."[29] Clearly, financial necessity made independent households impossible and drove some to take shelter in households headed by grown children.

When dependence was a necessity, residing with capable children could be a good solution. Unfortunately those suffering financial difficulties, like those with health problems, did not always find stable and appealing living arrangements available. This fact is poignantly illustrated by Revolutionary War pension applications describing transient men who could claim neither homes of their own nor the status of permanent dependence in someone else's household. Timothy Stephens, age seventy-one, a partially disabled laborer found shelter on a catch as catch can basis, explaining that "I have no family to take care of, but myself, and no place of residence but with those who employ me at work."[30] Similarly Edward Chapman had "no place of residence" except among those "whom I have formerly labored for."[31] Amos Curtis, a desperately poor sixty-eight-year-old without family, reported that he depended on the charity of friends for shelter. As a result he "resided in different families" over a period of several years.[32] Each of these men was alone—either with no family at all or none living with them. Too poor to keep residences of their own they performed an unsettling parade from one short-term housing situation to the next, deprived of the stability and comfort of a fixed residence.[33]

Bad as transience was, there may have been something even worse for economically disadvantaged old people unable to hang onto homes of their own. The poorhouse—an institutional household filled with needy dependents of all ages—was a possibility few can have relished. With their restrictive rules, strict discipline, and meager comforts, poorhouses cannot have been an attractive alternative for the elderly, but some were incarcerated nonetheless. We know for example that the septuagenarian Seth Boardman of Wethersfield spent at least a portion of his old age residing in the local poorhouse.[34] Boardman was not the only old person to experience this brand of institutional living.

Though records from Hartford's poorhouse are rare, the 1810 Census tells us that in that year at least 55 percent of poorhouse residents were forty-five or older.[35] This group almost certainly contained men or women who could be called old. When economic problems robbed the elderly of independent residences the aged might find satisfactory living arrangements as dependents in other's households. However, like infirm old people, they might also find themselves living in unstable or undesirable circumstances they no longer had the power to escape.

Poverty and poor health played a large role in transforming old people of both sexes into members of households that were not their own. For women, however, an additional force undermined autonomy in old age—the rules regarding widowhood. Early-American women did not customarily retain full control over marital property after their husbands death. One consequence of such limited property rights was that widows were sometimes required to yield to heirs who gained control over the conjugal home. The case of a woman named Mrs. Clark outlines this process. Mrs. Clark, a resident of Hampton, lived to witness the death of her seventy-two-year-old husband in 1798. As was typical, the widow Clark retained control of only some of her husband's property. The house she had occupied with her husband therefore was no longer her own. As a result, though she never moved, she saw her marital home transformed into her son's home within months of her husband's death. Her son Amasa, the home's new owner, immediately tore down part of the house and built new additions, developments that were probably rather disruptive for the grieving widow. While her house rapidly became the domain of Amasa and his young family, Widow Clark appears to have continued living there for at least a couple of years after her husband's death.[36] Losing her husband quickly transformed Mrs. Clark from a principle party in her own household to a subordinate member in her son's household. Men, even those who lost their wives, could assess their abilities and resources and decide for themselves when to break up housekeeping. Women had less chance to make this choice because widowhood often demanded new household arrangements, arrangements that made women secondary household members whether they liked it or not.

Some aged people may have freely and gladly dispensed with the responsibilities of maintaining an independent household. The bulk of the evidence suggests, however, that most did not. Old people enjoyed the familiarity, comforts, and security of their own homes and generally had to be pried away from them by compelling circumstances. Infirmity, economic difficulties, and widowhood were the unwelcome catalysts in the conversion from household autonomy to dependence in old age.

The loss of one's own home in old age could be taxing on several different levels. Even under the best of circumstances it could cause emotional upheaval. We have already seen how the aged John Bartlett complained "very forcibly" when he had to leave his own home for his son's. A seventy-eight year old widow from East Hartford named Eunice Stone also commented on the difficult adjustment she faced in departing from her familiar residence for her son's home in Milford. She wrote to a niece who remained in East Hartford:

> do write me I hear or no nothing of any friend I feel almost forgotten—& alone—altho' pleasantly situated with the family of my children, but the tryal of breakup & leaving [East Hartford] was no small tryal.[37]

Clearly Eunice Stone would have preferred living out her life independently in familiar East Hartford to living with even the most caring son in a place she did not know.

But emotional strain was not all uprooted elderly people had to worry about because when they exchanged independence for dependence they also gave up a large degree of control over their living circumstances. Sometimes this lack of control had few negative consequences. However, a number of aged people paid a high penalty for dependence when they found their living arrangements unsatisfactory, unstable, or simply unpleasant. Reduced by illness or lack of resources, these elderly had few means to improve their situation.

Underlying these challenges was the basic fact that living arrangements for the aged were neither predictable nor entirely reliable. Old age was a time of flux in which individuals were forced to alter their domestic environment to fit their changing needs. While we often cling to the pleasant idea that the aged had their residential needs met fully by warmly welcoming children, this vision fails to fully describe the realities aged men and women confronted. When dependence became necessary, living with children was only one possibility among many. Those who did not maintain independent households might live with neighbors or friends or employers, or they might pay kin or non-kin for boarding, or they might end up in the poorhouse. While some had the luxury of selecting their preferred living environment, others could only accept the less desirable situations dictated by necessity and hope that they were not too unlucky.

Together census data and qualitative sources provide a coherent description of the distinctive household experience of the elderly. Census data indicate that though some aged people retained residential independence, their households were smaller and more likely to be dissolved than younger people's. Because men and women sometimes disbanded their households in old age, the elderly were likely to become secondary members of others' households, sacrificing autonomy in the transition. Qualitative data put a human face on these aggregate findings. We find that the aged preferred independence but were forced, in many cases, to surrender it due to forces beyond their control. When they did, they found that just as there was no clear spiritual path in old age and no sure way to maintain economic security, there was also no one set arrangement for daily living. Instead individuals devised a variety of makeshift solutions and remained prepared to revise them to accommodate the vicissitudes of old age. Unfortunately the living arrangements available were not always good for the aged themselves, taking a significant toll on their comfort and peace of mind at a time of life when few were equipped to manage such stresses well.

NOTES

1. Thus for a household of eight people, for example, we know only the identity of its principal resident. There is no way to discern the relationship of the seven other residents to the head or to each other. Nor do we know the age even of the head since it is impossible to know from the census alone which of the eight tick marks in the various age columns represented the head. Compounding these difficulties are the age categories adopted by the United States census office. The 1790 census distinguished only between males under sixteen and males over sixteen and lumped women of all ages in a single category. From 1800 to 1820 more categories were introduced, but the elderly were still relatively undifferentiated as part of the "over forty-five" group. Only in 1830 did census officials begin to count individuals by more precise measures. For the first time adults were divided into ten-year groups.

2. The vital statistics data referred to here were compiled by the author from newspaper death notices and headstone inscriptions of Hartford deaths from 1790 to 1830. The resulting database contains birth and death information for over 14,000 Hartford men and women who lived during the early national period. See appendix A for a full description of this data.

3. I successfully matched age data to names in 53.6 percent of the cases in 1790, 53.7 percent in 1800, 51.9 percent in 1810, 49.6 percent in 1820 and 42.9 percent in 1830. Because this group was matched to age data, it probably tends to have the same biases as the vital statistics database—namely greater inclusion of wealthier people who persisted in Hartford over poorer, more transient people. Unfortunately, because heads were mostly male, only limited glimpses of women's domestic circumstances are possible from census data and comparison of the differences between men's and women's households is difficult.

4. See, for example, Robert V. Wells, "Family Size and Fertility Control in Eighteenth-Century America: A Study of Quaker Families," *Population Studies* 25 (March 1971): 73; and *Revolutions in Americans' Lives: A Demographic Perspective on the History of Americans, Their Families, and Their Society* (Westport CT: Greenwood Press, 1982), 44–45, 91–92.

5. However as Wells has pointed out, changes in fertility patterns did not affect all segments of the American population at once, and aggregate Hartford data may mask subtle trends in subgroups of the city's families. Wells, "Family Size and Fertility Control," 82. In addition, it is possible that the figures presented here are smaller than would be found a few decades earlier. Philip Greven shows that family size was already decreasing in Andover, Massachusetts by the early eighteenth century. See *Four Generations: Population, Land, and Family in Colonial Andover, Massachusetts* (Ithaca: Cornell University Press, 1970), 200–201. Finally household size is one indicator of changes in family life, but not the only one. Some of the domestic transformations that scholars have seen in this period may not be reflected in this figure. For example, Mary Ryan has documented the transition in the period from authoritarian, patriarchal families to more affectionate, nurturing families in *Cradle of the Middle Class* (New York: Cambridge University Press, 1981).

6. This was accomplished by finding all instances of households containing residents between one and nine, ten and nineteen, twenty and twenty-nine, etc., and then calculating the average size of their households.

7. The fact that women were more likely to live alone helps explain some of the gap between men's and women's household sizes shown in figure 6.3. Still, most of the differences in the household sizes of women compared to men are not very significant because they are probably explained by the fact that census takers counted a few very large "households" which were almost all male and most likely small manufactories, workshops,

or schools. The inclusion of these unusual households had the effect of raising the average number of males per household above that of women.

8. The wealth of the household head exerted an effect on household size. Because increased age and increased wealth were correlated as we saw in chapter 4, it is important to try to distinguish between the effects of the two. By analyzing 1790, 1800, and 1810 census data alongside tax information we can determine that increasing wealth (independent of age) generally meant larger households. With this in mind we can look back to figure 6.2 in which household size declined with the age of the head. If the effect of wealth (to inflate households) was subtracted from figure 6.2, households of those fifty and over—those who tended to be best off financially—would probably decline more dramatically than they do. In other words, when considering the household circumstances of those fifty and above we must be aware of two contrary forces operating—increasing age tending to depress household size and wealth tending to inflate it.

9. We are talking here about people, usually male, who were seen by census takers as "official" heads of household. Though other household members—including women—often played extremely important roles in household management and domestic life, they were not usually considered the "official" head due to social norms placing males in leadership roles. Because it is impossible to recover systematic information on who actually held the most responsibility in any given household, I have adopted the census's definition of "head" without intending to downplay women's contributions.

10. Males headed 86 percent of all Hartford households.

11. William Williams to Solomon Williams, 16 July 1810, Williams Family Papers, CHS.

12. Maltby Family Papers, 1811–1843, CHS.

13. Mary Vinton to Francis Vinton, 11 January 1825, Francis Vinton Correspondence, CHS.

14. Jonathan Brace to Francis Ann Brace, 21 October 1818, Bunce-Brace Correspondence, CHS.

15. James Cogswell, Diary, 10 November 1790, CHS.

16. Abiel Baldwin to John Maltby [Sr.], 14 February 1822, Maltby Family Papers, CHS.

17. Thomas Robbins, *Diary of Thomas Robbins*, ed. Increase Tarbox (Boston: Beacon Press, 1886–7), vol. 1, 7, 10 May 1825.

18. James W. Robbins to Thomas Robbins, 31 March 1825, Thomas Robbins Papers, CHS.

19. Peter Laslett has also pointed out that the fact that some elderly people lived apart from their families does not mean they were rejected by them. As seems to have been the case with Widow Robbins, some elderly people chose to guard their independence by retaining their own residences. See Peter Laslett, "The Traditional English Family and the Aged in Our Society," in *Aging, Death, and the Completion of Being*, ed. David D. Van Tassel (Philadelphia: University of Pennsylvania Press, 1979), 98–99. In addition, Terri Premo has found that early national widows in particular, "consistently expressed the desire to maintain their own homes" preferring "to maintain separate, independent living arrangements." (*Winter Friends: Women Growing Old in the New Republic, 1785–1835* [Urbana: University of Illinois Press, 1990], 35–36.)

20. James Henretta, "Families and Farms: *Mentalité* in Pre-Industrial America," *William and Mary Quarterly*, 3d series, 35 (January 1978): 32.

21. Shubael Bartlett, Diary, 8 October 1830, CHS.

22. Ibid., 30 June 1831.

23. Ibid., 16 July 1831.

24. John Thomas case, March 1780, CG.

25. Joanna Teel case, March 1797, CG.

26. Dorothy Eno case, 1806–1816, CG.
27. Phebe Brown to Mrs. Terry, 16 June 1818, Wadsworth Family Papers, CHS.
28. Ebenezer Darrow, 2 August 1820, RPA.
29. Charles Miller, 1 August 1820, RPA.
30. Timothy Stephens, 1 August 1820, RPA.
31. Edward Chapman, 1 August 1820, RPA.
32. Amos Curtis, 9 August 1820, RPA.
33. As pension applicants, such men may have enjoyed greater stability once a pension was received. However, their vagabond lives before such relief show that for the very poor, a fixed household could be elusive in old age.
34. Seth Boardman, 1 August 1820, RPA.
35. U.S. Census (manuscript), Hartford CT, 1810.
36. Jonathan Clark, Journal, 31 May 1798–2 March 1800, CHS.
37. Eunice Stone to Abigail Williams, 2 September 1824, Abigail Williams Correspondence, CHS.

VII

Family Lives of the Elderly

The previous chapter explored the very practical aspects of the elderly's domestic lives, discussing the sorts of people who were likely to live with the aged and the reasons for these arrangements. The household, defined as a group of people sharing the same dwelling, was our focus. Now we turn to consider the family, a category whose members sometimes but not always overlapped with the household. Family—defined here as the relations between husband and wife, parents and children, sisters and brothers, and grandparents and grandchildren—often figured prominently in the lives of old people, whether they were part of an aged person's household or not. To gain further perspective on the private lives of elderly men and women, this chapter considers the nature and quality of the elderly's family relationships.

The family has come up before. In chapters 2 and 3 dealing with ideas about the aged we saw that both published authors and ordinary folk alike valued good relations between the elderly and their kin. Commentators on the ideal relationship between old people and their families hoped the aged would be well-treated, perhaps even respected, by their families and that the aged would, in return, behave admirably toward their kin. This chapter adds another dimension to our understanding of the aged by drawing on personal papers and court records from Connecticut to compare these ideals with the actual behavior of ordinary men and women.

As we shall see, ideals do not always mesh well with reality. As the earlier analysis of the elderly's economic circumstances has already hinted, the quality of relations with spouses, children, grandchildren, and siblings varied tremendously among the aged. In the records, loving relationships characterized by tender affections are juxtaposed with contentious wrangling over money or property. Generous, mild-mannered elders appear alongside willful, intemperate patriarchs while dutifully caring children contrast with deceitful, difficult offspring. And of course many fell into the gray areas between these extremes. As some of the aged's most important social links, family could offer companionship, comfort, care, and affection to soften the blows of aging, but when relationships soured family could also be a source of pain. The evidence, unfortunately, does not allow us to estimate how likely or unlikely these different situations were. We can say that in the more or less random sample of documents used from the period no one type of family scenario seems to have dominated.[1] The huge range in the quality of the elderly's kin relations meant that a successful family life in old age was not guaranteed, no matter what early national rhetoric on the subject said. Moreover, though some historians have suggested that the elderly tended to have uniform family experiences in past times, the diversity found here simply cannot support any sweeping generalizations on the quality of family life in old age.[2]

THE IMPORTANT RELATIONSHIPS OF OLD AGE

Husband and Wife

In early national America, as today, the marital relationship formed the core of a family. Unlike children or other relatives who might live elsewhere, spouses almost always cohabited, sharing daily life in close proximity. As a result, for those with spouses in old age, the quality of the conjugal relationship played an important role in shaping existence.

For some, marriage was an intense and deeply fulfilling experience that enriched old age. The diary of the Reverend James Cogswell of Scotland, Connecticut, penned when he was between sixty-one and seventy-one years old, describes such a rich relationship. James Cogswell was married to Martha, a woman five years his senior. For both it was a second marriage, as each had been widowed earlier. At the start of Cogswell's diary, the couple had been married eight years. Yet though their time together had been relatively short their attachment was deep. Cogswell respected his wife, calling her "a kind

Family Lives of the Elderly

prudent Consort."[3] In addition, the couple shared religious values. James' diary records how the two spent many quiet evenings together reading sermons and sharing accounts of their spiritual experiences. Before each Sabbath James read the sermon he would later deliver from the pulpit to his wife so she could offer her opinion of it (which was almost always favorable). However, their care for one another was not only spiritual. Each nurtured the other through difficult times. When James lost a grown son to a gun accident he noted that, "Mrs. Cogswell comforted me especially."[4] And when Martha suffered from infirmities James wrote, "I am afflicted with her," and made every effort to soothe her.[5] On one occasion in 1791, for example, James explained:

> Mrs. Cogswell is poorer—grown fainter and weeker—went to Doctr. Cheney's he came to see Her & ordered some new Medicines—picked some Straw berrys for her. She has eat a few of them.[6]

The Cogswells thus shared a great deal of tenderness and affection based on a sympathetic understanding of one another and shared interests that undoubtedly enhanced their aged years.

Not all marriages offered so much to aged spouses. William Williams—a once prominent man in public affairs—seems to have found much less pleasure in wedded life than James Cogswell. Married for about forty years to the daughter of one of Connecticut's governors, in old age Williams seems to have taken very little account of his spouse. Though a number of his letters to his children survive detailing many aspects of his life, his wife Mary is never mentioned. Indeed though Mary cannot have been far away, he complained to his son in 1811 at the age of eighty that "I am poor & melancholly and destitute of all Society."[7] Whether his wife neglected him or he simply found her company unsatisfactory is unknown. The marital relationship apparently offered few charms to Williams.

In the case of William H. Lee, a destitute and disabled farmer, marriage was less than ideal for other reasons. He and his wife evidently raised a family and cohabited together until he was at least fifty-nine. Yet sometime over the next nine years his wife moved out to reside with her brother, so that by the age of sixty-eight Lee reported he "contributed nothing for the support of his wife." Instead Mrs.

Lee's brother supported her. Perhaps it was Lee's extreme poverty and inability to gain a living that drove Mrs. Lee to her brother's. Or perhaps the couple could no longer abide each other—after all, William Lee pointedly indicated that his wife had the use of the couple's bedding "which she uses in a room by herself in her brother's house."[8] In either case their marriage did not afford the kind of comfort, support, and affection some other couples enjoyed during their aged years.

Still, there were worse marriages than the Lees'. Old John Lewis of Middletown made himself and his hapless wife Martha the town scandal when he fornicated repeatedly with a neighboring widow. Not surprisingly, the couple's relationship deteriorated rapidly as vitriolic accusations and threats were hurled between them. Martha, in late middle-age at the time of these events, thus saw her chances of a fulfilling conjugal relationship in old age evaporate. Meanwhile her husband, who already was old, found a way to maximize marital strife at a time of life when other men were enjoying at least a degree of domestic peace. Clearly there was a wide range of possible marital experiences in old age. For some, aging together brought the chance for intimacy and mutual support. Boredom, dissatisfaction, or incompatibility neutralized marriage's positive qualities in other cases, or worse, sowed unhappiness for all involved.

Whether good or bad, a couple's relationship often underwent change over time, especially if serious health problems accompanied old age. For instance, we saw in chapter 6 how when Abiel Baldwin's wife Ann fell ill and lost not only her physical health but also her "mental faculties," he had to find a housekeeper to take over her practical duties.[9] Replacing Ann's less practical contributions to the marriage was not so easily solved. Abiel and Ann's relationship was transformed by his wife's sickness. Though she was still physically present, he lost the companion he had known and gained the responsibility of caring for an invalid.

Poor health could bring new stresses and burdens to a marriage. Joseph Dyer, a poor man from Granby, had once been a farmer. By the age of seventy-six, however, he was "wholly incompetent to manage his affairs—is intemperate—distracted, and improvident in his conduct and wholly incompetent to take care of himself and family."[10] Meanwhile it seems that his wife, aged sixty-seven, had been for a number of years "occasionally subject to fitts which render her incapable of pursuing her labor constantly."[11] The combination of Joseph's problems and his wife's must have complicated their relationship greatly, with Joseph's behavior adding only greater burdens to his wife's already difficult situation.

Health problems could certainly compromise the quality of a couple's relations. However, the greatest shock a marriage could endure was the death of a spouse. Mortality was a common theme in early national Connecticut, particularly in religious rhetoric. In addition, age itself necessarily brought death into closer proximity. As a result, the prospect of a spouse dying in old age was a very real one which could quite understandably cause trepidation. When James Cogswell's wife was suffering through an illness she told him that "perhaps the Time is now come that we must part, I am old & infirm and every attack [of illness] hastens The Time." On hearing her remarks, Cogswell wrote "I was affected & had reason to be." Still, the two found comfort in reflecting "that we had lived so happily together . . . [and] have sincerely laboured to promote each other's spiritual As well as temporal Interest."[12]

However when a spouse actually died, finding comfort was much more difficult. First of all, losing a spouse could lead to physical disruptions. As we saw earlier women faced the possibility of giving up or sharing their marital homes with their husband's other heirs. For men, the loss of a helpmeet also had the potential to alter daily routines. But emotional adjustments, especially for couples who had been close, were even more difficult to bear. Seventy-three year old Eliphalet Williams wrote his brother of his feelings on the death of his wife:

> Probably before this reaches you, you will hear the sorrowful tidings of the death of my beloved wife, who Expired l[a]st Thursday . . . I had long looked for my own dissolution but little tho't of my Partner's going before me; the unexpectedness of which stroak, adds much to ye weight . . . I feel that off of my side my better half is torn, while the rest lies bleeding & to mourn.

Though Williams sought comfort in religion, stating that "such is the will of the Lord; & I desire to acquiesce in it as right & good," this was no easy task as he reeled under the weight of grief.[13] Similarly, when John Maltby Sr. lost his wife at the age of sixty-three, his son-in-law wrote sympathetically, "I know, my dear Sir, that your loss is great—at your period of life, & in your circumstances, *irreparably* so."[14]

Even after the initial shock and pain of a spouse's death subsided, the surviving widow or widower faced long-term emotional challenges including loneliness. Timothy Maltby, a sixty-year-old widower living in New York, lamented in an epistle to his brother in Connecticut,

> I am A lonesom man . . . I am advised by my best friend to marry a gain but their is no body in my knowlage . . . that could make me a padner perhaps I should visit my nativ country [i.e. Connecticut] I might find some one that might share with me in my joys and sorrows in my old age.[15]

Though aged widows and widowers went on with their lives in old age, the loss of a spouse could be a source of profound and lasting distress.

Of course, remarriage (for those who could find a suitable candidate) was an option that could help to mitigate this distress. Evidence on how remarriage in old age was negotiated is scarce but the well-documented case of John Maltby Sr. provides a glimpse into the issues involved. His story shows that though remarriage may have been a desirable solution to widowhood, matrimony in old age posed special problems of its own. John Maltby Sr. lost his wife at the age of sixty-three in January of 1831. Evidently, however, life without a spouse was not something John Sr. wanted to endure for very long. The correspondence of his son John Jr.—a minister—reveals that by August of the same year the elder Maltby had already expressed an interest in remarrying and had identified a few possible brides. John Jr. agreed that "it is proper for you to be married again," but he added that the new connection should be "judiciously formed." And John Jr. admitted to having "some difficulties," with the principal candidate his father had in mind, a widow named Sarah Douglass.

First John Jr. was concerned that she was too young, noting that "I should rather see you connected with a person, about mother's age. I think there is propriety in it. The person in question is nearer our ages than your's." Second, John Jr. was anxious that Widow Douglass' "*notions & feelings* about life" might not match his father's, implying that her social status was inferior to his. Third, John Jr. worried that the terms of the marriage be well-thought out. In particular he raised the question of whether, if John Sr. remarried, his estate should not be at least partially protected from demands by his new wife should he die first. Rather than forming a union "as in early life, involving all that appertains to either party in one common interest," John Jr. asked whether "it would be better to form the union with some limitations and provisions in this respect?"[16] John Jr.'s comments on his father's remarriage indicate fears of both social embarrassment and dilution of the family estate.

John Sr. continued to correspond with his son on the topic of remarriage over the next few months while John Jr. kept in touch with his sisters and brothers. Everyone in the family was "much interested" in the outcome. By November John Jr. had concluded that Sarah Douglass' character "may be called a *safe character*" though he still urged prudence and cryptically told his father to hold off on any action until John Jr. had had a chance to investigate some aspect of Mrs. Douglass further.[17]

Meanwhile John Sr.'s daughter Julia-Ann was forming her own views on her father's possible matrimony. She wrote another sister that "I think a great deal of Father and hope he will not be left to act unwisely." Julia-Ann thus seems to have shared some of her brother's concerns about the suitability of the proposed match. However, she also recognized that the decision was her father's to make. As she put it, "I think we ought not to interfere too much if he should be made unhappy by marrying according to our wishes it would be worse than almost anything else."[18]

Clearly, for John Sr. at least, remarriage in old age involved considering far more than whom he fancied. Propriety, the disposition of his estate and his children's feelings also mattered. Ultimately, only about a year from his first wife's death, John Maltby found an path through this thicket of concerns and married Sarah Douglass with the blessing of his children. One son, Enoch, wrote to his father shortly after the wedding,

> I am happy in being able to think of you as not being alone and sorrowful and that the desolation at your table is repaird. And I trust that I do and ever shall exercise a

filial regard for her who has consented to be the companion of my Father in his declining years.[19]

All ended well in John Sr.'s remarriage bid as both he and his children were contented by the outcome. This case suggests, however, that remarriage in old age was a delicate matter, involving not only the prospective spouses but the entire family.

Though Maltby's story illuminates some dimensions of remarriage in old age, many are still obscure. The proportion of men and women who remarried in old age is unknown. John Faragher's work on seventeenth-century Wethersfield, Connecticut has shown that when people lost spouses after age fifty, remarriage was rare, at least in comparison with remarriage among younger widows and widowers.[20] Unfortunately Hartford demographic data from the early national period are insufficient to resolve whether this pattern still held true in nineteenth-century Connecticut. Meanwhile, Alexander Keyssar's study of eighteenth-century Massachusetts indicates that widows were quite unlikely to reestablish matrimonial ties in old age.[21] Likewise, Lisa Wilson has estimated that in early-nineteenth century Philadelphia over 80 percent of widows (aged or otherwise) never took another spouse.[22] And Terri Premo has found some evidence that early national widows may even have felt hostile toward the idea of remarriage at an advanced age.[23] Yet whether there were differences in male and female rates of remarriage or remarriage among different social groups in Hartford remains uncertain. Most likely individual circumstances—including emotional attachment to the deceased spouse, financial considerations, health, relations with family, and the availability of suitors—along with social expectations widened or constrained the aged's choices when it came to remarriage.

The marital relation could play a very important role in determining the quality of an old person's domestic life. Yet old age itself did not determine much about the quality of marital relations. Couples like the Cogswells experienced marriage at its best—as a relationship of mutual caring, intimacy, and support that helped them through old age. However for men like William Williams who took little notice of his wife, marriage offered fewer benefits. And John Lewis, the adulterer, must have found matrimony a positive burden faced as he was with a distraught and incensed wife. Unfortunately, pinning down what made some marriages successful in old age while others faltered is nearly impossible. Individual personalities certainly played a large role as did the quality of the union before the onset of old age. Certainly the aged were no more immune to marital strains than other age groups. Moreover marriage in old age was burdened with the possibility of intense grief and disruption if one partner died. Though remarriage may have softened the blow of widowhood in old age, remarriage was itself a tricky issue and one that may have been impractical or undesirable at an advanced age.

Parents and Children

On par with the marital relation in importance for many aged people was the filial relationship. This relationship, much more than the conjugal bond, attracted the commentary of prescriptive authors as well as Connecticut's men and women. As chapter 2 showed, religious literature counseled children to listen to the advice of their parents (especially regarding spiritual matters), to be attentive to parents and visit them often, and to support them if necessary. In addition children were told not to mistreat the aged, take advantage of their weaknesses, or despise them for their infirmities. Chapter 3 demonstrated that at least some Connecticut citizens took these ideas seriously. Though less dogmatic than religious writers, ordinary citizens, both young and old, echoed the notion that children were bound in obligation to their parents. And some parents clearly looked to their children as sources of comfort and assistance in their aged years. Turning now to evidence from diaries, letters, and court cases we are in a position to evaluate just how well these ideas were actually implemented in early national families.

Some parents and children attained the sort of relationship advocated by religious writers. The case of Shubael Bartlett, a minister from East Windsor, and his widower father John provides the best example of this. When Shubael's diary begins, father and son lived in different towns but Shubael visited his father when his ministerial duties permitted and wrote respectfully of him, almost always referring to John as "my honoured Father." When John's health worsened due to an infected leg and he came to live with his son, Shubael's dutifulness intensified. Caring for his father was difficult, unpleasant, time consuming, and sometimes competed with Shubael's pastoral duties but Shubael's efforts on his father's behalf never flagged. His diary records his frequent prayers to behave admirably toward his infirm parent. He wrote, for example,

> Oh that I may have the spirit of honouring my father in all things, amidst all the trials we have with him under the infirmities and sufferings of old age, that I may not dishonour GOD, in any thing, in thought, in word, or in deed concerning my honoured and Dear Father.[24]

And there is every indication that Shubael's behavior toward his father lived up to his prayer. Shubael conversed with his father on religion hoping to insure his eternal peace, he nursed his father patiently and dressed his infected leg, he helped his father relieve himself in the middle of the night, and in the last stage of his decline he watched over his father's bed while he slept. Though such tasks were far from convenient, Shubael prayed,

> May I always be enabled to wait on my parents as they need, according to the spirit of God's holy commandment which says, 'Honour thy father and thy mother that thy days may be long upon the land which the LORD thy GOD giveth thee.'[25]

Perhaps because he was a minister, Shubael Bartlett effectively embodied religious prescriptions of filial devotion. As suggested in published literature, he visited and respected his parent, cared for him when needed, and did not take advantage of his many weaknesses. Instead, Shubael used his father's infirmities as an opportunity for redoubled faithfulness.

Mason Cogswell, the son of the Reverend James Cogswell behaved similarly towards his aged father. A very busy physician in Hartford, Mason occasionally found time to visit his father and stepmother who resided six towns to the east in Scotland, Connecticut. During these visits father and son conversed on religious topics, and Mason seems to have listened attentively to his father's spiritual advice. Overall the relationship was a warm one and the elder Cogswell was quite satisfied with his son's behavior. After one visit James mused gratefully, "what thanks shall I render to God for such a son?"[26] Good relations persisted throughout James' old age and when he retired from the pulpit at eighty-four, he moved to Hartford to live with Mason. As a biographer explained,

> In his old age there was provided for him a most delightful home in the family of his son in Hartford, a seeming compensation to him for the provision he had made for his own aged parents many years before.[27]

Mason Cogswell, like Shubael Bartlett, was the ideally dutiful child, offering comfort and respectful companionship to his aged parent. He also carried on a family tradition of sheltering elderly parents toward the end of life.

However, good relations between aged parents and children did not depend on their living together, or even nearby one another. Indeed many affectionate filial relationships were carried on at a distance. Americans, especially young ones, were on the move in the early national period. Seeking fresh opportunities, Connecticut citizens migrated in large numbers to areas such as upstate New York, the rich Ohio River valley, and the northern reaches of New England. As one observer put it in 1819,

> within the last thirty years, the current of emigration from this State has swelled to a torrent . . . It may be safely estimated, that at the present time the emigrants from Connecticut, and their descendants amount to more than 700,000 souls.[28]

Even for those who remained in the Nutmeg State, it was not uncommon for children to reside in a town other than that of their parents as they married and pursued livelihoods of their own. As a result, many families were geographically scattered. Though such circumstances meant that children could not fulfill all the duties to their parents outlined in prescriptive literature, they did not necessarily interfere with satisfying filial relationships.

Benjamin Gilman, a New Hampshire man "advanced in years" had a married daughter named Clarissa as well as grandchildren in Norwich, Connecticut. Though living at a distance, Benjamin corresponded warmly with his daughter and visited on rare occasions.

Yet while he was fond of Clarissa and her family, Benjamin was fairly content with a long-distance relationship with his offspring. We know, for example, that in 1834 his granddaughter suggested that Benjamin and his wife move to Norwich so the family could be closer to one another. Though Benjamin found this invitation "gratifying," he nonetheless declined it explaining that, "we are highly favored at this place, There are but few streets to be found that are so pleasant, handsome, or healthy to live on as Court Street Exeter N.H."[29] For some aged people the ideal expressed in printed literature of children close at hand to aid their parents was not necessarily desired by all. For men like Gilman, occasional visits and an exchange of affectionate letters afforded satisfaction enough.

John Maltby Sr. and his wife Elizabeth of Northford also enjoyed a warm relationship with their son John Jr., a minister living in Sutton, Massachusetts. John Jr. was an affectionate child with a deep sense of gratitude and duty toward his parents. However as a minister he could not freely select his town of residence and hence found himself and his family removed from his parents in their old age. Of this he wrote:

> Dear parents I think of you often, & hope & trust I often pray for you . . . I would gladly be with you, & share with you your joys & sorrows. But this Providence seems not to intend. What have we then to do except to stand each in his lot, & give ourselves diligently to our respective duties till our work is done.[30]

In expressing himself this way, John Jr. acknowledged his wish to act as a helpful companion to his parents but he also indicated that fulfilling his calling took precedence. However, distance did not prevent John and his parents from sharing their thoughts and plans frequently by letter. Occasionally visits were also arranged, as in 1828 when John Jr. and his family announced by mail that, "your children are purposing to visit you soon. Monday the 1st of Sept. is the [date] fixed upon for setting out & we hope to reach your door, children & grandchildren, on Tuesday."[31] While most of the time John Jr. was physically separated from his parents, he nonetheless invested substantial energy in the relationship. Though this family may have preferred to live in closer proximity, strong filial bonds persisted that must have been satisfying to aging parents and children alike.

Unfortunately, not all parent-child relationships ran as smoothly as the cases just described. Though physical distance between an aged parent and a child did not necessarily strain the relationship, it could make interaction more difficult, especially if parents felt their children were not sufficiently attentive. Obedience Hoadley, the aged mother of a daughter named Elizabeth and a son named John, was one who suffered under a sense of neglect from her children. Residing in North Branford while her children lived in Northford and Windham respectively, Obedience yearned for more filial visits. Once when ill health prevented Elizabeth from traveling to see her mother, Obedience wrote plaintively, "I wish you was well anuff to Ride to North branford and see your Old mother."[32] On another occasion Obedience seemed to doubt her daughter's care for her. She pleaded, "Elizabeth my Dear Child I am afraid you Have forgotten that you had A mother in this world But I am yet alive and Still am your mother I think of you a great Deal."[33] Clearly Obedience was not satisfied with the level of attention she received from her physically distant daughter.

Yet even well-intentioned children sometimes could not avoid irking their parents in this way. For example, in March of 1829 when Obedience was ninety-three and ill her son John wrote explaining why he could not visit her,

> was it not for Insurmountable barriers I should come Immediately and see you but It Is a season of the year when it is all but Impossible for me to get across the North *River* and . . . I am compelled (though reluctantly) to wait until the Ice shall Break in the River, then soon as the wings of time can carry me . . . I shall be there . . . Do me the justice to Believe me as ever your affectionate son.[34]

John's defensive closing salutation suggests that his mother may have complained that he had been insufficiently dutiful in the past. Benjamin Franklin once observed (in relation to his own elderly sister) that "Old age, infirmities, and poverty joined, are afflictions enough. The neglect and slights of friends and near relations should never be added." Unfortunately, Franklin noted, people in such circumstances are "apt to suspect" neglect even when none is intended.[35] Whether Obedience's sense of being forgotten by her children was justified by their actions, or simply a suspicion brought on by a lonely, infirm existence is unknown. In either case, in Obedience's mind her children strayed from the ideal.

William Williams, the father of three children, likewise sensed the sting of neglect in his old age. Though one of his sons lived nearby, William Sr. complained that "William [Jr.] is a dear child & is kind to me but is swallowed up with his own farm and business that he affords me but very detached pieces of his time and company."[36] And later, when William Jr. was away at Hartford, the elder William groused that his letters were insufficient. "Dear son," he wrote, "I rec'd a very small sheet of a Letter from you on Fryday night it contained a little & a very little information . . . its shews how little time you can spare for or about me." William Sr. concluded this testy epistle by imploring his son to "write me long letters."[37]

Another of Williams' son named Solomon, though living at a distance, tried to behave dutifully. Solomon sent letters reminding his father and mother of his affection for them and how,

> I have for a few short years attempted, tho' most wretchedly, to devote [myself] to the comfort of those dear Parents, & which it wod still be my happiness to continue—but remote as I am, my heart alone is with you.[38]

In his father's view, however, Solomon's "heart" was not enough. At the age of seventy-nine, William informed his son that "Your . . . absence from me is inexpressibly grievous & renders my life much more uncomfortable & bitter than it wod be."[39] While other elderly parents accepted that children might live far away or be constrained in the amount of time they could spend with them, Williams resisted these ideas. Though his children appear to have respected and loved him, Williams' filial relationships soured when his children failed to meet his expectations in old age.

While inattentiveness on the part of children—whether real or merely perceived—could strain filial relations, conflict over money or property was an equally important source of tension. The court case of the septuagenarian Abel Carter and his three sons Abel Jr., John, and

Daniel (all of Southington) illustrates this point. Abel Carter was a wealthy man with an estate "worth twelve hundred pounds." In 1796, when the Carter case was heard in court, Abel had been married to a second wife for about twenty years. Abel's first wife, the mother of Abel Jr., John, and Daniel, had passed away long ago. The court records consist of a series of petitions—from the selectmen of Southington, Abel's sons, and from others who appear to have been neighbors or acquaintances—asking the court to appoint a conservator to Abel, because, the petitioners argued, Abel was no longer competent to administer his large estate.

The legal basis for this request was a Connecticut statute intended to deal with individuals who as a result of mental deficiency, insanity, or "distraction," were incapable of managing their own affairs. According to the law, suitable candidates for such action were those who through age or sickness had lost their understanding or people judged to be "likely to be reduced to Want by Idleness, Mismanagement, or bad Husbandry." The law allowed interested parties (such as children) as well as the town's selectmen to initiate proceedings to appoint conservators to such people to ensure that the individual in question was cared for and that his or her property was not squandered. In such cases court hearings were held to establish the competence of the intended conservatee at which petitions from interested parties were heard. If the individual was found incompetent, a conservator was appointed to manage his affairs and the conservatee lost the power to do so.[40] The practice of appointing conservators to those who are no longer physically or mentally capable is long-standing and similar statutes remain in force even today.[41] In the case of Abel Carter, his sons most likely organized the campaign to have a conservator appointed. Yet because Carter himself disputed the action, a family feud ensued that must have seriously embittered filial relations in the Carter family.

The petitioners painted a picture of a selfish father and a grasping stepmother unjustly depriving the sons of their rightful due. To begin with, several selectmen of Southington testified that Abel himself was in physical decline but that due to his tendency to be "Naturly Selfish and Self willed" he was "still verry Tenatious of his own Abilities." According to the selectmen, Abel's bull-headed insistence on managing his own estate even as his strength waned was made worse by the fact that his wife (the sons' step-mother) was, suttle and intriguing and appears to have uncommon influence and controul over her Husband also a Lover of ardent spirit which article is consumed in that Family to an unreasonable Degree.

As a result, the petitioners concluded that Abel's estate "for some years past and at present appears to be Rather wasteing" to the disadvantage of his sons who "have been verry instrumental of Procuring their Father his estate."[42]

A second petition submitted by another selectman furnished further details. According to this official, Abel "had not done justice to his children and had given too great a part of his Estate to his present wife." The petitioner also speculated that Abel's wife had employed undue influence over her husband "to wean his love and good will" from his sons. Her intent he suspected was to induce Abel to "give a considerable part of his Estate to her children [from her former marriage] which would be very unjust" since "She and her family were as poor as any Family whatever at the time he married her."[43]

Combined with this testimony was a petition from two other men who argued that Abel Carter's "age & Bodyly Infirmity" rendered him "incappible of conducting his Business in a proper manner" and that "there is Danger of his Disposing of his property greatly to the Detrement of his proper Heirs," namely his sons.[44] The final petition—from the sons themselves—agreed that Abel was "infirm and impotent." Though they did not comment on either their father or step-mother's character and conduct, the sons feared that unless someone else was given control over their father's property "the whole of his s[ai]d estate will be wasted and spent." In short the sons wanted the court to act "so that his estate may not be squandered away imprudently."[45]

Clearly Abel Carter did not wish to surrender control over any of his property to his sons in old age, a scenario that will seem familiar to readers of Philip Greven's work.[46] Perhaps the old man felt they did not need his resources since they were, as the selectmen acknowledged, "industrious, Laborious and Wealthy Men each."[47] Yet his sons and their co-petitioners attempted to wrest control from him nonetheless by publicly declaring him incompetent, maligning his wife's character, alluding to the aged couple's intemperance, and complaining that the sons were being mistreated. How true these

Family Lives of the Elderly 217

allegations were is unclear. We do know, however, that the court declined the petitioners' wishes and Abel remained the master of his estate. Yet, though the case ultimately came to nothing, the whole experience must have scarred the sons' relationship with their father irreparably, if in fact the Carters' filial bonds were not already broken beyond repair before the case even began. Abel Carter may or may not have behaved rightly towards his sons. But his sons most definitely defied the conventions of proper filial behavior by challenging their father in court and allying themselves with those who spoke evil of him. Thus while good filial relationship could be very good indeed, bad filial relationships could be extremely bad.

Another court case, involving ninety-nine-year-old Samuel Hooker and his son Samuel Jr. of Berlin, offers further evidence on how filial relationships could be strained over questions of property. In this case Samuel Jr. asked for a conservator to be appointed for his aged father due to his being "totally Deaf & Blind." The elder Hooker had a "Very Considerable Estate" and his son worried that "the same is dayly Exposed to be taken from him by Designing People."[48] In this case, the court felt the son's petition was justified—Samuel Hooker was indeed incapable of managing his own affairs—and in 1783 the court appointed Samuel Jr. as his father's conservator, empowering him to manage his father's estate.

However, Samuel Jr. seems not to have performed well in this capacity for by 1785 fourteen other "Heirs & children" of Samuel Sr. petitioned the court to remove Samuel Jr. as conservator. Though no one disputed that Samuel Sr. needed someone to look after him, this passel of relatives agreed that Samuel Jr. was "a very unfit person for the Trust." They believed Samuel Jr. "will neither Take prudent care of our Hond. Father nor his Estate and believe he will Suffer Grately for wont of proper care." In addition they claimed that were Samuel Sr. "capable of Judging for himself he would by no means [have] approved of his person & Estate being committed to his care for when he was capable of Judging he refused to appoint him Executor to his will."[49] Other testimony by a son-in-law of Samuel Sr. explained how while paying a visit to his father-in-law, Samuel Sr. had lamented that,

> he should be glad if he had some thing to treat me with as he used to have but his son Samu. had got the

> improvement of all his Estate into his hands & he had nothing but what his son Samu. allowed him. Day by Day he seldom had any thing for his Refreshment but his Common meals.[50]

Though a final petition filed by two selectmen and five other inhabitants of Berlin vouched for Samuel Jr.'s fitness as a caretaker, the court ultimately found the complaints against him "reasonable" and Samuel Jr. lost control of his father's property to another conservator.[51]

Like the Carter case, the Hooker case suggests far less than ideal relations between father and son. Most likely these tensions had been long simmering—Samuel Sr.'s refusal to appoint his namesake the executor of his will certainly suggests strain in the filial relationship. However conflicts over property probably worsened the situation. With Samuel Sr. both deaf and blind by ninety-nine, Samuel Jr. was in a position to gain the upper hand in such conflicts. If, as his siblings and relatives believed, Samuel Jr. did mistreat his father and take advantage of his weaknesses he strayed a long way from the path laid down in prescriptive literature.

The two cases described above are complex and it is difficult to know exactly how to assign blame for deteriorating filial relationships. However one final example is more clear cut. Here an elderly woman named Anna Rudd found herself the victim of her son Cephas' unscrupulousness. Evidently Anna was either very trusting of her son or had lost her mental acuity because her son found it easy to deprive her of an annuity he owed her. On a visit to her son's house Anna signed a paper which discharged Cephas of responsibility for paying her $8.88 annually. Two of Anna's grandsons explained how this transpired:

> Anna says that her s[ai]d son presented said papers to her for her to sign asking her if she could write her name on her answering in the affermative as she thought [he] wished her to sign them she did . . . but [she] did not know what was contained in said writings as they were not read in [her] hearing.[52]

That Cephas did not read the papers he wanted his mother to sign is not surprising—clearly he intended to relieve himself of a financial obligation to her without her knowledge. Only when a grandson of Anna Rudd learned what had happened were steps taken to restore the old woman's rights. Such behavior, which exploited either a mother's trust or an old woman's weakness, would have horrified not only the authors of prescriptive literature but ordinary Connecticut people alike who held to the idea that aged parents deserved the respect and care of their children.

Early national Connecticut was home to a full spectrum of filial relationships. The example of children who not only respected but also nursed their aged parents shows that for some, duty to family was a principal objective even if it was inconvenient and unpleasant. Meanwhile the tendency of many parents and children to sustain warm and satisfying relations, sometimes over long distances, speaks of the fundamental importance of the filial bond even in a world of increasing mobility and new opportunity. Yet it is a mistake to suppose that before the advent of our modern world most filial relationships were steeped in love and duty. Children might not visit as often as expected or pay the attention parents wanted. Or they might dispute with their parents over material resources or deny them comforts. For their part, parents might behave badly toward children, making peevish demands or failing to share their bounty with offspring. Therefore though good filial relationships were prescribed in printed literature and undoubtedly hoped for by aged parents, early national Americans were not entirely successful in taming the volatile mix called family to ensure love and respect for elderly kin.

Grandparents and Grandchildren

Relations with grandchildren, though less well-documented, seem to have run a similar gamut from very positive to abysmal in quality. In some cases, grandchildren and grandparents were extremely attached by an intense, affectionate bond. Frances Ann Brace, for example, was raised in the home of her Hartford grandparents, who took great pains to assure her welfare. When as a girl she was sent to school in Litchfield, five towns to the west of Hartford, Frances described an unexpected visit from her beloved grandparents:

> I catched up my bonnet and ran home, there saw my Grand Parents. It was so unexpected tears of joy immediately flowed, which I could not suppress, and they thought I was not pleased to see them but had they known my thoughts, they would have a different opinion ... I feel better contented than I did before they came though it was *hard parting*. Tears of a very different character, then showed themselves.[53]

Though Frances eventually married and moved away from Hartford she kept in touch through correspondence. In one letter she told her grandparents, "how frequently I have been reminded ... of the pleasant hours in the society of you both that have passed in former days, and the recollection of which inspires grateful feelings for your unremitted kindness."[54] Not long after, her grandfather reciprocated the sentiment telling her of his gratitude for his "dear relations" including "grandchildren, for all of whom, I entertain the tenderest affection."[55]

The grandfather of Eliza Staples, one "Grandpapa Wakeman," was similarly enmeshed in his granddaughter's life. Wakeman lived in Ridgefield, within easy distance of his daughter, son-in-law, and granddaughter Eliza in neighboring Redding. Because relations were good among this family there were frequent visits back and forth. For example, as a teen in the summer of 1814 Eliza recorded the following in her diary:

> June 16: Have come to Grandpa W's just at night.
> June 21: I have been to Ridgefield again; & stay to Grandpas all night.
> July 4: Went to meeting in Ridgefield ... we stayed to Grandpa's to tea.[56]

Though grandparent and grandchild lived in separate households, frequent visits brought them together often.

However, even grandchildren who did not see their grandparents regularly could form strong attachments to them. Benjamin Tompkins of Middletown, the grandson of Shadrach and Aletta Osborn of Southbury, lived quite a distance from his grandparents. However during a visit one summer a bond developed, inspiring him to address numerous fond letters to them. In 1819 he wrote,

> Altho I wrote you a lttr a few weeks since yet I think so much about Southbury that I can not help writing again . . . I long to see you all and expect that pleasure in a few weeks if I should not go to Southbury I hope you will come here for I want to see you more & more.

He concluded this epistle saying "I shall be highly gratified if you will take the trouble to write to your affectionate Grand Son."[57]

Perhaps because the grandparent-grandchild relationship was less immediate than the parent-child relationship more complete histories of interactions across three generations is lacking. However, evidence such as that quoted above suggests that the grandchild-grandparent relationship could be characterized by warm interactions enjoyed by both young and old. Though prescriptive literature on the filial relationship outlined specific duties children owed to parents, less was said about the responsibilities of grandchildren beyond the general injunction to respect the aged. It appears that though some grandchildren may indeed have respected their elders, they were also likely to regard them sentimentally. Thus on the death of his grandmother, a young man named Eliphalet Silliman wrote in his diary, "This morning... my much respected and beloved grandmother departed this life."[58] To Silliman respect and love mingled together best expressed his feelings toward his ninety-three-year-old grandmother.

However, the affection that characterized some relationships was strained or absent in others. One court case—that of Olive Montague of Wethersfield—provides a glimpse into grandparent-grandchild relations that were far from ideal. Olive Montague was, in 1820, a widow who "by reason of age sickness & other infirmity" could neither support nor maintain herself by her own toil. In addition, Olive was entirely destitute, "having no estate wherewithall she could be supported or maintained." As a result, Olive had called on the town of Wethersfield for aid and the town had in turn "laid out & expended for the maintenance of s[ai]d Olive in board lodging medicine & other necessaries about the sum of 150 dolls." However the town grew tired of supporting Olive, especially since she had no fewer than five grandchildren in Wethersfield, another five in neighboring Hartford, two more in nearby Berlin, and one grandson in Enfield all of whom were "of sufficient ability to support & maintain" Olive. Indeed they were not only able to aid their wretched grandmother, but were in fact legally obliged to under Connecticut law.[59] Yet all thirteen shirked their responsibility requiring the selectmen of Wethersfield to ask the court for an "order & decree" that the grandchildren pay not only the $150 that Wethersfield had already expended on Olive's behalf but also "such sums as shall be deemed just & reasonable for the support & maintenance of s[ai]d Olive" in the future. The court agreed that six of the grandchildren were indeed responsible for their aged grandmother's plight and ordered them to pay 34 cents each per week to provide her with necessities.[60] Had Olive Montague done something to deserve her grandchildren's neglect and apparent inhumanity toward her? We do not know. It is clear, however, that under some circumstances, grandchildren living in very close proximity to a grandparent could elect to ignore her suffering and allow her to face the indignity of becoming a town pauper without intervening. Though prescriptive literature laid down guidelines for good behavior across generations, the reality was that love and respect were not necessarily intrinsic to the grandchild-grandparent relationship.[61]

Sisters and Brothers

Bonds between elderly people and their sisters and brothers—who were frequently old themselves—were the final important component in the family lives of the aged. Born into the same family and sharing memories of early life together, siblings could remain strongly bonded even as the years advanced. Yet the passage of time frequently scattered siblings geographically, making contact more difficult.

For Rebecca Noyes of Stonington—who had never married and hence had neither a spouse, children, nor grandchildren—siblings were especially important, forming the core of her family life throughout old age. Indeed for her entire elderly life Noyes resided among her brother Thomas' family, along with another sister named Bridget. Thus Rebecca's daily life consisted of activities with siblings to whom she was greatly attached. She and her sister Bridget were particularly inseparable. Some entries from Rebecca's diary suggest the tenor of their shared daily routine:

> May 21: Sister B & myself repair'd our black bombazet gowns.
> May 31: Sister B & me were engaged in making our white flannel petticoat.
> July 29: Sister B and me went into a warm *bath*—we felt very comfortable after it.[62]

Not only did Rebecca and Bridget do everything together, they seemed to feel everything together as well. In addition, when difficulties arose the two shared the burden by caring for each other. When Bridget fell ill for a time in 1826, Rebecca watched over her carefully while recording her feelings in her diary. She wrote:

> May 12: I felt very gloomy about my Dear sister.
> May 13: She thinks she is a little better *I catch at a straw.*
> May 16: my heart is full. I wish I cou'd think my dear Sister B. was better.[63]

Bridget recovered and the relationship continued to flourish so that in 1830 Rebecca reflected, "I am blest with my Dear Sister Bridget's company she is all attention to me. What a comfort to have so kind a *Sister.*"[64] Having grown up together and shared many of their older years in the bosom of their brother's family, Rebecca and Bridget were closer than some spouses. Their relationship shows just how important and positive sibling relationships could be in old age.

Of course, for people who had raised families of their own sibling bonds were likely to be less central to daily life. Physical distance could also make visits difficult. Timothy Maltby lived in Richland, New York while his brother John Maltby Sr. resided in Northford, Connecticut. Though Timothy intended to pay John a visit in 1830, he told his brother, "I have been Confind at home taken sick . . . and [am] not yet able to meke you the visit which i Calculated on." He also explained that, even if his health were good, he had to wait until someone repaid him a debt in order to have enough cash for the journey.[65] Whether he finally traveled to Connecticut is unknown. In the meantime, correspondence helped bridge the distance between the two brothers, allowing them to share news and experiences with one another.

Distance similarly intruded between Elisha Niles of Chatham, Connecticut and his "Sister Kellogg" who resided somewhere in New York state. When, at fifty-two, Elisha Niles set out to see her he "had not seen my sister Kellogg nor her family for more than 20 years." Still, he arranged to visit her at last and happily "found all well & verry rich for a New Country." He estimated that on this trip, which included stops elsewhere, he covered "about 1260 miles" in all.[66] Given the commitment such a journey required both in time and money it is not surprising he did not visit his sister more often.

Still, despite separations, sibling relationships could remain very important to aged people. For example, the parents and siblings of Eunice Stone, even when long dead, lingered heavily in her memory. She wrote: "my dear friends and early relatives are gone—now sleeping in the dust . . . but distance or time—has not lessened my tender affections for any of them."[67] And on another occasion she reflected, "when I look back on the days of my youth—under the wing of parents—Brothers, sisters, [I] am lost & all seems a dream—where am I—[I] seem alone." For Stone, her relationships with her "early relatives" were like a fixed anchor in a "busy, bustling world" she no longer felt very connected to.[68]

Like relationships with grandchildren, evidence on sibling relationships is not plentiful. The cases cited above hint at the possibilities for very warm sibling relationships in old age and also at how time and distance could pull brothers and sisters apart.

This chapter demonstrates that family relations in old age were complex and that the behavior of the aged and their kin toward one another stubbornly resists easy categorization. Archival records document positive, satisfying relationships that enriched old age as well as abysmal relationships that can only have reduced the quality of life for elderly men and women. Between these extremes lay a thousand gradations of experience. Yet though the evidence does not create a tidy story or suggest a pattern of change over time in the period between 1790 and 1830, the elderly's relationships with family are nonetheless instructive on a number of counts.

The wide range of family experiences among the aged occurring in one specific place and time demonstrates that efforts to see the elderly's experiences as monolithic in the past are misguided. In the study of the aged it was once intellectually fashionable to try to label societies as "pre-modern" or "modern" on the basis of the elderly's family relations, ideas about the aged, and other factors. The assumption was that pre-modern and modern societies were each marked by a distinct set of characteristics that determined the experiences of the aged.[69] Scholars more recently have continued to describe the elderly's circumstances in overly simplified terms.[70] Evidence from early national Connecticut shows that even within a relatively homogeneous population, family relations varied tremendously. In other words, there was no single typically pre-modern or pre-industrial way of arranging family life or treating the elderly. Instead, American society two hundred years ago displayed the complexity that we sometimes like to think of as the peculiar province of our fast-paced world.

In addition, this chapter undermines the findings of David Hackett Fischer who has written of the early national period as a time of wrenching, revolutionary change in age relations. Specifically Fischer argues for a change in this period from "exaltation" of the aged to increasing denigration of the old—a change which according to Fischer was well underway by 1820.[71] The family situations described in Connecticut diaries, letters, and court documents can be seen as case studies of age relations. Contrary to Fischer's contention, they reveal no tidal wave of unidirectional change sweeping through age relations. Long-term changes in age relations may have been occurring in early national America. But if they were, they must have been far more subtle and uneven than has been suggested.

The evidence presented here also refutes the less scholarly but nevertheless widely believed idea that somehow the aged and their families meshed seamlessly in the past. It is appealing to assume that at one time old and young lived together in harmonious, solid families whose integrity was safe from the breakdown that seems to be rending twentieth-century families. This is a fantasy. Early national families had their share of discord. By showing both the dark and light sides of the aged's kin relations this chapter debunks a popular notion, replacing it with the knowledge that our social declension relative to the aged may not be as severe as many have assumed.

The evidence on old people's family lives also demonstrates the importance of looking not only at what people say or write about a subject but also at what they do. All societies formulate notions of ideal behavior, and such ideals relating to the elderly are probably found in most cultures. Yet understanding such ideals and expectations provides only half the story. How people actually behaved toward their parents, children, grandparents, and grandchildren is the other half. Connecticut sources show that while ideas may inform people, complex circumstances determine whether ideas actually get put into practice. People may have valued good relations between the aged and their kin, yet factors as diverse as personality, geographical dispersion, health, and finances could exert force that undermined ideal notions and effectively sabotaged relationships. In short, the world of ideas and the practice of daily life surely interweave, but they are far from the same thing.

Finally, the evidence on family indicates another area of challenge for old people. While there is no evidence that family relations were more difficult in old age than at other times, there is also no evidence that advanced age operated to ward off trouble with kin. However, if relationships with kin became embittered those saddled with the burdens of old age were at a disadvantage. More than others, the elderly depended on family. When family ties weakened or broke, the elderly were likely to suffer disproportionately, rendered especially vulnerable to the hardships of old age.

NOTES

1. Of course, the qualitative documents employed for this project were not selected in a truly random fashion. However, the author read diaries and letters she thought might contain information on old people without any other prior expectation of what else they might contain. No effort was made to seek out either positive or negative interactions between the aged and their kin. Court records—because they by nature concern contentious relationships—do tend to highlight difficulties among the aged and their families. These latter, however, have been used sparingly here.
2. David Hackett Fischer's claim that the aged were venerated in the period from 1607 to 1820 suggests a high degree of uniformity of (positive) experience among the aged in the past. See *Growing Old in America*, expanded ed. (New York: Oxford University Press, 1978), chapter 1.
3. James Cogswell, Diary, 27 January 1790, CHS.
4. Ibid., 2 September 1790.
5. Ibid., 13 March 1790.
6. Ibid., 4 June 1791.
7. William Williams to William T. Williams, 15 May 1811, Williams Family Papers, CHS.
8. William H. Lee, 1 August 1820, RPA.
9. Abiel Baldwin to John Maltby, 14 February 1822, Maltby Family Papers, CHS.
10. Joseph Dyer case, March 1832, CG.
11. Joseph Dyer, 1 August 1820, RPA.
12. Cogswell, Diary, 13 April 1790.
13. Eliphalet Williams to William Williams, 27 January 1800, Williams Family Papers, CHS.
14. Enoch Pond to John Maltby [Sr.], 4 January 1831, Maltby Family Papers, CHS.
15. Timothy Maltby to John Maltby [Sr.], 11 February 1830, Maltby Family Papers, CHS.
16. John Maltby [Jr.] to John Maltby [Sr.], 23 August 1831, Maltby Family Papers, CHS.
17. Ibid., 25 November 1831.
18. Julia-Ann Pond to Selina Maltby-Foote, 11 December 1831, Maltby Family Papers, CHS.
19. Julia-Ann and Enoch Pond to John Maltby [Sr.], 14 February 1832, Maltby Family Papers, CHS.
20. John Faragher, "Old Women and Old Men in Seventeenth-Century Wethersfield, Connecticut," *Women's Studies* 4 (Special Issue 1976): 18. Faragher's findings are based on a sample of approximately 180 Wethersfield households from 1640 to 1700.
21. Alexander Keyssar, "Widowhood in Eighteenth-Century Massachusetts: A Problem in the History of the Family," *Perspectives in American History* 8 (1974): 83–119.
22. Lisa Wilson, *Life After Death: Widows in Pennsylvania 1750–1850* (Philadelphia: Temple University Press, 1992), 2. Wilson's book covers many aspects of widows lives, although she does not focus on aged widows particularly.
23. Terri Premo, *Winter Friends: Women Growing Old in the New Republic, 1785–1835* (Urbana: University of Illinois Press, 1990), 24.
24. Shubael Bartlett, Diary, 14 July 1831, CHS.
25. Ibid., 16 July 1831.
26. Cogswell, Diary, 30 July 1790.
27. E.O. Jameson, *The Cogswells in America* (1884), 119.

28. John C. Pease and John M. Niles, *Gazetteer of the States of Connecticut and Rhode Island* (Hartford CT: William S. Marsh, 1819), 11.
29. Benjamin Clark Gilman to Eliza G. Odiorne, 24 August 1834, Benjamin Clark Gilman Correspondence, CHS.
30. John Maltby [Jr.] to John [Sr.] and Elizabeth Maltby, 2 October 1829, Maltby Family Papers, CHS.
31. Margaret Maltby to John [Sr.] and Elizabeth Maltby, 23 August 1828, Maltby Family Papers, CHS.
32. Obedience Hoadley to Elizabeth Maltby, undated, Maltby Family Papers, CHS.
33. Ibid., undated.
34. John Ives to Obedience Hoadley, 4 March 1829, Maltby Family Papers, CHS.
35. Benjamin Franklin, *Benjamin Franklin's Autobiographical Writings*, ed. Carl Van Doren (New York: Viking Press, 1945), 101.
36. William Williams to Solomon Williams, 16 July 1810, Williams Family Papers, CHS.
37. William Williams to William T. Williams, 15 May 1811, Williams Family Papers, CHS.
38. Solomon Williams to William Williams, 1 January 1807, Williams Family Papers, CHS.
39. William Williams to Solomon Williams, 16 July 1810, Williams Family Papers, CHS.
40. *Acts and Laws of the State of Connecticut* (Hartford CT: Hudson & Goodwin, 1796), 232–237; *The Public Statute Laws of the State of Connecticut*, book 1 (Hartford CT: Hudson & Goodwin, 1808), 382–387; *The Public Statute Laws of the State of Connecticut* (Hartford CT: S.G. Goodrich & Huntington & Hopkins, 1821), 274-278.
41. Current California law is very similar to that employed in early national Connecticut. Now as then, conservators are appointed by the court in response to a petition from an interested party. Modern conservators are bound, as were their early national counterparts, to administer the estates of their charges prudently and to account for their actions to the court. Current law, however, is somewhat more refined. There are now several different types of conservatorships as well as more elaborate procedures and safeguards. Conservatorships today are used most frequently to provide for mentally retarded, mentally ill, or aged people who are too physically weak or mentally impaired to manage on their own. However, though in the early national period courts probably took a stronger hand in investigating and managing the property of those accused of "idleness, mismanagement, or bad husbandry," it is still possible to have a conservator appointed in cases in which an individual appears to be incompetently wasting his or her property (by, for example, making large donations to questionable parties).
42. Abel Carter case, Selectmen of Southington to Hartford County Court, 27 May 1796, CG.
43. Ibid., E. Andrews to Hartford County Court, 30 May 1790.
44. Ibid., John Curtis and Timothy Clark to Hartford County Court, 30 May 1796.
45. Ibid., John Carter, Abel Carter Jr. and Daniel Carter to Hartford County Court, 31 May 1796.
46. Greven shows that fathers in colonial Andover, Massachusetts often tended to resist turning over their land to sons until their deaths. The effect of this was to keep sons dependent, and therefore obedient, to fathers until relatively late in their lives. Though the Carter saga suggests that some fathers continued to resist parceling out property in the early national period, it is unclear how prevalent this tendency was. In any case, the elder Carter's lack of generosity appears neither to have ensured his sons' obedience nor prevented their economic independence. See *Four Generations: Population, Land, and Family in Colonial Andover, Massachusetts* (Ithaca: Cornell University Press, 1970).

47. Abel Carter case, Selectmen of Southington to Hartford County Court, 27 May 1796, CG.
48. Samuel Hooker [Sr.] case, Samuel Hooker Jr. to Hartford County Court, 28 June 1783, CG.
49. Ibid., Moses Gilburt et al. to Hartford County Court, 20 October 1785.
50. Ibid., Testimony of Samuel Hart, 18 November 1785.
51. Ibid., Testimony of Elias Beckley et al., 24 October 1785.
52. Document signed by G.[?] Brigham & Artemas Gurley[?], 19 January 1819, Norman Brigham Correspondence, CHS.
53. Frances Ann Brace to "Dear Aunt," 22 July 1822, Bunce-Brace Correspondence, CHS.
54. Frances Ann Brace to Jonathan Brace, 24 June 1831, Bunce-Brace Correspondence, CHS.
55. Jonathan Brace to James M. Bunce, 29 June 1831, Bunce-Brace Correspondence, CHS.
56. Eliza Ann Hull Staples, Diary, 16, 21 June, 4 July 1814, CSL.
57. Benjamin W. Tompkins to S. Osborn, 2 November 1819, Shadrach Osborn Papers, CHS.
58. Eliphalet Silliman, Journal, 29 October 1821, CSL.
59. Public relief was a last resort. By law family held primary responsibility for supporting needy kin. Thus if a child or grandchild of a needy parent or grandparent was capable of supporting that person, they were obliged to do so and public aid was not supposed to be given. How strictly these laws were enforced in the early national period is unknown at present. For a detailed discussion of Connecticut's poor laws see Edward Capen, *The Historical Development of the Poor Law of Connecticut*, Studies in History, Economics and Public Law, vol. 22 (New York: Columbia University Press, 1905), 75–76, 116.
60. Olive Montague case, March 1820 and August 1820 sessions, HCC.
61. For some colonial evidence on grandparent-grandchild relations see John Demos, "Old Age in Early New England," in *Aging, Death, and the Completion of Being*, ed. David D. Van Tassel (Philadelphia: University of Pennsylvania Press, 1979), 127–129. For another perspective on grandmothers particularly see Premo, *Winter Friends*, chapter 3.
62. Rebecca Noyes, Diary, 21, 31 May, 29 July 1820, CHS.
63. Ibid., 12, 13, 16 May 1826.
64. Ibid., 13 February 1830.
65. Timothy Maltby to John Maltby [Sr.], 11 February 1830, Maltby Family Papers, CHS.
66. Elisha Niles, Diary, 31 October 1816, CHS.
67. Eunice Stone to Abigail Williams, 3 December 1829, Abigail Williams Correspondence, CHS.
68. Ibid., 23 April 1829.
69. Vern Bengtson et al., "Modernization, Modernity, and Perceptions of Aging: A Cross-Cultural Study," *Journal of Gerontology* 30 (November 1975): 688–695, provides a good example of this kind of thinking.
70. The most glaring example is Fischer, *Growing Old in America*.
71. Ibid., chapter 2.

VIII

Age, Wealth, and Community Leadership

In 1784 Hartford was incorporated as a city. Not long afterwards, in early 1785, its citizens decided on an official seal to represent the new civic body. Hartford's voters agreed that the best graphic symbol for their home would consist of the

> Connecticut River, represented by the figure of an Old Man, crown'd with Rushes, seated against a Rock, holding an Urn with a Stream flowing from it—At his feet a net & fish peculiar to the River, lying by it, with Barrels and Bales—over his head an Oak growing out of a Cleft in the Rock—Round the whole these words Sigillum Civitatis Hartfordiensis.[1]

The citizens of Hartford thus selected an old man amidst plenty for their official public seal—an image that remained in use until 1852.

Symbolically then, the old had a central place in Hartford's civic life. Yet the reality of public life was somewhat different. This chapter offers one perspective on the elderly's involvement in community affairs. Specifically it looks at the role of the aged as leaders in Hartford. By investigating two characteristics of leaders—age and wealth—we learn both who Hartford's people considered worthy and appropriate custodians of their public institutions, and equally important, who actually held the reigns of power. In the process, the place of the aged in public life becomes clear.

When the records of local government, churches, voluntary associations, and institutions such as schools and hospitals are examined closely it becomes plain that the aged assumed a more marginal role in civic affairs than might be inferred from the city's seal. Indeed the elderly did not generally lead and manage Hartford. While the experience that came with age was valued in leaders, this held true only to a point—men in middle age were preferred to those of other ages. However, being middle-aged was not in itself sufficient qualification for leadership and responsibility. Wealth counted for a great deal and most of Hartford's civic leaders possessed substantially more than their fellow citizens. In short, while the elderly might lead, qualities other than old age were generally preferred. Thus, though scholars have sometimes argued that early national Americans looked to old men for leadership, the Hartford evidence does not bear this out.[2]

Indeed, Hartford was far from a gerontocracy. Yet though the influence of the aged in civic affairs was limited, there is no evidence that it declined from 1790 to 1830. Rather, it appears that leadership patterns in early national Hartford were similar to patterns already well-established in the eighteenth century or earlier, undermining any attempt to link declining public power among the elderly with the social and economic changes that were transforming the lives of early national Americans.

SOURCES AND METHODS

All communities have leaders—men or women who act as "guiding or directing heads" of the people around them.[3] In general leaders can be divided into two groups: those whose influence is informal (authors or wealthy philanthropists for example), and those whose influence stems from connection to formalized institutional structures such as government. Because no systematic records of informal leaders exist, I focus exclusively on formal leaders—officeholders—who left records as participants in institutions.

Leaders were elected regularly to head four different types of Hartford organizations—local government (the City of Hartford and the Town of Hartford), churches, voluntary organizations, and institutions (schools and hospitals).[4] In many instances the names of these leaders, their positions, and their dates of service have survived, yielding a dataset of about 4,400 observations.[5] By matching this information to age data from elsewhere—which was possible for just

Age, Wealth, and Community Leadership 233

over 80 percent of all leaders—a fairly complete age profile of Hartford's influential men emerges.[6] And by matching officers' names to information from Hartford's tax rolls—which was possible for about 76 percent of leaders in the years for which tax records exist—a good picture of their wealth relative to non-leaders becomes clear.[7]

Because the vast majority of Hartford's formal leaders—from mayors to deacons to trustees—were voted into office by their fellow citizens, it stands to reason that these officers reflected the taste of the voting population.[8] Understanding voter preferences is important to grasping the place of the aged in public life. Though I have not conducted an exhaustive survey of all aspects of leadership, an examination of age and wealth provides ample evidence that the elderly did not occupy a central role in leading Hartford.[9]

AGE AND LEADERSHIP IN HARTFORD

What relationship did age have to leadership in early national Hartford? Were older leaders preferred to younger men? How important were the aged in the community's public affairs? These questions can be answered by taking several different perspectives on Hartford's officeholders. To begin with we look at trends in the ages of leaders over the forty-year period from 1790 to 1830 to see if Hartford's guiding men were generally getting older or younger. Next we consider leaders by the types of organizations they led to discern whether government, church, voluntary association, and institutional leaders differed substantially from one another in terms of age. And finally we analyze leaders in even smaller subsets—by the precise offices they held—to see if within certain types of organizations, different offices tended to be filled by men of different ages.

Trends in Leaders' Ages Over Time

Looking at leaders' ages over time can indicate whether the involvement of Hartford's elderly people in civic affairs was in flux or relatively stable. Examining leaders' mean and median ages for every year from 1790 to 1830, shown in Figure 8.1, is a good way to begin. Two features of the graph stand out. First, it is immediately obvious

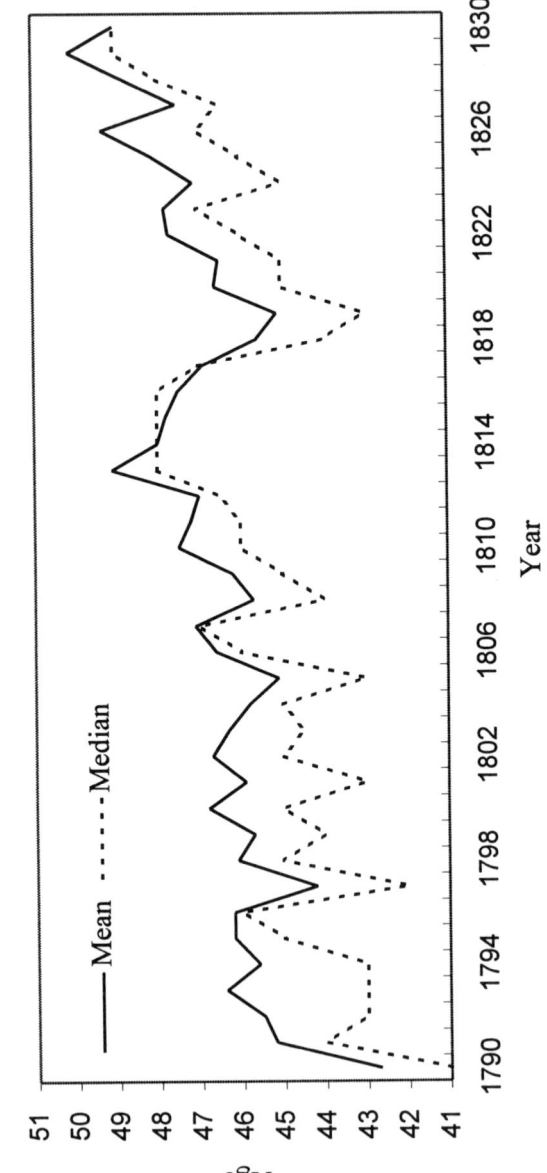

Figure 8.1. Average Ages of Hartford Leaders, 1790-1830

Source: The approximately 80 percent of all Hartford leaders for whom age information is available. See appendix C.

Age, Wealth, and Community Leadership

that Hartford's leaders were, on average, middle-aged rather than especially old or young. Indeed, in every year except one both the mean and the median ages of leaders fell between forty-one and fifty. Overall, the mean age of officeholders for the entire period was forty-seven years and the median forty-six years. These figures quickly make obvious that the aged were not the dominant participants in Hartford's public life at any time during the early national period.

Second, while the average ages of officeholders never stray from solid middle-age, there is a noticeable trend toward slightly older officeholders over the period. This is somewhat surprising since Hartford, like most growing locales in the early national period, was home to more and more organizations with leaders over time. Voluntary organizations accounted for most of the increase. These fledgling bodies provided more opportunities for leadership than had existed earlier. In addition because they could be formed by anyone, and officers were elected from the members only, we can guess that it was easier to become a leader in such an organization than in more established organizations such as local government or churches. And as Mary Ryan has shown, young men and women were quite active in such voluntary associations.[10] For all these reasons we would expect the average age of leaders to drop over the period from 1790 to 1830 as opportunities to lead widened.[11] The fact that average age seems to have risen despite these changes is evidence that Hartford citizens may have valued older leaders more over time rather than less. Still, leadership in early national Hartford was dominated by the middle-aged while the elderly played a stable, but peripheral role.

Figure 8.2 provides another perspective on the ages of Hartford's public figures by showing the percentages of leaders of different ages for different decades. As in the previous graph, figure 8.2 shows the later decades having somewhat more older officeholders than the earlier decades. However, aside from these relatively slight variations, the data from all decades are quite similar. In each decade, men in their twenties made up a small proportion of all leaders—from about 4 to 7 percent. Men in their thirties were much more active as leaders, comprising about 21 to 28 percent of all leaders. Men in their forties were always the dominant age group, making up from about 26 to 35 percent of leaders. Men past their forties found fewer places in Hartford's leadership. Those in their fifties comprised from about 19

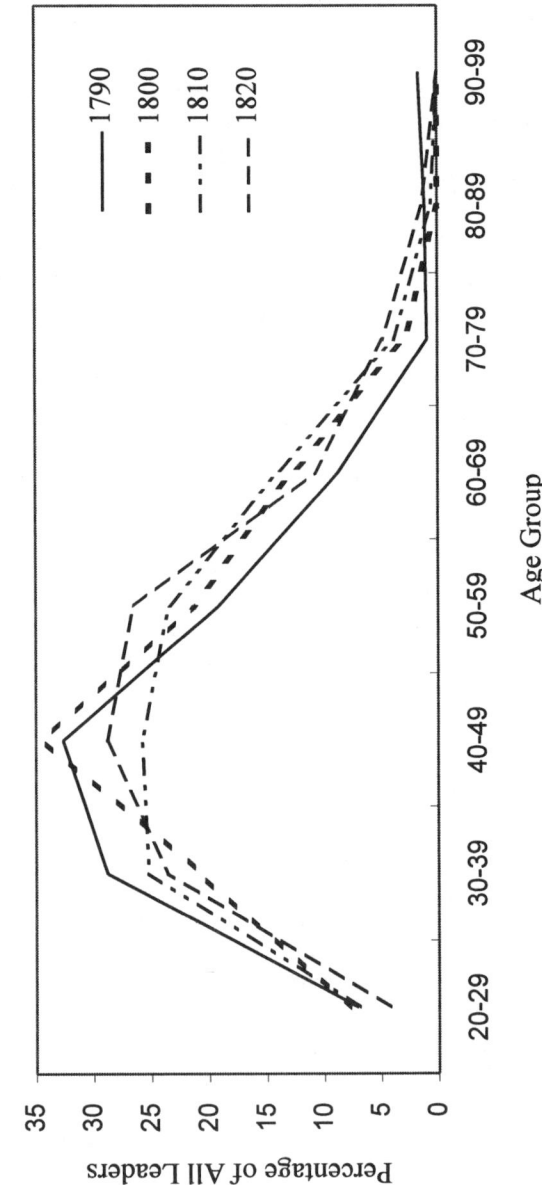

Figure 8.2. Ages of Hartford Leaders by Decade, 1790-1830

Source: The approximately 80 percent of all Hartford leaders for whom age information is available (excluding two leaders under age twenty). See appendix C.

Age, Wealth, and Community Leadership

percent to 27 percent of all leaders, while those in their sixties formed an even smaller 8 to 14 percent. Men in their seventies were even more rarely active as civic officials—always making up less than 5 percent of all leaders. Very few leaders—less than 3 percent—were either in their eighties or nineties. This graph thus confirms the dominance of middle-aged men—especially those between age forty and forty-nine—as leaders, but indicates that men in early old age (their fifties) were often active as well. With more advanced age, leadership declined sharply with the result that very few truly elderly men participated in Hartford's public affairs. That these results are similar over the whole period again suggests that Hartford's citizens were not in the process of dramatically altering their preferences in leaders either to the advantage or detriment of older people from 1790 to 1830.

While it is useful to know the sheer percentages that each age group contributed to Hartford's leadership, such figures can be better understood when compared to the population at large. Reliable data on the age breakdown of Hartford's population is available for one year—1830—when federal census-takers began enumerating residents' ages in detail. When presented alongside information on leaders' ages from the 1820s, this data is quite illuminating as seen in figure 8.3. Here it becomes clear that Hartford's leaders were not drawn proportionately from the population of adult males in general. For example, young men in their twenties were a very large segment of the total male population—about 45 percent—yet men of this age made up only about 4 percent of all leaders in the 1820s. Men in their thirties were much better represented among leaders, with about an equal share in leadership and the population. Since men in their twenties held so few offices, older men obviously had to hold disproportionately more—a fact that is evident in looking at men in their forties. About twice as many men of this age were leaders than we might expect from their share in the overall population. Even more surprising is the disproportion among fifty-year-olds. Though comprising only about 7 percent of adult male Hartfordians in 1830, they made up about 26 percent of all leaders. Men in their fifties thus held the most power and influence in public affairs per capita of any age group. Indeed, though the pool of men this age was relatively small, Hartford's citizens clearly found this group generally attractive

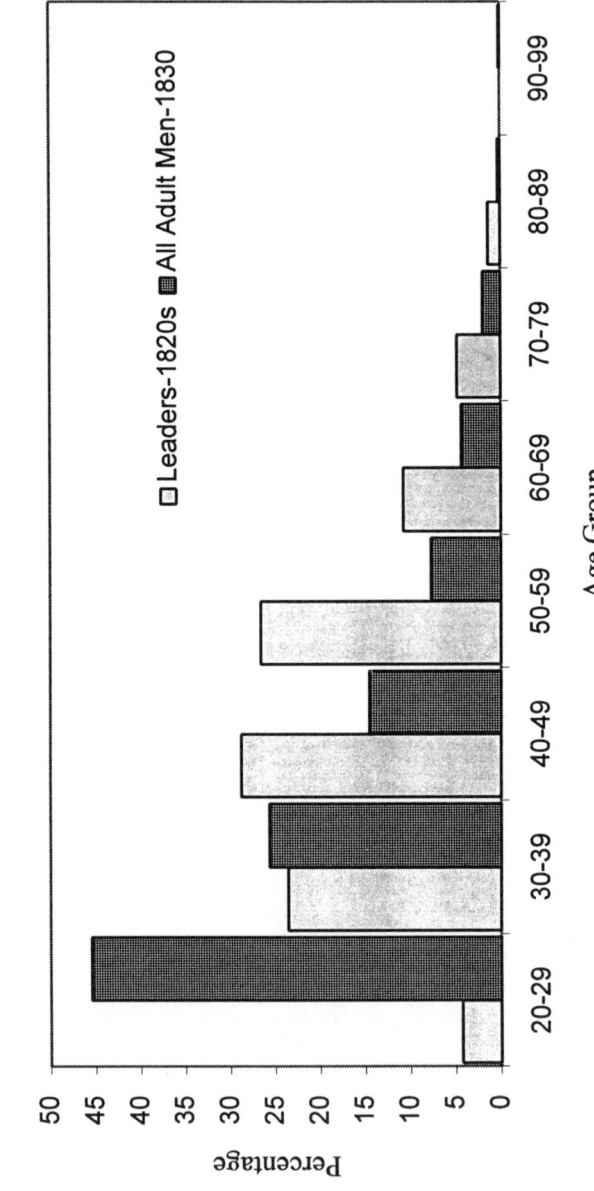

Figure 8.3. Ages of Leaders Compared to Ages of All Adult Men

Source: Hartford leaders from 1820 through 1830 for whom age data are available (1334 observations). See appendix C.

Age, Wealth, and Community Leadership 239

as leaders. Sixty-year-olds were also disproportionately active as leaders, though significantly less so than fifty-year olds. And even men in their seventies and eighties retained a larger share of leadership positions than expected. These findings serve to balance the evidence presented earlier showing the aged as relatively minor participants in Hartford's civic affairs. While older men were never the majority of Hartford's leaders, old men played a larger leadership role than expected because their fellow Hartfordians chose them disproportionately.[12]

We have gained some important insights into Hartford's early national civic leaders. To begin with, the "average" leader was middle-aged rather than old. We have also found that leadership tended to decline with age and that in terms of sheer numbers, the old—and especially the very old—played relatively limited roles in public life. Yet tempering this is the knowledge that the aged often played a greater role than we would expect from their share in the larger population. Since these findings hold true from 1790 to 1830, continuity rather than change can be said to have characterized the position of the elderly in public life during the period. Though it is true that Hartford was not ruled by the aged, there is no reason to believe that elderly men were in the process of losing what share of influence they had. By the same token, there is no conclusive evidence of any increase in public power or participation by aged citizens in civic life.

Leaders' Ages by the Type of Organization They Headed

Having considered the basic age structure of Hartford's leaders and the question of change over time in this structure, we can consider leaders from another perspective—by the type of organizations they headed. There were four main types of organizations in Hartford with leaders: local government, churches, voluntary associations, and institutions (a category consisting of schools and hospitals). By looking at the ages of their leaders separately we discover that within the large trends described above there were variations in the extent of the elderly's involvement.

Figure 8.4 and table 8.1 show some of this variation by presenting the mean and median ages of officeholders for the different types of

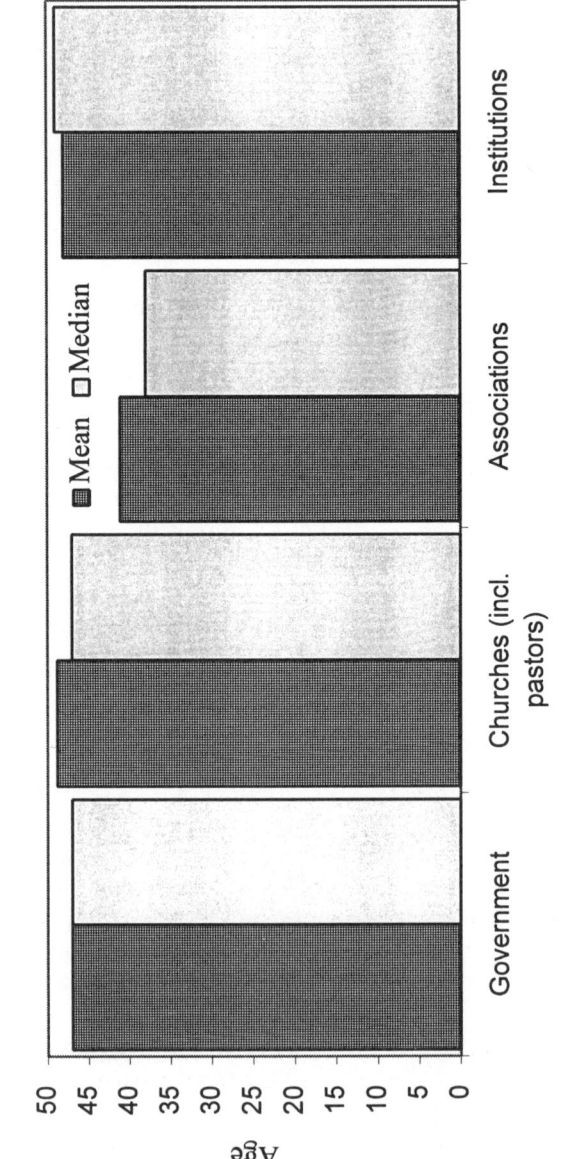

Figure 8.4. Average Ages of Leaders by Type of Organization, 1790-1830

Source: The approximately 80 percent of all Hartford leaders for whom age information is available. See appendix C.

organizations. As we saw earlier, the mean age of all officeholders was forty-seven, while the median was forty-six. Yet different kinds of organizations called for somewhat older or younger leaders. Churches and institutions, for example, tended to have older leaders than average. In the case of churches, this can be explained in large part by the fact that deacons (a type of leader most churches selected) seem often to have been chosen at advanced ages and retained until death. The reasons why institutional leaders were older than other kinds of officers is less clear. One hypothesis is that such leaders were expected to make large financial contributions to the organizations they led. As chapter 4 explained, men in Hartford tended to reach their peak economic health in late middle age and early old age. Thus somewhat older men who were likely to be wealthier may have been desired over younger men. Officers in local government meanwhile were quite average agewise. However, those who headed associations tended to be especially young. This is not surprising since voluntary associations could be established by any group of mutually interested individuals and run according to the tastes of the group alone. A candidate for office in the Hartford Peace Society, for example, would only have to appeal to his peers in the group. In addition, the responsibilities of officers in voluntary associations (in contrast to government) were likely to be less weighty. These factors probably all contributed to the younger ages of association leaders.[13]

Table 8.1. Mean and Median Ages of Officeholders by Type of Organization

Type	Mean	Median	Obs.
Government	47.0	47	1348
Churches	48.8	47	1208
Associations	41.1	38	456
Institutions	48.0	49	540
All Types	47.0	46	3549

Source: See appendix C.

The averages just discussed can be better understood by considering figure 8.5, which illustrates the age structure of leaders in different types of organizations. This graph confirms the distinctiveness of each type of organization. Voluntary associations stand out most in that they had many more youthful leaders than any

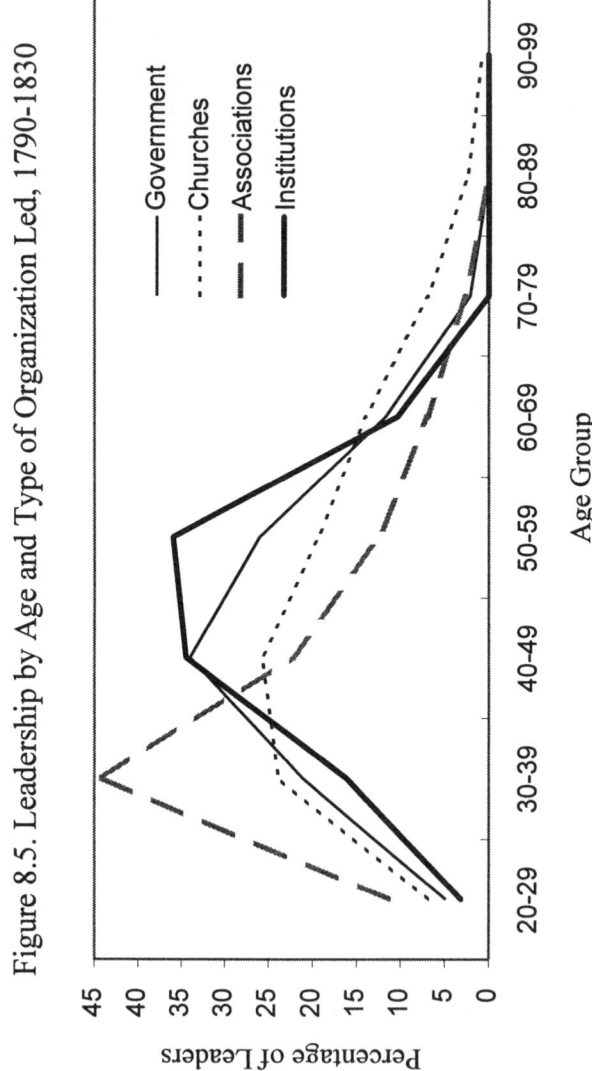

Figure 8.5. Leadership by Age and Type of Organization Led, 1790-1830

Source: The approximately 80 percent of all Hartford leaders for whom age information is available (excluding two leaders under age twenty). See appendix C.

Age, Wealth, and Community Leadership

other type of organization. About 12 percent were in their twenties, and the largest group—nearly 45 percent—were in their thirties. From this high point there was a steep decline in leadership among older men with the result that only about 22 percent of associational leaders were aged fifty or older. These findings are consistent with those of Mary Ryan who notes that associations tended to bring together people of similar ages into "voluntary peer groups."[14] In a society as youthful as early national America, this no doubt resulted in many associations comprised of relatively young people who would elect leaders from amongst themselves.

Government leaders follow another pattern. The largest segment of local government officials were in their forties with a decline in leadership after that age. In all, men aged fifty and over made up about 40 percent of all government posts, a fraction almost twice as high as that of associations. Churches show an even greater tendency to select older men as leaders. As with government officers, the largest group of church leaders are in their forties. Yet the decline in leadership with age among church leaders is gentler. As a result about 43 percent of all church leaders are fifty or older. In addition, churches are the only organizations with very elderly men—those in their eighties and nineties—serving as leaders. Finally, institutions also favored somewhat older leaders as seen by the fact that the largest segment of such leaders were in their fifties and about 46 percent of all leaders were over that age. Yet institutions evidently preferred older men only to a point. Only about 10 percent of all institutional leaders were sixty or over and none were aged seventy or more.

The public career of Josiah Beckwith, a Hartford leader, illustrates some of the patterns just described. Beckwith held his first post at the age of forty when he was elected town constable. Very active in civic life over the next seventeen years, Beckwith eventually occupied offices in city government, voluntary associations such as the Hartford Evangelical Tract Society and the Sunday School Society, and his church as well. However, as he moved into his late fifties, Beckwith's leadership activities narrowed. Elected to his last job in government (as councilman) at age fifty-seven, he subsequently held offices only in churches, serving both as Trustee to the First Methodist Church and as Deacon in the First Congregational Church.[15] Thus by the time of his death at age sixty-one, Beckwith had, except for religious leadership, eased out of public life.

Anecdotal evidence such as this combined with the aggregate findings make clear that though Hartford's people generally selected men to lead them from the ranks of the middle aged, they also considered the circumstances of leadership in making selections. In some contexts, such as voluntary organizations, younger men offered their services as leaders and were accepted, while in other contexts they were likely to be rejected. The same was true for the elderly. Even the very old found leadership roles open to them in churches, while men of the same age were evidently undesired in other types of organizations.

Leaders' Ages by Office

Hartford's leaders and the place of the aged among them can be further understood by looking at the ages of leaders in specific offices. We have just seen how different types of organizations called for officers of diverse ages. A look at specific offices indicates that there was further age differentiation even within organizations. To illustrate this point tables 8.2 through 8.5 present the mean and median ages of leaders in various posts. Though it is difficult to precisely rank most offices by prestige and level of responsibility, the most important office in each category is easily identified and is listed first (i.e. mayor, moderator, pastor, and president).[16]

Looking first at the city government offices it is evident that the job of mayor, the city's foremost executive office, tended to be filled by men quite a bit older than any other city office. At an average age of sixty-four, Hartford's mayors were generally old. Aldermen, the second ranking post, were also on average older than most other city officials. Meanwhile middle-aged men in their forties were generally selected for the city's other posts. The youngest of these were the sheriffs. It is likely that relatively youthful men were selected as sheriffs because the job, unlike other major offices, could make strenuous physical demands on its holders. Overall, in city government older men were preferred for the most important jobs though middle-aged men filled more offices.

While we might expect town government to operate the same way it did not. Here the moderator—or what might be called the chairman today—was unlikely to be the oldest officer, though his position was the highest one. Instead the clerk/register was the oldest officer. However by the standards of Hartford leaders in general, the moderator was still older than average. Indeed, voters seemed to have preferred most town officers to be in early old age. Four out of six offices were held by men who were on average fifty or sixty years old, while only two posts (the less prestigious jobs of constable and grand juryman) were held by men on average thirty or forty years old.

Table 8.2. Leaders' Ages in Government Offices, Hartford, 1790–1830

	Office	Mean	Median	Obs.
City	Mayor	64	64	41
	Alderman	51	52	145
	Councilman	47	46	423
	Clerk	45	47	41
	Treasurer	45	44	41
	Collector	46	47	32
	Auditor	48	46	22
	Sheriff	42	41	67
Town	Moderator	55	54	33
	Selectman	51	49	140
	Clerk/Register	64	63	26
	Treasurer	55	54	35
	Constable	43	43	120
	Grandjuryman	36	34	182

Source: See appendix C. Note: Averages have been rounded to the nearest year.

Thus even between the two branches of local government—city and town—voters displayed different preferences in terms of leaders' ages, with town officers more advanced in years than their city counterparts. Yet because the responsibilities of town and city officers were similar, it is hard to believe that voters selected men of different ages for any practical reason or due to any rigid conception of age relations. More likely such choices were simply a matter of custom. As Edward Cook has demonstrated, notions of appropriate ages for town offices were not fixed but instead could vary significantly by locality. For example, in some towns constables might be under forty while other towns preferred constables over this age.[17] Habit or tradition, rather than some universally held sense of age relations, helped determine who got which jobs. This factor probably accounts for much of the difference in city and town officers' ages.

Hartford's church members likewise selected men of different ages depending on the specific job. As table 8.3 shows, the average pastor was in his forties. However, pastors, unlike other leaders who faced regular election, were usually chosen only once with the expectation of life tenure. Thus, while it is worth noting pastors tendency to be in mid-life, their ages are not very revealing of their parishioners tastes. Lay officers' ages tell us more. Deacons tended to be relatively old, as a result of the fact that once chosen they were often retained until death. Yet other church posts typically went to younger men. It is likely that individuals new to church leadership would begin their careers as clerks and later take on other posts, perhaps eventually becoming a deacon after years of proven service. The leadership activities of George Beach, a Hartford man in the paint and dye business, follow such a pattern.[18] Beach began his career as a church leader when he was chosen a member of the Episcopal Christ Church vestry at age thirty. Three years later he became treasurer. Then at the age of thirty-eight Beach was selected junior warden of the church and finally, one year later, senior warden.[19] Beach steadily worked his way through his church's offices as he aged.

Table 8.3. Leaders' Ages in Church Offices, Hartford, 1790–1830

Office	Mean	Median	Obs.
Pastor	47	45	191
Deacon	60	61	318
Manager[a]	49	47	1208
Treasurer	46	46	66
Clerk	38	38	123

Source: See appendix C. Note: Averages have been rounded to the nearest year.
[a] Includes Committee of Church, Committee of Society, and Prudential Committee members, Junior Wardens, Senior Wardens, Vestry, Trustees, and Collectors.

Voluntary association offices were also somewhat age stratified. Those who became presidents—the highest and most important office—were older on average than any other officers. Thus even though voluntary associations generally opted for younger leaders than other types of organizations, their members placed the older men from within this young group at the helm. Meanwhile, secretaries of voluntary associations tended to be especially young. Indeed, secretaries were about twelve or thirteen years younger than presidents on average. The other offices tended to go to men between these extremes. Even though voluntary associations in general were more open to younger leaders than other types of organizations, their participants nevertheless made age distinctions in selecting men for specific offices.

Table 8.4. Leaders' Ages in Voluntary Association Offices, Hartford, 1790–1830

Office	Mean	Median	Obs.
President[a]	45	44	64
Vice President	40	38	20
Director[b]	42	39	259
Secretary	33	31	41
Treasurer	42	37	41
Misc.[c]	37	38	31

Source: See appendix C. Note: Averages have been rounded to the nearest year.
[a] Includes all Presidents as well as Masters of the Masonic lodge.
[b] Includes the following officers (similar in function): Leaders, Directors, Managers, Trustees, Officers, and Committee Members; as well as all Masonic offices except Master and Tyler, namely Senior Wardens, Junior Wardens, Senior Deacons, Junior Deacons.
[c] Includes Librarians, Subscription Committee members, Auditors, Collectors, General Agents for Tract Distribution, Tylers, and Foremen.

Table 8.5. Leaders' Ages in Institution Offices, Hartford, 1790–1830

Office	Mean	Median	Obs.
President	56	56	13
Vice President	53	54	91
Director[a]	47	47	397
Treasurer	51	51	20
Auditor	53	53	5
Secretary	42	43	14

Source: See appendix C. Note: Averages have been rounded to the nearest year.
[a] Includes Directors, Prudential Committee members, Trustees, and Commissioners of Funds.

Leaders of institutions also varied by age depending on the offices they held. The top institutional office—president—tended to go to men of greater age than any other post. The average age of presidents was fifty-six. However, as with voluntary associations, secretaries tended to be younger. Possibly the role of secretary, as recorder of events and decisions rather than active participant, was seen as more appropriate for younger, less experienced leaders. Most other institutional offices were filled by men whose average age ranged from the late forties to the early fifties.

The fact that in three of the five cases reviewed here—in institutions, voluntary associations, and city government—the highest office was home to the oldest officeholders suggests that for Hartford people significant maturity was an important characteristic in major leaders. While younger men were seen as appropriate for lesser posts, Hartfordians appreciated greater age for some of the community's most visible, important roles.

All leadership positions in Hartford were not alike. Voters, whether they were freemen, parishioners, members of associations, or organizers of institutions, recognized this fact and selected men not only for specific types of organizations but for specific offices as well. Though it is difficult to establish a precise ranking of offices and the influence and power they carried, it appears from the figures in tables 8.2, 8.3, 8.4, and 8.5 that Hartford voters made at least some connection between older age and higher office and younger age and lesser office. However this connection should not be overstated for several reasons. First, though age is an easily observable characteristic, age *per se* may not have been what voters were considering when selecting leaders. Instead, in filling high posts voters may have looked for experience, stability, or proven commitment to the community—all characteristics that take time to establish and therefore require greater age. Conversely voters may have selected less experienced men (likely to be younger) for lesser jobs.[20] Second, though we do observe some distinctions in filling offices by age, most leaders still remained within the general category of middle-aged and as such were more similar agewise than different. Which leads us to perhaps the most significant point. Whatever distinctions were made by age in selecting leaders, voters generally preferred men in mid-life over the aged. Though the elderly found some niches in public life, once past middle age extra years were more of a liability than an asset. The next obvious question is why. Why were middle-aged men more desirable as leaders than the aged? Before addressing this question fully we must consider a second important characteristic of leaders—their economic status.

WEALTH AND LEADERSHIP IN HARTFORD

Hartford's citizens considered age when choosing their leaders but age was not their only concern, wealth mattered too. Here we explore the relationship between financial status and leadership. As in our analysis of age, we look at leaders' wealth from three perspectives: how it changed over time, how it varied by type of organization lead, and finally how it varied by specific office held. As seen earlier, Hartford voters did not consider the wisdom of old age an important criterion for leadership. In fact, old age was not a particularly desirable trait in most leaders. Our analysis here illuminates what they did value in leaders—money and presumably the high social standing that went with it.[21] Respect for wealth thus seems to have been far more important than respect for age when it came to selecting leaders.

Trends in Leaders' Wealth Over Time

Tax records from Hartford's early national period are incomplete. However for many of the years between 1790 and 1814 records have survived, permitting an analysis of leaders' financial status for much of the period.[22] By ranking the taxpayers listed in these records into quartiles based on the size of their "lists"—with the first quartile consisting of poorest taxpayers and the fourth quartile the richest—and then looking at leaders' rankings we can draw conclusions about leaders' wealth relative to other citizens.[23] We begin by considering leaders' wealth over the period of approximately twenty-five years for which data is available to determine whether changes in leaders' financial status were underway.

Figure 8.6 depicts the financial standing of Hartford's leaders for every year from 1790 to 1814. For each year the percentage of leaders in each of the four quartiles is shown. Two general features are notable. First, it is plain that leaders were quite well-to-do compared to their fellow citizens. There are always far more leaders in the fourth (richest) quartile than in any other. In every year, men whose wealth placed them in the top 25 percent of all Hartford taxpayers made up from around 55 to 75 percent of all leaders.[24] In short, this group dominated Hartford's public life, claiming twice to three times more

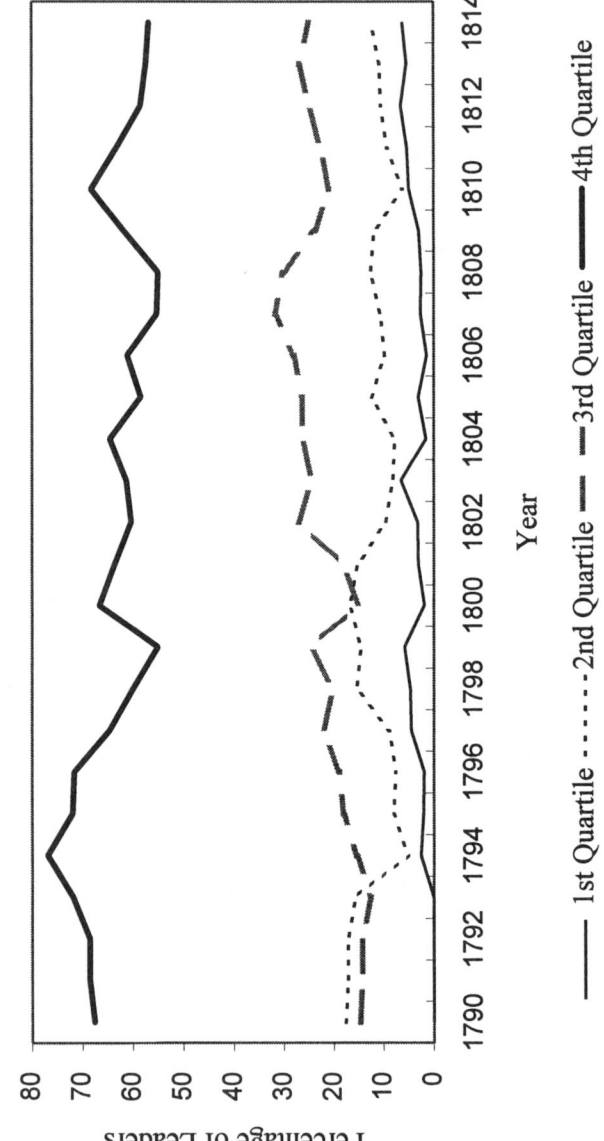

Figure 8.6. Hartford Leaders' Tax Quartiles, 1790-1814

Source: The approximately 76 percent of all Hartford leaders for whom tax information is available. See appendix C.

leadership roles than we would expect based on their numbers among taxpayers. Moreover, the tendency for leaders to be concentrated in the upper ranks of Hartford society was probably even more dramatic than it appears in this graph. Tax rolls did not include some of Hartford's poorest residents whose taxes were abated. Hence those on the tax rolls were a wealthier group than the general population. To be among the wealthiest of this already wealthy group was indeed a distinction. A second notable feature of figure 8.6 is that it shows that across the spectrum of taxpayers, increased wealth meant increased leadership. In every year, men in the first (poorest) quartile held the smallest share of offices—ranging from none at all to about 7 percent.[25] Meanwhile, men in the second quartile, though definitely not rich, were always more successful as leaders than their poorer neighbors. And those in the third quartile, with a few exceptions, garnered more leadership posts than less prosperous citizens. And as just noted, men in the top quartile did even better. Thus in selecting leaders, Hartford's voters were prepared to make distinctions in wealth at all levels.

Beyond these general facts which hold true throughout the period, figure 8.6 also illustrates change over time. To begin with, it appears that from 1790 to 1814, opportunities for leadership increased somewhat for men in the poorest quartile. No leaders came from the first quartile before 1793, but after this year the numbers increase sporadically and slowly. Meanwhile, the second quartile started off at a high point at the beginning of the period, experienced dips and rises in leadership participation and then leveled off at around 10 percent after 1802. The result for the second quartile is no clear trend over time. Leadership among men in the third quartile, however, seems to have risen over time. In 1790, about 15 percent of leaders came from the third quartile. After 1802, from about 20 to 32 percent came from this group. Gains among men in the third quartile probably account for the trend observed in the fourth quartile. Over time, men in the fourth quartile lost some of their dominance as leaders. Beginning in 1790 with a 68 percent share of offices, this figure hovers nearer 60 percent later in the period. Without the benefit of tax data spanning a longer period we must be cautious reaching conclusions. However, the data suggest that leadership may have become more accessible to men from a wider range of economic circumstances as time passed. Still, even though there may have been some redistribution of leadership roles throughout the period, those with above-average wealth—the third and fourth quartiles—nevertheless retained a very large share of Hartford's important public offices.

The authors of the *Gazetteer of the States of Connecticut and Rhode Island* remarked in 1819 that Connecticut people tended to "attach an undeserved importance to *property*," a tendency which was rooted "in part to the prevailing spirit and habits of trade; but principally to civil institutions, and the established principles and customs of society."[26] The analysis of leaders reveals that a preference for wealth was indeed strong among Hartfordians. This fact can begin to explain why voters generally selected men who were neither especially young nor old to lead them—such men tended to be at their financial peak.[27]

Leaders' Wealth by the Type of Organization They Headed

Voters' preference for wealthy leaders permeated every type of civic organization in Hartford. Those who held offices in government, churches, voluntary associations, or institutions all tended to be substantially better off than the general population. Both figure 8.7 and table 8.6 provide evidence that wealth was a significant criterion for leadership in all branches of Hartford's civic life.

Looking first at government officeholders, we see that almost two-thirds ranked among the wealthiest of all taxpayers in the fourth quartile. Roughly a quarter more were in the third quartile. Thus almost 87 percent of government officers held more wealth than average.[28] Clearly many government leaders were not, as two examples will illustrate, part of the common mass of Hartford's citizens. Thomas Seymour was mayor of the city from its incorporation in 1784 until 1812. Not simply wealthy (he ranked in the top 10 percent of all taxpayers), Seymour was also a Yale graduate, a former King's Attorney, an officer in Connecticut's militia during the Revolution, a long-serving member of the state's House of Representatives, and an assistant to the Governor, as well as Chief Judge of Hartford's County Court.[29] Thomas K. Brace, a councilman and alderman in the 1820s, was likewise wealthy and distinguished. Brace owned a line of passenger and freight ships, was a founder and president of the Aetna Insurance Company, and helped promote the

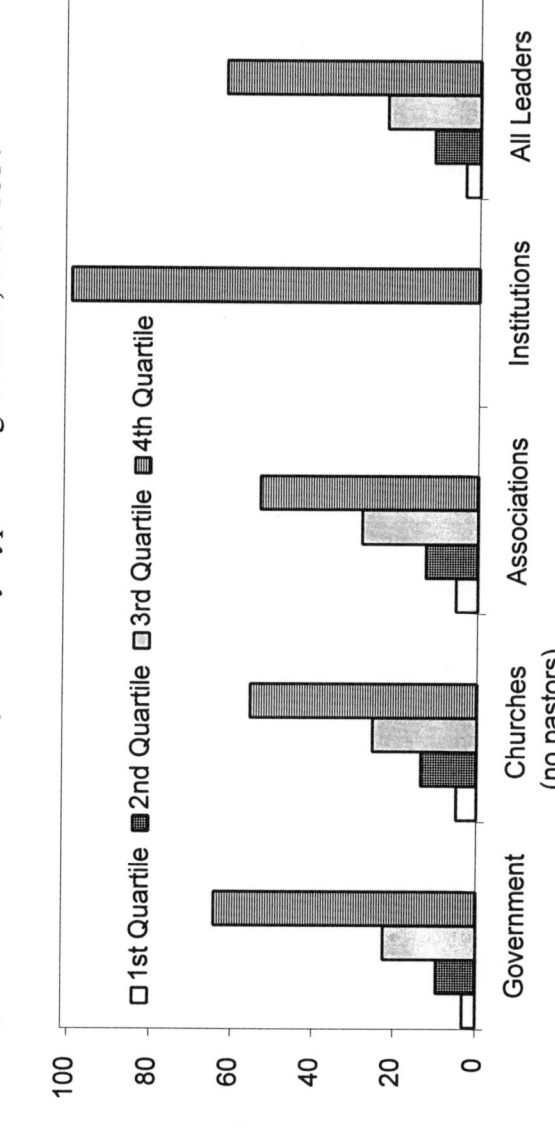

Figure 8.7. Leaders' Tax Quartiles by Type of Organization, 1790-1814

Source: The approximately 76 percent of all Hartford leaders for whom tax information is available. See appendix C.

253

city's banking industry. As a member of the Society of the Cincinnati, Brace too had served as an officer during the Revolution.[30] Hartford's local government was thus home to the wealthy and socially prominent. Meanwhile, less than 10 percent of government officers fell into the second quartile and only about 3 percent were amongst the poorer first quartile.

Though churches utilized slightly less prosperous leaders, over 55 percent were nevertheless ranked among the richest taxpayers in Hartford. Another quarter of church leaders possessed more resources than most of their fellow citizens. A perusal of Hartford's church records shows that lay officers were sometimes among the largest contributors whenever congregations needed to raise funds.[31] Thus when church members selected leaders who were wealthy they may have done so not simply out of abstract respect for wealth but because they expected their leaders to actively support the church financially. However, though wealthier men dominated church leadership there was some room for less prosperous leaders. Compared to government, churches selected more leaders from the second quartile—about 14 percent—and more from the first quartile as well—about 5 percent. This slightly more egalitarian approach may have been due to the preference in churches for elderly deacons. Such men were often quite advanced in years and thus were likely to have somewhat diminished fortunes. Parishioners selecting officers may also have considered qualities not linked to material wealth, such as piety, more than those who elected government officers.

Table 8.6. Percentage of Leaders in Each Tax Quartile by Type of Organization

Organization Type	First Quartile	Second Quartile	Third Quartile	Fourth Quartile	Obs.
Government	3.2	9.6	22.6	64.3	768
Churches	4.9	13.6	25.5	55.7	461
Associations	5.2	12.7	28.4	53.5	211
Institutions	0	0	0	100.0	98
All Leaders	3.5	11.2	22.8	62.4	1538

Source: See appendix C.

The wealth levels of voluntary association leaders were quite similar to those of churches. With about 54 percent of all leaders coming from the fourth quartile, the wealthy dominated leadership but not as strongly as was the case in government. As with churches, slightly more than one quarter came from the third quartile. And with about 14 percent of all posts going to men in the second quartile and another 5 percent or so to those in the first quartile, men of lesser means found more access to leadership in voluntary associations than they would have in government. However, though the wealth patterns of church and voluntary association leaders were very similar, the reasons for them were different. In churches, the wish for older men in some offices (as well as a possible preference for qualities unrelated to wealth) probably acted to decrease the overall wealth level of leaders. In contrast, the tendency for voluntary association leaders to be younger than average probably explains why they were not quite as wealthy as their government counterparts. As younger men they would have been in the process of accumulating fortunes, rather than at their financial peak.[32] The greater flexibility of voluntary associations, which could be formed by any group of mutually interested people for almost any reason, may also have allowed less prosperous men into leadership positions.

Institutions appear in figure 8.7 and table 8.6 as utterly dominated by men in the wealthiest quartile. Indeed, the fourth quartile appears to have furnished 100 percent of all institutional leaders. However for the years between 1790 and 1814 when tax data exist, only one institution—namely the Hartford Grammar School—was in operation. Thus while we can definitively say that high wealth was an absolute requirement for leaders of this school, we know little about leadership patterns in the institutions founded after 1814. However, anecdotal evidence suggests that wealth continued to be important, though perhaps not to the degree shown here. Ward Woodbridge, for example, held the vice-presidency of the Connecticut Deaf and Dumb Asylum (Thomas Gallaudet's pioneering school founded in 1816) from 1817 until at least 1830.[33] Woodbridge was perhaps the third wealthiest man in Hartford, having made his fortune in dry goods, cotton manufacturing, and insurance.[34] Though he may not have been chosen vice-president solely because of his prosperity, Woodbridge's assets no doubt helped make him an attractive leader.

Though the precise extent to which wealthy men dominated varied somewhat by the type of organization, the data make one thing clear—the wealthy did dominate. In every case more than 80 percent of all offices went to men ranked in the top half of taxpayers, and no less than 53 percent went to those in the top quarter. Across the board, in every kind of civic organization, Hartford's voters valued wealth and its accompanying social status in their leaders.

Leaders' Wealth by Office

In selecting officers, however, Hartford voters did make some distinctions among offices. Table 8.7, for example, shows that voters tended to select wealthier men more for the higher offices in government and less for the lower. In the key city posts of mayor, alderman, and councilman, the vast majority of officers were in the fourth quartile. Meanwhile the less important jobs drew men from a wider financial spectrum. In town offices the same tended to be true. Here the moderator and selectmen were almost always among Hartford's wealthiest people, while some of the less prestigious posts were filled by more ordinary men.

Table 8.7. Percentage of Government Leaders in Each Tax Quartile by Office, 1790–1814

	Office	First Quartile	Second Quartile	Third Quartile	Fourth Quartile	Obs.
City	Mayor	0	0	23.1	76.9	13
	Alderman	0	1.2	11.2	87.6	89
	Councilman	0	0.3	11.7	87.9	273
	Clerk	0	17.4	65.2	17.4	23
	Treasurer	0	47.6	28.6	23.8	21
	Collector	33.3	5.6	44.4	16.7	18
	Auditor	0	0	10.0	90.0	20
	Sheriff	0	18.8	62.5	18.8	48
Town	Moderator	0	0	15.4	84.6	13
	Selectman	0	0	7.1	92.9	42
	Clerk/Register	0	0	5.5	94.4	18
	Treasurer	15.8	31.6	21.1	31.6	19
	Constable	12.3	27.7	36.9	23.1	65
	Grandjuryman	7.5	22.6	32.1	37.7	106

Source: See appendix C.

In the case of church leaders, deacons, managers, and treasurers tended to be better off than clerks. As we saw earlier, clerks were likely to be fairly young. Because clerkship may have been seen as an "entry-level" position in church leadership, parishioners may have been more willing to accept candidates of lesser financial status.

Table 8.8. Percentage of Church Leaders in Each Tax Quartile by Office, 1790–1814

Office	First Quartile	Second Quartile	Third Quartile	Fourth Quartile	Obs.
Deacon	2.8	20.1	25.9	51.1	139
Manager[a]	4.8	4.4	29.6	61.1	226
Treasurer	0	9.3	15.6	75.0	32
Clerk	12.5	34.4	15.6	37.5	64

Source: See appendix C. Note: Pastors do not appear in this table because tax data almost never exists for them as they were generally exempt from taxes.
[a] Includes Committee of Church, Committee of Society, Junior Wardens, Senior Wardens, and Vestry.

Table 8.9. Percentage of Association Leaders in Each Tax Quartile by Office, 1790–1814

Office	First Quartile	Second Quartile	Third Quartile	Fourth Quartile	Obs.
President[a]	0	13.6	4.5	81.8	22
Vice Pres.	0	0	100.0	0	1
Director[b]	0.8	9.3	37.3	52.5	118
Secretary	11.1	0	50.0	38.9	18
Treasurer	0	12.5	4.1	83.3	24
Misc.[c]	28.6	35.7	14.3	21.4	28

Source: See appendix C.
[a] Includes all Presidents as well as Masters of Masonic lodge.
[b] Includes Leaders, Managers, Trustees, Committee of Appropriations members, as well as all Masonic offices except Master and Tyler, namely Senior Warden, Junior Warden, Senior Deacon, and Junior Deacon.
[c] Includes Librarians, Subscription Committee members, Auditors, Collectors, Tylers, and Foremen.

With voluntary association leaders, we again see some connection between wealth and the importance of the job. Here the vast majority of presidents were wealthy enough to be among the fourth quartile of taxpayers. With the exception of treasurers—whose case suggests that the connection between wealth and higher office did not always hold—all other officers were generally filled by men with fewer resources than presidents.[35]

Patterns of wealth among leaders in institutional offices are somewhat more obscure. As noted earlier, records from only one school are available for the period from 1790 to 1814. Since this school elected only one sort of officer—shown in table 8.10 below—we can say little about different wealth levels by office.

Table 8.10. Percentage of Institution Leaders in Each Tax Quartile by Office, 1790–1814

Office	First Quartile	Second Quartile	Third Quartile	Fourth Quartile	Obs.
Director[a]	0	0	0	100	98

Source: See appendix C.
[a] The Hartford Grammar School was the sole institution in Hartford prior to 1814 for which leader information exists. Therefore the figures reported reflect only its Trustees.

We have looked at the financial standing of Hartford's leaders from three perspectives—over time, by type of institution, and by specific office. Each perspective confirms the importance of significant wealth for success in public life. Drawing on the analysis of age patterns presented earlier, we can conclude that wealth, along with middle age, was the ideal combination in the eyes of Hartford's citizens. Old age, in contrast, was not sought after in leaders. These patterns appear to have changed little from 1790 to 1830.

INTERPRETING AGE AND WEALTH PATTERNS

We now have a fairly clear picture of the aged's limited role in Hartford's public life. We can gain further insight by placing this case study into larger context. To do so we must consider several questions: Had the aged once been sought after leaders? Were they, at some point, displaced by a new value system that exalted wealth and relative youth instead? In short, were the elderly in early national America suffering a decline from former prestige and power?

The findings of several scholars suggest such a shift. David Hackett Fischer, for example, describes deep changes in the history of old age occurring in the period from 1770 to 1820, in which the aged lost prestige while youth was increasingly glorified. Likewise, Thomas

Cole identifies a "cultural devaluation of old age" taking place in roughly the same period.[36] Given these views one might anticipate a diminution in whatever public power and influence the elderly had as confidence in their value declined. Meanwhile, the findings of Gordon Wood provide even more reason to suspect a decline in the aged's public position over time. Wood sees the Revolution as unleashing vast change in almost every aspect of life. According to Wood public life in particular was transformed in the decades following the war as an old system of deference gave way to a new environment of rough and tumble contention.[37] Thus if the aged had once enjoyed the respect of others and benefited from deference, we would expect these advantages to be stripped from them in the early national period.

Yet we have seen that within the period from 1790 to 1830 the position of the aged in public life was not worsening. This in itself provides some reason to doubt that a major shift in the elderly's civic roles was underway. Moreover, when the findings from Hartford are considered in the context of other studies of leadership, it becomes patently obvious that, despite expectations, the aged were not experiencing a slide from power. Indeed the work of other scholars suggests that the patterns of leadership seen in Hartford—specifically the preference for wealthy, middle-aged leaders rather than old leaders—was far from new.

Keith Thomas' work on early-modern England demonstrates that "important offices were normally assumed by the solidly middle-aged." Indeed, despite the prevalence of a "gerontocratic ideal" in seventeenth-century English society, Thomas notes that "if some of the elderly retained authority, it was because of the material resources at their disposal" rather than their age. Given these findings he concludes that "it is therefore wrong to regard the depreciation of old age as a recent affair."[38] In Thomas' view, any decline in power and influence on the part of the aged, if it ever occurred, must have come before the seventeenth century in England.

Likewise Daniel Scott Smith's study of old age in colonial Hingham, Massachusetts has shown that "old age was honored and respected, but it did not command continued wealth or leadership position."[39] Indeed, there were "more important principles of stratification than age" and when it came to office-holding these principles were clear—"during ordinary times wealth and to a lesser extent family and education counted more than age and experience."[40]

Though Smith sees wealth as becoming a more significant basis for social inequality through the colonial period, this was simply a matter of degree since "wealth had always been the most important basis of inequality in New England towns."[41] Like Hartford people later, Hingham's voters showed no strong preference for elderly leaders. Indeed, except for a brief period after the town's founding, they rarely selected men of very advanced years for public office. In short, Hingham was, as Hartford would be, "dominated not by the old but by the middle aged."[42] Thus, Smith would probably agree that by the early national period, any depreciation of the aged that might have occurred was certainly not a recent affair.

Edward Cook's detailed analysis of eighteenth-century town officials has similarly noted the tendency of New Englanders to select "prosperous townsmen" in middle age to lead them.[43] According to Cook,

> the normal practice in eighteenth-century New England was to elect middle-aged town leaders ... careers in town politics had a predictable rhythm. Until his middle thirties, an aspiring town leader served his town in the minor offices, if at all, while devoting most of his time to a growing family and, he hoped, a growing estate. Then, as he approached middle age, a man became eligible for the responsible town offices that served as a practice ground for potential leaders, and finally, if his service proved satisfactory, he could expect to become a leader sometime before his fiftieth year.

However with greater age, men did not continue to hold office. Cook states that leaders typically departed from office "as old age approached," yielding to the next generation of leaders.[44] Closely resembling Hartford's pattern somewhat later, Cook finds that "most leaders stood somewhere in the top quarter of their town's tax list."[45]

Bruce Daniels' study of leadership in eighteenth-century Hartford and New Haven provides further documentation of the tendency of Connecticut people—and Hartfordians specifically—to place other criteria above old age in selecting leaders. According to Daniels, "Hartford progressed from a small Puritan village to a large New Light town and to an incorporated city in 1784 at the end of the Revolution

Age, Wealth, and Community Leadership

under basically the same class of leaders." Old age was never an important feature of this class of men. Instead, "prosperity and family connections were the two key criteria and together brought the greatest chance for success in town politics."[46] Like Thomas, Smith, and Cook, Daniels uncovers no evidence that the aged ever held central leadership roles.

There was nothing new in early national Hartford's patterns of leadership. Hartford voters in the years from 1790 to 1830 behaved as generations before them had, selecting men for public office from a pool with the desirable characteristics of middle-age and prosperity. Just as it appears that America's elderly never had a firm grip on the reigns of power, it also seems that the well-to-do have ever had the upper hand in leadership. Therefore neither an alleged decline in the cultural value of the aged, the democratization of politics after the Revolution, nor any of the other social changes transforming America in the first decades of the republic were to blame for the elderly's marginal role in public life because their share of public power had never been large.[47]

WHY DIDN'T THE ELDERLY LEAD?

Why didn't the aged lead? And what, in contrast, made middle-aged men so appealing? Unfortunately, no contemporary sources address these questions directly. However, several likely answers suggest themselves.

The first has been touched on before. As we have seen, wealth was quite desirable in leaders. This may have been due simply to a general respect for material success. Or voters may have, as Edward Cook points out, considered the practical fact that well-to-do men could better absorb the costs (both in time and money) of holding office.[48] Whatever the appeal, we know from earlier chapters that old age was likely to be a time of declining fortunes, as a man's ability to earn decreased while his expenses remained level or even increased. It is possible, therefore, that some old men were seen as less desirable candidates for office due to diminished financial standing. In addition, facing greater financial burdens in old age, some men may have been reluctant to take on unpaid work in public office, preferring to devote their time to ensuring their own welfare and that of their families.

One of the reasons men's wealth tended to decline with age—illness or protracted debility—probably also played a significant role in limiting elderly men's participation in public life. Old age was not infrequently accompanied by diminished physical or mental health. When considering candidates for civic offices, voters may have understandably opted for healthy, robust men over more feeble individuals. Meanwhile men in poor health were less likely to be candidates for office in the first place, because few infirm people can have wished to further burden themselves by taking on the extra responsibilities of leadership. One case—that of Samuel Wyllys—indicates how health problems worked to push men out of public life. Wyllys was the scion of an established family, a Yale graduate, a respected veteran officer of the Revolutionary War, and an attorney. In his health he held several posts in local government as well as performing as Connecticut's Secretary of State. But a "paralytic shock" disabled him at the age of seventy, forcing his retirement from public office.[49] Though he lived to eighty-five, Wyllys never again resumed a public role. Far from it, he lived his final years as a "lunatic" under the care of a conservator.[50] Thus, though old men such as Wyllys surely had more experience than younger men, this experience was outweighed by the negative features of aging.

Table 8.11. Ages of White Males, Hartford, 1830

Age Group	Total Number	Percentage of All Males	Percentage of Adult Males[a]
0–9	999	21.60	—
10–19	1181	25.54	—
20–29	1111	24.03	45.47
30–39	626	13.54	25.62
40–49	354	7.65	14.49
50–59	188	4.06	7.69
60–69	106	2.29	4.33
70–79	48	1.03	1.96
80–89	6	0.12	0.24
90–99	3	0.06	0.12
100 & Up	1	0.02	0.04

Source: U.S. Census, Hartford, CT, 1830.
[a] Age twenty and over.

Age, Wealth, and Community Leadership

Finally, even if Hartford people had evidenced a strong preference for elderly men as leaders, the aged probably still would not have taken on the majority of leadership roles. Most likely there simply were not enough able old men around to fill all the offices. Though we do not know the precise age breakdown of Hartford's population for much of the period, 1830 census data reveal that the numbers of men fifty and over were relatively small. As table 8.11 illustrates, only about 7.4 percent of all males in the town were fifty or over in 1830. When we look solely at their proportion of adult males (twenty and over) they still only comprised about 14.3 percent. A strict gerontocracy simply would not have been practical since the number of possible candidates for office decreased dramatically with age. With such a small pool, finding enough men of leadership caliber and ability would have been difficult indeed.

Clearly there were good reasons why the aged generally did not lead. But this does not explain fully why the middle-aged did lead. Presumably Hartford's people could have selected more youthful men to fill their public offices instead. Most likely what swayed voters toward the middle-aged was their tendency to combine experience, wealth and health in an attractive balance. Middle-aged men had enough experience to make them capable leaders. Yet unlike the aged, who had even more experience, they were also likely to be at their financial peak, adding to their allure. In addition, many would be free of the debilitating health problems that often afflicted older men. Young men on the other hand, though generally healthy, were likely to be deficient in experience and have less wealth than men in mid-life. They were also likely to be busy establishing livelihoods and building families, perhaps decreasing their interest in public service. Middle-aged men were therefore ideal—they were old enough to reap some advantages from age but not too old that liabilities overwhelmed these advantages. This balance of qualities probably accounts for their popularity as leaders not only in early national Hartford but in other places and times as well.

This chapter has shown that elderly men did not dominate Hartford as leaders. Though some men remained civically active in old age, voters evidenced no real preference for old men as a group. Instead they most often selected middle-aged men of substantial means to manage the town's affairs. Yet though the elderly were not centrally important in public life, there is little evidence that their position was worsening over time. These basic facts do much to illuminate the workings of early national public life and the aged's role in them.

These findings also enrich our general understanding of old age in the past. Previous chapters have demonstrated that growing old could disrupt familiar routines and alter the quality of life. Chapters 4 and 5, for example, analyzing the economic position of the elderly, showed that old age was likely to be a time of diminishing fortunes. This chapter suggests that decline in old age was not just financial. Men were likely to surrender control not only of resources but also of public influence and power as they aged. And, as I have suggested, these two losses were probably linked. Meanwhile control over private life could be simultaneously threatened. As chapters 6 and 7 described, fewer elderly men headed their own households than middle-aged men and some old people found themselves entirely dependent on others, unable to manage their own affairs or even care for themselves. By looking at leaders we see a parallel decline. Just as power over private matters—a household or even oneself—diminished, influence in public affairs was likely to wane too. Thus several facets of a man's power could be simultaneously whittled away in old age.

Overall then, this chapter, along with several others, indicates that growing old could mean making the adjustment from occupying a central place in economic, family, and civic life to a more marginal role at the periphery. The degree to which this occurred depended on many factors. And, of course, those people—including most women—who never held much private or public power at any stage of life were unlikely to experience this shift.[51] Nevertheless, the procession of men out of power provided a visible spectacle for all to see, helping to define old age as the "declining years."

NOTES

1. City of Hartford, Court of Common Council Records 1784–1811, vol. 11, 21 February 1785, Town Clerk's Office; City of Hartford, Records of City Meetings, 22 February 1785, Town Clerk's Office.

2. David Hackett Fischer argues this most strongly. For example, by assigning the term "gerontocratia" to the entire period from 1607 to 1820 Fischer rather strongly implies a rule of the aged. He also argues for this same period that "the prestige of age was often translated into political power." (*Growing Old in America*, expanded ed. [New York: Oxford University Press, 1978], table of contents, 48.) In a more recent book, Fischer similarly suggests that old age and leadership in New England were positively correlated. He states that respect for age affected patterns of office holding with the result that "the higher the office, the older the incumbent was likely to be." (*Albion's Seed: Four British Folkways in America* [New York: Oxford University Press, 1989], 103–111, 106.) W. Andrew Achenbaum also sees a relation between old age and tendency to lead. Achenbaum states that "Americans between 1790 and 1860 respected the wisdom of years and considered it appropriate to rely on the elderly's experience and expertise." And he notes that in terms of public office holding "old age often seemed to enhance rather than to reduce a candidate's attractiveness." However, unlike Fischer, Achenbaum acknowledges that his conclusions are mostly about "perceptions" of the aged and that "the frequent references to the honor due age do not mean that the elderly *in fact* wielded vast power or held extraordinarily prestigious positions." Achenbaum may well be correct that early national Americans valued the old as leaders rhetorically—his observation that Americans personified their nation as an aged "Uncle Sam" is remarkably similar to Hartfordians choice of an old man as their symbol—yet this chapter demonstrates that rhetoric and actual practice could diverge and that the aged were not particularly valued as leaders. (*Old Age in the New Land: The American Experience since 1790* [Baltimore: Johns Hopkins University Press, 1978], 11, 20, 11, 25.)

3. *Random House Dictionary of the English Language* (New York: Random House, 1966), 814.

4. Government, voluntary associations, and institutions generally conducted elections yearly, while churches selected their leaders more sporadically.

5. Each observation consists of a leader's name, his office, and the year held. Not surprisingly, records on government leaders are most complete and lists of officeholders for every year from 1790 to 1830 are easily found. Information on Hartford's other leaders is not as complete. For churches, voluntary associations, and institutions, records have not survived for some years. In addition there were undoubtedly several Hartford organizations that have left no trace at all in the historical record. Despite these lacunae, enough information is available to draw conclusions about Hartford leaders. See appendix C for a complete list of the Hartford organizations included in this analysis.

6. See appendix A for a complete description of this age data. The age data used have some biases—relevant here is the tendency to under-include information on infants and children. However this bias does not affect findings on the ages of leaders since leaders were never infants or children. Thus there is no reason to believe that the 20 percent of leaders for whom age data is unavailable were distinct agewise (i.e. generally younger or older) than the 80 percent I was able to match with age data. As a result the fraction that was successfully matched can be used with confidence to represent the ages of leaders in general.

7. Only those leaders holding office between 1790 and 1814 were matched to tax data since this is the period for which suitable tax rolls (i.e. town lists) exist. See appendix B for a detailed description of these tax records. Like age records, tax records have biases. Of concern to us here is the fact that Hartford tax rolls seem to have underrepresented poorer

men (those whose taxes were abated were rarely listed). Thus in our analysis of leaders it is possible that their wealth levels are somewhat inflated due to the absence of tax information on poorer men and hence poorer leaders. However this chapter's findings suggest that, in fact, there were probably relatively few poor leaders anyway. If a man's taxes were abated he would have likely fallen into the poorest tax quartile (first) had he appeared on a tax list. Those with somewhat more wealth would have fallen into the second quartile. Yet as this chapter will demonstrate, there were very few leaders even in the second quartile. Given this fact and the large number of leaders in the third and fourth quartiles, it is logical to assume that even if men in the first quartile played a slightly larger role than the tax records indicate, it was still a minor role.

8. Of course for different offices there were different groups of voters. City officers were elected by enfranchised males of the city, while church officials were selected by members of the congregation, and voluntary association and institutional leaders were chosen by their peers. In each case, however, a group of voters expressed its preference by choosing among candidates. However in all cases voters were likely to be male. Thus the results discussed below reflect a definite gender bias. To begin with, women were not generally considered for public office, so looking at public officers tells us little about women's roles as community leaders or indeed if women acted as leaders at all. (Although looking at public officers alone does tell us that women were not preferred by voters for formal leadership roles.) Unfortunately this problem is not easily solved. As noted above, information on informal leaders (a group more likely to include women) is scarce, thus it is very difficult to capture what role, if any women might have played in this respect. A second problem stems from the fact that because voters for public officers of almost every kind were men, a study of elected officers will not illuminate women's preferences in leaders or if they differed from men's. Yet because there is no way to uncover women's attitudes toward elected officials, we must accept male preferences as our guide to tastes in general. Thus while for the purposes of this analysis it is assumed that those men who held office did so because they possessed characteristics desirable to Hartford people in general, the limitations just described should be borne in mind.

9. Clearly these two elements do not fully summarize what distinguished leaders from non-leaders. Scholars, including Edward M. Cook, Jr. and Bruce Daniels, have effectively considered other factors such as education, family background, experience in minor offices, and church membership in determining who held power in New England towns. There is no doubting the value of these more exhaustive approaches, but space and time limitations required a more pared-down strategy here. See Cook, *The Fathers of the Towns: Leadership and Community Structure in Eighteenth-Century New England* (Baltimore: Johns Hopkins University Press, 1976); Bruce Daniels, "Large Town Power Structures in Eighteenth Century Connecticut" (Ph.D. diss., University of Connecticut, 1970).

10. Mary Ryan, *Cradle of the Middle Class: The Family in Oneida County, New York, 1790–1865* (New York: Cambridge University Press, 1981), 127–132.

11. Indeed as figure 8.4 and table 8.1 illustrate, leaders of voluntary associations were generally younger than other leaders in Hartford. However, their relative youthfulness was not significant enough to pull down, or even prevent an upward trend, in the average ages of all leaders.

12. The precise percentages are as follows: In the 1790s, men fifty and over accounted for about 32 percent of all leaders. In the next decade they were 37 percent. The figure rose again in the 1810s to about 42 percent and by the 1820s was about 43 percent.

13. There is another way to think about age variations by type of organization. For each type of organization we can calculate the average age at which leaders last held office and the interval between the year this last office was held and death. To do so we must consider only those leaders for whom both age and year of death are known and who died in 1830 or prior (since I have no data on leaders after that period and hence no way of

Age, Wealth, and Community Leadership 267

determining for men who died after 1830 when their last office was held). Such constraints result in 131 observations, all for men who were more likely to lead in the earlier part of my period than the later. The results, presented in table C-1 in appendix C, are worth cautious consideration. Though inconclusive due to the small number of observations, the data suggest that church and institutional leaders tended to retire from office later than average while associational leaders left their posts exceptionally early.

14. Ryan, *Cradle of the Middle Class*, 106.

15. HTR; Henry F. Smith, *Municipal Register of the City of Hartford 1900* (Hartford CT: E.M. Ward Co., 1900), 756–776; Hartford Evangelical Tract Society, *Constitution of the Hartford Evangelical Tract Society* (1816); *First Report of the Hartford Evangelical Tract Society* (1817); *Second Report of the Hartford Evangelical Tract Society* (1818); Hartford First Church of Christ, Records 1684–1930 (includes Conference Association records), vol. 18, reel 503, CSL; Hartford First Church of Christ, Records 1684–1930 (includes Sunday School Society records), vol. 22, reel 504, CSL; George Leon Walker, *History of the First Church in Hartford* (Hartford CT: Brown & Gross, 1884), 413–414; Trustee Records of the First Methodist Church 1823–1846, box 136, vol. 5, CSL.

16. In terms of churches we should make the distinction between the religious head (the pastor) and the lay head (perhaps a deacon or other official).

17. Cook, *Fathers of the Towns*, 32.

18. *Passbook to a Proud Past and a Promising Future* (Hartford CT: Connecticut Printers, 1969), 27.

19. *History of the Parish of Christ Church Hartford*, (Hartford CT: Belknap & Warfield, 1895), 528–529.

20. Edward Cook explores these possibilities in depth for the eighteenth century. Cook shows how younger men often worked their way up through relatively menial, non-leadership posts in town government (such as hog reeve). In the process they gained experience on their way to more important and responsible leadership positions. Thus though "towns filled their offices with men from a broad but predictable range of age groups," younger men were likely to be concentrated in the non-leadership offices while middle-aged men garnered the important posts. (*Fathers of the Towns*, 33 and chapter 2 generally.)

21. While a more extensive analysis of leaders would uncover other important characteristics Hartfordians expected in their civic officers (education or an established family, for example), a look at wealth is sufficient to demonstrate that old age was much less attractive to voters than other factors.

22. I have used Hartford's town tax lists in the following analysis rather than valuation lists, which deal only with real property. The lists used are from 1792, 1795, 1796, 1798, 1802, 1805, 1806, and 1814 for the North District and 1794, 1798, 1807, 1808, 1809, and 1811 for the South District, CHS. See appendix B for a full account of these records.

23. See appendix B for an explanation of how a taxpayer's "list" was arrived at. Though lists were not straightforward assessments of wealth, they can be used as a proxy for wealth.

24. All leaders for whom tax information is available, that is. As mentioned earlier, tax data was matched to leaders' names in 76 percent of all cases—a large fraction but nevertheless not the entire population of leaders.

25. Some interpretive caution is in order regarding the first quartile due to the fact that very poor men were likely to be left off the rolls. Such men, had they been listed, would surely have fallen into the first quartile. Yet because those who were not listed could not be matched to leaders' names, it is possible that the findings presented in this chapter underestimate the number of leaders in the first quartile. Despite this uncertainty, there is reason to believe any such bias would be small. Because there is a clear pattern in the second, third, and fourth quartiles of greater leadership with greater wealth, it seems unlikely that the first quartile would have produced many more leaders than what we see in figure

8.6. And even if it did, it is highly unlikely that men in the first quartile would have done better as leaders than those in the second. In short, there may be a bias in the data but it is probably not large enough to affect overall findings.

26. John C. Pease and John M. Niles, *A Gazetteer of the States of Connecticut and Rhode Island* (Hartford CT: William S. Marsh, 1819), 13.

27. For evidence of this point see chapter 4.

28. Again, because tax rolls tended to exclude the poor, those who appear on tax rolls and hence were ranked into quartiles were a wealthier group in general than all Hartford citizens. Even those taxpayers at the bottom of the third quartile can be considered better off than the average Hartfordian.

29. Memorial plaque located in Hartford City Hall, Hartford CT.

30. Smith, *Municipal Register of the City of Hartford 1900,* 756-776; *Passbook to a Proud Past,* 24.

31. Several of the largest donors to the Universalist Church's building fund were church officers. See Donald Watt, *From Heresy Toward Truth* (West Hartford CT: 1971), 14-17. Similarly when the North Congregational Church was raising money for the purchase of an organ in 1828, some of the most generous contributions came from church leaders. See Hartford Park Congregational Church Papers 1823-1891, vol. D, reel 521, CSL.

32. It is worth noting that though voluntary association leaders were somewhat less well-to-do than government leaders, both types of leaders were probably of similar social standing, though at different stages along the path of resource accumulation. In other words, given a few more years, most voluntary association leaders would probably have come to resemble government leaders wealthwise.

33. *Report of the Committee of the Connecticut Asylum for... Deaf and Dumb Persons* (Hartford CT: Hudson & Co., 1817), 2; *Second Report of the Directors of the Connecticut Asylum for... Deaf and Dumb Persons* (Hartford CT: Hudson & Co., 1818), 3; *Third Report of the Directors of the Connecticut Asylum for... Deaf and Dumb Persons* (Hartford CT: Hudson & Co., 1819), 2; *Fourth Report of the Directors of the American Asylum at Hartford for... the Deaf and Dumb* (Hartford CT: Hudson & Co., 1820), 2; *Fifth Report of the Directors of the American Asylum at Hartford for... the Deaf and Dumb* (Hartford CT: Hudson & Co., 1821), 2; *Sixth Report of the Directors of the American Asylum at Hartford for... the Deaf and Dumb* (Hartford CT: Hudson & Co., 1822), 2; *Seventh Report of the Directors of the American Asylum at Hartford for... the Deaf and Dumb* (Hartford CT: W. Hudson & L. Skinner, 1823), 2; *Eighth Report of the Directors of the American Asylum at Hartford for... the Deaf and Dumb* (Hartford CT: W. Hudson & L. Skinner, 1824), 2; *Ninth Report of the Directors of the American Asylum at Hartford for... the Deaf and Dumb* (Hartford CT: W. Hudson & L. Skinner, 1825), 2; *Tenth Report of the Directors of the American Asylum at Hartford for... the Deaf and Dumb* (Hartford CT: W. Hudson & L. Skinner, 1826), 2; *Eleventh Report of the Directors of the American Asylum at Hartford for... the Deaf and Dumb* (Hartford CT: 1827), 2; *Twelfth Report of the Directors of the American Asylum at Hartford for... the Deaf and Dumb* (Hartford CT: Hudson & Skinner, 1828), 2; *Thirteenth Report of the Directors of the American Asylum at Hartford for... the Deaf and Dumb* (Hartford CT: Hudson & Skinner, 1829), 2; *Fourteenth Report of the Directors of the American Asylum at Hartford for... the Deaf and Dumb* (Hartford CT: Hudson & Skinner, 1830), 2.

34. *Passbook to a Proud Past,* 18.

35. The wealth of treasurers is somewhat surprising and difficult to interpret. One might guess that voters appreciated wealthy treasurers since treasurers handled an

organization's money. However this logic is not fully convincing since treasurers in other types of organizations were not always exceptionally wealthy.

36. Fischer, *Growing Old in America*, chapters 1 and 2; Thomas R. Cole, *The Journey of Life: A Cultural History of Aging in America* (New York: Cambridge University Press, 1992), 56.

37. Gordon Wood, *The Radicalism of the American Revolution* (New York: Vintage Books, 1991), chapters 14 and 16.

38. Thomas, "Age and Authority in Early Modern England," 211–212, 246–247.

39. Daniel Scott Smith, "Old Age and the Great Transformation: A New England Case Study," in *Aging and the Elderly: Humanistic Perspectives in Gerontology*, ed. Stuart Spicker, Kathleen Woodward, and David D. Van Tassel (Atlantic Highlands NJ: Humanities Press, 1978), 291.

40. Ibid., 292, 294.

41. Ibid., 292.

42. Ibid., 291.

43. Cook, *Fathers of the Towns*, 185.

44. Ibid., 109–111.

45. Ibid., 81.

46. Daniels, "Large Town Power Structures," 99, 68.

47. Though we are principally concerned here with the elderly, the findings from Hartford can also be applied to the general question of deference and its decline after the Revolution. Though scholars, such as Gordon Wood in *The Radicalism of the American Revolution*, have argued that deference to social superiors was waning, reshaping the nature of politics at every level, the persistent preference on the part of Hartford voters for wealthy local officials suggests Hartfordians were not so quick to change. Perhaps Hartford, as a hotbed of Federalism, experienced the shift to more democratic politics later than other localities. See Wood's chapters 14 and 16.

48. Cook, *Fathers of the Towns*, 86.

49. Franklin Bowditch Dexter, *Biographical Sketches of the Graduates of Yale College*, vol. 2 (New York: Henry Holt & Co., 1896), 562–563.

50. Samuel and William Wyllys case, petition of 5 November 1822, CG.

51. Though women infrequently headed households, pursued independent economic lives, or held public office, they did exert influence in many less formal ways. John Faragher makes the interesting suggestion that because of the different nature of women's and men's roles, women were ultimately able to retain a more central place both in family and community life and therefore avoid marginalization in old age more successfully than men. He states, "Whereas women's nurturing roles were still usable in old age and valuable in the larger community, men's productive skills were greatly lessened in the older years and there was little place for them outside the economic unit of the family." Unfortunately few sources exist to show whether this held true for early national Hartford. See "Old Women and Old Men in Seventeenth-Century Wethersfield, Connecticut," *Women's Studies* 4 (Special Issue 1976): 27.

IX

Perspectives on the Aged

In different ways each aspect of the elderly's lives was marked by risk and difficulty. Ideological formulations of old age posed the first challenge to aging people. Though scholars have argued for the dominance of single ideas in the thinking about old age—stressing veneration, for example—in fact early national Americans had to sort their way through contradictory approaches which together provided little clear direction to people attempting to come to terms with growing old.

Even if one settled on the dominant religious view of old age, difficulties were likely. Religious formulations lent purpose and meaning to growing old but at the same time made demands of the aged that were so rigorous as to be unrealistic. Clerics pledged that those who successfully met these demands would enjoy both present rewards and future bliss but these promises were not reassuring when expectations were set so high. Moreover, religious ideas on aging were negative, stressing decay as the fundamental characteristic of old age. And they emphasized the severe consequences (eternal damnation in particular) for those unable to fully enact religious prescriptions. Given these problems, the chances of gaining spiritual comfort from such an approach were slim.

Attempts by ordinary people to implement ideas on old age indicate just how faulty these concepts were. Though the religious formulation of old age resonated most among Connecticut people, few successfully implemented its high flown notions. Instead ordinary people were required to alter religious principles to make them usable in everyday life or to ignore them as hopelessly irrelevant. Yet despite these modifications, people who took religious prescriptions seriously found spiritual comfort elusive because they could rarely meet the demands made of them. The irresolvable tension between the ideal and the real caused at least some old people worry and even anguish in their declining years. Thus, while it has been argued that ideas about aging of the period provided satisfying existential meaning for those growing old, meaning which twentieth-century American society is sorely lacking, such existential promise had a high price.[1] In many cases the stiff material of ideology simply could not be made to conform to the curves of daily life, leaving the aged with no powerful or fully compelling way to understand senescence.

Compounding these ideological difficulties were economic challenges. Advancing age generally brought declining resources. This pattern meant that financial stability in old age required foresight and planning. Just as individuals plan for old age today, early national Americans attempted to make allowances for the special economic demands of growing old, eager to ensure a degree of comfort in their waning years. Unfortunately such efforts were often cut short due to circumstances, such as illness, beyond the elderly's control. The failure of individual efforts to remain economically afloat in old age put the aged at the mercy of an unreliable familial safety net. Sometimes families did extend ample economic assistance to the needy elderly but not always. And when adequate aid failed to materialize, penury was the result. This disastrous fate befell a significant fraction of old men and women in early national America. No longer able to garner a livelihood and disappointed in their hopes of assistance from kin, the indigent aged could rely only on the rudimentary and piecemeal aid provided by public and private charity. Because old age and economic insecurity went hand in hand and because economic supports for the needy aged were defective, the old were particularly exposed to economic crisis and hardship.

As the elderly coped with spiritual challenges and economic decline, many also contended with upheaval in their domestic circumstances. Connecticut people preferred to maintain independent households in old age, but unfortunately control over households tended to slip out of old people's grasp. When it did aged men and women had to adapt to subordinate roles in other's households, no longer fully able to determine daily routines and sometimes painfully separated from familiar people and places. Surrendering domestic independence also laid the aged open to the possibility of an unsettled, uncomfortable existence which they had no power to correct. The disruptive descent from a central domestic role to a marginal one was especially trying for aged men and women already battling decline on several other fronts.

Given these hardships, the family potentially played a key role in easing the aged's trials. In some cases family did serve this function, assisting and comforting elderly people as they adapted to their changing circumstances. However, as in all other areas of life for the aged, family relations involved risk. Despite early national rhetoric advocating good treatment and respect for the aged, a successful family life could never be taken for granted. Indeed the elderly's neediness was not necessarily correlated with their families' willingness or ability to give, either emotionally or materially. As a result the elderly might have satisfying kin relationships but they could also suffer with abominable ones, adding additional trials to the lives of those made vulnerable by old age. Thus, while it has been argued that old people have lost the respect and centrality they once had in families, evidence from the early national period suggests that these were accorded only contingently even in past times.

Something similar can be said of the aged's roles in community life from evidence on leadership. Old age has been thought by some to have been a desired characteristic in leaders in past times. Scholars have suggested that a high regard for older men's special qualities translated into political power. In fact, while elderly men might play significant roles in their communities, they did so in spite of their age rather than because of it. Indeed, middle age and wealth were far more popular features in leaders than advanced age. As a result, men who gained influence with middle age were likely to ease out of public life with advancing years. These patterns cannot be attributed to a devaluation of the aged due to the rising tide of democracy, economic development, urbanization, or social flux that characterized the period. Instead the place of the aged at the sidelines of community life was long-established even by the turn of the nineteenth century. Therefore in public life, just as in aspects of private life, growing old diminished rather than enhanced stature, leaving the aged on the margins of power and influence.

In tracing each of these aspects of the elderly's lives in the early national period it is important to consider the question of change over time, especially because this era has been described by one influential historian of old age as a watershed in age relations in which an established system of veneration of the elderly was replaced by a new system which devalued them.[2] Was the early national period actually a dramatic turning point for old people? The evidence offered here does not suggest that the position of the elderly was undergoing a dramatic change in the forty years between 1790 and 1830. The themes presented in published work on the aged are remarkable more for their constancy than for any abrupt change. And the ways that ordinary Connecticut people conceived of old age do not appear to have altered much from 1790 to 1830. Nor are there strong trends in the economic circumstances of the elderly over this same period. Though specific events (such as the economic downturn associated with the War of 1812) may have temporarily worsened or improved the financial circumstances of the aged, such shifts cannot be linked to any change in the position of old people *per se*. Meanwhile, neither the domestic arrangements of the elderly nor their family relations indicate widespread modifications in the experience of old age over the period. Finally, in terms of the elderly's community roles it is quite clear that no alteration was underway. Therefore, the evidence provides little support for the view that the early national period was a time of profound change in age relations. Of course it is possible that far more subtle changes were occurring in various facets of old people's lives. Further studies will be needed to demonstrate the existence and nature of any such transformations.

In confronting the question of change over time, it is worthwhile to consider arguments scholars have made about the early national period more broadly. The decades after the Revolution have been characterized as a time of tremendous upheaval in social relations of all sorts. Scholars have particularly emphasized a change from patriarchal, hierarchical, and deferential interaction to a more democratic, egalitarian style.[3] Anticipating that the lives of the elderly might shed light on this transition, I have been attentive to signs of such change. Yet the stories of old men and women in Connecticut reveal consistency more than ruptures with the past. The elderly were, of course, only one segment of all Americans. Nevertheless their stories indicate that while social change was surely underway from 1790 to 1830, it may have been less dramatic and sweeping than some have concluded.

To sum up, the aged in early national America were distinctive from other age groups. Though there were variations in experience based on whether one was male or female, rich or poor, sick or healthy, and loved or forlorn, the aged lives were shaped by one basic fact: old age in was a risky time of life often fraught with decline and hardship. This state of affairs was probably not new to the period between 1790 and 1830. For as long as the aged had relied primarily on their own efforts to ensure a good old age (and when this failed on the largely informal networks of family and community), difficulties were to be expected.

Given these facts, how does old age in early national America compare to old age today? Beginning with the similarities, the biological nature of growing old remains essentially unaltered. Though therapeutics have evolved, the physiological changes that come with time continue to shape the experience of aging. And nothing can alter the fact that the inevitable decays of old age are precursors to death. Ways of coping with death have shifted over time but mortality remains intimately bound up with growing old. Moreover, many of the factors that helped determine the quality of old age for early national Americans continue to play significant roles today. Sex, economic position, family relations, individual personality, and health still shape how well or poorly men and women fare as age advances. These fundamentals of old age seem to transcend time.

In other respects growing old has changed. Old age itself now starts later than it once did and according to a more rigid chronological schedule. In addition, twentieth-century ideas about old age are no longer formulated along religious lines as they once were. Old people are generally not required or even expected to work until their health gives out as they typically were two hundred years ago. Instead leisure, an unfamiliar and certainly suspect concept in the early national period, has become a principle activity of the aged. Meanwhile, modern old age is far more bureaucratized and institutionalized than it once . was. Government agencies, social programs, senior centers, and retirement homes organized to serve the needs of the aged now exist where previously there were none. Entire branches of inquiry including geriatrics and gerontology have sprung up for the scientific study of aging. And more elaborate treatments for the ailments of old age have followed in their path. At the same time the number of old people in America today (both in sheer terms and proportionately) is far larger than ever before, with important effects on the nation's cultural, social, and economic life. People, especially women, live much longer.

These changes taken together are what distinguish old age in early national America most from today. Men and women from 1790 to 1830 were essentially on their own, required to meet the challenges of aging by fashioning old age for themselves on an individual basis with far less guidance than they receive today. Early national society did not do things for its members. Though family and community might assist the aged, no bureaucracies led them down a well-worn path, no senior programs existed to shape their lives, and no foolproof safety nets were extended to protect them in old age. Making old age, and making it secure, were individual projects. As such, people had a certain latitude to make choices about how they would live and grow old. Yet while men and women might successfully construct old age, the project was risky and the consequences of failure severe. Quite ironically then, what distinguishes the experience of growing old in the past is that it was more individualistic and less communitarian than it is today.

This book, by bringing to mind the complexities of growing old in the past and drawing these comparisons between past and present, permits fresh reflection on an issue that has preoccupied scholars—the aged's decline over the course of American history. In the literature on old age much has been made much of a downward slide in the position of aged people over time. Though American scholars have formulated the exact nature of this decline differently, this theme has remained central to interpretations of old age history from its beginnings to the present.[4] While it is easy to reject the crudely deterministic version offered early on by modernization theorists, other interpretations cannot be dismissed as lightly. And because this book covers only a small segment of the American past, it cannot prove or refute a general decline in the lives of old people in any case. However, several questions arising from the findings presented here may provoke reconsideration of the question. For example: Is the demanding and difficult ideology of growing old found in the early national period better for elderly people than ideas held about old age today? Is it better to be required to labor in old age out of necessity as most were two hundred years ago than to be encouraged not to work under today's system of retirement? Given the range in the family lives of the aged in the past, can we really say that family relations were better than they are today when a similar variety prevails? Can we assume that the elderly were better attended to in a society that managed their problems informally than in a society that handles them formally and institutionally? Are aged widows living under the system of dower better off than elderly widows today? And is it better for fewer people to survive to old age or for more to survive?

Simple responses to these questions are impossible. Certainly however, the answers would not suggest that old age was categorically better or easier in the early national period than it is today. A realistic appraisal of old age in the past shows it had a full complement of negative features. Therefore, while in specific areas the aged's lives may have worsened over time, other areas have surely improved. Thus it is far from obvious that an overall decline has plagued the elderly or that it is even useful to formulate an understanding of old age history in these terms. More productive approaches and a truer account of change will come as scholars continue working to uncover the diversity of the aged population and the determinants of the elderly's experiences in all eras of our past.

NOTES

1. Thomas Cole makes this point in *The Journey of Life: A Cultural History of Aging in America* (New York: Cambridge University Press, 1992).
2. David Hackett Fischer, *Growing Old in America*, expanded ed. (New York: Oxford University Press, 1978), chapter 2.
3. Gordon Wood describes this transition as both dramatic and relatively swift in *The Radicalism of the American Revolution* (New York: Vintage Books, 1991). Others who have charted the demise of patriarchal hierarchy include Jay Fliegelman, *Prodigals and Pilgrims: The American Revolution Against Patriarchal Authority 1750–1800* (New York: Cambridge University Press, 1982); and Mary Ryan, *Cradle of the Middle Class: The Family in Oneida County, New York, 1790–1865* (New York: Cambridge University Press, 1981).
4. The preoccupation with decline began with the development of modernization theory. Despite the general rejection of this model by historians of aging, the theme has continued to resonate. See for example Fischer, *Growing Old in America*; W. Andrew Achenbaum, *Old Age in the New Land: The American Experience Since 1790* (Baltimore: Johns Hopkins University Press, 1978); Carole Haber, *Beyond Sixty-Five: The Dilemma of Old Age in America's Past* (New York: Cambridge University Press, 1983).

Appendix A

Hartford Vital Records

No systematic records of births and deaths were kept in Hartford for the period from 1790 to 1830. However, in order to pursue a study of the elderly birth and death (and hence age) information on Hartford's people was absolutely essential. To know the ages of the hundreds of people encountered in archival records it was necessary to construct a directory of sorts, gathering together the names and vital information for those alive in the city from 1790 to 1830.

Since no systematic records exist it is impossible to recover age data for every man, woman, and child who lived in Hartford. However, by compiling information from two sources I was able to capture at least some vital information on more than 13,000 individuals. Newspaper death notices are the first source. As part of their extensive genealogical collections, the Connecticut State Library maintains compilations of death notices from numerous Connecticut papers published during the early national period. I extracted names, dates of death, and any other vital information provided on Hartford people from three principle Hartford newspapers of the time—*The Connecticut Courant*, *The American Mercury*, and *The Hartford Times*. Anyone alive for any portion of the period from 1790 to 1830 was included. A second equally extensive source provided additional vital information on Hartford people. During the 1930s the W.P.A. assigned workers to canvass Connecticut recording information from tombstones in every cemetery large and small. The result was the Hale Headstone Collection, also housed at the Connecticut State Library.[1] Birth and death information from twenty-seven Hartford cemeteries containing the remains of hundreds of people who lived from 1790 to 1830 are included in this collection.

When combined into a database, these two sources provided the essential age information needed to go forward with many aspects of this book. Not only was I frequently able to identify the ages of men and women mentioned in qualitative documents such as diaries and letters, but I was also able to match age information to other sources including tax records, probates, censuses, and leadership data.

However this age data is not entirely free of problems for the historian. To begin with, the data capture only people who actually died or were buried in Hartford. Many people were born in Hartford or moved there, but died and were interred elsewhere. Thus the data are generally biased towards more established people rather than more transient individuals. Second, because people included in these sources had to have a newspaper death notice or a tombstone durable enough to remain standing and legible in the 1930s, there is a bias towards adults and more prosperous people. Infants and children were less likely to have tombstones or death notices than their older relatives. Indeed, analysis of the database indicates that there is a persistent under-representation of children throughout the period.[2] In addition, it is likely that poorer people of all ages escaped the notice of newspaper editors more often than their well-to-do peers, while their families must have frequently foregone the expense of a quality tombstone. Hence poorer people probably show up less frequently in the dataset than they did in the general population. When relevant these flaws have been noted at various points throughout the book.

NOTES

1. The Barbour Collection, of which newspaper death notices form a part, and the Hale Headstone Collection are only two components of the vast genealogical collections of the Connecticut State Library.

2. Though it appears that by the 1830s (perhaps with the sentimentalization of both death and children) there was a trend towards more elaborate burial practices for children than prevailed in the 1790s, this does not seem to correct the bias entirely.

Appendix B

Hartford Tax Records

Tax lists are invaluable sources for the historian. However, they pose certain methodological problems and have some biases. Two types of tax lists from Hartford, Connecticut are used in this study—town lists and valuation lists. While most of these records are in the collections of the Connecticut Historical Society in Hartford, a few are located at the Connecticut State Library, also in Hartford.

TOWN LISTS

Town lists were compiled each year by one or more Hartford men and contained the name of each taxpayer along with the items he was liable to be taxed for. These included land (broken down into different kinds such as plowland, meadow, etc.), buildings, fireplaces, livestock, bank stock, carriages, and luxury items such as gold watches and silver plate. Rather than assessing such property on the basis of its market value if sold, tax assessors aimed at determining its yearly income value for the owner. The town lists also included a "faculty" assessment which was an estimate of the yearly income one might earn from a given trade. Anyone practicing a trade such as blacksmithing, tanning, or medicine was assessed a sum that varied by trade and also by the value of an individual's practice. Tax assessors received guidelines to assist them in determining what individual trades and practices were worth. Many people—most farmers for example—practiced no formal trade and hence had no "faculty" assessment added to their list. The general principle guiding the assessment of both property and faculties was thus their yearly income value, rather than their total value.[1] Finally, the town list also contained the number of "polls" or head taxes a person was responsible for. In contrast to property and faculty assessment, the poll was a flat tax. Set at a fixed $60 (or £18 before 1796), polls were levied on men between twenty-one and seventy years of age. A "minor" poll rate of $30 (or £9 before 1796) applied to youths between eighteen and twenty-one. However, it should be noted that there were several classes of men who were excused from paying polls. Though the law varied over the period, men disabled by lameness or infirmity, militia members, and clergymen were relieved of the poll tax at various times. There is evidence that the poor's poll taxes were abated as well.

The grand total of all the items included on the town list was called a person's "list," and from this list a person's actual taxes were calculated. For example, in 1809 Hartford's town officers decided on a tax of three cents per list dollar.[2] Thus functionally at least the list was similar to today's "adjusted gross income" in that it formed the base from which tax payments were derived.

Hartford was bisected by the Mill River into two parts—north and south. Tax assessors adopted this division, collecting information on the North District and South District separately. Unfortunately there is only one year for which records of both districts survive—1798. For the North District alone we have lists from 1792 through 1796, 1802, 1805, 1806, and 1814. For the South District alone the 1794, 1807 through 1809, 1811, 1816 and 1817 lists have been preserved.[3] Given the different characters and populations of these districts each is analyzed separately in the present study.

Obviously, though town assessors aimed at determining taxpayers' ability to pay by estimating their probable income, town lists do not give direct or exact information on income or overall wealth. However, since the goal here is to see how the elderly fared relative to other groups rather than to determine their absolute holdings, tax records can be used fruitfully.[4] Connecticut's system of taxation attempted to spread the burden of taxes fairly. While during the period there was some contention over how best to levy taxes to achieve maximum equity, we can nevertheless assume that the existing system determined with reasonably accuracy an individual's ability to pay.[5] Town lists which take real estate, some moveable property, bank stock, and some luxury goods into account are thus quite suggestive of the relative standing of individuals in the community. Though such assessments were initially made to determine income rather than wealth, the fact that real property was the most important item subject to taxation means they also indicate quite a bit about a taxpayer's overall wealth. The poll tax—at a flat rate for everyone who paid it—is the only feature of these lists that does not bear relation to wealth or income. To correct for this I have subtracted the poll tax from the total list in all my analyses of these records.

In addition these records can be used successfully to indicate changes in individual's fortunes over time. Since the method of drawing up the lists remained fairly constant over the period under discussion, the varying size of a person's list over a period of years hints strongly at his or her changing economic circumstances.

Indeed the main interpretive problem posed by town lists revolves around what information was not included rather than what was. Those who were included on town lists were evaluated by one set of fairly consistent rules. Yet for reasons that are not completely clear, in any given year a significant fraction of Hartford's citizens did not appear on the tax lists at all. For example, Hartford's population in 1790 was 4,072. Of these the manuscript census for the city of Hartford reveals that about 663 were heads of household. Meanwhile the tax lists for the nearest years (1793 for the North district and 1794 for the South district) have a total of 597 entries. At first glance one might guess that the tax records contained many of the heads of household listed in the census along with some other property-owners who did not head households. However a comparison of the census and the tax lists reveals that this intuition is not altogether correct. In fact, only about 359 people on the tax lists or 54 percent can be matched to household head's names on the census. Clearly then not all heads of household were included on tax lists and many people who did not head households were included. A comparison of the 1810 census with the nearest years for which tax lists exist bears out a similar result.[6] There were 1,248 heads of household listed in the census and only 916 names on the tax lists, some of which undoubtedly did not match the census.

The important criteria for inclusion on a tax list were: 1) being a male of poll tax age, and/or 2) ownership of property of the type that was being taxed—land, a house, livestock, a carriage, bank stock, or luxury goods, and/or 3) practice of a trade subject to a faculty tax.

We know that some men were relieved of the obligation to pay a poll tax. Still, it was possible to appear on the tax lists and be liable for property or faculty taxes even when poll taxes were not assessed. This probably would have been the case for those classes of men who were granted exemption from poll taxes (such as militia members and the disabled) as well as for property owners who did not reside in Hartford and hence would not have been liable for the poll.

However, while such men would have met at least one of the criteria for inclusion on tax lists, others met none and were therefore not listed. Town records indicate that from time to time a "Board of Relief" was selected "to grant Relief upon appeals from the doings of the [tax] Assessors, & to equalize the list."[7] This suggests that there was an effort to relieve those in straitened circumstances from their poll obligations. If those receiving such poll abatements also lacked property and a taxable trade, they would not be included on the tax rolls. It is these men who had their poll tax abated and neither owned taxable property nor had a faculty liability that constitute a shadow population of Hartford men who never made it onto the tax lists.[8] Such men, lacking real property and a taxable trade and considered worthy of poll tax abatement, were almost surely in the poorer ranks of the city's population. As a result, the people who appeared on tax lists are unlikely to be a cross-section of the population but rather the middle and upper strata of society.

In addition, men over the age of seventy were automatically relieved of the poll tax which introduces an additional bias into the tax lists. The fact that in other age categories men who were only liable for a poll tax were included in the town list (and thus when the poll is subtracted had a list total of $0), while after seventy they were not tends to decrease the proportion of men over seventy relative to other ages that were included in the tax lists. We can estimate the number of men who may have disappeared from tax lists in this way by noting that the percentage of men in their sixties who had lists equal to $0 was on average 7.5 percent of identifiable sixty-year-olds on the town lists.[9] About 70 percent of these men with lists equal to $0 probably survived to age seventy.[10] Thus we can imagine that on average around 5.2 percent of all sixty-year-olds dropped off the lists when they reached their seventieth year due to relief from the poll tax. The elimination of such men probably had the effect of pushing up the average list size for those over-seventy-year-olds who remained (who by definition must have had tax liabilities other than the poll and hence lists larger than $0). Thus the reader should be aware that the circumstances of the over-seventy set appear more favorable in the tax data than they probably were.

Women were also generally absent from the tax rolls as there were no poll obligations for women and few held the type of property that was taxed. However a small percentage of the names on all tax lists are women's. Generally these seem to have been widows or women who had inherited property in their own names. Most adult women's financial fortunes, however, depended on their husbands' resources and as such tax records provide indirect evidence on the circumstances of women.

Unfortunately, tax records do not give the ages of the people they list. Therefore in order to make tax records useful, names that appeared in them had to be linked with available birth and death dates. (See appendix A for a description of how vital data was collected and its limitations.) For each tax list I was able to match between 44.4 and 59 percent of names with age information. The analysis of tax records is based on the portions of the lists successfully matched.

Though necessary, paring down the tax records in this way introduced additional biases in the data—biases that are built into the vital statistics database. The relevant effects of matching tax records with vital records are twofold. First, matching probably intensified the bias already present in the tax records towards wealthier people. Second, matching tended to favor people who persisted in Hartford (those who actually died there) over more transient or shorter-term residents, thus most likely giving a better picture of trends among more well-established families, than families with weaker connections to Hartford. Though these problems should be kept in mind, none of them are grave—town lists provide a detailed look at many Hartford citizens that cannot be had from any other source.

VALUATION LISTS

The second type of tax record that has survived—valuation lists—provide more direct information on individual assets than town lists. These lists were compiled under order of the United States Collector of Revenue after federal direct taxes were instituted to finance the War of 1812. These records name every person who owned Hartford land, dwelling houses, or slaves (the last an irrelevant category for Connecticut by this time), along with the dollar value of their property. Unlike town lists, which attempted to assess the revenue value of property, valuation lists based their assessment on the market value of property if sold. Valuation lists for Hartford exist for three years—1813, 1815, and 1816—and include both the North and South districts each year.[11]

These records do not pose the same problems of inclusion that the town lists do. There was one simple criteria for being on a valuation list—ownership of real estate in Hartford. Age, sex, and other circumstances were irrelevant. Thus valuations give a fairly complete picture of the distribution of real estate among different age groups. However because valuation lists only consider real property, they naturally tended to include the more prosperous segments of the population while excluding the poor. In addition, it is quite possible that there were middling or wealthy craftsmen or merchants in Hartford that owned little or no real estate. The economic standing of such men, whose resources were more likely to be invested in shops or store inventory, are thus underrepresented by valuation lists. Although Hartford had tradesmen and merchants in all age groups, this bias would probably effect middle-age to older men most as they were more likely to own large concerns than men just beginning in the world of business. Thus the valuation figures presented in this book potentially underestimate the overall holdings of those in their forties and above.

Like town lists, valuation lists had to be matched to vital records to determine the ages of property owners. The same method as with the town lists was used, with the result that vital information was found for from 48.3 to 54.3 percent of the people on each list. As described earlier, the matching process tended to favor more established members of the community, adults, and the more well-to-do. However, the latter problem is not as important here as it is for the town lists since valuation lists already excluded almost all truly poor people. Likewise the under-representation of children in the vital records database poses no real problem here since very few children owned real estate. Because valuation records contain different information on the resources of Hartford people than town lists, they add another dimension to the analysis of the elderly's financial circumstances.

NOTES

1. For an overview of the Connecticut system of taxation see Diana Ross McCain, "As True as Taxes: An Historian's Guide to Direct Taxation and Tax Records in Connecticut 1637–1820," (Master's thesis, Wesleyan University, 1981).
2. 29 December 1809, HTR.
3. Hartford Tax Lists, CHS.
4. The question of whether information derived from these tax records on individual's economic standing might be skewed by cohort effects has been raised. This seems unlikely since assets were reassessed each and every year. However, because Hartford town tax lists are only extant for the period from 1792 to 1816 it is impossible to evaluate any cohort effects that might be seen in the long run.
5. Diana McCain discusses some of the tensions over early national Connecticut taxation in "As True as Taxes," chapters 2–4.
6. In this case the nearest years are 1811 for the North district and 1814 for the South.
7. 26 September 1825, HTR.
8. Unfortunately, systematic lists of those who received poll tax abatements or explanations of why specific abatements were given rarely survive. I have found only one list entitled "Abatement of County Taxes on List 1826" (Hartford County, County Court Papers by Subject 1715–1855, Box 555, CSL), though this list is obviously too late to be helpful in conjunction with Hartford's extant town tax and valuation lists.
9. This figure comes from dividing the number of men with lists of $0 by all men in their sixties for whom we have age information.
10. This death rate is based on the fact that 3.8 percent of identifiable men in their sixties on the tax lists died per year. Over ten years this produces an estimated death rate of 31.25 percent (i.e. 3.8 to the tenth), and consequently a survival rate around 70 percent.
11. List of Taxes payable... 1813, Connecticut, 4th District, Hartford County, CSL; List of Taxes Payable... 1815, U.S. Collector of Revenue, Connecticut 4th District Records, CHS; and for the 1816 valuation list, Hartford Tax Lists, CHS.

Appendix C

Information on Hartford Leaders

In order to find out about Hartford's leaders in the period from 1790 to 1830 I combed through all the records—both published and unpublished—I could find from local government bodies, churches, voluntary associations, and institutions that existed in early national Hartford. (These Hartford sources are listed in detail in this book's bibliography.) The result was a database of about 4,400 observations on leaders, or about 110 per year for the period from 1790 to 1830. Each observation includes a leader's name, his office held, and the year the office was held.

LOCAL GOVERNMENT

The local government offices included in the database are those of both the Town of Hartford and the City of Hartford, which were administratively distinct bodies in this period. The Town's important offices were: Moderator, Clerk/Register of Deeds, Treasurer, Selectmen, Constables, and Grand Jury members. The City meanwhile elected a Mayor, Clerk, Treasurer, Collector, Auditor, Sheriffs, Aldermen, and Councilmen.[1] As in other New England towns there were also many lesser officers who inspected goods and buildings, controlled animals, or saw to the upkeep of roads, fences, and boundaries. These lesser posts have not been analyzed here because my interest was in the leaders of local government rather than in all functionaries both major and minor. In distinguishing between major and minor posts I was aided by the City and Town record keepers themselves, who tended to group the election of each separately.

CHURCHES

An attempt was made to collect leaders names from all churches that existed in Hartford from 1790 to 1830. Complete or partial leadership information was gathered for Hartford's First Congregational Church, Second Congregational Church, North Congregational Church, West Hartford Congregational Church, First Baptist Church, Church of the Redeemer (Universalist), First Methodist Church, and Christ Church (Episcopal).

VOLUNTARY ASSOCIATIONS

Hartford voluntary associations for which partial or complete leadership information survives are the Charitable Society, Conference Association, Female Beneficent Society, Hartford Auxiliary Colonization Society, Hartford Evangelical Tract Society, Hartford Library Company, Hartford Peace Society, Jubal Society, Mechanics Society, Park Congregational Church Gentleman's Association, St. Johns Lodge Freemasons, South Engine Company, Sunday School Society, and the Widows Society.

INSTITUTIONS

Hartford's institutions for which leadership information can be found are the Hartford Grammar School, Hartford Female Seminary, Connecticut Retreat for the Insane, and the American Asylum for the Deaf and Dumb.

MATCHING LEADERS TO AGE AND TAX INFORMATION

In its raw form the database of approximately 4,400 observations was not very useful because it lacked the ages of officeholders. Hence leaders' names were matched to age data collected from newspaper death notices and headstone inscriptions.[2] In this way age information for just over 80 percent of all officeholders in my leaders database was

Information on Hartford Leaders 293

recovered. The analysis of age trends presented in chapter 8 is based on this sizable fraction.

To gain further insight into the nature of Hartford's leaders, officers' names were also matched to information from Hartford's tax rolls (town lists) to determine how leaders' wealth compared to that of non-leaders.[3] Of all the leaders in the database between 1790 and 1814 (roughly the period when suitable tax records exist), about 76 percent were successfully matched with tax information. The basic method was as follows: For every year that suitable tax records exist, all taxpayers were assigned rankings (quartiles) based on the size of their tax lists. These rankings were then matched to leaders' names. Because Hartford tax rolls were compiled in two parts (Northside and Southside) and because rolls for both sides are lost for several years, leaders' names in any given year were matched to tax information from the nearest extant tax lists. Thus, for example, leaders holding office in 1793 were matched to tax information from the 1792 (Northside) and 1794 (Southside) tax rolls. In other words, every effort was made to determine leaders' wealth as closely as possible to the time they held office, if not in the very year of office holding. The analysis in chapter 8 of leaders' wealth is based on this sizable fraction.

Table C-1. Average Age at Retirement and Interval to Death by Type of Organization

Type	Age Last Office Held		Yrs. Between Last Office & Death		
	Mean	Median	Mean	Median	Obs.
Government	50.4	49.0	9.5	7.0	70
Churches	59.3	59.0	2.0	5.2	39
Associations	40.4	35.0	8.1	6.5	15
Institutions	60.0	60.5	1.0	0	7
All Types	52.2	50.5	7.6	4.5	131

Source: See note 13, chapter 8 and appendix C.

NOTES

1. It is worth noting that the mayor and the first two aldermen elected each year also served as the three judges of civil and criminal matters for the Hartford City Court. See Henry F. Smith, ed., *Municipal Register of the City of Hartford 1900* (Hartford CT: E.M. Ward Co., 1900), 17.
2. Refer to appendix A for a complete description of this age data.
3. See appendix B for more information on these tax records.

Selected Bibliography of Primary Sources

PERSONAL PAPERS

Diaries

Zeloda Barrett Diary, CHS.
Shubael Bartlett Diary, CHS.
Abby Jane Bigelow Diary, CHS.
Oliver Boardman Diary, CHS.
Jonathan Clark Journal, CHS.
James Cogswell Diary, CHS.
Jennet Cowles Memory Book, CHS.
Mary Ann Cowles Diary, CHS.
Peter Wallace Gallaudet Diary, CHS.
George Gillet Diary, CSL.
Mary Treadwell Hooker Record Book, CSL.
Susan Johnson Diary, CHS.
Joseph Joselin, Jr. Diary, CHS.
Martha Mortimer Starr Lewis Record Book, CHS.
Mercy Morris Journal, CHS.
Sophia Munroe Diary, CHS.
Elisha Niles Diary, CHS.
Rebecca Noyes Diary, CHS.
Edwin Olmsted Diary, CSL.
William Seward Pierson Diary, CSL.
Humphrey Pratt Diary, CHS.
Eliphalet Silliman Diary, CSL.
William Silliman Diary, CSL.
Eliza Ann Staples Diary, CSL.

Lucinda Storrs Diary, CSL.
Samuel Talcott Diary, CHS.
Ransom Warner Diary, CHS.
Austin Williams Diary, CHS.

Manuscript Collections

Norman Brigham Correspondence, CHS.
Bunce-Brace Correspondence, CHS.
Mason Fitch Cogswell Account Books, CHS.
Robert Dinsmoor Papers, CHS.
Benjamin Clark Gilman Correspondence, CHS.
Goodwin Papers, CHS.
Maltby Family Papers, CHS.
Shadrach Osborn Papers, CHS.
Samuel Richards Papers and Letters, CHS.
Thomas Robbins Papers, CHS.
Samuel Tuttle Papers, CSL.
Francis Vinton Correspondence, CHS.
Daniel Wadsworth Papers, CHS.
Wadsworth Family Papers, CHS.
Whitman Family Correspondence, CHS.
Abigail Williams Correspondence, CHS.
Williams Family Papers, CHS
Wyllys Papers, CHS.

PUBLISHED WORKS RELATING TO OLD AGE

The Adventures of Old Dame Trudge. Philadelphia: William Charles, 1811.
Allen, Anson. *Allen's New-England Almanac, for 1806*. Hartford CT: Lincoln & Gleason, 1805.
Association for the Relief of Respectable, Aged, Indigent Females. *The Constitution and First and Second Annual Reports*. New York: J. Seymour, 1815.
———. *The Third Annual Report and By-Laws*. New York: J Seymour, 1816.

———. *The Fifth Annual Report*. New York: J. Gray & Co., 1818.
Beddoes, Thomas. *Hygeia; or Essays Moral and Medical*. 3 vols. London: J. Mills for R. Phillips, 1802–1803.
Beers, Andrew. *The Farmer's Calendar; or New York & Vermont Almanack for the Year 1805*. Troy: Wright & Wilbur, 1804.
———. *Beers's Almanac for . . . 1806*. Hartford CT: Hudson & Goodwin, 1805.
———. *The Farmer's Almanac, and Register for the Middle District; for . . . 1806*. Kingston NY: Buel for J. Freer, 1805.
The Benevolent Old Man of the Rock: An Entertaining Story for Youth. Boston: Thomas Wait & Co., 1810[?].
The Best and Easiest Method of Preserving Uninterrupted Health to Extreme Old Age. London: R. Baldwin, 1748.
Bickerstaffe, Isaac. *The New England Almanack, or Lady's and Gentleman's Diary for . . . 1805*. Providence RI: John Carter, 1804.
———. *He Would if He Could: Or an Old Fool Worse than Any*. New York: David Longworth, 1808.
Bridge, William. *A Word to the Aged*. Boston: 1679.
Buchan, William. *Domestic Medicine*. Leominster MA: Adams & Wilder for Isaiah Thomas, 1804.
Buckland, James. *The Wonder of Wonders or the Remarkable Discovery of an American Hermit Who Lived Upwards of 200 Years*. Kennebunk ME: James Remich, 1815.
Carlisle, Anthony. *An Essay on the Disorders of Old Age, and on the Means for Prolonging Human Life*. Philadelphia: Edward Earle, 1819.
Chapin, Calvin. *A Sermon, Delivered at the Funeral of Rev. John Marsh*. Hartford CT: G. Goodwin & Sons, 1821.
Cicero, Marcus Tullius. *Cato Major; Or a Discourse on Old Age*. Translated by Benjamin Franklin. Philadelphia: W. Duane, 1809.
Cogswell, James. *Faithfulness in the Service of Christ . . . Being a Sermon Preached at Lebanon, March 4, 1776*. Hartford CT: Lincoln & Gleason, 1806.
The Conversion of an Aged Sinner. New York: Hopkins and Seymour for Forrest, 1804.
Cornaro, Luigi. *The Probable Way of Attaining a Long and Healthful Life*. 6th ed. Portsmouth: George Jerry Osbourne, 1788.

Daboll, Nathan. *The New England Almanack, and Gentlemen and Ladies' Diary for . . . 1804*. New London CT: Samuel Green, 1803.

———. *The New England Almanack, and Gentleman and Ladies Diary for . . . 1805*. New London CT: Samuel Green, 1804.

Dod, John. *Old Mr. Dod's Sayings*. Cambridge MA: Marmaduke Johnson, 1673.

Dunlap, John. *Short Addresses to Children, &c.*. Cambridge NY: Tennery & Stock, 1805[?].

An Easy Way to Prolong Life. 4th ed. Dover NH: Samuel Bragg for William T. Clap, 1796.

Ely, Zebulon. *A Gospel Minister, Though Young, Should be Respectable by his Example*. Hartford CT: Lincoln & Gleason, 1806.

———. *A Ripe Shock Seasonably Gathered. A Discourse Occasioned by the Death of the Honourable William Williams*. Hartford CT: Hudson & Goodwin, 1812.

Emblems of Mortality. Hartford CT: Printed by John Babcock, 1801.

Emerson, William. *A Sermon, Delivered in Brattle Street Church, Boston . . . Madam Elizabeth Bowdoin . . . Who Departed Life May 5, 1803, in the Seventy Second Year of Her Age*. Boston: 1803.

An Explanation of the Ten Commandments . . . by an Aged Schoolmistress. Keene NH: Henry Blake & Co., 1794.

The Farmer's Almanac for the Year of Our Lord 1805. Fredericktown MD: 1804[?].

Father Abraham's Almanac, for . . . 1805. Philadelphia: Stewart for B., J., and R. Johnson, 1804.

Floyer, John. *Medicina Gerocomica: Or, the Galenic Art of Preserving Old Men's Healths*. London: Printed for F. Isted, 1724.

Gardiner, John. *The Widowed Mourner*. Boston: 1791.

Gay, Ebenezer. *The Old Man's Calendar*. 4th ed. Dover NH: Eliphalet Ladd, 1793.

Gratton, John. *A Journal of the Life of that Ancient Servant of Christ, John Gratton*. Stanford NY: Daniel Lawrence for Henry and John Hull, 1805.

Griswold, Stanley. *The Good Man's Prospects in the Hour of Death*. Litchfield: T. Collier, 1801.

Hartford Evangelical Tract Society. *An Exhortation to Sick Persons.* Hartford CT: 1816.
———. *Monitor to Parents.* Hartford: 1816.
———. *Account of Sir Matthew Hale.* Hartford CT: 1817.
———. *Happy Poverty or the Story of Poor Blind Ellen.* Hartford CT: Hudson & Co., 1817.
———. *Way of Salvation.* Hartford CT: 1817.
———. *Address of a Minister to His Parishioners.* Hartford CT: 1821.
———. *The Blind Irishman, Restored to Sight.* Hartford CT: 1821.
———. *The Contrast.* Hartford CT: 1821.
———. *The Happy Shepherd.* Hartford CT: Hudson & Skinner, 1823.
———. *Address to Mothers.* Hartford CT: Hudson & Skinner, 1824.
———. *Memoir of Mr. John Cooper.* Hartford CT: Hudson & Skinner, 1824.
Hill, John. *The Old Man's Guide to Health and Longer Life with Rules for Diet, Exercise, and Physic.* Philadelphia: Dunlap, 1775.
The History of Old Bridget. A True Story. Philadelphia: William Bradford, 1818.
Hoare, Prince. *My Grandmother, A Musical Farce in Two Acts.* New York: Thomas Longworth, 1819.
Jameson, Horatio Gates. *The American Domestick Medicine.* Baltimore: F. Lucas, 1817.
Kitchener, William. *The Art of Invigorating and Prolonging Life, by Food, Clothes, Air, Exercise, Wine, Sleep, &c..* 2d ed. London: Printed for Hurst, Robinson, & Co., 1821.
Lathrop, Joseph. *The Infirmities and Comforts of Old Age. A Sermon to Aged People.* Springfield MA: Henry Brewer, 1805.
———. *Old Age Improved: A Sermon.* Springfield MA: T. Dickman, 1811.
A Letter to the Clergy of the Colony of Connecticut. New York: Parker, 1760.
Lord, Benjamin. *The Aged Minister's Solemn Appeal to God, and Serious Address to his People.* Norwich: John Trumbull, 1783.
Martin, Sarah Catherine. *A Curious Account of the Comic Adventures of Old Mother Hubbard and her Dog.* New York: William Charles, 1807.
Mather, Cotton. *Addresses to Old Men, and Young Men, and Little Children.* Boston: R. Pierce, 1690.

Methodist Episcopal Church. Trustees of the Fund for the Relief and Support of the Itinerant, Superannuated, and Worn-Out Ministers and Preachers. *Articles of Association*. New York: J.C. Tollen for Daniel Hill and Thomas Ware, 1814.
My Grandfather; A Poem. Philadelphia: William Charles, 1817.
My Grandmother, A Poem. Philadelphia: William Charles, 1817.
New England Tract Society. *Tracts Published by the New England Tract Society*. Vol. 2. Andover: Flagg and Gould, 1814.
Old Age. New York: Samuel Wood, 1810.
The Old Bachelor's Masterpiece. Fairhaven VT: J.P. Spooner, 1797.
Old Grand-papa and Other Poems. Philadelphia: Warner, 1817.
Orton, Job. *Discourses to the Aged*. Salem: J. Cushing for T.C. Cushing, 1801.
Osborn, Elizabeth. *The Loving Invitation of Christ to the Aged, Middle-Aged, Youth and Children*. Exeter NH: C. Norris & Co., 1811.
Parkinson, James. *The Town and Country Friend and Physician*. Philadelphia: Printed by James Humphreys, 1803.
Perkins, Nathan. *Sermon Delivered at the Interment of Rev. Timothy Pitkin*. Hartford CT: Hudson & Goodwin, 1812.
A Remarkable Instance of Longevity. 1803.
Rush, Benjamin. *Medical Inquiries and Observations Upon the Diseases of the Mind*. Philadelphia: Merritt for Kimber & Richardson, 1812.
———. *Medical Inquiries and Observations*. 2 vols. 4th ed. Philadelphia: Printed for Johnson & Warner, 1815.
———. "Commonplace Book." In *The Autobiography of Benjamin Rush*. Edited by George C. Corner. Princeton: Princeton University Press, 1948.
Scudder, John. *An Inaugural Dissertation on the Diseases of Old Age*. New York: Van Winkle & Wiley, 1815.
Society for the Relief of the Widows and Orphans of the Clergy of the Protestant Episcopal Church. *Rules of the Society . . . in the State of South-Carolina; Adopted the 21st Day of October, 1818*. Charleston: A.E. Miller, 1819.
Stanford, John. *Six Short Sermons Adapted to the Aged*. New York: T. and J. Swords, 1829.
———. *The Aged Christian's Companion*. New York: Stanford and Sword's, 1852.

Strong, Nathan. *A Sermon, Delivered at Hartford, January 6, 1807 at the Funeral of the Rev. James Cogswell.* Hartford CT: Hudson & Goodwin, 1807.
———. *A Sermon on the Uses of Time; Addressed to Men in the Several Ages of Life.* Hartford CT: Peter B. Gleason & Co., 1813.
Tenney, Caleb. *Ministers Must Die. A Sermon, Preached, September 16, 1821. The Sabbath After the Interment of the Rev. John Marsh.* Hartford CT: George Goodwin & Sons, 1821.
Thomas, Robert B. *The Farmer's Almanac . . . for the Year of Our Lord 1805.* Boston: Munroe & Francis for John West, 1804.
———. *The Farmer's Almanack, Calculated . . . for . . . 1806.* Boston: John West, 1805.
Thomson, Alexander. *The Family Physician.* New York: James Oran, 1802.
To the Public. New York[?]: 1780.
Tullar, Martin. *A Concise System of Family Duty.* Windsor VT: Nahum Mower, 1802.
Wells, William. *Eight Letters, from an Aged Minister to the Young Men and Youth.* Brattleborough VT: J.R. Caldwell, 1818.
Wesley, John. *Primitive Physic.* 25th ed. Philadelphia: Solomon W. Conrad, 1801.
Wilkins, Henry. *The Family Adviser.* 3d ed. Philadelphia: Conrad for Cooper, 1801.
Wirt, William. *The Old Bachelor.* 2 vols. Baltimore: Fielding Lucas, 1818.

HARTFORD AND CONNECTICUT SOURCES

Manuscript

Charitable Society, Papers 1792–1871, CHS.
Christ Church Cathedral, Hartford, Papers 1795–1815, CSL.
Christ Church Parish, Hartford, Records 1795–1927, CSL.
Church of the Redeemer, Hartford, Pastor's Register 1824–1923, CSL.
City of Hartford, City Accounts, Town Clerk's Office, Hartford, Conn.
City of Hartford, Court of Common Council Records 1784–1830, Town Clerk's Office, Hartford, Conn.

City of Hartford, Records of City Meetings 1784–1845, Town Clerk's Office, Hartford, Conn.

City of Hartford, Treasurer's Ledgers 1796–1853 and 1785–1835, Town Clerk's Office, Hartford, Conn.

City of Hartford, Treasurer's Reports 1815–1854, Town Clerk's Office, Hartford, Conn.

Constitution of the Female Beneficent Society, Hartford, 29 May 1811, Samuel Tuttle Papers, CSL.

First Baptist Church, Hartford, Records 1789–1909, 6 vols., CSL.

First Church of Christ, Hartford, Records 1684–1930, 29 vols., CSL.

First Church of Christ, Hartford, Records 1698–1811, CSL.

First Congregational Church, West Hartford, Records 1713–1933, CSL.

First Congregational Church, West Hartford, Records 1736–1920, CSL.

First Ecclesiastical Society, Hartford, Records 1737–1824, CHS.

First Methodist Church, Hartford, Records 1825–1844, 13 vols., CSL.

First Methodist Church, Hartford, Trustee Records 1823–1846, CSL.

First Universalist Church, Hartford, Correspondence, Receipts, etc. 1825–1885 CHS.

Hartford County Temperance Society, Records 1829–1840, CHS.

Hartford Female Seminary, Records and Minutes of Meetings of Trustees 1827–1890, CHS.

Hartford Grammar School, Trustees Records 1791–1947, CHS.

North and Park Congregational Church, Hartford, Records 1823–1926, CSL.

Park Congregational Church, Hartford, Papers 1823–1891, CSL.

Park Congregational Church Gentlemen's Association in the North Ecclesiastical Society, Constitution and Records 1825–1833, CSL.

Second Congregational Church, Hartford, Records 1792–1912, 2 vols., CSL.

Second Ecclesiastical Society, Hartford, Records 1767–1920, CSL.

Society of Friends, Quaker Records 1800–1823, CSL.

South Engine Company, Account Book 1807–1827, CHS.

Town of Hartford, Meetings of Town Officers 1799–1832, Town Clerk's Office, Hartford, Conn.

Town of Hartford, Town Votes No. 3 1796–1863, Town Clerk's Office, Hartford, Conn.

Bibliography

Published

American Asylum for the Education and Instruction of Deaf and Dumb Persons. *Fourth Report of the Directors of the American Asylum for . . . the Deaf and Dumb.* Hartford CT: Hudson & Co., 1820.

———. *Fifth Report of the Directors of the American Asylum for . . . the Deaf and Dumb.* Hartford CT: Hudson & Co., 1821.

———. *Sixth Report of the Directors of the American Asylum for . . . the Deaf and Dumb.* Hartford CT: Hudson & Co., 1822.

———. *Seventh Report of the Directors of the American Asylum for . . . the Deaf and Dumb.* Hartford CT: W. Hudson & L. Skinner, 1823.

———. *Eighth Report of the Directors of the American Asylum for . . . the Deaf and Dumb.* Hartford CT: W. Hudson & L. Skinner, 1824.

———. *Ninth Report of the Directors of the American Asylum for . . . the Deaf and Dumb.* Hartford CT: W. Hudson & L. Skinner, 1825.

———. *Tenth Report of the Directors of the American Asylum for . . . the Deaf and Dumb.* Hartford CT: W. Hudson & L. Skinner, 1826.

———. *Eleventh Report of the Directors of the American Asylum for . . . the Deaf and Dumb.* Hartford CT: 1827.

———. *Twelfth Report of the Directors of the American Asylum for . . . the Deaf and Dumb.* Hartford CT: Hudson & Skinner, 1828.

———. *Thirteenth Report of the Directors of the American Asylum for . . . the Deaf and Dumb.* Hartford CT: Hudson & Skinner, 1829.

———. *Fourteenth Report of the Directors of the American Asylum for . . . the Deaf and Dumb.* Hartford CT: W. Hudson & L. Skinner, 1830.

Andrews, Frank D., comp. *Directory for the City of Hartford for the Year 1799.* Vineland NJ: 1910.

At an Adjourned Meeting of the Inhabitants of the Town of Hartford, Held on the 30th Day of December, 1822. 1822.

Ballou, Hosea. *A Sermon Delivered at Hartford, Conn . . . at the Dedication of the New Universalist Meeting House*. Boston: H. Bowen, 1824.

Bickford, Christopher P. *The Connecticut Historical Society 1825–1975: A Brief Illustrated History*. Hartford CT: Connecticut Historical Society, 1975.

Bird, Viggo E. *Early Beginnings of Connecticut Industry*. Princeton: Newcomen Society, 1937.

A Brief Historical Sketch: Aetna Insurance Company, Hartford Connecticut 1819–1905. Hartford CT: Aetna Insurance Co., 1905.

A Brief History of the American Asylum, at Hartford for the Education and Instruction of the Deaf and Dumb. Hartford CT: Case, Lockwood & Brainard Co., 1893.

A Brief History of the Formation of the North Church in Hartford, Connecticut. Hartford: Goodwin & Co., 1832.

A Brief Summary of Christian Doctrine and a Form of Covenant Adopted by the First Church in Hartford. Hartford CT: Hudson & Co., 1822.

Burpee, Charles W. *First Century of the Phoenix National Bank of Hartford*. Hartford CT: 1914.

———. *History of Hartford County Connecticut 1633–1928*. 3 vols. Hartford: S.J. Clarke Publishing Co., 1928.

Burr, Grace Tallman. *Widows' Society of Hartford, Connecticut: History, Work, Future*. Hartford CT: 1938.

Capen, Edward. *The Historical Development of the Poor Law of Connecticut*. Studies in History, Economics and Public Law, vol. 22. New York: Columbia University Press, 1905.

Centennial History of the Society for Savings of Hartford, Connecticut 1819–1919. New York: Brearley Service Organization, 1919.

Centennial Memorial of the First Baptist Church of Hartford, Connecticut, March 23d and 24th, 1890. Hartford CT: Press of the Christian Secretary, 1890.

Charitable Society. *Constitution of the Charitable Society*. Hartford: 1793[?].

The Charter and its Amendments and the Revised By-Laws of the City of Hartford. Hartford CT: Case, Tiffany & Co., 1856.

Clark, George L. *A History of Connecticut: Its People and Institutions*. 2d ed. New York: G.P. Putnam's Sons, 1914.

Connecticut Asylum for the Education and Instruction of Deaf and Dumb Persons. *Report of the Committee of the Connecticut Asylum for . . . Deaf and Dumb Persons.* Hartford CT: Hudson & Co., 1817.

———. *Second Report of the Directors of the Connecticut Asylum for . . . Deaf and Dumb Persons.* Hartford CT: Hudson & Co., 1818.

———. *Third Report of the Directors of the Connecticut Asylum for . . . Deaf and Dumb Persons.* Hartford CT: Hudson & Co., 1819.

Connecticut Historical Society. *The Act of Incorporation, and the Constitution of the Connecticut Historical Society.* Hartford CT: Charles Babcock, 1825.

The Connecticut Historical Society and Associated Institutions. Hartford CT: Connecticut Historical Society, 1889.

Connecticut Retreat for the Insane. *Charter of the Hartford Retreat.* 1822.

———. *Third Report of the Directors of the Connecticut Retreat for the Insane.* Hartford: 1827.

———. *Report of the Medical Visitors of the Connecticut Retreat for the Insane.* Hartford CT: Hudson and Skinner, 1830.

———. *Seventh Report of the Medical Visitors of the Connecticut Retreat for the Insane.* Hartford CT: Hudson and Skinner, 1831.

Constitution and By-Laws of the Grand Lodge of Connecticut and By-Laws of St. John's Lodge, No. 4. Hartford CT: Elihu Geer, 1861.

Contributions to the History of Christ Church, Hartford. Hartford CT: Belknap & Warfield, 1895.

Crawford, Elijah. *History of the Methodist Episcopal Church in Hartford: A Discourse Delivered on Fast Day April 6, 1849.* Hartford CT: Case, Tiffany and Co., 1849.

Dunkleberger, George S. *An Early History of St. John's Lodge, No. 4 A.F. & A.M. Hartford, Conn. 1762–1937.* Hartford CT: Case, Lockwood & Brainard Co., 1937.

Erving, Henry W. *The Connecticut River Banking Company: One Hundred Years of Service 1825–1925.* Hartford CT: 1925.

Gall, Henry R. and William George Jordan. *One Hundred Years of Fire Insurance: Being a History of the Aetna Insurance Company.* Hartford CT: Aetna Insurance Co., 1919.

Grand Lodge of Connecticut. *Constitution and Bye-Laws . . . Adopted by the Grand Lodge of Connecticut.* Hartford CT: Elisha Babcock, 1799.

Grant, Ellsworth and Marion H. Grant, *The City of Hartford 1784–1984.* Hartford CT: Connecticut Historical Society, 1986.

Grew, Henry. *Reasons for the Secession of a Number of Members from the Baptist Church in Hartford.* Hartford CT: 1824.

Hall, William H. *West Hartford.* Hartford CT: West Hartford Chamber of Commerce, 1930.

Hartford Auxiliary Colonization Society. *Constitution of the Hartford Auxiliary Colonization Society.* Hartford CT: Lincoln & Stone, 1819.

Hartford City Directory for 1828. Hartford CT: Ariel Ensign, 1828[?].

Hartford City Mission. *Constitution.* Hartford: P.B. Gleason & Co., 1831.

Hartford Evangelical Tract Society. *Constitution of the Hartford Evangelical Tract Society.* 1816.

———. *First Report of the Hartford Evangelical Tract Society.* 1817.

———. *Second Report of the Hartford Evangelical Tract Society.* 1818.

———. *Third Report of the Hartford Evangelical Tract Society.* 1819.

———. *Fourth Report of the Hartford Evangelical Tract Society.* 1820.

———. *Eighth Report of the Hartford Evangelical Tract Society.* Hartford CT: Hudson & Skinner, 1824.

Hartford Female Beneficent Society. *A Report of the Hartford Female Beneficent Society for the Year 1833.* Hartford CT: Hanmer & Comstock, 1833.

Hartford Female Seminary. *The Annual Catalogue of the Hartford Female Seminary.* Hartford CT: George F. Olmsted, 1831.

Hartford National Bank and Trust Company. Hartford CT: 1942.

Hartford Orphan Asylum. *Hartford Orphan Asylum: The 69th Annual Report of the Managers.* Hartford CT: Case, Lockwood & Brainard, 1902.

———. *Report of the Corresponding Secretary of the Annual Meeting of the Corporators of the Hartford Orphan Asylum, 1944.* 1944.

"Hartford Town Votes Volume 1 1635–1716." *Collections of the Connecticut Historical Society* 6 (1897): v–410.

Historical Catalogue of the First Church in Hartford 1633–1885. Hartford CT: First Church, 1885.

History of the Parish of Christ Church Hartford. Hartford CT: Belknap & Warfield, 1895.

Linsley, Joel H. *The First Annual Address Delivered Before the Hartford Peace Society . . . with the First Annual Report.* Hartford CT: Philemon Canfield, 1829.

Loomis, Dwight and J. Gilbert Calhoun, eds. *The Judicial and Civil History of Connecticut.* Boston: Boston History Co., 1895.

Manual of the Congregational Church in West Hartford, Conn.. Hartford CT: The Fowler & Miller Co., 1884.

Mechanics Society of Hartford. *Act of Incorporation and By-Laws of the Mechanics Society of Hartford.* Hartford CT: P.B. Gleason & Co., 1829.

Memorial Sketches. 1893.

Morse, Jarvis M. *A Neglected Period of Connecticut's History 1818–1850.* New Haven: Yale University Press, 1933.

Murray, William C. *St. John's Lodge No. 4 1762–1962.* Hartford: Connecticut Printers Inc., 1962.

125 Years of the Connecticut Historical Society 1825–1950. Hartford CT: Connecticut Historical Society, 1951.

Page, Charles W. "Dr. Eli Todd and the Early Days of the Hartford Retreat." In *Transactions of the Connecticut Medical Society.* 1913.

Parker, Edwin Pond. *History of the Second Church of Christ in Hartford.* Hartford CT: Belknap & Warfield, 1892.

Passbook to a Proud Past and a Promising Future. Hartford CT: Connecticut Printers, 1969.

Pearce, G. Hazard. "History of the Quaker Cemetery So. Quaker Lane West Hartford, Connecticut." Photocopy. Connecticut State Library, Hartford, Conn.

Pease, John C. and John M. Niles. *A Gazetteer of the States of Connecticut and Rhode Island.* Hartford CT: William S. Marsh, 1819.

The Pocket Register for the City of Hartford. Hartford CT: Benjamin H. Norton, 1825.

Potter, Rockwell Harmon. *Hartford's First Church.* Hartford CT: First Church of Christ, 1932.

Report of a Committee of the Connecticut Medical Society Respecting an Asylum for the Insane with the Constitution of the Society. Hartford CT: Bowles & Francis, 1821.

Report of the Physician of the Connecticut Retreat for the Insane from the Opening of the Institution . . . to the 1st of April 1825. Hartford CT: P.B. Goodsell, 1825[?].

A Review of the Records of the Widows' Society of Hartford 1825–1892. Hartford CT: Case, Lockwood & Brainard Co., 1892.

Roth, David M. *Connecticut: A Bicentennial History.* New York: W.W. Norton & Co., 1979.

St. John's Lodge. *Souvenir Program, Sesqui-Centennial Anniversary of St. John's Lodge No. 4 A.F. & A.M..* Hartford CT: 1912.

Smith, Henry F., comp. *Municipal Register of the City of Hartford 1900.* Hartford CT: E.M. Ward Co., 1900.

Society for the Relief of the Insane . . . Annual Meeting at Hartford. Hartford CT: W. Hudson & L. Skinner, 1823.

Spinka, Matthew. *A History of the First Church of Christ Congregational, West Hartford, Conn..* N.p., n.d.

Sumner, George and Gurdon W. Russell. *Sketches of Physicians in Hartford.* Hartford CT: Case, Lockwood & Brainard Co., 1890.

Trumbull, J. Hammond. *The Memorial History of Hartford County Connecticut 1633–1884.* 2 vols. Boston: Edward L. Osgood, 1886.

Two Hundredth Anniversary: The First Church of Christ West Hartford, Connecticut. 1913.

Walker, George Leon. *History of the First Church in Hartford 1633–1883.* Hartford CT: Brown & Gross, 1884.

Watt, Donald. *From Heresy Toward Truth: The Story of Universalism in Greater Hartford and Connecticut, 1821–1971.* West Hartford CT: The Universalist Church, 1971.

Weld, Stanley B. *The History of Immanuel Church 1824–1967.* Hartford CT: Connecticut Printers, 1968.

Woodward, P.H. *One Hundred Years of the Hartford Bank.* Hartford CT: Case, Lockwood & Brainard Co., 1892.

Index

Adultery: in old age, 75–76, 79, 204, 208
Aetna Fire Insurance Company, 157, 252
African-Americans: elderly, 13, 16–17, 46–47
Afterlife: anxiety about, 64–66
Age: and household composition, 171–186, 272–273; relation to leadership, 231–249, 258–264, 273
Age consciousness, 63
Age relations: change in, 225, 258–261, 273–274
American Asylum for the Deaf and Dumb, 7, 155, 255, 292
American Revolution. *See* Revolutionary War
Annuities, 151–152, 156–157, 218–219
Association for the Relief of Respectable, Aged, Indigent Females in New York, 11
Associations. *See* Voluntary associations
Auxiliary Colonization Society, 7

Baptists, 7
Beddoes, Thomas, 42
Beer, Andrew, 24, 26
Behavior of elderly: prescribed, 30–38, 39–40, 41–43, 44–45, 57; described in popular literature, 46–48, 50–51; actual, 57–82, 84–85
Benefits of old age, 38–39, 57
Bickerstaffe, Isaac, 11, 48
Birthdays, 62–63
Birth control, 132, 173
Boarding, 125, 145, 190–192, 196, 221
Bridge, William, 32, 33, 36

Carlisle, Anthony, 11, 41, 42, 43–44
Census, United States, 172–173
Cent Society, 7
Charitable Society, 7, 139–141, 142
Charity: toward elderly, 125, 138–143, 193, 272
Childrearing: in old age, 132
Children, 201; duties to parents, 38–39, 82–84; economic support from, 129–134, 148–150, 153; dependent on elderly, 132–133, 145; as help to elderly, 190, 192–193, 195–196; relations with parents, 206–208, 209–219, 224, 226
Christ Church, 246
Churches, 291, 292; charity toward elderly, 140, 141–142; leadership of, 231–233, 235, 239–244, 246, 248, 252–257
Cicero, Marcus Tullius, 50
Civic affairs: elderly's role in, 231–249, 258–264, 273
Climate: prescribed for elderly, 42
Community: economic support for elderly from, 121, 134–143, 150–153, 159–160, 221–222, 272; elderly's role in, 231–249, 258–264, 273, 274
Congregationalism, 7, 8, 30, 32, 36, 37, 40, 47, 51, 57, 66, 76; persistence in Connecticut, 60
Congress: pension legislation, 122–124, 138
Connecticut, 60, 122, 135, 137, 139, 201, 211, 215, 252

309

Connecticut Deaf and Dumb Asylum, 7, 155, 255, 292
Connecticut Medical Society, 155
Connecticut Retreat for the Insane, 8
Connecticut River, 4, 5, 231
Conservators, 152–153, 157, 158, 191–192, 215–218, 262
Cornaro, Luigi, 11, 41, 43

Death: elderly warned about, 32, 36–37, 63–64; preparation for, 32–33, 34–37, 57, 61–66, 72–76, 205; quality of, 38, 40; effect on households, 186; effect on family life, 205–206, 209
Demographics: in colonial period, 12; in early national period, 13–17; change in, 173, 179; at present, 275–276
Detachment from world: in old age, 35, 72–76, 186
Diet: prescribed for elderly, 41–42, 43, 57
Dunlap, John, 38

Economic activity: in Hartford, Connecticut, 5–6
Economic circumstances: of youth, 89, 96–99, 101–113, 115–117; of middle aged, 89, 96–113, 115–117; of elderly, 89, 96–110, 112–117, 121–160, 192–194, 264, 272, 274; of elderly women, 103–104, 148, 153–154, 156–157, 158, 159, 218–219, 221–222; of leaders, 249–263. *See also* Poor elderly; Middling elderly; Wealthy elderly
Economic life cycle, 103–104, 109, 110–117
Economic support: for elderly, 121, 122, 153, 159; from family, 126, 129–134, 148–150, 156–157, 159, 221–222, 272; from community, 134–143, 150–153, 159–160
Elderly: definition of, 8–12, 275
Emotional problems: in old age, 195, 205–206
Episcopalians, 7
Exercise: prescribed for elderly, 42, 57

Family, xviii, 47; duties to elderly, 38–39, 82–84, 129, 130; in popular literature, 49–50; economic support from, 121, 122, 126, 129–134, 143, 148–150, 153, 156–157, 221–222, 272; experience of elderly with, 171, 187–189, 194, 201–226, 273, 274, 276–277; as help to elderly, 187–188, 189, 190, 192–193, 195–196, 273. *See also* Children; Grandchildren; Grandparents; Parents; Siblings; Spouses
Female Beneficent Society, 7
First Church of Christ, 141–142
First Congregational Church, 243
First Methodist Church, 243
Floyer, Sir John, 23, 41, 42, 43
Franklin, Benjamin, 50, 135, 213–214

Gallaudet, Thomas, 7, 255
Gardiner, John, 48
Gay, Ebenezer, 9, 22, 26, 32, 34, 35
Geriatrics, 275
Gerontology, 275
Government, local, 7, 291; leadership of, 231–233, 235, 239–246, 248, 252–256, 260–261
Grandchildren, 201; duties to elderly, 83; dependent on elderly, 133; as help to elderly, 188; relations with grandparents, 211–212, 219–222, 226
Grandparents, 201; in popular literature, 47, 49–50, 80; economic responsibilities of, 133; relations with grandchildren, 79, 83, 211–212, 219–222, 226
Griswold, Stanley, 9, 23

Hartford, Connecticut, 153, 154; as area for study, 3–4; in early national period, 3–8; population of, 4; North District, 4, 90, 91–92, 95–98 *passim*, 100–102 *passim*, 284, 285, 288, 293; South District, 4, 90, 91, 93, 95–97 *passim*, 99–102 *passim*, 284, 285, 288, 293; economic activity in, 5–6; political role

of, 7; religion in, 7; voluntary associations in, 7, 139–141, 292; community life in, 7–8; elderly population of, 13–17; tax records from, 89–91, 115, 283–288, 293; stratification in, 110–111, 116, 117; poor relief in, 135–137, 139, 142, 194; households in, 172–185; leadership in, 231–264, 291–293
Hartford City Court, 157
Hartford Convention of 1814, 7
Hartford County, Connecticut, 122–124, 136–137
Hartford Evangelical Tract Society, 7, 243
Hartford Female Seminary, 8
Hartford Grammar School, 255, 258
Hartford Peace Society, 241
Hawes, Joel, 9
Health: improvement in old age, 41–45; economic importance for elderly, 122, 126, 127–129, 134, 143, 153, 155, 158, 272. *See also* Infirmity in old age
Hill, John, 10, 23, 42, 43
Historiography of old age, xiv–xvii, 225, 276
Hospitals, 239, 292
Household headship, 172, 176, 179–186; maintaining in old age, 187–189; loss in old age, 189–196, 209–211, 272–273
Households, 171–172, 179–186, 201; linked to census data, 172–173; composition of, 172–179; arrangement in old age, 186–196, 272–273
Housing, 125, 145

Ideas on old age: religious, 22–23, 25–26, 28, 29–40, 51, 57, 201, 221, 226, 271–272; medical, 23–24, 27, 29, 40–44, 51; in popular literature, 24, 26–27, 29–30, 45–51; of ordinary people, 24–25, 27–29, 57–85, 271–272, 274; religious compared to medical, 44–45, 57; religious applied to daily life, 59–85, 209–219; medical applied to daily life, 70–71

Ideological climate: for elderly, 21, 29–30, 40, 44–45, 51, 59–60, 66, 84–85, 271–272, 276
Infirmity in old age: described by medical authors, 23–24; described by ordinary people, 25; purpose of, 32; mitigation of, 41–45, 51; treatment for, 43–44; coping with, 67–71; economic effects of, 127–129, 159, 218–219, 272; legal provisions for, 152–153, 157–158; effect on household arrangement, 172, 186, 188, 190–192, 194, 195, 209–211; effect on family life, 204–205, 209–210; effect on leadership, 262. *See also* Health
Inheritance practices, 154, 156–157, 158, 194
Institutions: leadership of, 231–233, 239–243, 247–248, 252–256, 258, 291, 292
Insurance, 151; industry in Hartford, Connecticut, 6

Kitchener, William, 41, 42, 44

Lathrop, Joseph, 9, 26, 28, 30–31, 32, 33, 35, 81
Law, 129, 130, 152–153, 222
Leadership, 232–233; by elderly, 231–249, 258–264, 273; by middle aged, 232, 234–248, 258–263; by young, 233–238, 241–243, 244–248, 260, 263; and wealth, 241, 249–263; sources of information on, 291–293
Leisure, 275
Life cycle: economic, 103–104, 109, 110–117
Life expectancy: in past, 12, 13; modern, 276
Life insurance, 151
Life span: predicted, 9
Linnean Botanic Society, 7
Literature, popular: ideas on old age in, 24, 26–27, 29–30, 45–51
Longevity: methods for increasing, 41–43

Manufacturing: in Hartford, Connecticut, 5–6
Marriage: in old age, 202–209. *See also* Remarriage
Mather, Cotton, 33, 34, 39
Mechanics Society, 7, 152
Medical ideas on old age: 23–24, 27, 29, 40–44, 51; compared to religious, 44–45, 57; applied to daily life, 70–71
Medical treatment: of elderly, 43–44, 70–71, 275
Memory loss, 26, 27
Mental decline: in old age, 25–28, 127, 145–146, 218–219, 262; legal provisions for, 152–153; effect on household arrangement, 188, 190–192; effect on family life, 204–205
Methodists, 7, 243
Middle aged: economic status of, 89, 96–113, 115–117; as taxpayers, 92–96; households of, 176–185; as leaders, 232, 234–248, 258–263, 273
Middling elderly: in tax records, 90; economic circumstances of, 121, 143–153
Ministers Annuity Society, 152
Mobility: geographical, 211
Modernization theory: applied to elderly, xiv–xvi, 225, 276; problems with, xv

Number of elderly: 12–17, 275–276

Old: definition of, 8–12, 275
Orton, Job, 28, 32, 34, 35, 38–39, 40

Paine, Thomas, 135
Parents: 201; relations with children, 206–208, 209–219, 226
Peace Society, 7
Pennsylvania Company for Insurance on Lives and Granting Annuities, 151
Pension applicants, 125–140, 142–143, 193
Pensions: federal, 122–124, 135, 138, 142
Poor elderly: in tax records, 90–91; economic circumstances of, 109, 121–134, 159, 221–222; family life of, 129–134, 204; households of, 129–130, 192–194; support for, 134–143, 159–160, 192–193, 221–222, 272. *See also* Poverty, old age
Poorhouse, 135–137, 142, 193–194, 196
Poor relief: charitable, 125, 138–143, 193, 272; public, 135–138, 142–143, 159–160, 193–194, 221–222, 272
Poverty, old age: 121, 122, 124–125, 150, 160, 192–194, 204, 221–222, 272; frequency of, 123–124, 134; causes of, 126–134; relief of, 134–143. *See also* Poor elderly
Prescriptive literature: on old age, 21–45, 51, 221, 271–272; compared to actual behavior, 57–85, 201–202, 209–219, 226
Property: holding by young, 91–117; holding by middle aged, 92–117; holding by elderly in general, 92–117; disposal of in old age, 101, 103, 108, 114–115, 116, 150, 156, 157, 191, 207, 216–217; holding by poor elderly, 124–125; holding by middling elderly, 144; holding by wealthy elderly, 153–157; conflict over, 214–219
Propriety: in old age, 30–31, 33–34, 76–80, 206
Public life: elderly's role in, 231–249, 258–264, 273
Purpose of old age: in religious view, 30–33, 46, 51; in medical view, 45; in popular literature, 45–46, 51; for ordinary people, 61, 64

Quakers, 7, 141

Real estate: assessment of, 90; distribution of, 95–96, 104–109
Religion: in Hartford, Connecticut, 7; anxiety about, 64–66, 85, 271–272
Religious ideas on old age: 22–23, 25–26, 28, 29–40, 51, 57, 201, 221,

Index

226, 271–272; compared to medical, 44–45, 57; applied to daily life, 59–85, 209–219
Religious instruction: role of elderly, 30–32, 36, 80–82
Remarriage: in old age, 77, 206–209
Retirement, 115, 129, 148, 211, 262, 276, 293. *See also* Work
Revolutionary War, 154, 259, 274; pensions from, 122–124, 135, 138, 142; veterans of, 125–140, 142–143, 193
Rush, Benjamin, 24, 27, 42–43

Savings: 121, 122, 126, 134, 143, 146, 153–154, 158
Schools: in Hartford, Connecticut, 7–8, 239, 255, 258, 292
Scudder, John, 24, 44
Servants, 188–189
Sexuality: in old age, 47–48, 75–76, 79, 204
Siblings, 201, 222–224
Social change, 274
Spouses, 201; relations in old age, 202–209
Status of elderly: decline in, xv–xvii, 276–277
Strong, Nathan, 31, 32–33, 36, 39
Submission: in old age, 32–34, 67–72, 205
Sunday School Society, 7, 243

Tax, poll, 90–91, 95, 96, 97, 284, 285–287
Tax assessment, 90–91, 283–285, 286
Taxpayers: ages of, 91–96
Tax records, 233, 249, 251; described, 89–91, 115, 283–288; matched to leader information, 293. *See also* Town lists; Valuation lists
Tenney, Caleb, 9, 36–37
Thomas, Isaiah, 11
Thomson, Alexander, 41, 42
Town lists, 89–93, 95–104, 109–114, 249, 283–287, 293.
Tracts, religious, 37–38, 39, 40
Trinity College, 7
Tullar, Martin, 38

Valuation lists, 89–91, 94–96, 104–109, 287–288.
Veneration: of elderly, 51, 271, 274

Veterans: of Revolutionary War, 125–140, 142–143, 193, 252, 254, 262
Vital statistics, 91, 279–280, 287, 288, 292
Voluntary associations: in Hartford, Connecticut, 7, 291, 292; aid offered elderly by, 139–141, 142, 152–153; leadership of, 231–233, 235, 239–244, 246–248, 252–257
Voter preferences: in selecting leaders, 233, 237, 245–246, 248, 251, 252, 256, 258, 263

War of 1812, 5, 274, 288
Washington College, 7
Wealth: and household composition, 179; relation to leadership, 241, 249–263, 273
Wealthy elderly: in tax records, 90–91; economic circumstances of, 121, 122, 124, 153–159
Weaning from world: in old age, 35, 72–76, 186
Wesley, John, 23
Widowhood, 103–104, 156–157, 158, 195
Widows, 123, 140–141, 142, 148, 149–150, 153–154, 221–222, 277; living arrangements of, 187, 188–189, 192, 194, 205, 206; remarriage of, 206–208
Widows' Society, 7, 141, 142
Wisdom: in old age, 28–29, 249
Women, 205, 218–219, 264; in elderly population, 13–17, 276; duties in old age, 34; in popular literature, 46–47; preparing for death, 75; in tax records, 91; working in old age, 128, 129; as dependents, 132; economic circumstances of, 103–104, 148, 153–154, 156–157, 158, 159; poor, 140, 221–222; households of, 178–179, 191–192, 194; as household heads, 181, 183–185, 187. *See also* Widows; Widowhood
Work: in old age, 101, 115, 121, 122, 134, 143, 146–148, 153, 155, 158, 275, 276; occupations of elderly, 126, 127–128, 129,

Work (con't)
    144; cessation of, 127–129.
    See also Retirement

Yale College, 154, 155, 252, 262
Young: duties to old, 48–50, 82–84; economic status of, 89, 96–99, 101–113, 115–117, 130; as taxpayers, 91–96; dependent on elderly, 132–133, 145; households of, 176–185; as leaders, 233–238, 241–243, 244–248, 260, 263

3326800 0293495 7

DATE DUE

MAR 0 7 1997			

Demco, Inc. 38-293